古原覓蹤

The Guyuan Mizong Collection
A Study of Inner Asian Steppe Bronzes

Emma C. Bunker | Ursula Brosseder

Contributions by
Yiu-Kang Hsu | Bo Lawergren | Donna Strahan

Photographs by
Rainer Wolfsberger

2022
Harrassowitz Verlag · Wiesbaden

7   *Acknowledgments*

9   *Artifacts from Inner Asia during the First Millennium BCE and their Cultural Significance*

Chapter 1
31 *Bronze Age Inner Asian Artifacts, Thirteenth to Eleventh Century BCE*
32 *Entries 1–6*

Chapter 2
44 *Dynastic China's Northeast Eurasian Regional Cultures during the First Millennium BCE*
Chapter 2a
46 *Artifacts Found East of the Taihang Range*
52 *Entries 7–21*
Chapter 2b
76 *Artifacts Associated with Mountain Cemetery Sites in the Jundushan*
84 *Entries 22–37*

Chapter 3
112 *Inner Asian Artifacts Found West of the Taihang Range during the First Millennium BCE*
Chapter 3a
115 *Inner Eurasian Artifacts from South-Central Inner Mongolia West of the Taihang Range*
122 *Entries 38–46*
Chapter 3b
141 *Artifacts Associated with the Ordos Region of Southwestern Inner Mongolia, Shanxi, and Shaanxi Provinces*
144 *Entries 47–67*

Chapter 3c
180 *Southern Ningxia Hui Autonomous Region, the Qingyang Plateau of Southeastern Gansu, and Parts of the Xinjiang Uyghur Autonomous Region*
199 *Entries 68–94*

Chapter 3d
255 *Ancient Chinese and Eurasian Cultural Connectivity*
266 *Entries 95–100*

Chapter 4
282 *Belt Plaques from Inner Asia and China, Third Century BCE to First Century CE*
286 *Entries 101–138*

Chapter 5
348 *Xianbei*
350 *Entries 139–140*

Chapter 6
353 *Artifacts with Exotic Overtones in the Arts of Dynastic China and the Neighboring Pastoral World during the Latter Half of the First Millennium BCE*
354 *Entries 141–150*

Chapter 7
374 *Beyond Inner Asia: Artifacts Relating Visually to Inner Asian Materials*
378 *Entries 151–167*

Chapter 8
414 *Individual Pieces beyond the Scope of the Guyuan Mizong Collection*
415 *Entries 168–170*

Chapter 9
420 *Forgeries and Modern Productions*
422 *Entries 171–179*

Chapter 10
436 *Production and Distribution of Belt Plaques in Inner Asia: Preliminary Insights from the Guyuan Mizong Collection Ursula Brosseder and Yiu-Kang Hsu*

Chapter 11
458 *Using Music Archaeological Methods to Establish a New History of Chinese Strings Bo Lawergren*

Appendices
Appendix 1
474 *CT-Scan Documentation of the Tuning Key with Recumbent Goat-Man*
Appendix 2
479 *Casting the Qin Tuning Keys in the Freer and Sackler Collections / Donna Strahan*
Appendix 3
486 *Alloy Compositional Data*

503 *Bibliography*
534 *Index of Places*
541 *Picture Credits*

Acknowledgments

This book is dedicated to Emma C. Bunker (1930–2021). For decades, she was a leading scholar of the ancient pastoral cultures of the vast territories of Northern China, Southern Siberia, and Central Asia, a field too often marginalized in the discourse of Asian art experts. Starting with her co-authorship of *Animal Style from East to West*, an exhibition and catalogue produced by the Asia Society New York in 1970, she became the foremost expert on the art and the technologies that these peoples applied to create their objets d'art. From early on in her career, she consulted with leading specialists in metallurgy and was interested in the composition of the alloys and their geographical attribution. She was, for example, able to understand a silvery surface on the bronze plaques as tinned, a process that had not been previously discussed. As a result, each object in this volume was submitted to a metallurgical analysis. Her constant curiosity and tenacity also led her to define a hitherto-unnoticed casting process dubbed "lost textile," which involved actual textile fragments being inserted into the casting. Moreover, because she always insisted on consulting the backside of an object for valuable information, each of the works contained in this volume is also shown in reverse. Needless to say, she travelled widely in China from the early 1980s onward, when such journeys were still a rather complex affair. She cultivated close relationships with Chinese experts, as well as with Russian researchers exploring Siberia. Since she herself had lived for long periods in rural lands and was endowed with a deep familiarity with horses, she understood the hands-on ways of the steppe peoples, and thus the conditions lying at the origin of these objects. But above all, she had a wonderful personality: She was always generous in giving advice from her vast storehouse of experience and knowledge, impatient with false pretense, and a hard worker with unceasing curiosity and interest. On this, her final book, she worked until the end of her days.

The title *Guyuan Mizong* (古原覓蹤) refers to the effort of this book to trace, by way of their artifacts, a culture and its people in an ancient place, which have largely been forgotten among the great waves of history. It was written in a spirit of collaboration by Emma C. Bunker and Ursula Brosseder. While the Introduction, Chapter 1, and Chapters 5 through 9 were written jointly, Chapter 3d was written by Ms. Bunker alone. Dr. Brosseder was solely responsible for Chapter 4. For Chapters 2 and 3a to 3c, Ms. Bunker provided the initial text, which was revised by Dr. Brosseder, who also added the steppe perspective and the maps.

The coming into being of his volume involved a long journey. The authors were supported by many people who graciously donated their time, energy, knowledge, and vast experience—and who can only be repaid with deep gratitude.

Katharina Schneider served as a scientific assistant to the catalogue and bibliography for an extended period of time.

John Stevenson, Jenny So, and Chad Jorgenson reworked the text in their capacity as English-language editors.

Bo Lawergren and Donna Strahan provided contributions that fill out our picture of the tuning keys in the collection, which have been the focus of extensive discussion, while Yiu-Kang Hsu added to the chapter exploring the production and distribution of belt plaques in Inner Asia.

Katheryn Linduff, Sergei Miniaev, and James Lally shared their views and were open to discussion.

Wang Dong-Ning, Bryan Miller, and Margarete Prüch helped with pinyin transliteration, as well as with navigating the complex sea of Chinese publishing.

Pieter Meyers, Ester Ferreira, and Jens Stenger conducted all the metallurgical analyses.

Walter Frei conserved many of the objects and prepared them to be measured.

Throughout the years, Rainer Wolfsberger laid the visual foundation for this book, with photographs taken over the course of multiple sessions.

Regula Schorta took upon herself the entire coordination, management, and final editing of the extensive manuscript.

Franziska Schott and Marco Schibig gave the book its form and design.

The actual book was produced by the team of Abächerli Media AG.

Artifacts from Inner Asia during the First Millennium BCE and their Cultural Significance

Introduction

The ancient Chinese, Greeks, and Romans, who formed the urban civilizations at the eastern and western termini of the Eurasian steppe, described the pastoral peoples in their writings as "barbarians" and "nomads," emphasizing their mobility, their lack of literacy, and, as a consequence, their deficient cultural status. These urban gazetteers regarded their mobile pastoral neighbors as "cultural others," that is, as peoples whose cultures they held to be clearly inferior. Much archaeological literature today still continues to refer to the Inner Eurasian Frontier regional zones as "peripheral," "out of the way," or other similar derogatory terms.

Archaeological investigations have made clear that the artifacts belonging to the ancient Inner Asian pastoral peoples were created as personal accessories to be worn on the body and clothing, or as objects to identify their horse harnesses and weaponry. All these physical objects, distinguished by their lively zoomorphic motifs and often romantically described as "Animal Style," must have had serious symbolic meaning for their various pastoral owners. Beautifully illustrated picture books full of artifacts from the northern regions of China distinguished by zoomorphic motifs suggest the amazing diversity of such items (Tian and Guo 1986; Wu En 2008; E'erduosi bowuguan 2013), but offer few explanations for the visual similarities between many of the examples or establish whether or not they share cultural connections. Because similarity of design does not, in itself, prove cultural transmission or the existence of shared beliefs, such resemblances must be investigated before any broader relationship is postulated. The popularity of these beautiful artifacts, especially among early collectors, was partly the result of their romanticized attachment to the idea of the "noble savage" and to the visual appeal of the zoomorphic decorations. However, the contextual study actually carried out on these artifacts did not match the level of fascination for them.

In the past, the cultural history of northern China was written on the basis of ancient Chinese texts by modern scholars specializing primarily in Chinese history. The result has been a strongly Sinocentric perception of the inhabitants of Inner Asia, specifically of the pastoral peoples of the steppe areas of northern China. They were seen as ruthless mounted warriors, constantly harassing their more civilized and settled dynastic Chinese neighbors, and little interest was taken in their distinctive beliefs or in the significance of their material culture.

However, not only Eurasian steppe artifacts, but also dynastic Chinese objects, would be easier to interpret if scholars were more knowledgeable about pastoral practices, horseback riding, and zoology. The case of the famous bronze *you* in the Cernuschi Museum in Paris—described as being cast in the form of a "tiger devouring a boy," who is, in turn, thought to be a "barbarian"—is one prominent example. This extraordinary vessel appears to have been included in a volume devoted to Qin Shihuang's terracotta warriors (Liu Yang et al. 2012/2013, 204–5, fig. 1) to represent "barbarian" beliefs in contrast to Chinese superiority, a long-outdated Sinocentric approach. If the author of that volume had understood feline habits, however, he would have recognized that the scene is, in fact, benign. Mouthing is a protective action, not an attempt to secure a future meal, as we can see in the case of the late Western Zhou-period bronze tiger holding her cub carefully in her jaws (So and Bunker 1995, 43, fig. 13). Anyone who works with artifacts from ancient eastern Eurasia and dynastic China must therefore understand zoology, as such imagery had serious iconographic meaning, just as some long-forgotten myth must have inspired the scene on the Cernuschi *you* mentioned above.

Dynastic China and its Inner Asian neighbors, which produced the artifacts in the present collection, were not as culturally separate as people have tended to believe.[1] Taking into account the advances made over the past decade in the archaeology of Mongolia, it becomes clear that the various pastoral groups of the Inner Asian steppes and dynastic China had been culturally interconnected for millennia, resulting in cultural hybridity, adoptions, and borrowings.

The Guyuan Mizong Collection

The types, styles, and iconography of the artifacts contained in the present collection display an amazing variety of animals and animal narratives, mostly associated with the pastoral peoples who inhabited the vast eastern Eurasian steppes

---

1   Linduff et al. 2018; So 2019; Rawson 2017; Rawson et al. 2020.

stretching from the northern Chinese grasslands in the south to southern Siberia in the north, and from Manchuria in the east to the Inner Asian mountain corridor in the west.

The majority of these artifacts represent a time period spanning more than one thousand years, from the late second millennium BCE to the second century CE. For the most part, they were initially acquired in the early twentieth century by European and American collectors, who were attracted by their fascinating zoomorphic motifs, but who took little interest in their broader cultural context before they were gathered together in this collection. The artifacts were acquired with a connoisseur's eye for aesthetics and variety, not with a view to creating a systematic showcase of Inner Asian cultures. Thus, the objects represent neither a coherent nor a comprehensive survey of materials from every region of Inner Asia and, in this respect, the collection is comparable to many other collections of steppe bronzes that have been published in the past.[2]

Nevertheless, this study will make use of these objects in order to determine the broader contexts of steppe art and archaeology, as well as to suggest more accurate terminology for referring to them and to discuss certain aspects of their production. By reconstructing their cultural contexts and arriving at a better understanding of how they were produced, we will work toward a more enlightened approach to understanding the pastoral groups who produced, commissioned, and used them.

Our main aim here is to propose an individual context for each artifact in the present collection—insofar as possible—by comparing them to excavated pieces that exhibit visual analogies and which are often dismissed, without further explanation, as "exotica." Most of the artifacts in this collection come from various areas of northern China, which was not a homogenous geographic sphere, but appears to have been divided ecologically by the Taihang Mountains that run north and south along the western border of Hebei and Shanxi provinces (fig. 1). Each of these two areas is, in turn, divided into several sub-regions, which are distinguished by specific choices of artifacts and the symbolic motifs that adorn them. Metal artifacts are also distinguished by their production methods, which usually indicate regional foundry techniques. Consequently, the objects in this

---

2 To name but a few: Barbier 1996; Bunker et al. 1997; Bunker et al. 2002; Wagner and Butz 2007; Jäger and Kansteiner 2011; Art animalier 2012.

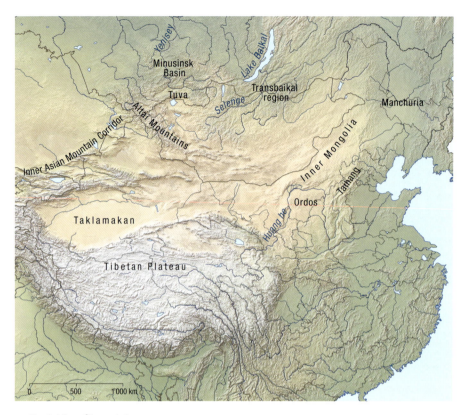

Fig. 1: Map of Inner Asia.

volume are divided on regional lines, via a comparison to examples with known excavated parallels, and then catalogued individually in geographically organized sections.

In Chapters 1–3 objects from northern China are discussed, while Chapter 4 is devoted to belt plaques from Inner Asia, most of which also belong to northern China and only some to Mongolia or southern Siberia. Chapter 6 brings together those artifacts with "exotic overtones," while Chapter 7 deals with the numerous plaques and ornaments that are not directly related culturally to those associated with Inner Asia, but are nonetheless visually similar. A few pieces falling outside of the general timeframe of this volume are discussed in Chapter 8.

It is of great significance that the owner of the Guyuan Mizong Collection has arranged for the majority of pieces to be tested to determine their alloy composition. A comprehensive evaluation of all of the metallurgical results for each piece is beyond the scope of this publication—and beyond the limits of our expertise. We will therefore focus on the production and circulation of belt plaques from

Inner Asia, not only because they are a well-studied group of artifacts, but also because abundant published compositional data is available for a more comprehensive analysis (see Chapters 4 and 10). Even when we do not comprehensively discuss all of the metallurgical results—as, for example, Chase and Douglas (1997) did for the pieces in the Sackler Collection—we offer the data as a reference point for future studies. The metallurgical testing also enabled us to identify some modern forgeries among the pieces (Chapter 9).

We also considered it important to show the backside of each piece, since these not only potentially enable an evaluation of their production technique, but also reveal their fastening system, which is, in certain cases, crucial for identifying the area in which the artifact was produced and used. Unfortunately, only a few publications provide this information (Wagner and Butz 2007; see also von Falkenhausen 2012, 453).

Metallurgical analyses and detailed documentation may justify the renewed publication of some well-known pieces, such as the "goatman" tuning key (Chapter 3d, entry 98; Appendix 1). Because of new findings about the tuning keys, which demonstrate that the "goatman" tuning key is not only visually unusual, but was also cast differently from all of other tuning keys, we decided to also include the tuning keys kept in the Freer Gallery of Art and Arthur M. Sackler Gallery, Washington DC, in order to illustrate this point further (Appendix 2).

Our attempt to provide a cultural context for each piece in this collection met with several challenges: First, there is the great cultural diversity between regions within northern China ranging from the Ordos area through Inner Mongolia, west of the Taihang range, and the areas east of the Taihang range, all the way to Manchuria, each with its own local cultural traditions and practices. Second, different fields with their own research traditions meet in Inner Asia. The field of eastern Eurasian archaeology is dominated by research traditions from the former Soviet Union and Russia, while the field of Chinese archaeology has been dominated for a long period of time by an interest in the Central Plains and has only fairly recently dealt more comprehensively with the archaeological heritage of the peoples living in the steppe areas of northern China. Western scholars who study the archaeology of these regions have usually been trained in one of the two fields and are less knowledgeable in the other. Third, research bearing on the eastern end of the Eurasian Steppe has recently gained momentum as a result of the tremendous advances that the archaeology of Mongolia has made over the past two decades. These discoveries have changed and are still constantly changing our understanding of the pastoral peoples living there and led to a growing awareness of the interconnectedness between the steppe areas of China and the regions farther to the north and west.[3] However, while the archaeology of Mongolia is a fast-changing field, with new discoveries being made each year, its findings have not yet reached a wide audience.

While it remains a challenge to understand the context for each specific piece from across Inner Asia, we hope that our combined expertise and our respective perspectives, which are rooted predominantly in Chinese archaeology, on the one hand, and the archaeology of eastern Eurasia, on the other, will help us give a more comprehensive account of each piece. That said, for some pieces we can only make suggestions, while mistakes seem inevitable given the limits of our respective expertise.

The artifacts in this collection and their analogues in the territories of Inner Asia, but also further west, show that these objects, mostly preserved in the solemn context of burial, marked highly varied fields of exchange, throughout which technology, ideas, and goods were carried. Today, these artifacts from antiquity can be studied in order to garner clues as to how that world and its network system flourished, enriched, and sometimes transformed societies in its path. The examples mentioned here are presented as hints that help us understand that system—people learn, borrow, copy, appropriate, adopt, and adapt, as part of the very basic, everyday human process of communication. The images and artifacts presented here document that course of exchange, and hopefully this publication will encourage further dialogue about such visual conversations of the past across this vital part of the world. Sorting out the various exotic motifs and artifact types reveals much about the Inner Asian pastoral cultures and enriches our understanding of their contributions to world history.

We propose multiple sources for their iconography, some of which can be traced back to the ancient Near East, southern Siberia, and dynastic China, as well as to other more obscure locations. Such a careful analysis, as well as an approach that considers the region not as a periphery to dynastic China, but as a

---

3   See for instance Bunker 1992b; So 2014; Shelach-Lavi 2015b; Rawson 2015a; Rawson 2017; Rawson et al. 2020; Linduff et al. 2018.

well-connected region in its own right, leads to a more nuanced understanding of the use and cultural meaning of such materials.

The Region

The diversity and complexity of the forms and iconography of the metal artifacts in the present collection is staggering. Such an extraordinary variety of types, styles, and imagery should not, however, appear unusual, since the artifacts reflect the economies, fauna, and beliefs of people living within a specific, regional steppe environment. Given the great variety of environmental conditions and a subsistence economy, housing traditions and forms of mobility vary significantly, ranging from sedentary, agricultural homesteads to mobile tents called yurts (*ger* in Mongolian).

Numerous terms have been employed to designate the geographical area we are interested in here, which covers the northern areas of China from Dzhungaria, the Ordos area, and the Taihang range through to Manchuria, while, further north, it encompasses Mongolia, southern Siberia together with the Transbaikal region, Tuva and the Minusinsk Basin, the Altai, and the Inner Asian Mountain Corridor. Especially during the time period under consideration here, namely the late second and first millennium BCE to the first century CE, this region was highly interconnected.

"Inner Eurasia or Central Asia refers to a region that has not always been geographically understood in the past, but today this region includes the former Soviet States of Kazakhstan, Turkmenistan, Uzbekistan, Tajikistan, and Kyrgyzstan, along with the western reaches of China (Xinjiang), Mongolia," and perhaps Afghanistan and Azerbaijan (Hanks 2013, 5). Denis Sinor used the term "Inner Asia" as a synonym for the whole of central Eurasia stretching from the Pacific Ocean to the Black Sea, with the steppe areas as the key to understanding the role of this region in world history (Sinor 1975; 1990, 6–7).

The term "Inner Asian Frontier" refers to the eastern end of the vast Inner Eurasian land mass, which includes the steppe belt running from the Pacific westward for thousands of kilometers through central Siberia. It covers what has been called the Northern Zone (*beifang*) of dynastic China, as well as Mongolia and southeastern Siberia. Ultimately its contacts reached as far as the Carpathian Mountains of eastern Europe. However, the term "frontier" still projects onto eastern Eurasia a Chinese perspective, seeing it in relation to dynastic China.

For our purposes here, we use the term Inner Asia to designate the area outlined above (fig. 1). "Central Asia" designates those former Soviet states to the west of the Inner Asian Mountain Corridor.

The steppe zone itself is composed of deserts, forests, lakes, mountains, rivers, and seas that create small geographical pockets that are not environmentally homogenous. Instead, each area has a distinctive terrain and ecology that appears to have shaped communities' lifeways, beliefs, and specific priorities, which are revealed through their choice of artifacts, clothing, and iconography. These communities participated in a vast, culturally interconnected, globalized Inner Eurasian world, where their regional identities, gender, prestige, sacred beliefs, and values systems appear to have governed their choice of dress and sacred zoomorphic symbols, which they displayed on the artifacts that accompanied them in life and death (Linduff and Rubinson 2008). As we study the many metal items from the first millennium BCE in the present collection, it will become evident that these artifacts had significance for the mounted pastoralists, as well as associated agropastoral and agricultural communities, but their specific meaning must have differed across regions.

"Animal Style"

Due to the lack of a precise archaeological context, the specific origins of the many Inner Asian artifacts from collections have been described by a plethora of ambiguous and sometimes pejorative terms, such as "Animal Style," "Barbarian," "Early Nomads," "Nomadic," "Ordos," "Sino-Nomadic," "Sino-Siberian," and "Scytho-Siberian." These terms have no archaeological validity and are not universally understood or applicable. Instead, they were invented by art historians as a means of dealing with the fact that the pastoral groups left no indigenous written literature to describe their artifacts and zoomorphic iconography (So and Bunker 1995, 13). Whereas the dynastic Chinese possessed their ritual vessels and historical texts, precious treasures that attested to their beliefs, power, wealth, and status, which they displayed in temples and palaces, the pastoralists displayed the artifacts that reflected their beliefs and activities on their bodies or on their horses.

Ellis Minns, an archaeologist, paleographer, and scholar of Eurasian Steppe bronzes in the first half of the twentieth century, discussed the zoomorphic motifs and noted their visual similarities to various artifacts from other cultures,

Fig. 2: Wild boar hunt. Right-hand belt plaque; gold, blue smalt and coral; third to second century BCE. Siberian collection of Peter I. The State Hermitage Museum, St. Petersburg, inv. no. Si.1727-1/69.

but refrained from connecting them on the cultural level, making instead the following observation:

> In the matter of [this North Asian art], it has been denied occasionally that there is anything that deserves a name at all. Twenty years ago, I ventured to write: 'Scythic art has a character of its own. When we have made all the allowance for foreign influence there remains something unlike anything else, the basis of the whole development, that to which imported elements had to conform or else degenerate beyond recognition.' But I don't seem to have arrived at any definition of what that something is. A love for beast forms, joined with a tendency to conventionalize them and adapt them to fill completely the space dealt with, *horror vacui*, an indulgence in superficial and incongruous detail and a way of turning extremities into subsidiary beast forms, this is as far as I got (Minns 1930, 3).

In other words, a frank, art-historical *je ne sais quoi*. Is it possible to suggest terms that could be universally accepted?

Karl Jettmar, the most eminent twentieth-century expert of steppe art, wrote of the term "Animal Style": "In fact there is no general 'style' of this kind … the

'Animal Style' has always been a concession to museum officials and private collectors so as to bring objects of different origin, some related in fact, and others with only superficial similarities, under a general and highly impressive heading … Rostovtzeff popularized this rather ambiguous term [and] did so when he was an emigrant and had to regard the interested layman and the owners of the treasures he published and explained so splendidly" (Jettmar 1972, 256–58). Ann Farkas tried valiantly to explain the term in her text for the Asia Society Gallery exhibition in 1970 entitled *"Animal Style": Art from East to West*, indicating that the field was so confusing that "there is enough evidence to support almost any hypothesis" (Bunker et al. 1970, 20).

Numerous scholars have attempted to explain the profusion of zoomorphic decoration as "hunting magic," but the mentality of the mounted pastoralist was not the same as that of the Paleolithic hunter. While there may be coincidental similarities in their art forms, their contexts and therefore their meanings were fundamentally different. Paleolithic hunting scenes may have been subsistence symbols, while a mounted hunter pursuing a boar on a later Iron Age belt buckle might, for example, connect its elite owner to an episode from the oral epic tales that would bolster his right to rule (fig. 2). The epic tales sung by bards, celebrating their pastoral origins and heroic heritage, would have been psychologically satisfying, acting as a means of constructing social memory and asserting social control.

In lieu of indigenous written records, Inner Asian artifacts specific to certain regions can provide visual clues that reveal information about the sociopolitical background of a given region's peoples and their local economies, sacred beliefs, gender identification, dress, and sacred iconography employing primarily zoomorphic motifs. These cultural indicators, along with an understanding of the foundry techniques that produced their metal objects, may result in a more accurate understanding of this ancient world (Bunker 2009, passim). Further comparisons with material culture found at sites in Mongolia, southern Siberia, Xinjiang, Kazakhstan, and Afghanistan makes it clear that dynastic China's frontier regions were not independent entities, but rather an integral part of a vast, shared, globalized Eurasian world that had long-distance cultural interactions with much of the rest of the Old World.

Pastoralist Lifeways and the Emergence of Pastoralism

Few scholars dealing with the field have adequate first-hand knowledge of the pastoral world or how its inhabitants lived, including their herd management and breeding practices.

In the recent publication, *Nomads as Agents of Cultural Change: The Mongols and their Eurasian Predecessors* (Amitai and Biran 2015), the Inner Asian pastoral herders, traditionally described in vague, now-obsolete terms without illustrations, are credited with being important facilitators and catalysts of social change beneficial to ancient dynastic China.

> The nomads … had a distinctive material culture, comprised especially of small, light, and precious artifacts that could be worn or carried along by themselves or on their horses. Gold, the color of the sun that stands for durability and authority, played a major role in this material culture, and golden objects, such as belt plaques, daggers, knives, horse equipment, often decorated with zoomorphic designs (known as the "animal style"), were among its most typical artifacts throughout history (Biran 2015, 4).
>
> Despite the barbarian image often created by sedentary peoples … it can be argued that a sophisticated nomadic culture existe[d] … This culture is mainly political (Biran 2015, 2).

In other words, their material culture has been fundamentally ignored and given poor press. The earlier, Sinocentric approach missed the social context that existed between dynastic China's northern pastoral neighbors and other distant steppe pastoralists revealed by extensive comparative studies of their artifacts. Their similar design details and metallurgical techniques suggest a commercial relationship that would have fostered the pastoral groups' role "as agents of social change" and helped to clarify how such change occurred (Amitai and Biran 2015, passim).

The seasonal migration between summer and winter pastures is a major herding practice, capable of precipitating an explosive increase or decrease in the number of animals grazing on marginal land. It is a way of life that differs from that of the settled, semi-urbanized agricultural peoples. Survival under these conditions required skillful animal management and husbandry, courage, and endurance, in order to maintain the herds. The wealth and survival of herding pastoralists depended on successfully providing sufficient food and water in early spring to support the birth of the next generation of animals. Those animals then needed to be nurtured and fed until they reached maturity. In the case of groups that were also dependent on hunting, proper conservation management of their wild game was imperative. Sometimes "only a few members of each community, shepherds and herders, accompanied their herds and flocks on migration," rather than large-scale nomadism. Consequently, the terms "nomadic" and "nomadic style" are meaningless in relation to the specific Inner Asian pastoral world under discussion in this volume. Instead, the word "nomadic" often appears to be used pejoratively by scholars, to suggest a lack of structure and sophistication on the part of the pastoralists and to emphasize their status as uncivilized "others." Both are inaccurate assessments. J. R. R. Tolkien put it more aptly in another context, writing: "all those who wander are not lost" (Tolkien, The Fellowship of the Ring).

The recently established field of bioarchaeology has reconstructed, using the analysis of stable isotopes, that the pastoralists' subsistence involved the "intensive exploitation of domesticated livestock for a variety of renewable and post-mortem foodstuffs, including milk, blood, fat and meat, and other non-edible products, including fiber and skin" (Makarewicz 2018, 141). Depending on environmental conditions, pasture availability, cultural traditions, and the individual herder's knowledge and skill, pastoralists employ a variety of husbandry strategies. Anthropological and ethnographic research have documented a huge variety of pastoralist diets, while bioarchaeological studies now help us to reconstruct the strategies of animal and plant exploitation used in each setting. These can include "plant agriculture accompanied by some animal herding, intensive livestock husbandry accompanied by regular low-level cultivation of crops or more opportunistic plant horticulture, and multi-resource pastoralism that draws simultaneously from multiple wild and domesticated plant and animal resources" (Makarewicz 2018, 142).

Few bioarchaeological studies provide evidence for the variety of animal-management strategies that are adapted to local ecologies (Makarewicz 2018). Some reveal the use of sheep foddering during the winter season, which allowed for the extension of the lambing season and the prolongation of the availability of dairy products throughout the year (Ventresca Miller et al. 2020; Makarewicz 2017).

One major topic that has yet to be fully resolved is the emergence of pastoralism in Inner Asia. It has been recognized that it emerged in different ways in the various ecological and geographic regions of Inner Eurasia (Frachetti 2012) and the contours of its beginnings in the central and the eastern Eurasian steppes have begun to be identified by recent bioarchaeological studies.[4]

According to those studies, sheep (*Ovies aries*) are attested in Afanas'evo contexts of the end of the fourth millennium BCE in the Altai region (Hermes et al. 2020), while by 3000 BCE a pastoralist subsistence economy is known for Mongolia (Jeong et al. 2020). From another study, we learn that dairy production was firmly established in northern Mongolia by 1300 BCE (Jeong et al. 2018). The first evidence for horse milking, which is nowadays associated with alcohol production, is known from around 1200 BCE in Mongolia (Wilkin et al. 2020a; Jeong et al. 2020, 893).

Fish is another resource that is regularly exploited by pastoralists (Makarewicz 2018, 143), and the depiction of fish in Iron Age Pazyryk culture may reflect its importance (Rudenko 1970, pl. 167D).

Besides animal products, grain too plays a role in discussions of pastoralist economies, since it has long been thought that pastoralist economies depend on grains imported from neighboring agricultural societies. Initially crops were dispersed from east to west (millet) and from west to east (wheat and barley) in the Bronze Age (Stevens et al. 2016). Millet was consumed by Bronze Age pastoralists at low levels throughout the second millennium BCE (Ventresca Miller and Makarewicz 2019) and it has been suggested that the initial westward dispersal of millet was facilitated by the pastoralists (Hermes et al. 2019). In Mongolia, millet consumption began around 800 BCE and increased during the Xiongnu empire in the late first century BCE (Wilkin et al. 2020b). The more insights we gain into the actual practices for their subsistence economies, the more differentiated our perspectives become and we can overcome long-held beliefs about the dependency of the pastoralists from their settled agricultural neighbors.

Patterns of seasonal migration can vary greatly according to the ecological zone and the landscapes the pastoralists inhabit. Transhumance—the seasonal movement between higher pastures in summer and lower valleys in winter—is practiced, for example, in western Mongolia in the high mountains of the Altai. In central Mongolia, data suggests that seasonal pastoralists movements of the Late Bronze Age only covered a few kilometers (Houle 2010). Their seasonal migratory

---

4   E.g., Jeong et al. 2018; Hermes et al. 2019; Wilkin et al. 2020a; Wilkin et al. 2020b.

pattern appears to be similar to the one seen today, when pastoralists move from their summer camp close to the river to their winter camp—which is located just a little way up the hill, where they are less exposed to the wind—continuing a migratory pattern that may have been established already in the Bronze Age by their predecessors. The distance between the two camps is only a few kilometers, so it would appear that they followed an almost "stationary" migratory pattern. Lifeways and subsistence bases also vary greatly in the areas of northern China (see Linduff et al. 2018).

Another field that is rapidly changing our knowledge about the mobility and migration of groups in Eurasia is the study of ancient genetics (e.g., Narasimhan et al. 2019; Jeong et al. 2020). In Inner Asia, by the Late Bronze Age, there were three genetically distinct clusters (Jeong et al. 2020, 893–94). The genetic data for the Late Iron Age, the Xiongnu period which corresponds roughly to the Western Han dynasty (2nd century BCE to 1st century CE) shows that the Xiongnu empire formed by integration and mixing local and distant groups and that, in its later stages, an influx of western and eastern gene pools can be observed (Jeong et al. 2020, 896–97).

The History of Horses

Horses play an important role for most pastoral societies, and especially for the pastoralists of Inner Asia. The horse was first domesticated, Anthony argues, in the Pontic-Caspian steppes as a source of winter meat (Anthony 2007, 201). He states that, "horses were linked symbolically with humans and the cultured world of domesticated animals by 4800 BCE … and added yet another element to the burst of economic, ritual, decorative, and political innovations that swept across the western steppes with the initial spread of stockbreeding about 5200–4800 BCE" (Anthony 2007, 201). Riding might have begun in the Pontic-Caspian steppes and/or in the early Botai-Tersek culture in northern Kazakhstan, a hypothesis suggested by research on bit-wear on horse teeth from burials, which is taken as evidence of riding or driving (Anthony 2007, especially 205–21). More recent studies have suggested that horses were first tamed, probably for the purposes of milking and herding, in the Botai culture area no later than around 4000 BCE (Olsen 2008). While this first domestication event is fairly well understood, the history of the horse in our region of interest, Inner Asia, is as of yet unclear. Ancient DNA studies have revealed that the horses of Inner Asia from the late second and first millennium BCE—and all modern horses—are not descendants of the Botai horses, but that present-day populations of Przewalski horses are feral descendants of the Botai horses.[5] Furthermore, a study by Gaunitz et al. (2018) showed that the genetic makeup of domestic horses changed dramatically in the third millennium BCE (Orlando 2020, 24.5). This could be explained either by a second, independent domestication of horses or, alternatively, by massive introgressive capture that completely supplanted the horses' Botai ancestry (Gaunitz et al. 2018, 113; Orlando 2020, 24.5). Given the paucity of horse bones in the central Eurasian archaeological record of the third millennium BCE, the disentangling of these two scenarios poses a challenge (Orlando 2020, 24.5). Currently, we do not know where in the Eurasian steppes this independent horse domestication event took place. Given the importance of the horse in the rich petroglyph art of the Altai, we may suspect that the Altai people of the third and second millennium were heavily involved in or connected with this process.

The horse may have been considered a significant cosmic symbol associated with the sun, gold, rebirth, and the heroic warrior in the burial rituals of the migrating pastoralists, as has been suggested for West and South Asia (Kelekna 2009, 64; 78–79; 136, map 30–31). But horses played many roles throughout the Inner Asian pastoral world, as they play a key role in enhancing mobility. At first, horses were of critical importance for two-wheeled carts and chariots, and Rawson and her colleagues see the transmission of the chariot into Shang China as being driven by their northern neighbors (Rawson et al. 2020).

Later, horse riding, and fighting from horseback, was an innovation that was also adopted by dynastic China. The adoption of cavalry from their neighbors along the Inner Eurasian Frontier by Prince Wu Ling of Zhao, during the late fourth century BCE, is recorded in ancient Chinese texts. One wonders whether his conversion to cavalry was really accomplished as rapidly as claimed and just how proficient his cavalry became. They would have been mounted archers, but this form of archery is not a skill capable of being learned overnight, especially without stirrups, which had not been invented by 307 BCE, the date given in the *Shiji* for Prince Wu Ling's military innovation (*Shiji* 43.1806–9).

John F. Haskins, an art historian and accomplished horseman, as well as a colleague of Emma Bunker, always questioned how the "war horse" was invented

---

5   Gaunitz et al. 2018; Fages et al. 2019; Orlando 2020.

and then adopted by the Zhao state to form their cavalry. "To train a large, nervous animal, whose main defense is flight, to stand under attack and even press forward against an armed enemy even at the risk of the horse's own life begs an explanation. To ride a horse for transport is one thing, and to ride a horse on the chase is another thing, but to transform mounted archers and horses into a complex war machine, combining both psychological as well as physical unity would have been incredibly complex and begs an explanation. One wonders if the Zhao actually adopted the concept of cavalry from the Inner Eurasian Frontier pastoralists by hiring mounted steppe warriors as mercenaries to fill the bill, as the Chinese have never been known as accomplished horsemen" (Haskins, April, 1991, personal letter).

One also wonders about the effectiveness of the cavalry, after the Zhao state adopted this military innovation. It is quite possible that Zhao's first cavalry was primarily for show; true cavalry must have developed later in China. Mounted horsemen charging fleeing foot soldiers would have been so disruptive against infantry that Zhao's military success would have been inevitable. The terracotta cavalrymen from the Qin Shihuang tomb complex, Pit 2, appear to be experienced horsemen and are shown holding their horses' reins (Michaelson 1999, 40–41; Liu Yang et al. 2012/2013, pls. 78–79).[6]

Metallurgy

Historically, Inner Eurasia has been a territory that has facilitated the transfer of ideas and technology between East and West (Hanks 2013), especially the diffusion of early metallurgical technology. Already in the late third millennium and the early second millennium BCE, with bronzes of the Seima-Turbino phenomenon, the metal industry of China was impacted from the steppes (Rawson 2015a; Rawson 2017). Subsequently, sites on the Central Plains, such as Erlitou, provide evidence of a shift towards using bronze in an entirely local context (Rawson 2017, 379). The later Karasuk-style bronzes, typical for the Minusinsk Basin of the second half of the second millennium BCE, are also found across northern China (Legrand 2006; Zhang Liangren 2017, 101, fig. 1). Short swords and daggers testify to engagements on the part of the Zhou and the Late Shang

---

6   The suggestion that, with stirrups not yet invented, the riders were "possibly tied to the saddle," is not only ludicrous, but would have been suicidal (Michaelson 1999, 41, quoting Robert Temple, *The Genius of China*, London 1991, 89–90).

with their northern neighbors (Rawson 2017, 381, fig. 4). Details of the dissemination of Karasuk metallurgy have been outlined and extensively discussed, but are not yet fully resolved.⁷

Religion

We may presume that the pastoralists who inhabited Inner Asia were animists, who believed that "spiritual powers permeate and animate nature, inhabiting animals, plants, rocks and other objects in the environment… In Animism, such beliefs together with their associated taboos, rituals, and practices may help manage and conserve the natural environment. Animism is the religion common to most indigenous traditional hunting-gathering, fishing, farming, and herding societies throughout the world… Animism is not anthropomorphic, but an ecocentric world view that opposes the excessive abuse of the land" (Sponsel 2012, 9–11). Such beliefs manifest themselves visually in different ways, in accordance with the various ecologies found throughout the world.

Dress, Textiles, and Belts Signifying Status and Rank

Among pastoral peoples, the need for personal identification and recognition of status was of profound importance, with many moving seasonally and returning to some kind of home base in wintertime. These pastoral groups led highly structured lives organized around prescribed seasonal activities, including both daily excursions and longer migrations to customary water sources, pastures, and hunting grounds. This way of life was reflected in choices of dress and artifacts, which had specific functions and were highly portable. Visual symbols, primarily zoomorphic, adorned their dress, providing clues to clan associations, as well as to specific individual markers of prestige, sacred beliefs, and gender. The zoomorphic, human, and vegetal motifs that adorn many artifacts would probably have served to identify the person whose artifacts displayed them. They played a significant role among many pastoral peoples inhabiting the Eurasian Steppe east of the Urals during the late second and first millennium BCE. Their artifacts reveal details about daily life, regional characteristics, and exotic foreign contacts, often through long-distance, down-the-line trade and exchange.

---

7 Novgorodova 1970; Legrand 2006; Zhang Liangren 2017.

Fig. 3: Straight tubular pants made of blue tapestry-weave woolen cloth, excavated from Zaghunluq cemetery, Qiemo county, find no. 85QZM4:50; first half of the first millennium BCE. Urumqi, Xinjiang Uyghur Autonomous Region Museum.

Metal belt ornaments are one of the most distinctive artifacts associated with the pastoral peoples inhabiting Inner Asia. Belts were not just a practical means of holding up and fastening items of clothing. To the pastoral peoples of northern Eurasia, belt ornaments appear to have been indispensable regalia, which they adorned with visual symbols that reflected their diverse individual values and concerns, such as spiritual beliefs, economy, kinship, gender, rank, prestige, valor, and wealth. The source for detached metal belt plaques strung on some sort of perishable material, such as fabric or leather, is somewhat obscure, but belts embellished by metal were already in fashion during the third millennium BCE in the ancient Near East, where they are found with small personal weapons suspended from them in burials at Ur (Moorey 1967, 83–85). According to So, "belts formed by multiple ornaments seem to have appeared almost simultaneously in both east and west around the beginning of the first millennium BCE, suggesting they originated from a common, as yet undetermined source" (So 1997, 70–71). Belts distinguished by a series of plaques first gained popularity during the first millennium BCE.[8]

---

8   So 1997; Bunker et al. 2002; Brosseder 2011, 349–55; see also Chapters 3 and 4, this volume.

Such belts became extremely popular among the pastoral peoples of the eastern Eurasian steppes, for whom such regalia continued to hold a magico-mythical power. Ultimately, belts became signature items for successive pastoral peoples, such as the Yuezhi (Rouzhi), Xiongnu, Turks, Qidan, and Mongols. Although a few belts distinguished by bronze and gold ornaments have been found in Western Zhou-period Chinese graves (Bunker 1993, 38, figs. 6; 7), they are not typical Central Plains accessories; their presence represents rather an intrusion in a dynastic Chinese setting. The belt hooks that became fashionable with the dynastic Chinese were elaborately decorated, elongated hooks, attached by a raised button on the back, that—through the richness of their production—reflected power, prestige, and wealth. It is doubtful, however, that their highly diverse decorations were ever intended to reflect clan or rank (So and Bunker 1995, 77–85).

Evidence of clothing from eastern Eurasia varies according to the class, gender, and status of those who were buried wearing them and textiles played an important role in the transmission of cultural features (e.g., Allsen 1997; Keller and Schorta 2001). The dynamic cultural changes that occurred throughout the Eurasian steppes during the second millennium BCE were heralded by the development of tailored clothes, especially the invention of riding trousers. Examples have been found among grave goods in Xinjiang and in frozen tombs in the Altai (fig. 3). "Made from three pieces of cloth, one for each side covering the lower abdomen and the leg, and one for the crotch" (Beck et al. 2014, 4–5; 6, fig. 5; see also Zaghunluq 2016, 157–59), riding trousers were created to make sitting astride a horse more comfortable by protecting the genitals, which the garments of urban dwellers could not do. Recent literature on the subject is essential reading for today's scholars, many of whom appear to have never ridden or driven a horse. I do not wish to criticize my colleagues, but the knowledge gained from having a horse between one's legs clarifies many issues about Inner Eurasian culture. To date, there seems to be no mention of pants for women or any accommodations made for their riding comfort, although, as will become apparent, women wearing wide skirts did ride, and presumably wore some kind of protective undergarment.

Elite clothing often displayed zoomorphic designs, sometimes in the weave, and sometimes through metal, leather, or wooden attachments. Surprisingly, scientific tests have determined that the dyes and weaves of woolen clothing recovered from elite kurgans at Arzhan, Tuva, and Pazyryk in the Altai, for example, are not local but eastern Mediterranean in origin, providing evidence of the far-ranging globalization that characterized contact among Inner Asian steppe cultures in the first millennium BCE (Polos'mak and Barkova 2005, 228–29). The important role played by textiles in the transmission of cultural features throughout Inner Asia is exemplified by the study of the impressive long skirts with zoomorphic decoration found at Shanpula, in Xinjiang, research which was supported by the Abegg-Stiftung (Bunker 2001a, 39–45; Schorta 2001, 79–87).

According to Polos'mak's interpretation based on numerous Altaic burials, the clothing reflected "the social and marital status of the wearer as well as his [or her] tribal affiliation" (Polos'mak and Barkova 2005). Polos'mak's survey of numerous burials in the Altai dating to the latter half of the first millennium BCE reveals the continuous use of headdresses enhanced by zoomorphic images suggesting some animistic shamanistic beliefs.

Tattoos featuring zoomorphic motifs embellish the skin of many bodies found in Altaic burials (Barkova and Pankova 2005), the designs of which are beautifully conceived and probably represented major sacred beliefs. Interestingly, their significance within Altaic culture was the opposite of that accorded to them by the dynastic Chinese, who considered tattoos to be marks of "barbarian" inferiority and used them as a degrading form of punishment (Lullo 2013).

Early Chinese historical literature, such as the *Shiji*, completed around 94 BCE, identified pastoralists by the type of material from which their garments were made. "Felts and furs" were traditional Xiongnu garb, typifying the Xiongnu's pastoral lifestyle. By the fourth century CE, the phrase "stripping off felt and fur" was used to epitomize the transformation from "nomadification" to the dress requirements of Sinification (Honey 1992, 3–4). Ancient references of this kind provide serious evidence for the importance of textiles and dress in identifying status and affiliation in antiquity—in other words, there was definitely "a language of clothes" (see also Elkina et al. 2019).

Outlook

Our desire to publish this collection reflects our view that the Inner Asian communities left a rich and deeply intriguing cultural heritage, which it is worth our while to puzzle out. The connectivity between the steppe communities and dynastic China during the late second millennium BCE to the first centuries CE is fascinating and becomes most visible in steppe innovations that made their way into dynastic China, like the chariots in dynastic Shang graves (see recently Rawson et al. 2020) or the practice of including belt plaques in royal tombs of the Western Han dynasty (e.g., Kost 2017). These instances reveal much about China's appropriation of exotic material for their own political reasons. On the other hand, steppe communities profited from agricultural innovations from dynastic China, like the farming of millet, architecture (in the late first millennium BCE), and especially exotica or prestigious goods. Long-distance trade and the desire for luxury items among the pastoral elite fueled down-the-line trade networks, perhaps controlled by special mobile, militant pastoral bands (Stark 2012; Brosseder 2015).

The attribution of each piece or motif to a specific time period and cultural context can only be work in progress, since the landscape of knowledge in Inner Asian archaeology is constantly undergoing rapid change, while the highly diverse cultural expressions are challenging, especially for singular pieces. Innovations like groups of mounted warriors, which inevitably changed the history of warfare, and numerous empires, including the largest empire in the world, the Mongol World Empire, all came out of this region. Our contribution—however limited—aims at highlighting this often-overlooked region of the world, which deserves more attention, in order to assume its rightful place in world history.

Chapter 1

Bronze Age Inner Asian Artifacts, Thirteenth to Eleventh Century BCE

Inner Eurasian-style metal artifacts found at Bronze Age sites reveal the early presence in northern China of agro-pastoralists engaged primarily in animal herding, an economy significantly different from dynastic China's settled agrarian economy (So and Bunker 1995, 33). Bronze knives with integrally cast hilts designed to be carried on the body became signature artifacts for this region, often with zoomorphic pommels that ultimately derive from the Karasuk culture.[9]

Inner Asian bronze knives and daggers with integrally cast hilts were often enhanced with zoomorphic pommels (entry 1). Such artifacts continued a type known from much earlier sites in northern Eurasia (Loehr 1956), which are ancestral to examples found in late Shang-period chariot burials with foreign horse and chariot specialists. These specialists were probably slaves brought from Inner Asia, since their skills were not indigenous to ancient dynastic China (So and Bunker 1995, 36–37). The earliest evidence of horse-drawn chariots in dynastic China occurs at Yinxu, Anyang, in the tomb of Fu Hao (M5), the royal consort of Wu Ding, herself an elite member of an Inner Eurasian group who was married off to the Shang ruler, Wu Ding. This connection would help explain the chariot's transmission into the dynastic Chinese world.[10]

The pommels of certain Inner Asian-type tools were slit to form rattles that produced non-tonal noise (entry 2), a characteristic of noisemakers related to the practice of animism, a belief system associated with hunting and herding peoples (So and Bunker 1995, 35; Eliade 1964, 91). Jingles were also attached to the underside of ritual vessels, an exotic feature introduced into the dynastic Chinese world from beyond the northern frontiers (So and Bunker 1995, 34–35; Shelach 2009, 128), marking the cultural connectivity between the steppe and the sown.

---

9   Chlenova 1976; Legrand 2004, 154, figs. 5.4–5; Legrand 2006, 843–79; Matsumoto 2018, 139–218.
10 Suggested by So and Bunker 1995, 26–27, 36; Linduff 2003; Rawson 2017.

1 | Knife

Northwest China
13th–12th century BCE

Length 24 cm
Width 3.5 cm
Weight 73.2 g

Bronze inlaid with turquoise, alloy composition by J. Stenger: Cu 74%; Sn 11%; Pb 5%; As <1%

Ex Mathias Komor, New York, February 1945; Myron S. Falk Jr. Collection, New York, no. 531; Christie's New York, 16 October 2001, lot 174

Published: Bunker et al. 1970, 86, no. 54; So and Bunker 1995, 101–2, no. 15; 34, col. pl. 4; Falk Collection 2001, 222–23, no. 174

This handsome knife has a pommel embellished with an ibex head. The circular eyes and nostrils are inlaid with turquoise, as are the eye sockets of the stylized long-beaked bird head that forms a suspension loop beneath the ibex's muzzle. The pommel, hilt, and blade are all integrally cast, with a projecting ridge marking the transition from handle to blade. A longitudinal sawtooth pattern marks the middle of the hilt with a perpendicular series of parallel raised lines just below the pommel, perhaps reflecting an earlier pre-metal production method for hafting a stone blade. A faint mold mark on the hilt indicates that this knife was cast in a two-piece section mold.

Knives with gently curved blades and integrally cast hilts are signature steppe tools, which are usually found in non-Chinese contexts in Inner Mongolia, northern Shaanxi, Shanxi, and Hebei (Wu En 1985, 138–39; Tian and Guo 1986, 15–32). A virtually identical example was recovered at Suide county in Shaanxi (He Guang and Zhu Jieyuan 1975, 83, fig. 3). The appearance of this type of knife in Shang-period burials at the capital of Anyang, Henan (Yinxu 1980, pl. 66.1), represents an exotic intrusion associated with the introduction of wheeled transport from Inner Asia, probably as the result of the intermarriage of Shang rulers with elite foreign women. The use of colored-stone inlays is also a northern ornamental device (So and Bunker 1995, 101–2, no. 15; Bunker et al. 1997, 121, no. 6).

Knives with animal-headed pommels are also characteristic of southern Siberia and Mongolia (Matsumoto 2018, 139–218, type A2), often minus inlays (e.g., Ancient Culture 2009, 51; Èrdènèchuluun 2011, 286–89, no. 282; Matsumoto et al. 2019). Most knives found at Inner Asian sites are utilitarian tools, but those with elaborate inlaid pommels may also be prestige items that signify rank and clan affiliation. Those knives with fine workmanship possibly originated in northwestern China, rather than in Siberia (Loehr 1956, 101–5; Wu En 1985, 147–48; So and Bunker 1995, 101; Bunker et al. 1997, 121, no. 6).

2 | Dagger

Northwest China
13th–11th century BCE

Length 24.5 cm
Width 4.7 cm
Weight 182.4 g

Bronze,
alloy composition
by J. Stenger:
Cu 70%; Sn 7%; Pb 12%;
As <1%

Ex Eugene V. Thaw
Collection, New York and
Santa Fe

This dagger is distinguished by a slightly curved hilt, with a pommel formed of a rattle that produced noise when shaken. A tiny ring placed at the juncture of the rattle and the hilt serves as a suspension device. The flat hilt is marked by longitudinal raised lines, one of which continues past the notched guard to form a pronounced midrib that runs the length of the blade. The hilt and the long triangular blade are integrally cast in a two-piece mold, as indicated by the presence of mold marks running along the sides of the hilt.

The pronounced raised rib along the length of the blade—which occurs on many modern hunting blades—was a practical feature for hunters, as it would increase the flow of blood when the blade was withdrawn. An almost-identical dagger was discovered near the deceased's right shoulder in a grave of the Lijiaya culture in Shangdongcun, Ji county, Shanxi (Linduff 1997, 23, fig. A3; after Yan Jinzhu 1985, 848, fig. 2). The rather crude manner in which the rattle is formed "may represent the vestiges of a more primitive smithy metalworking tradition that created earlier rattles by slashing the top off a hollow tube, bending the slashed ends, inserting a pellet, then soldering a metal sheet over the top" (So in So and Bunker 1995, 100, no. 14, based on Loehr 1949, 29–34).

3 | Ritual Implement

Northwest China
13th–11th century BCE

Length 30.8 cm
Width 2.7 cm
Weight 127.1 g

Bronze,
alloy composition
not analyzed

Ex Mathias Komor,
New York, January
1948; Myron S. Falk Jr.
Collection, New York,
no. 524; Christie's
New York,
16 October 2001, lot 173

Published:
Falk Collection 2001,
222, no. 173

This ritual implement terminates in a stylized alligator head, with a separate movable tongue secured between the open, flat jaws with a vertical pin. The alligator's elongated pointed tail is shown in relief along the median of the blade, while the backside of the blade is flat. A double-spiral guard marks the juncture between the handle and the long blade with a rounded tip that curves slightly upward. The openwork handle was once inlaid with turquoise. Mold marks running along each side of the handle represent evidence of casting in a two-part mold.

Implements of this kind were produced along the northern frontiers of ancient dynastic China by non-Shang groups, with whom the Shang peoples interacted (Bunker et al. 1997, 114–15; Linduff 1997, 25). Several examples similar to this piece have been found over the last thirty years at sites in Shilou county, Shanxi, with dates contemporaneous with the Shang dynasty (Guo Yong 1962, 34, fig. 4; So and Bunker 1995, 99–100; Linduff 1997, 25, fig. A9).

Scholars disagree on the function of this type of artifact, but a common suggestion is that they served as shamans' wands. The loose tongue jingles when shaken, a feature that connects this implement with other noisemaking artifacts found in northwestern China, thus supporting an association with animism. Such objects have traditionally been described as snake-shaped, but, zoologically speaking, there is nothing snake-like about them. Also the frequent reference in scholarly literature to these reptiles as crocodiles is zoologically inaccurate (Bunker 1979, passim). Instead, they can be convincingly identified as alligators, which have a similar bony central ridge running from the eyes to the snout (Bunker et al. 1997, 114–15). In antiquity, alligators lived to the west of the Taihang Mountains, near the Yellow River in Shanxi province, and thus would have been a logical choice of zoomorphic motif for the peoples of that region.

4 | Ornament with Two Wild Asses

Northeast China
12th–10th century BCE

Height 9.2 cm
Width 9.7 cm
Weight 96.3 g

Bronze,
alloy composition
by J. Stenger:
Cu 66%; Sn 9%; Pb 13%;
As trace

This ornament was cast in the form of a slit circle with flaring ends, with two confronted, long-eared wild asses with striated manes standing in profile on the inner edge. The ornament is hollow at the back, and the remains of mold seams on the edges suggest it was cast in a two-piece mold.

Although no identical example has been published, similar images are displayed on several other ancient artifacts. A gold earring from the Mynshukur burial, Taldykorgan region in southeastern Kazakhstan, and dating to the twelfth to tenth century BCE, is similar in concept, displaying two wild asses standing on the inner edge of a circle (Basilov 1989, 9–10; Popescu et al. 1998, 119, no. 38). The wild ass inscribed on the base of a bronze ritual *gui* from Jingjiecun, Shanxi, is shown with its legs angled slightly forward, as if braced (Linduff 2003, fig. 2). The same pose is struck by the two asses on our ornament here, as well as by the two jade horse images found in Fu Hao's tomb (M5) at Anyang (Linduff 2003, fig. 1). The slit circle with flaring ends is the same shape as a gold earring from Liujiahe, Pinggu district, outside Beijing, and was based on foreign prototypes (Bunker 1993, 37, fig. 1), as were two gold bracelets from a Lower Xiajiadian site (An Jimin and An Jiayuan 2008, fig. 1). On this basis, it is possible that our ornament is contemporary with the late Shang dynasty and associated with pastoralists living in the Inner Asian regions to the north of ancient dynastic China. A stylistically related object displaying a frontal human face above two standing wild asses, all within a rounded frame with two flaring terminates, is held in a private collection in China, but was published without any origin being given (Wang Fei 2009, 87).

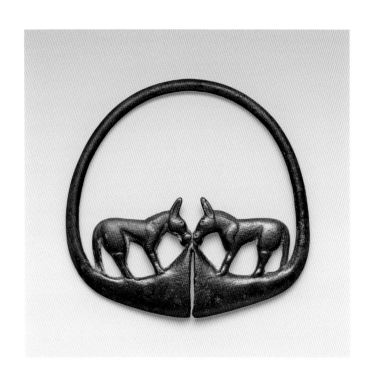

5 | Harness Cheek-Piece in the Shape of a Dragon Head

North-central China, late Western Zhou
ca. 9th century BCE

Height 5.8 cm
Width 9.6 cm
Weight 44.1 g

Cast bronze, alloy composition by J. Stenger:
Cu 75%; Sn 12%; Pb 2%; As trace

Ex Edgar and Hedwig Worch Collection, Paris and New York; Christie's New York, 2 June 1994, lot 44 (part); Therese and Erwin Harris Collection, Miami, Florida; Christie's New York, 16 March 2017, lot 830 (together with entry 6)

Published: Christie's 1994, 22–23, no. 44 (part); Harris Collection 2017, 37, no. 830

This curved cheek-piece is cast in the shape of a stylized dragon head with a ribbed body. The head is looking backward and a long crest sweeps back to form a D-shaped ring, enabling it to be attached to the bridle of a chariot horse. Originally, there would have been another cheek-piece cast in mirror image.

The reverse of the present cheek-piece has three tubular attachment loops, as well as a hole in the middle to accommodate one end of the bit, to which one of the driving reins would have been attached. Such cheek-pieces were created for chariot horse bridles and not continued after the end of the Western Zhou period, according to Magdalene von Dewall (1967, 503–70).

Horse gear of this kind has been found at Xincun in Henan and was decorated by late Western Zhou craftsmen with animal motifs, a tradition also generally characteristic of later Inner Asian steppe art in Siberia, as it is found, for example, in Bashadar and in Pazyryk kurgans in the Altai (Watson 1972, 147 and pl. 1c). Such similarities provide evidence for cultural exchange in antiquity that has not always been recognized or understood, especially when pieces lack the cultural context of burial, since contact between the various cultural regions was never merely unidirectional, but rather frequent and highly complex.

6 | Harness Piece

North-central China, late Western Zhou
ca. 9th century BCE

Height 4.8 cm
Width 5.4 cm
Weight 44.1 g

Cast bronze, alloy composition by J. Stenger: Cu 76%; Sn 14%; Pb 6%; As trace

Ex Edgar and Hedwig Worch Collection, Paris and New York; Christie's New York, 2 June 1994, lot 44 (part); Therese and Erwin Harris Collection, Miami, Florida; Christie's New York, 16 March 2017, lot 830 (together with entry 5)

Published: Christie's 1994, 22–23, no. 44 (part); Harris Collection, 2017, 37, no. 830.

This ornament has a large loop on the back side and depicts a zoomorphic face with two large spirals. When it was associated with cheek-piece no. 5 is unclear. The function remains uncertain: It possibly served as a decorative plaque for straps on the harness and was thus potentially part of a set. No close analogies are known to us.

Chapter 2

Dynastic China's Northeast Eurasian Regional Cultures during the First Millennium BCE

Only recently have the widely spread Inner Asian regional cultures of the first millennium BCE been studied with the goal of understanding the sociopolitical backgrounds and the diverse, but often closely interrelated, material cultures of the region's various inhabitants. New research suggests that past observations concerning their regional characteristics and associated artifacts may need to be rethought.[11]

Ancient dynastic China's northern Eurasian frontier lands were geographically divided along the western border of present-day Hebei province (fig. 4). The ecological differences between these areas are reflected in the range of local economic systems, artifact types, visual symbols, artistic styles, and metallurgical production techniques, some of which appear to have been region specific (Bunker 2009).

The Inner Asian regions northeast of the Taihang range include what are now Heilongjiang, Jilin, and Liaoning provinces, as well as parts of the southeastern Inner Mongolia Autonomous Region and tangential areas in Hebei province and Korea (Nelson 1995, 1–4). The land is marked by many rivers and thus was able to sustain small-scale cropping and settled stockbreeding that did not require long-distance migration in search of adequate pastures. At the same time, the mountainous regions also promoted hunting, trapping, fur trading, and leatherwork, allowing the inhabitants to maintain sedentary home bases, from which small groups might make seasonal expeditions in search of suitable grazing, fishing, and hunting grounds.

The northeast has been known for millennia as a major source of fur, leather, and other useful animal products, commodities that the Chinese tended not to produce themselves. Leopard and tiger skins are specifically listed as coming from

---

11   Linduff 1997; Linduff and Hanks 2009; Indrisano and Linduff 2013; Bunker et al. 1997; Bunker 2006; Bunker 2009; Kost 2014.

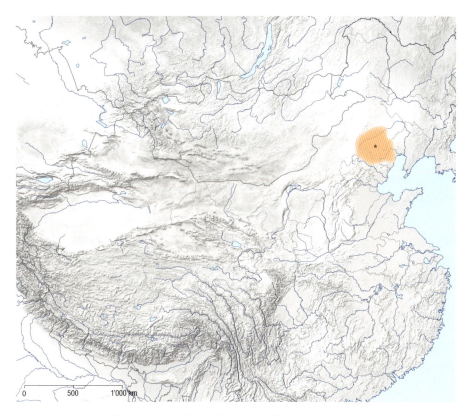

Fig. 4: Extension of the Upper Xiajiadian Culture named after the site Xiajiadian in Chifeng, northeastern Inner Mongolia.

the northeast in the *Huainanzi*, a Daoist anthology compiled in dynastic China during the first century BCE (Major 1993, 164).

The people living east of the Taihang range also had contact with Inner Asian pastoral groups living far to the northwest, in southern Siberia, via the "Fur Road," an ancient trans-Eurasian exchange route leading north via the Amur Valley, then westward to the Caspian Sea, and on to southeastern Europe, roughly the same route followed by the trans-Siberian railroad today (So and Bunker 1995, 65; Kuz'mina 2007).

It is important to point out that the Fur Road appears to have had almost no cultural impact on the Inner Asian cultures located west of the Taihang range. As a result, the practice of riding astride, certain metallurgical techniques, and specific zoomorphic symbols appear much earlier at sites located east of the Taihang range.

Chapter 2a
Artifacts Found East of the Taihang Range

Many artifacts found in burials east of the Taihang range illustrate the importance of hunting for local cultures. An eighth-century BCE bone fragment from tomb 102 at Nanshan'gen, Ningcheng county, southeast Inner Mongolia Autonomous Region, portrays a hunter with drawn bow, standing near two horse-drawn vehicles accompanied by a pair of hunting dogs, about to shoot two deer (fig. 5 A).

Numerous bronze fittings display images of mounted hunters chasing their quarry, providing visual evidence for the practice of riding astride in the northeastern frontier regions of dynastic China. For example, one bronze excavated from tomb 3 at Nanshan'gen, Ningcheng county, southeast Inner Mongolia Autonomous Region, is decorated with two mounted hunters chasing a hare (fig. 5 B). Another similar bronze fitting with a pendant rattle depicts two mounted hunters and their dogs pursuing a doe (Bunker et al. 2002, 60, no. 26). Rattles of this kind have a tiny pebble inside that produces non-tonal noise. Rattles figure prominently in many forms of shamanism, which consider the pebbles to be imbued with animistic spirits (Eliade 1964, 91; 178).

These hook-shaped bronzes belong to a group of artifacts that are often described as suspension devices (entry 7), without any indication as to what was suspended from them (Bunker et al. 2002, 60–63). A damaged exemplar, missing the riders and rattle, was found on the belly of the deceased at Xiaoheishigou, Ningcheng county, a site associated with the Upper Xiajiadian culture, suggesting that it might have been attached to the belt (Liu Bing 2006, 78).

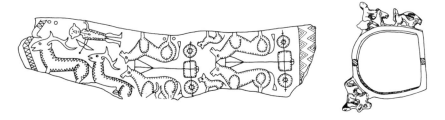

Fig. 5: A. Bone fragment with depiction of a hunter, excavated from tomb 102 at Nanshan'gen, Ningcheng county, southeastern Inner Mongolia; eighth century BCE. B. Bronze fitting with depiction of two mounted hunters chasing a hare, excavated from tomb 3 at Nanshan'gen, Ningcheng county, southeastern Inner Mongolia.

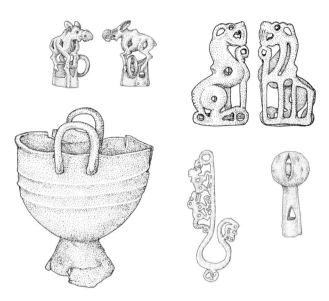

Fig. 6: Bronze items deposited in a cauldron found at Korsukova, Kachugskiĭ district, north of Irkutsk, Baikal area of south Siberia.

The Xiajiadian culture, named after a site near Chifeng, is a collective term used for much of the archaeological material found in the northeast, with the earliest material referenced as Lower Xiajiadian and later material as Upper Xiajiadian, a period tentatively dated to the eighth to sixth centuries BCE (Bunker et al. 1997, 154; Shelach 2009, 32, fig. 2.11; 37). The Chifeng region in northeastern China, previously known as Manchuria, has yielded a rich variety of these hook-shaped artifacts.

Some scholars consider the Upper Xiajiadian examples to be later versions of earlier symmetrical bow-shaped fittings associated with Shang and Zhou chariot burials (Wu En and Wagner 1999, passim; Wu En 2008, 47, fig. 29.3; 51, fig. 33.2). Earlier bow-shaped fittings of this kind also occur in Karasuk burials in the Minusinsk Basin of southern Siberia, where they are considered "components of the Karasuk weapon/tool kit on male belts" placed on the body along with knives with animal-head pommels (Wu Hsiao-yun 2013, 37–49; 40, fig. 2.12; 48, fig. 2.19). Wu En and Wagner (1999, passim) have suggested that fittings found in burials associated with a chariot should be regarded as rein guides. Bow-shaped and hook-shaped fittings are also depicted on deerstones in Mongolia (cf. Novgorodova 1989, 198), such as one located in Uushgiĭn Övör, which shows the fitting hanging from the belt (Takahama et al. 2006, 102, pl. 20.1). However,

Deerstone at Bayantsagaany khöndiï (central Mongolia, Arkhangaï aïmag, Ikhtamir sum; Törbat 2018a, 63, no. 33).

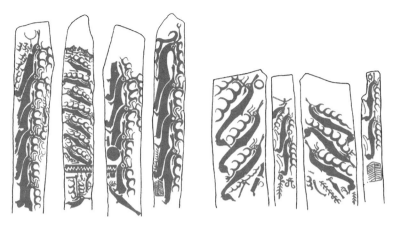

Fig. 7: Deerstones with images of knives and daggers with animal-shaped pommels hanging from the waist. Left: Deerstone from Uushgiĭn Övör, Mongolia. Right: Deerstone from Zuny gol, Mongolia.

Hsiao-yun Wu has recently demonstrated that the early bow-shaped artifacts were found with arrowheads and associated with archery, as "components of the weapon/tool set on elite male belts," precluding the identification of the later Upper Xiajiadian bronze hook-shaped items as a later version of the bow-shaped fittings of the Karasuk culture (Wu Hsiao-yun 2013, chapter 2, especially 53–56). Instead, the Upper Xiajiadian hook-shaped artifacts must have had some practical purpose connected to the region, since they seem to have been exclusive to the northeast and are not associated with herding peoples living elsewhere. That said, similar hook-shaped fittings have been found in the Baikal area: once as part of a deposit of bronze items in a cauldron northeast of Irkutsk (fig. 6) and once in a slab burial (Turkin 2003, 88–91, figs. 10–12). Both cases are indicative of long-distance contact with the far northwest.

One artifact contained in the present collection (entry 8), which is stylistically related to these hooks, shows a deer fleeing from a predator that is nipping at its tail. The deer's legs are depicted in such a way that the hind legs folding forward overlap with the forelegs folding backward, a pose that has traditionally been described as "recumbent" by scholars specializing in deer imagery (Schiltz 1975, 190, nos. 171–72). Deer in a hurry move differently than horses, so it is tempting to wonder whether this particular configuration of the deer's bent legs, as is found in entry 8, might have sometimes been intended to suggest speed (see discussion below, in Chapter 2b, entry 28). These representations of deer with folded legs also contain antlers, which are represented as a stylized series of interlinked

Fig. 8: Bronze helmet from Xiaoheishigou, Ningcheng county, Inner Mongolia (eighth century BCE) and felt headdress from tomb 1, Ak-Alakha site 1, Ukok plateau (early third century BCE) both topped with horse images.

curvilinear forms, an artistic convention that appears to have derived from more naturalistic deer images seen on earlier petroglyphs and deerstones. This stylization later recurs in the cervids represented on artifacts belonging to Scythian groups living in the Black Sea region.

Other Artifacts

Certain artifacts with zoomorphic imagery from Inner Eurasian regions east of the Taihang were primarily destined for personal use, such as garment plaques, tiny spoons, and tools, especially knives used for butchering and skinning (So 1997, 70–78; Bunker et al. 2002, 84). The zoomorphic images that distinguish many northeastern Inner Asian artifacts reflect the local fauna and beliefs associated with the various animal-oriented activities of the region's inhabitants. Images of copulating wild animals abound, probably intended as fertility amulets to encourage the proliferation of the wild herds upon which successful hunts depended. Such sexual images never appear on ornaments created for the mobile herding pastoralists living west of the Taihang range—where animal reproduction was supervised, as it still is today—except as the result of interregional artifactual exchange. By contrast, artifacts associated with the pastoralist groups living west of the Taihang are marked by animal-predation motifs that served as visual power themes and kinship markers, in an economy where water and grazing rights were the major issues (So and Bunker 1995, 64–65).

Wild animals depicted in raised lines on knife and dagger hilts (entry 9) also suggest connections with pictorial traditions represented in petroglyphs and on deerstones found throughout Mongolia and southern Siberia (Novgorodova 1980; Törbat 2018a; 2018b). Deerstones also show images of knives and daggers with animal-shaped pommels hanging from the waist (fig. 7; Novgorodova 1989, 186; Wu En 2003, figs. 1–3). Aside from hunting and semisedentary livestock raising, small-scale cropping also played an economic role in certain regions in the northeast containing rich, well-watered soil. An emphasis on fertility is often characteristic of peoples with an agricultural economy, which may explain the presence of penis-shaped handles that distinguish a few bronze ladles found at Upper Xiajiadian sites near Chifeng (Liu Bing 2006, 62–63).

Cultural connections with hunting groups to the far north are suggested by similarities between a bronze helmet surmounted by a horse image excavated at Xiaoheishigou, Ningcheng county, southeastern Inner Mongolia Autonomous Region, dated to the eighth century BCE, and a felt headdress topped by a wooden horse image from tomb 1 in Ak-Alakha 1 (fig. 8) on the Ukok Plateau in the Altai belonging to the Pazyryk culture of the early third century BCE, as noted by Polos'mak and Barkova (2005, 90).

In the past, the Inner Eurasian inhabitants living east of the Taihang were collectively referred to as the *Donghu* (eastern barbarians), a meaningless term with no tribal significance. As Shelach points out, "the very attempt to correlate the archaeological record of the Northern Zone with specific groups of people who inhabited the area prior to the fourth or third century BCE is not only fruitless but is also misleading and destructive" (Shelach 2009, 16; Linduff 1997, 67–73).

The artifacts in this chapter have been associated with northeastern China based on similarities to pieces that have been excavated or collected from areas east of the Taihang range. The northeast appears to have been home to various non-Chinese groups dependent on various animal-oriented economic practices that were semisedentary in contrast to the more mobile herders living west of the Taihang. Therefore, it should not be surprising that many later foreign groups, such as the Xianbei, the Turks, the Qidans, the Jurchins, the Mongols, and the Manchu, were also semisedentary unlike the herders located west of the Taihang.

7 | Fitting, Bronze Hook with Jingle and Turquoise Inlay

Northeast China
8th–7th century BCE

Height 11.4 cm
Width 5 cm
Weight 86.6 g

Bronze, turquoise, alloy composition by J. Stenger:
Cu 52%; Sn 6%; Pb 8%; As <1%

This bronze fitting is cast in the shape of a crouching leopard with bared, jagged teeth and a long, gracefully curved tail from which a rattle depends. The figure of a boar standing on the leopard's head and forepaws shows wear, suggesting that it likely served as a suspension loop. Turquoise inlays mark the leopard's shoulder, haunch, leg joints, and paws. The piece appears to have been lost-wax cast, using a wax model formed in a two-piece mold. Two similar examples are contained in the Thaw Collection (Bunker et al. 2002, 60–61, nos. 26–27). This fitting belongs to a group of artifacts that have been published in several Chinese archaeological books with limited details. In general, they are cast in the round and relate stylistically to pieces excavated in northeastern China and southeastern Inner Mongolia associated with the Upper Xiajiadian culture (So and Bunker 1995, 119, no. 34). A fitting of this type has been discovered in Irkutsk, southern Siberia, providing evidence for more long-distance contact between northeastern China and peoples living in the distant northwest (i.e., in southern Siberia) than has been acknowledged (Berdnikova et al. 1991, 129, fig. 6).

8 | Fitting

Liaoning
ca. 7th–6th century BCE

Height 9.2 cm
Width 6.7 cm
Weight 62.5 g

Cast bronze, alloy composition by J. Stenger: Cu 61%; Sn 11%; Pb 11%; As high

This bronze suspension device is formed by a reptilian loop terminating in snake heads seen from above. The reptilian body is represented by ribbed lines perpendicular to a central line that runs longitudinally. A zoomorphic predation scene on each of the artifact's outer sides appears to show a deer being pursued by two carnivores, one of them nipping at its tail, but extensive wear and poor-quality casting make positive species identification difficult. The piece is formed in the round without attachment loops, but evidence of wear at the top between the two carnivores suggests that a suspension strap produced the wear. The deer are represented with their legs folded as they flee the predators behind them, suggesting that this pose may sometimes be intended to indicate speed. No similar piece has been found by archaeologists, but the snake image seems to relate stylistically to the snake frame of a bronze plaque excavated at Shiertaiyingzi on the banks of the Daling River, which is twelve kilometers southwest of the Chaoyang county seat in Liaoning (Linduff 1997, 71–72, fig. A107). At the same time, the deer with backswept antlers resemble those portrayed on multiple deer-shaped plaques found in the Yuhuangmiao cemetery, located north of Beijing (Jundushan 2007, vol. 4, 380–83), indicating contact between the two regions. However, the question of where and by whom these plaques were actually cast remains unanswered.

9 | Knife

Eastern Mongolia or southern Siberia
ca. 8th–7th century BCE

Length 22.4 cm
Width 2.2 cm
Weight 93.6 g

Cast bronze, alloy composition by J. Stenger: Cu 85%; Sn 3%; Pb 3%; As <1%

Two recumbent caprids with cloven hooves decorate the flat hilt of this knife on one side, while three standing, horned bovines are portrayed on the other side. The animals are depicted in procession, with their bodies represented in profile relief against a plain-troughed space. The pommel is merely a flat, roof-like slab that protrudes on one side and contains a horizontal open slit below for attachment purposes. A spur marks the transition between the hilt and the blade, which are integrally cast. The remains of mold marks along the sides of the hilt indicate that the knife was cast in a two-piece mold.

Knives with similar roof-like pommels and spurs, which are vestigial remainders of the transverse ridge on earlier knives, marking the transition from hilt to blade, have been collected throughout eastern Mongolia and southern Siberia, but are difficult to date because their specific cultural contexts are unknown. A similar piece from a private collection in Mongolia is reported to come from Sükhbaatar province in eastern Mongolia (Ėrdėnėchuluun 2011, 307, no. 307). The Sackler Collection contains a large number of knives that were acquired from various missionaries, who bought them during the early twentieth century as curios (Bunker et al. 1997, 136–139; 144–153; 155–164; 183).

10 | Knife

Northeast China and southeast Inner Mongolia
8th–7th century BCE

Length 24.7 cm
Width 2.5 cm

Cast bronze, alloy composition by J. Stenger: Cu 89%; Sn 3%; Pb 3%; As trace

Ex Therese and Erwin Harris Collection, Miami, Florida, by 1978; Christie's New York, 16 March 2017, lot 816

Published: Oriental Bronze Metallurgist 1978, no. 29; So and Bunker 1995, 122–23, no. 40; Salviati 1996, 24, fig. 4; Harris Collection 2017, 26, no. 816

This knife has an integrally cast, curved blade and an openwork hilt formed of intertwining serpentine bodies. A small, oblong loop with a projecting, flat D-shaped tab at the end of the hilt serves as a device enabling the knife to be hung from the owner's belt.

A wonderful example of a knife with a similar entwined serpentine hilt is found in the Ordos Museum Collection, having been purchased without any indication as to the cultural context (Cao Wei 2012, 125). Knives with similar pommels have been traditionally associated with southeastern Mongolia, where hunting was widespread. A knife with a similar intertwined openwork design was recovered from one of the large tombs at Nanshan'gen, Ningcheng county, southeast Inner Mongolia (Liaoning and Zhongguo 1973, pl. 9.5; So and Bunker 1995, 122–23, no. 40).

11, 12, 13 | Three Knives

Northeast China, Upper
Xiajiadian culture
7th–5th century BCE

11 | Knife (left)
Length 21 cm
Width 3 cm
Weight 83 g
Bronze,
alloy composition
by J. Stenger:
Cu 54%; Sn 17%;
Pb 5%; As <1%

12 | Knife (middle)
Length 23.2 cm
Width 2.3 cm
Weight 104.1 g
Cast Bronze,
alloy composition
by J. Stenger:
Cu 78%; Sn 10%;
Pb 11%; As <1%

13 | Knife (right)
Length 23 cm
Width 2.5 cm
Weight 102.1 g
Bronze,
alloy composition
by E. Ferreira:
Cu 59.8%; Sn 14.7%;
Pb 3.4%

These three bronze knives each have an animal-shaped pommel, a single-edged blade, and a flat hilt, with all three elements integrally cast in a two-piece mold. Each blade turns upward almost imperceptibly at the tip, a characteristic that would have prevented a hunter from piercing and damaging the pelt when skinning an animal. The first knife (no. 11) has a U-shaped twin-horsehead terminal, the second (no. 12) has a terminal formed by a short-legged horse, while the third (no. 13) has a pommel formed by a standing wild boar.

Knives with similar animal-shaped pommels integrally cast with their hilts have counterparts among the numerous artifacts excavated from Upper Xiajiadian sites in northeastern China and southeastern Inner Mongolia, dating between the seventh and fifth century BCE. A knife with the same pommel design as no. 11 was excavated from an Upper Xiajiadian burial (Shelach 2009, 32, fig. 2.11). The knife with horse-shaped terminal, no. 12, has two known counterparts: one in the Thaw Collection in the Metropolitan Museum (Bunker et al. 2002, 93, no. 58), and another that was found in Ningcheng county (Wu En 2008, 97, fig. 58.7). Knives were very common among the non-Chinese peoples who inhabited the northern frontier zone, east of the Taihang Mountains, where such implements were designed as utilitarian tools used in hunting and skinning, rather than as weapons for hand-to-hand combat, as suggested by some scholars.

No. 13 has a pommel cast in the shape of a standing boar, an artifactual type that can be traced back to a Tagar-culture knife type of the sixth century BCE (Gossel-Raeck and Busch 1993, 223, no. 139).

14 | Vulture-shaped Garment Plaque

Northeast China
8th–7th century BCE

Height 4.7 cm
Width 4.2 cm
Weight 6.2 g

Bronze,
alloy composition
by J. Stenger:
Cu 88%; Sn 9%;
Pb 1%; As high

This small garment plaque takes the form of a vulture shown in flight with spread wings and an outstretched tail. Raised striations suggest wing and tail feathers, while raised chevrons indicate the long scrawny neck specific to vultures. A tiny vertical loop for attachment is placed behind the head on the reverse. A mold mark that runs along the length of the loop and down the back indicates that the loop was integrally cast with the plaque in a multipiece mold. Two vulture-shaped plaques similar to the present item have been discovered in northeastern China at Zhoujiadi, Aohan banner, southeastern Inner Mongolia, a site that has been dated to the eighth or seventh century BCE (Zhongguo 1984, 422, fig. 10.1–2). Seventeen similar examples have been excavated at Nanshan'gen, Ningcheng county, southeastern Inner Mongolia, another site with the same date (Zhongguo 1975, fig. 19.2, pl. 7.11–12).

The same bird occurs also in the Slab burial culture, for example on a plaque from the Dvoretzky cemetery in the eastern Transbaikal area (Chlenova 1992, pl. 101.16; Miniaev and Smolarski 2002, 19, no. 3), on a knife from eastern Mongolia (Novgorodova 1980, 102, top image), and on rock art attributed to the slab-burial culture (Novgorodova 1980, 111, fig. 71).

The bird on the present plaque resembles the vulture depicted on a mirror excavated at Shangcunling, near Sanmenxia, Henan, a site dated from the late Western Zhou to the early Spring and Autumn period, or about the eighth century BCE (Zhongguo 1959, 27, fig. 21). This mirror is an exotic intrusion at Shangcunling, probably having been made far to the northwest and acquired via exchange.

The vulture is a scavenger bird of prey common to northeastern China and the Eurasian steppes; it was associated with death in many ancient cultures, such as on the Sumerian Stela of the Vultures, from the third millennium BCE found in Girsu, Iraq (World's oldest writing 2016, 33).

15 | Two Coiled Feline Garment Plaques

Northeast China and the
Mongolian Plateau
6th–5th century BCE

15a | Garment Plaque
(left)
Diameter 3.2 cm
Weight 5.1 g
Bronze,
alloy composition
by J. Stenger:
Cu 75%; Sn 15%; Pb 8%;
As trace

15b | Garment Plaque
(right)
Diameter 3.2 cm
Weight 6.9 g
Bronze,
alloy composition
by J. Stenger:
Cu 83%; Sn 15%; Pb 21%;
As trace

These two circular, openwork garment plaques are each cast in the shape of a coiled leopard, with its body in profile and its head frontally facing the viewer. The shoulder and rump of each leopard is marked by intaglio, concentric tear-shaped lines. The eyes are indicated by intaglio dots within intaglio circles, and the nostrils by circular holes. The hip, shoulder, and tip of the tail each display a single, round cell, which may be residual inlay cells. Each plaque was piece-mold cast and displays two tiny attachment loops on the flat reverse side. The motif of a zoomorph coiled into a ring has an early eastern Eurasian origin, occurring on Hongshan Neolithic jades, and later on dynastic-Chinese bridle ornaments from the Western Zhou period, circa eleventh century to 771 BCE (Watson 1971, 108, fig. 48; Bunker et al. 2002, 24; Shao and Yang 2016, 57–58, fig. 11.4–9). A coiled carnivore motif also occurs on deerstones in Mongolia and southern Siberia, and subsequently on a bronze breastplate from a horse's harness excavated at Arzhan 1 in the Republic of Tuva, southern Siberia (Griaznov 1984, 37, fig. 15.4; Bokovenko 1995b, 270, fig. 8k). A feline with its face shown frontally, as we find on the two plaques under discussion, is considered a specific, coiled feline motif found at Upper Xiajiadian-culture sites in northeast China, according to Lin Yun (Lin Yun 2008, passim; Shao and Yang 2016, 58, fig. 11). A similar plaque is also reported from south-central Mongolia (Ėrdėnėchuluun 2011, 213, no. 218).

A small, gold version of the present plaques was one of the highlights of the Kempe Collection sold by Christie's, New York (Masterpieces 2019, 27, no. 502), and indicates the existence of a hierarchy of metals among the local elite.

The coiled feline motif was also transmitted west to Central Asia, where it appears in Saka art, and then further northwest, where it occurs in Scythian art (Chlenova 1967, 31; Schiltz 1975, 146, no. 51), but the faces are not shown frontally.

16, 17 | Two Spoon-shaped Pendants

Northeast China and
southeast Inner Mongolia
6th–5th century BCE

16 | Pendant (left)
Height 4.1 cm
Width 1.1 cm
Weight 5 g
Bronze,
alloy composition
by J. Stenger:
Cu 70%; Sn 5%;
Pb 18%; As <1%

17 | Pendant (right)
Height 4.3 cm
Width 1.3 cm
Weight 6.8 g
Bronze,
alloy composition
by J. Stenger:
Cu 84%; Sn 6%;
Pb 13%; As high

Two stylized, long-beaked raptor heads link a suspension loop to an elongated oval bowl on each of these two tiny spoons. The heads are shown in profile with the eyes represented by pierced circular holes. Each of the two spoons appears to have been cast in a two-piece mold, as indicated by a faint mold line along the edges. The casting quality of one spoon is far superior to that of the other.

A small spoon in the Arthur M. Sackler Collections has two long-beaked raptor heads similar in design to those depicted on these spoons (Bunker et al. 1997, 173, no. 87). Similar beak heads are also found on two daggers excavated at Xiaoheishigou, Ningcheng county, southeastern Inner Mongolia, in a sixth- to fifth-century context (Ningcheng et al. 1985, 37, fig. 32.3–4).

Such tiny spoons must have had some ritual function, but they have thus far received little scholarly attention. According to Sergei Miniaev, such pendant artifacts "were distributed in the steppe zone from the Transbaikal area to northeastern China" (e.g., Miniaev and Smolarski 2002, 23, no. 7; Ėrdėnėchuluun 2011, 456–58), but are not found among grave inventories in the Ordos Loop.

18 | Garment Plaque

Northeast China, Upper Xiajiadian culture
7th–6th century BCE

Height 5.9 cm
Width 4.5 cm
Weight 32.1 g

Cast bronze, alloy composition by E. Ferreira:
Cu 70%; Sn 9.2%; Pb 8.5%; As 0.7%; Fe 0.1%

Two crouching dogs, one above the other in perfect profile, adorn this openwork garment plaque. Each dog has a raised tail terminating in a raptor head looped over its back. The body of each dog is marked by ribbed, concentric ovals surrounded by raised lines that accentuate the dog's shoulders and haunches, while a concentric circle indicates the dog's eyes. The jaws are represented by jagged lines that suggest a fierce appearance. The reverse displays four small, vertical loops, one at each corner for attachment purposes. Flashing in the openings indicates that the plaque was cast in a two-piece mold.

Two plaques in the Thaw Collection at the Metropolitan Museum, New York (Bunker et al. 2002, 157, no. 134), depict canine images similar to those on the present plaque and are associated with the Upper Xiajiadian culture. Another plaque, also in the shape of a dog with a raptor-head tail tip, was found in Birja, close to Minusinsk in Siberia (Salmony 1934, 9, fig. 12). The close similarities between all these pieces suggest an as yet unidentified collaboration in the production of the artifacts. Were they made in both regions, Chifeng and Minusinsk, or only one in location and then transferred to the other? An analysis of the metal alloy compositions might help answer this question.

19 | Garment Plaque

Northeast China and southeast Inner Mongolia, Upper Xiajiadian culture
7th–6th century BCE

Height 5.6 cm
Width 4.2 cm
Weight 48.6 g

Cast bronze, alloy composition by J. Stenger:
Cu 70.0%; Sn 13%; Pb12 %; As trace

Two crouching dogs shown in raised profile with ovals marking their shoulders and haunches stand one on top of the other on the rectangular garment plaque. Each dog has a raised short tail, and the eyes are indicated by small, round, worn sockets. Their mouths are each indicated by an X-shape typical of many Upper Xiajiadian images of carnivores. The reverse of the plaque is hollow; it displays four vertical loops, two behind each dog, that appear to have been soldered onto the plaque, which has been cast in a two-piece mold.

The dogs are similar to those represented on a bronze stand excavated from M9601 at Xiaoheishigou, Ningcheng, in southeastern Inner Mongolia Autonomous Region (Xiajiadian 2007, 348–49, no. 205). Dogs have always been essential companions for hunters in this region. Compare the canine images depicted on the bone fragment from Nanshan'gen, showing a hunter accompanied by two dogs standing near his two carts (Linduff 1997, 69, fig. A102; see above fig. 5.A, p. 46).

20 | Spoon

Northeast China
7th–6th century BCE

Height 9 cm
Width 2.7 cm
Weight 16.5 g

Bronze,
alloy composition
by J. Stenger:
Cu 98%; Sn 2%;
Pb 5%

A recumbent, antlered cervid cast in the round surmounts the handle of this small spoon and serves as a suspension loop. Inner Asian steppe peoples often suspended small spoons from their belts. Numerous spoons have been found throughout Inner Asia, but are difficult to date, since most of them are surface finds whose specific cultural context is unknown. A spoon with an elongated bowl in the Borowski Collection has been associated with the Upper Xiajiadian complex (Jäger and Kansteiner 2011, 113, no. 159). Several other small spoons in the Sackler Collection associated with northeastern China date to the sixth–fifth century BCE (Bunker et al. 1997, 173–74). It is interesting to note that the present spoon has no trace of arsenic in its alloy, while the others do. Hopefully future archaeological discoveries will yield more precise information.

21 | Awl

Northeast China
First millennium BCE

Height 9.9 cm
Width 2.2 cm
Weight 18.2 g

Cast bronze,
alloy composition
not analyzed

The lower part of this awl has a square cross-section and a rounded shank. A standing carnivore surmounts the shank and serves as a suspension loop. The hilt is marked by horizontal lines and two diamond designs. A mold line bisecting the carnivore figure longitudinally and continuing down the shank indicates that the awl was cast in a two-piece mold.

An awl is a pointed tool for piercing or marking leather and wood, a tool that appears to have been part of the tool kit of the northeastern steppe world for a long time, but is difficult to date precisely (Shelach 2009, 28). The Arthur M. Sackler Collections include several Northern Zone awls and cases with geometric and zoomorphic decoration (Bunker et al. 1997, 104–06, no. 70). The royal burial at Arzhan 2, tomb 5, includes a bronze awl surmounted by an argali ram (Čugunov et al. 2010, pl. 77.6a–b). Awls tend to be recovered mostly from the graves of females (Linduff and Rubinson 2008, 172); we presume that females did most of the leatherwork.

Chapter 2b
Artifacts Associated with Mountain Cemetery Sites in the Jundushan

Cemetery sites in the rugged Jundushan terrain, east of the Taihang Mountains in the Beijing region, reveal burial customs and artifacts that are distinct from those associated with the Upper Xiajiadian culture located further east in Liaoning and the Chifeng area of southeastern Inner Mongolia. The Jundushan cemetery sites, traditionally associated with horse-riding hunting peoples who were sometimes referred to as "Shanrong" in ancient Chinese texts, have yielded a profusion of metal grave goods: necklaces, pectorals, belt plaques, and garment plaques, along with daggers, knives, arrowheads, and horse bits.[12]

According to ancient Chinese texts, the Shanrong moved eastward from northern Shanxi around 714 BCE and attacked the state of Zheng located in modern Henan (Bunker et al. 1997, 175–76). In 706 BCE, the Shanrong attacked the state of Qi in what is now Shandong province; they went on to attack the powerful Yan state located in northern Hebei in 664 BCE. A year later, the Qi state came to the aid of Yan, helping to drive the Shanrong northward, where they remained, forming important alien enclaves within Yan territory.

The Shanrong are described pejoratively in ancient dynastic Chinese texts as uncivilized and stateless, without distinctive characteristics that would allow any specific ethnic identification (So and Bunker 1995, 51, no. 27). The name Shanrong appears to be a generic term with a geographic modifier that can be roughly translated as "mountain warriors" (Hsu 1999, 549). Recent research by Linduff and Shelach indicate that such tribal names are not specific, nor are they historically accurate (Linduff 1997, 62–67; Shelach 2009, 16; 148–49). We have no idea what these peoples called themselves and we should thus avoid using ancient Sinitic renditions of non-Sinitic names that are meaningless, rather than illuminating. Numerous Rong groups are located in many places in ancient dynastic Chinese texts, but with no ethnic specifics (Di Cosmo 1999, 922–24; Wu Xiaolong 2013, 122; 134). Large cemetery sites, such as Yuhuangmiao, Hulugou, and Xiliangguang in the Jundushan, suggest that these hunting peoples had permanent residences from which small groups rode out to hunt and trap.

12   Linduff 1997, 63–67, fig. A87; Bunker et al. 1997, 175–76; Bunker et al. 2002, 20, fig. 25.

Long-distance contact with other non-Chinese Inner Asian groups was probably achieved through Zhangjiakou in present-day northern Hebei, long the starting point of an ancient route that led north to Lake Baikal and then west toward the Black Sea regions.

The extensive publication in 2007 of large numbers of grave goods from three Jundushan cemeteries—Yuhuangmiao, Hulugou, and Xiliangguang—is critical for anyone researching the exotic northeastern Eurasian non-dynastic peoples (Jundushan 2007). The more than 60,000 grave goods from 594 burials include personal ornaments, as well as the remains of heads and legs of horses, cows, goats, and dogs. The Yuhuangmiao cemetery alone yielded some 400 graves (Jundushan 2007, vol. 3, 1658), containing a plethora of artifacts, many of which relate stylistically and art-historically to artifacts found elsewhere in northern Chinese frontier regions, highlighting cultural relationships that we are only now beginning to discuss and try to explain. A few Jundushan burial sites, such as Qingzigou and Ganzibao, are not included in the large 2007 Jundushan publication, but are cited in the Sackler Collection entries, based on the author's personal observations (Bunker et al. 1997, 175–201).

A recent publication by Xiaolong Wu mentions the "remains of a tomb that have been identified with the Xianyu, often considered a sub-group of the White Di" (*Bai Di*) (Wu Xiaolong 2017, 27–28, fig. 2.1). The grave goods display characteristics that are both Zhou and northern, such as gold tiger plaques, similar to a pectoral plaque in the present collection (entry 22) that has been identified as being lost-wax cast. Far from being uncivilized, these horse-riding hunters possessed sophisticated cultural values made visible by the personal symbols that adorned their dress, indicating kinship relationships and various degrees of power, gender, and wealth. Comparative studies of their grave goods suggest the importance of personal adornment in acknowledging status, especially pectorals, some of which were made of gold.[13] For example, pectorals cast in specific zoomorphic shapes appear to be both region- and gender-specific. An elite female buried in M58 at Qingzigou, Xingzhou, displays an openwork bronze plaque on her chest, representing a frog encircled by a pair of snakes, possibly a fertility symbol (Bunker et al. 1997, 188, no. 110). By contrast, the chests of elite males are marked by crouching felines (So and Bunker 1995, 50; Jundushan 2007,

---

13 So and Bunker 1995, 46–50; Linduff 1997; Linduff and Sun 2004; Jundushan 2007, vol. 2, 897, fig. 561.

vol. 1, 301, fig. 54), some of which are also cast in gold (Jundushan 2007, vol. 2, 897, fig. 561), such as entry 22 in this chapter.

The large Yuhuangmiao publication contains numerous drawings of feline-shaped plaques, some of which are said to retain evidence of contact with textiles on their surfaces (Jundushan 2007, vol. 3, 1178–79). Whether such felines represent leopards or tigers is the subject of debate, but the slightly pointy ears and slim bodies (entries 22 and 23) suggest that the animal in question is intended to be a leopard rather than a tiger, which has more rounded ears and a more heavy-set body (MacDonald 1985, 36–38; 44–47).

Casting Observations

The bronze feline-shaped plaques are piece-mold cast, a manufacturing technique whose use is confirmed by the presence of metal flashing within the design openings (entry 23). However, the gold feline-shaped examples are lost-wax cast (entry 22), indicating a different choice of casting process for precious metal and revealing a sophisticated understanding of the different properties of gold and bronze (Bunker et al. 2002, 171–72, no. 157). Such technical knowledge may suggest the participation of non-local Eastern Zhou state metallurgists in the production of ornaments for the neighboring hunting elites, since no casting debris has been recovered locally in the Jundushan. Random mentions in ancient dynastic texts note the existence of commercial contacts between several Eastern Zhou states and nearby hunting groups that were valuable sources of fur, specifically tiger and leopard pelts (Di Cosmo 1999, 923).

A superb circular gold openwork plaque (entry 24) depicting a coiled doe within a frame of linked raptor heads with steppe associations may have once belonged to the peoples treated in this chapter. A circular gold plaque depicting a coiled feline in the Ordos Museum suggests that such personal ornaments were important personal markers in antiquity.[14] The two gold ornaments in the present chapter, the crouching leopard (entry 22) and the coiled doe within a border of linked raptor heads (entry 24), serve as important benchmarks for confirming the gold-to-silver ratio used in antiquity, which represents vital information for the study of large numbers of gold artifacts in collections around the world lacking specific scientific provenance.

---

14   E'erduosi Qingtongqi 2006, 244, no specific provenance mentioned. Emma Bunker is most grateful to Director Wang Zhihao for sending her this important Ordos Museum catalogue.

fig 9: Mirror from Shangcunling cemetery near Sanmenxia city, Henan, find no. M1612:65, diameter 6.7 cm; circa eighth century BCE.

Zoomorphic Image Sources

Many zoomorphic symbols that embellish the dead in the Jundushan cemeteries portray images of wild animals that have earlier traditions in the Sinitic artistic vocabulary, rather than in that of the Inner Eurasian steppe. For example, the coiled animal symbol has a far earlier priority, traceable to the Hongshan culture located in southeastern Inner Mongolia and northeastern China during the third millennium BCE. The symbol continued to distinguish certain Shang-period jades and Western Zhou chariot-horse cheek-pieces (Chang Kwang-chih 1986, 181–88, fig. 150; Watson 1971, 107–8, fig. 48).

The crouching feline image also has an earlier dynastic Chinese priority, such as entry 93 (Chapter 3c) that is similar to an earlier plaque excavated at Yucun, Ning county, Gansu, with Western Zhou bronzes and a dagger similar to entry 94 (Chapter 3c). Both Yucun-type artifacts in this collection are very similar to later counterparts among the grave goods at northeastern sites, such as the Jundushan Yuhuangmiao examples discussed here, providing artifactual evidence for the textual tradition that the so-called Jundushan mounted hunters had moved eastward from northwestern China to the Jundushan during the late eighth century BCE.[15] Stylized images of coiled felines have also been identified on an eighth-century BCE mirror that is stylistically related to an exotic mirror (fig. 9), excavated from M1612 at Shangcunling, a Guo state cemetery site

---

15 See discussion in Bunker et al. 1997, 175, and in this chapter.

near Sanmenxia, Henan, dated to the period of the late Western Zhou to early Spring and Autumn, circa eighth century BCE (Zhongguo 1959, 27, fig. 21; O'Donoghue 1990, 138–39, figs. 19 and 22). Such mirrors represent an Inner Asian steppe style from somewhere beyond dynastic China's northern frontier (cf. also Bunker et al. 2002, 156, no. 133), as does a highly stylized coiled feline image, such as the example in this chapter (see entry 37).

The Shangcunling mirror also displays a vulture image very similar to the Upper Xiajiadian vulture-shaped plaque in the present collection (Chapter 2a, entry 14). This is similar to an excavated example from Eastern Transbaikal (Chlenova 1992, pl. 1.16), suggesting a distant non-Chinese origin for such mirrors, located far to the north. This kind of artifactual evidence for long-distance globalized relationships points to the existence of less-known Eurasian Steppe exchange networks that we are only now beginning to recognize (Davydova and Miniaev 2008, 9). The presence in Yuhuangmiao (Jundushan 2007, vol. 1, 279, fig. 29; vol. 2, 989, fig. 602; 994, fig. 606), as well as in Shangcunling, of arrowheads of both the three-bladed and two-bladed types, is also relevant evidence of far-reaching connections throughout the Eurasian Steppe (see Watson 1971, fig. 56).

The appearance in Kazakhstan, in the sixth to fifth century BCE, of a coiled lupine image with fearsome open jaws further substantiates the existence of a vast, globalized sacred symbolism that appears to have permeated certain regions of the Eurasian steppe world by the middle of the first millennium BCE (Popescu et al. 1998, 149, no. 186). Curiously, however, the coiled carnivore image did not occur in the Ordos region west of the Taihang until the fifth to fourth century BCE, when it was introduced as a result of the processes set in motion by the Central Asian campaigns of the Persian leader, Cyrus, followed by those of Alexander the Great of Macedonia (Bunker 1992b; Kuz'mina 2007).

The extraordinary similarity between the two bronze felines with their paws transformed into tiny coiled feline images (entry 26) echoes the iconography displayed by the famous gold feline with paws also formed by tiny coiled felines that was excavated at Kelermes, the great Scythian seventh- to sixth-century BCE kurgan in the Black Sea region (fig. 10; Gossel-Raeck and Busch 1993, 48–49; Jacobson 1995, fig. 122). Another motif that distinguishes numerous metal plaques from various Jundushan cemeteries is the ubiquitous cervid image

Fig. 10: Gold feline from Kelermes kurgan in the Black Sea area; seventh to sixth century BCE. The State Hermitage Museum, St. Petersburg, inv. no. Ku.1903-2/1.

with backswept antlers, such as entries 29, 30, and 31. Backswept antlers on later images have been transformed into a series of tangent circles, as is the case with certain objects in this chapter, including entry 28 (Jundushan 2007, vol. 3, 1234, fig. 723.8–25; vol. 4, 347, fig. 4), creating a stylized image that has a long history throughout the eastern Inner Eurasian steppe world. The visual evolution of these deer images reveals much about trans-Eurasian Steppe contacts.[16] The image may have originally been based on a cervid motif that appeared earlier in Siberian petroglyphs of the second to first millennium BCE and on Mongolian deerstones, stylized human figures with unknown ritual connotations related to safe passage into the afterlife for the person memorialized (fig. 11) (Novgorodova 1980; Jacobson-Tepfer 2001, 33–34; 38). The original cervid symbol, probably a reindeer, was later altered to reflect the local species in the various regions to which it was diffused. Subsequently, the motif was transmitted eastward from Siberia to the Inner Asian borders of dynastic China and westward through Central Asia to the Black Sea region where, altered through contact with Near Eastern and Greek artistic conventions, it became the leitmotif of the Scythians (Amandry 1965). The wide range of territory in which this cervid image was portrayed suggests a common source in northeastern Eurasia, from which the symbol would

16   Chlenova 1963, 66–67, tables 1 and 2; Shelach 2009, 132, fig. 5.8; Jacobson 2006b.

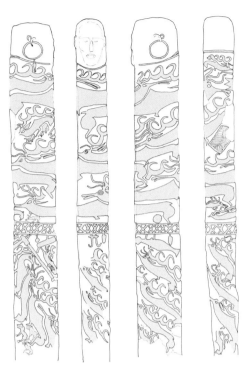

Fig. 11: Deerstone with human face from Uushgiĭn Övör, northern Mongolia.

have diffused to the east and west, rather than by a simple one-way transmission (Bunker et al. 2002, 17–18; Bunker 2006, 99–102).

Some artifacts with a Mongolian association are included in this chapter because they depict motifs that are similar to images found in Eastern or Inner Mongolia, such as the coiled leopards on entry 27, a personal ornament that has a counterpart collected in Mongolia (Volkov 1995, 323, fig. 2d). Mongolia is centered in Inner Asia, and shares borders with the Altai region of Russia, Tuva, and Transbaikalia (Volkov 1995, 319). The high-altitude environment encouraged and supported the successful development of a cattle-breeding economy. It is still the case today that we often lack sufficient information to understand the precise relationship between artifacts found in Mongolia and similar artifacts found elsewhere.

Riding-horse gear, such as bits and cheek-pieces, are standard features in northern Hebei burials belonging to the resident mounted hunting groups (Linduff 1997, 37, fig. A23; 63). These hunters appear to have been extremely self-sufficient and active traders, working on an equal basis with their nearby dynastic Chinese neighbors. The profusion of daggers in their graves has inspired a few scholars

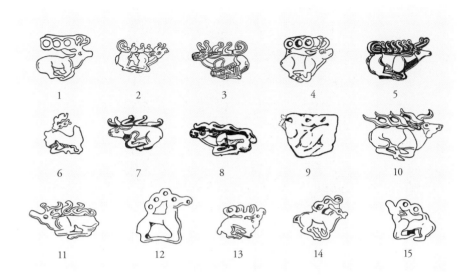

Fig. 12: A variety of deer images from Eurasia. 1, 2 – North Black Sea region:
1 – Siniavka, barrow no. 100, gold; 2 – Litoĭ kurgan («Melgunov hoard»), gold;
3–6 – North Caucasus: 3 – Kelermes, gold; 4 – Ul'skiĭ aul, gold;
5 – Kostromskaia barrow, gold; 6 – Verkhniaia Rutkha, bronze;
7 – Iran, Ziwiyeh, gold; 8 – South Ural regions, Gumarovo barrow no. 1, gold;
9, 10 – East Kazakhstan: 9 – Bobrov burial ground, bronze;
10 – Chilikty, barrow no. 5, gold; 11, 12 Minusinsk Basin:
11 – Verkhniaia Koia, bronze; 12 – Saianskaia, bronze;
13–15: North China, Ordos region; 13 – bone; 14, 15 – bronze.

to attribute a warlike character to these hunters, but no evidence of violence has so far been found in the archaeological records in the region. Several daggers appear to be later examples of an earlier dagger type, such as entry 94 (Chapter 3c) in the present volume. Knives were primarily hunting tools, and daggers were invaluable for a hunter, when it came to despatching trapped animals and stabbing at close range, rather than as a battle-ready weapon (Bunker et al. 2002, 74). Two millennia later, this same mountainous region became the Qing emperor Kangxi's favorite hunting grounds. Fur trading and leather tanning are still the major economic occupations there, especially in Zhangjiakou, a city in northern Hebei that still reeks of tanning chemicals today. It has long served as a point of departure for northern Eurasian destinations, such as Ulaanbaatar in Mongolia and Lake Baikal in Siberia.

22 | Pectoral Plaque

Jundushan region,
north of Beijing
6th–5th century BCE

Height 2.2 cm
Width 4.5 cm
Weight 9.7 g

Cast gold by lost-wax,
alloy composition by
P. Meyers (June 22, 2013):
Au 88%; Ag 7.5%;
Sn ca. 2.5%

This wonderful crouching gold leopard, represented in profile, originally served as a pectoral ornament to indicate the clan, gender, and prestige of its owner. Pierced circles mark the leopard's eye, ear, shoulder, haunch, leg-joints, and paws. Some of these circles may have originally been inlaid with turquoise, as is the case with circular marks of this kind on several gold examples excavated from graves associated with pastoral hunting groups living north of the present-day Beijing region (Hebei and Hebei 1980, pl. 50.1; 26; pl. 170). The mouth is represented with jagged jaws, but extensive wear makes this feature difficult to see.

The reverse is hollow and displays two vertical attachment loops extending from edge to edge, one behind the neck and the other behind the haunch. The loops were integrally cast with the plaque by the lost-wax process. Similar gold feline-shaped pectoral ornaments have been excavated from elite male graves in Yuhuangmiao, Jundushan, Yanqing county, Beijing (Jin Fengyi 1990, 6; So and Bunker 1995, 50, fig. 18; Bunker et al. 1997, 65, fig. A91; Jundushan 2007, vol. 3, 1178–79).

23 | Pectoral Plaque

Jundushan,
north of Beijing
6th–5th century BCE

Height 3.5 cm
Width 7.8 cm
Weight 28.1 g

Bronze,
alloy composition
by J. Stenger:
Cu 59%; Sn 15%; Pb 13%;
As trace

Ex Edgar and Hedwig
Worch Collection, Paris
and New York; Christie's
New York, 2 June 1994,
lot 49 (part)

Published:
Christie's 1994, 24–25,
no. 49 (part)

This bronze plaque takes the shape of a crouching leopard shown in profile, the bronze version of the previously discussed gold plaque (entry 22). Similar plaques have been found at cemetery sites in the Jundushan where they served as pectoral ornaments worn high on the chest to indicate clan, gender, power, and prestige. Many examples similar to the present plaques can be found in numerous Western collections, such as the Arthur M. Sackler Collections (Bunker et al. 1997, 189, no. 112), with images in the immense excavation publication of the Jundushan cemeteries (Jundushan 2007, vol. 3, 1179–84).

The reverse displays two vertical loops, one behind the shoulder and the other behind the haunch. The loops were pre-cast and then cast on to the plaque in a two-piece mold. The differences in production methods for casting pectorals made of different metals—gold and bronze—suggests that they were cast in different foundry workshops.

Analysis by Pieter Meyers indicates that the bronze alloy of the present plaque is different from that of the crouching feline plaque (entry 58, Chapter 3b) associated with northwestern China, demonstrating how careful one needs to be when suggesting a specific place of origin for artifacts associated with the greater Inner Eurasian world.

24 | Personal Ornament

Northeast China
6th–5th century BCE

Diameter 5.4 cm
Weight 48 g

Gold with turquoise inlay, alloy composition by P. Meyers (2013): Au 88%; Cu 3.8%; Ag 7.1%; Sn 2%

Ex Adolphe Stoclet Collection, Brussels; Eugene V. Thaw Collection, New York and Santa Fe

Published:
Bronzes Chinois 1934, no. 422;
van Goidsenhoven 1956, 356–57

This spectacular circular gold ornament is cast in the shape of a coiled doe surrounded by a border formed by eight linked raptor heads with inlaid turquoise eyes. The reverse shows a tiny loop at the edge of the plaque. Some of the gold leopard-shaped plaques excavated from burial sites in the Jundushan are also distinguished by turquoise inlay (Hebei and Hebei 1980, 96; pl. 170).

Gold inlaid with colored stone was foreign-inspired and suggests contact with the pastoral peoples of the Eurasian steppes. Their love of color, which can be observed from their grave goods at Pazyryk (Rudenko 1970, passim), may ultimately be traced back to the ancient kingdom of Ur in southern Mesopotamia, in present-day Iraq (So 2019, passim).

No circular plaques with this precise design have been discovered archaeologically, but a circular gold plaque with a coiled animal in the center in the Ordos Museum suggests that many such plaques may have been produced in antiquity (E'erduosi Qingtongqi 2006, 244, top). There are also numerous circular bronze examples with a plain domed boss shown within a frame formed by eight similar profile raptor heads with long, hooked beaks, such as those in the present publication (see entry 25) and several other examples in the Arthur M. Sackler Collections (Bunker et al. 1997, 195, no. 127).

Recent scholarship suggests that the raptor heads depicted on all of these plaques may be vultures, as indicated by their elongated beaks. The present gold plaque was cast by lost-wax, whereas the plaques made of bronze are piece-mold cast, the same difference in workmanship displayed by the gold and bronze leopard-shaped pectoral plaques in the current chapter (see entries 22 and 23).

25 | Two Garment Plaques

North of Beijing
and western Liaoning
6th–5th century BCE

25a | Garment Plaque
(left)
Diameter 2.1 cm
Weight 7.4 g
Cast bronze,
alloy composition
by J. Stenger:
Cu 70%; Sn 5%;
Pb 10%; As <1%

25b | Garment Plaque
(right)
Diameter 2.1 cm
Weight 7.7 g
Cast bronze,
alloy composition
by J. Stenger:
Cu 72%; Sn 4%;
Pb 5%; As <1%

These two circular garment plaques each represent a domed boss surrounded by a border formed by seven linked raptor heads with long, hooked beaks that appear to represent vultures. Each plaque has an integrally cast rounded loop across the hollow back and was cast in a multi-piece mold integrally with its loops, as indicated by mold marks on the sides and around the bases of the loops.

Circular bronze plaques with raptor-head frames have been found at many sites in northern Hebei, where numerous examples enhanced the dead in burials, as Emma Bunker observed at the museum in Longhua county in 1993. Several plaques similar to those under discussion are included in the Arthur M. Sackler Collections (Bunker et al. 1997, 195, nos. 126, 127).

26 | Two Garment Plaques

Northeast China
6th–5th century BCE

26a | Garment Plaque (top)
Height 1.9 cm
Width 2.9 cm
Weight 5.7 g
Bronze,
alloy composition
by J. Stenger:
Cu 57%; Sn 1%; Pb 9%

26b | Garment Plaque (bottom)
Height 2.1 cm
Width 3 cm
Weight 5.7 g
Bronze,
alloy composition
by J. Stenger:
Cu 71%; Pb 21%

These two plaques are each cast in the form of a crouching feline with a slightly pointed ear shown in profile. The feline intended may be a leopard, a species known to have inhabited the mountainous regions of what is today northern Hebei. The eye is indicated by a rounded depression and the mouth by a hole with the remains of fangs. The back of each plaque is slightly concave and displays two vertical loops that were integrally cast in multipiece molds.

The paws and tail appear oversized and each of them may represent a tiny, styled coiled feline. This unusual iconography also adorns the paws and tail of the gold crouching feline that once decorated a Scythian shield from the Kelermes kurgan in the Black Sea region, dated to around the seventh to sixth century BCE (Rolle 1989, color fig. 19; fig. 10, p. 81). The iconographic similarities between artifacts found enormous distances apart are too great to be coincidental, but the transmission routes remain unclear.

27 | Ornamental Fitting with Two Coiled Leopards

Mongolia or Inner Mongolia
7th–6th century BCE

Height 2.4 cm
Width 4.9 cm
Weight 14.1 g

Bronze, alloy composition by E. Ferreira:
Cu 86.2%; Sn 3%; As 2.9%; Fe 0.2%

This small bronze fitting is formed by two coiled leopard images shown in profile, their jaws open revealing their fangs and the tail tips touching their heads, in order to accommodate the fitting shape. The eye and the ear of each carnivore are pierced, and the paws are represented as circles with indented centers. The reverse shows a vertical bar running from the bottom edge of the top leopard to the bottom edge of the leopard below, thus forming a kind of fitting from which something could be suspended. A fitting in the Ordos Museum is similar in shape to the present object and features animals stylistically similar to images associated with northeastern China (E'erduosi Qingtongqi 2006, 212).

A small fitting in the State Hermitage Museum in St. Petersburg displays an object that is identical in form to the present example. The Hermitage piece was a chance find discovered in "Ol sum," Mongolia, in 1926 by Pyotr K. Kozlov (Hermitage 1981, no. 11; Gossel-Raeck 1991, 229, no. 151; Bogdanov 2006, 154, no. 1). The Kozlov discovery was also published by Volkov but, again, with no specific information about the cultural context (Volkov 1995, 323, fig. 2.d). An unprovenanced fitting of this shape in the Barbier-Mueller Museum displays an image of copulating ibex figures that relates it to Upper Xiajiadian fertility motifs (cf. Bunker 2006, 92, fig. 2). However, the Upper Xiajiadian region is an area where ibex images are not common.

Such similarities suggest that, although these coiled feline motifs are visually akin to motifs found in the Jundushan, it is doubtful that the present fitting originated there, but instead probably represents exotica obtained through exchange, marriage alliance, or trade. For example, coiled feline images appeared in Central Asia in Saka art, and then, later on, further northwest in Scythian art (Chlenova 1967, 31; Schiltz 1975, 146, no. 51).

28, 29, 30, 31 | Six Deer-shaped Ornamental Plaques

Northeast China
ca. 6th century BCE

28a | Height 2.5 cm
Width 3.1 cm
Weight 5.2 g
Cast bronze,
alloy composition
by J. Stenger:
Cu 61%; Pb 20%

28b | Height 2.3 cm
Width 3.2 cm
Weight 4.8 g
Cast bronze,
alloy composition
by J. Stenger:
Cu 77%; Sn 3%;
Pb 13%

29a | Height 2.7 cm
Width 3.3 cm
Weight 7.2 g
Cast bronze,
alloy composition
by J. Stenger:
Cu 87%; Sn 3%;
Pb trace; As very high

29b | Height 2.8 cm
Width 3.3 cm
Weight 8.3 g
Cast bronze,
alloy composition
by J. Stenger:
Cu 87%; Sn 3%;
Pb 2%; As high

These six bronze plaques are each cast in the shape of a deer shown in profile, with highly stylized curvilinear backswept antlers arched from the head to the hindquarters (no. 29a, b). The legs are shown drawn up and folded beneath the body, such that the back legs overlap the front legs. Four plaques have two attachment loops on the reverse that were integrally piece-mold cast, as indicated by mold marks at the juncture of the loops and along the edges. The antlers are transformed into tangential circles, an artistic convention characteristic of cervid images related to the northeastern Eurasian frontier world east of the Taihang range (Loehr 1955). The single plaque (no. 30) is badly worn with parts of the antlers broken off; there is one loop behind the neck and a broken one behind the rump. The depiction of this particular deer plaque with the legs folded to form a straight base distinguishes it from the pairs previously discussed and makes it difficult to locate its origin.

Some of the present examples appear to have belonged to large sets of deer-shaped plaques, such as those found in burials dating to about the seventh or sixth century BCE at Ganzibao, Huailai county, northern Hebei (He Yong and Liu Jianzhong 1993; So and Bunker 1995, 160–61; Bunker et al. 1997, 171–72; Wu Hsiao-yun 2013, 83, fig. 3.23.2).

According to Chlenova, these deer images, with bent or folded legs, all similar in details, appeared during the Scythian era and can be subdivided into two variants—eastern and western—with the image concept originating somewhere in Central Eurasia between the seventh and fourth centuries BCE (Chlenova 1994, 505–6; 530, fig. 11). With the new archaeological research on deerstones it has become clear that the earliest depictions of deer images occur on the deerstones in Mongolia dating between 1200 and 700 BCE (fig. 7, p. 49; cf. Bunker et al. 1997, 171, fig. 82.1; Volkov 2002; Törbat 2018a; 2018b).

The recent publication of numerous cervid images among the grave goods in burials at Yuhuangmiao (Jundushan 2007, vol. 1, 270, fig. 18; vol. 3, 1234, fig. 723.8–25) adds additional information to the study of

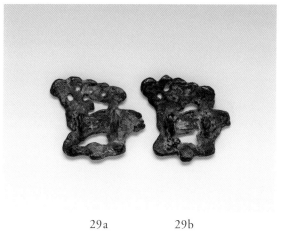

28a 28b 29a 29b

30 | Single Plaque
Height 3.6 cm
Width 5 cm
Weight 10.4 g
Cast bronze,
alloy composition
not analyzed

31 | Single Plaque
Black Sea Region
ca. 6th century BCE
Height 4 cm
Width 6.7 cm
Weight 35.7 g
Cast bronze,
alloy composition
by J. Stenger:
Cu 80%; Sn 3%; Pb <1%

the iconic cervid image with backswept antlers that became the Scythian icon *par excellence*.

Deer images visually similar to these bronze plaques were long associated by scholars in the past with the Scythians, since such images were already known in the Black Sea region by the seventh century BCE (fig. 12, p. 83). Such early northeastern deer images, or the memory of them, may have been retained by mobile pastoral groups who possibly brought their images from their eastern Eurasian homeland to western Eurasia, where they combined with Near Eastern and Greek elements to form what was to become a major hallmark motif of Scythian art (Chlenova 1963; Amandry 1965, 149–50; Williams and Ogden 1994, 135, no. 79; Bunker et al. 2002, 180–81). The Tagar culture cervid images associated with Minusinsk are Siberian in origin and are quite realistically portrayed (Bokovenko 1995a, 312, fig. 21). In this light, the "Ordos region" appears not as a Chinese borderland, but rather as a steppe outpost (Loehr 1955, 67–71). An in-depth study of the origins of the local variants of the cervid images in the Eurasian world can be found in articles written by Max Loehr in 1955 and Natal'iia Chlenova in 1994 that are still relevant today.

Cervid motifs on gold and bronze ornaments, as well as body tattoos, occur over enormous distances, suggesting long-distance contact throughout the northern Eurasian steppe world. During this time, many images were altered to reflect the local fauna of the region in which they were created, with the aesthetic styles through which the various images are represented often yielding clues regarding their respective production regions.

The gold cervid images associated with the Almaty region in Kazakhstan, dated to the seventh to sixth century BCE, display antlers that are naturalistically portrayed (Stark and Rubinson 2012, 27, fig. 1-9); by the late sixth century BCE, however, the deer images in question display antlers represented by a series of tangential circles (see entry 28). These were presumably cast by metalsmiths who depicted the antlers in typical Sinitic symmetrical fashion, indicating that they were probably cast by a nearby Zhou state and exchanged with local hunters. The deer intended here are probably wapiti (*Cervus canadensis*), which are known to inhabit

Manchuria and Mongolia (MacDonald 1985, 528), whereas the cervid images carved on several deerstones may be reindeer, given the presence of brow tines that occur only in reindeer, as is the case of the cervid no. 31. This item may actually have been cast further west, near the Black Sea region and is similar to the deer image from the Kostromskaia shield that has brow tines (Schiltz 1975, 134–35, no. 17).

30 31

32 | Spoon with Cervid Image

North of Beijing
6th–5th century BCE

Length 11.2 cm
Width 2.8 cm
Weight 23.2 g

Bronze,
alloy composition
not analyzed

A deer shown in profile with folded legs and flowing antlers transformed into tangential circles surmounts the long handle of this spoon. The ears are represented by small depressions and the eyes are indicated by a circular pupil within a circular rim. The whole object was cast in the round. Flashing in the holes suggests that the whole spoon was cast in a two-piece mold. The deer image here is the same one represented on the plaques discussed in the previous entry and can be stylistically associated with plaques from the hunters' tombs in the Jundushan. The diffusion of this image throughout the Eurasian steppes has been carefully documented by Natal'iia Chlenova (1963; 1994).

33 | Plaque Depicting a Female Ibex and Kid

Northern Beijing and western Liaoning
6th–4th century BCE

Height 3.8 cm
Width 3.3 cm
Weight 6.1 g

Cast bronze, alloy composition by J. Stenger: Cu 77%; Sn 12%; Pb 8%; As trace

This plaque is cast in the shape of a female ibex, with her kid represented standing underneath her belly. Her eye is indicated by a depression within a circular rim and her mouth by a triangular depression. Regular anterior ridges mark the horns, which are characteristic of both male and female ibexes, in contrast to sheep, where only males have horns. Many plaques with this design are so worn that the scene has been misinterpreted as a female ibex nursing her kid (Bunker et al. 1997, 191, no. 116). Drawings of examples published in Chinese collections now make it clear that the kid is not suckling (Wu En 2008, 236, fig. 154.1.2.5). The present plaque has a flat back with no attachment loops and was probably cast in an open mold that left minimal flashing in the design openings.

The ibex (*Capra ibex*) is a wild goat that thrives in mountainous regions, such as those in Luanping county in present-day northern Hebei, where numerous plaques with this image are found (personal observation in 1993). Two plaques with this design were also collected in Manhanshan in Liangcheng county, but not in an archaeological context (Tian and Guo 1986, 90, fig. 59.3–4). Such plaques have also been published as characteristic of the Maoqinggou culture based on information in Wu En (2007), but this observation cannot be confirmed archaeologically (Kost 2014, 46, fig. 7). There is also no evidence that plaques such as the present one can be associated with the later Xiongnu period as has been suggested in the past (Yu Ping and Dai Ge 1985, 41, fig. 14).

34 | Garment Plaque

North of Beijing or western Liaoning
6th–5th century BCE

Height 5 cm
Width 1.5 cm
Weight 10 g

Bronze, alloy composition by J. Stenger: Cu 79%; Sn 13%; Pb 8%; As trace

This tiny openwork plaque depicts two wild-ass protomes with folded front legs and heads turned back, with both ears shown and pierced. The eyes are rendered by a rounded boss surrounded by a circular ridge; slight depressions mark the nostrils and mouth. The back of the plaque is slightly concave and has no attachment loops, so presumably attachment was made possible through the openwork design. Mold marks around the edges of the rectangular frame indicate that the plaque was piece-mold cast.

A plaque in the Sackler Collections exhibits four of these wild-ass protomes within frames with references to an excavated example with four such protomes discovered at Ganzibao, Huailai county, north of Beijing (Bunker et al. 1997, 198, no. 131). Plaques of this type belong to a group depicting a limited number of stereotyped ungulate images within rectangular frames (see Bunker et al. 1997, 198–200).

35 | Garment Plaque

Northeast Inner Mongolia and north of Beijing
ca. 6th–5th century BCE

Height 2.2 cm
Width 3.6 cm
Weight 8.3 g

Bronze, alloy composition by J. Stenger:
Cu 83%; Sn 9%; Pb 15%; As trace

This tiny plaque is cast in the shape of four tangent wild-ass heads shown frontally with circular depressions to mark the eyes and elongated ovals within raised rims to represent the ears. Two tiny vertical loops are provided on the reverse close to each edge for attachment purposes. Mold marks next to the integrally cast loops on the reverse suggest casting in a multipiece mold.

Plaques with similar ass-head motifs can be found in numerous collections around the world (Andersson 1932, pl. 29.8–9; Tian and Guo 1986, 167, fig. 115.3–4; Bunker et al. 1997, 169, no. 77). Plaques representing two tangent ass heads are recorded as having been acquired in Khadainsume, present-day Zhangbei in northern Hebei. Other small animal-head plaques found in sets west of the Taihang range, such as no. 43 (Chapter 3a), are superficially similar, but the way they are cast and their attachments loops are distinctly different, which suggests that they were not cast east of the Taihang and that they were made for different pastoral groups.

36 | Belt Hook

Northern Hebei
ca. 6th century BCE

Height 5 cm
Width 12 cm
Weight 63 g

Bronze, alloy composition by J. Stenger: Cu 66%; Sn 9%; Pb 12%; As trace

This belt hook represents a fantastic feline with the body shown in profile and the head with full face turned back to touch its tail. The animal's body is marked by raised linear spiral designs, and raised lines rib the tail. The paws each have three prominent, curled claws, which is characteristic of the way in which claws are depicted on some northern Hebei artifacts (Bunker et al. 1997, 197, no. 130). The long, slender hook extends from the feline's rump and terminates in a dragon head.

The reverse of the present hook carries two round buttons on projecting stems for attachment purposes, an unusual feature, since most belt hooks have only one attachment button on the back (So and Bunker 1995, 169, no. 95). A small group of animal-shaped belt hooks outfitted with two buttons on the back have been recovered from Jundushan, Yanqing county, in northern Beijing, dated to about the sixth century BCE (So and Bunker 1995, 170, no. 96).

37 | Coiled Feline-shaped Plaque

Inner Asia
ca. 8th century BCE

Height 6.8 cm
Width 8.4 cm
Weight 81.6 g

Bronze with turquoise inlay, alloy composition by E. Ferreira: Cu 88.5%; Sn 6.3%; Pb 4.3%; As 0.3%; Fe 0.1%

This plaque is formed by a stylized feline with open jagged jaws and a coiled body marked by thread-relief spiral patterns. Turquoise inlay marks the eye and rump; the inlay for the shoulder is missing. The reverse displays four horizontal hooks facing inward and thus may represent an early type of buckle. Flashing along the edges of the pierced areas indicates that the piece was probably cast in a multipiece mold integrally with the hooks.

A feline with similar jagged teeth and spiral body marks is represented on a mirror excavated from tomb M1612 at Shangcunling in Henan, where it has long been considered exotica (O'Donoghue 1990, 138, fig. 22). A mirror in the Hans Bidder Collection displays a coiled feline with similar jagged open jaws and thread-relief details (O'Donoghue 1990, 138, fig. 19; Wagner and Butz 2007, 56–57, no. 45). Another mirror decorated with a coiled wolf represented in thread relief was excavated from tomb 165 of graveyard no. 4 at Chawuhu Gully in Hejing county, Xinjiang Uyghur Autonomous Region, dated circa eighth century BCE (Xinjiang 1998, 246; Wagner and Butz 2007, 57, fig. 45-2). To date, no specific casting source for the bronze mirrors with thread-relief decoration has been identified. Hence, this plaque has been included here, since it seems to be stylistically related to the coiled carnivore images depicted on these mirrors and could eventually provide clues to their origins. The presence of turquoise inlay also relates this buckle to the use of turquoise inlay to mark the gold feline-shaped pectoral images associated with the hunting peoples of the Jundushan. However, since the treatment of the surface is distinctly different from anything associated with the Jundushan, its origin remains unclear.

Chapter 3

Inner Asian Artifacts Found West of the Taihang Range during the First Millennium BCE

West of the Taihang range, dynastic China's Inner Asian borderlands encompass large areas of grasslands, which are separated geographically and ecologically into three regional zones (fig. 13), each with its own local herding strategies and significant cultural variations (Linduff 1997). The first zone includes cemeteries in Liangcheng and Horinger counties located in south-central Inner Mongolia. Burial sites in northern Shaanxi and the greater Ordos region of southwestern Inner Mongolia form a second zone, while a third cultural zone was located in the southern Ningxia Hui Autonomous Region, the Qingyang plateau of southeastern Gansu, and parts of the Xinjiang Uyghur Autonomous Region.

In the past, artifacts from all three zones were often referred to collectively as "Ordos" bronzes, a name derived from a small desert region in southwest Inner Mongolia. Their zoomorphic imagery has been described as "animal style," a term that is neither historically nor archaeologically corroborated and that is now considered obsolete. More recently, the archaeological material from these three zones has occasionally been identified with reference to regional type-site names, which have been accompanied by drawings of artifacts that are claimed to be characteristic of each zone. However, there has not yet been sufficient comparative research.[17] Recent scholarship suggests that these three zones were far more culturally complex than has traditionally been acknowledged and that they should no longer be defined in scholarly literature by type-site names located on contemporary maps.

Further study reveals that, in many instances, certain artifacts said to be characteristic of one zone may, in fact, be an exotic intrusion from another zone, while others may be so ubiquitous throughout all of the zones that the original

---

17 Wu En 2007, a system that has been discussed and amended by Kost 2014, 41–59.

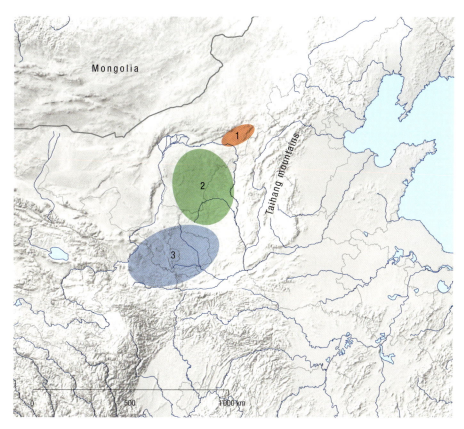

Fig. 13: Detail map of the Ordos region mentioned in the text and dealt with in Chapters 3a–c. 1 – Liangcheng and Horinger counties, south-central Inner Mongolia. 2 – Northern Shaanxi and the greater Ordos region of southwestern Inner Mongolia. 3 – Southern Ningxia Hui Autonomous Region, the Qingyang plateau of southeastern Gansu, and parts of the Xinjiang Uyghur Autonomous Region.

production source is difficult to identify. Hence, even when an artifact is found in a burial in a specific region, this does not necessarily indicate that it was actually made there. Often, the motifs found on the various artifacts are visually similar to zoomorphic designs found in the art of southern Siberia, but, at the same time, there are also clear associations with the art of northern dynastic China.

The three zones located west of the Taihang were never culturally homogenous, although they were at times interconnected. Instead, the economy of the pastoral peoples resident in each zone during the first millennium BCE was dependent on their individual ecological environment, which in turn governed their choice of artifacts, as well as the visual symbols that distinguished them as groups with their own specific elite regional markers.

The artifacts associated with the pastoralists living west of the Taihang display fascinating zoomorphic symbols reflecting their lifeways and regional beliefs. In general, personal ornaments associated with pastoralists living west of the Taihang are significantly different from those found at sites east of the Taihang: Prominent belt buckles and plaques enhanced by zoomorphic symbols replaced the pectorals used as group identifiers and status indicators to the east. Research is now beginning to reveal that belt plaques with certain iconography are also often gender-specific (Linduff and Rubinson 2013; Kost 2014). Belt plaques and prominent buckles, the major personal ornaments for the elite west of the Taihang, are often marked by predators and predation scenes involving tigers, wolves, raptors, and various ungulate victims. Such motifs bestowed status and prestige on the owner and may also have served as totems and clan markers confirming a group's rights to specific grazing lands and water sources. These concerns are still major issues for herders on open rangeland today, as Emma Bunker knows well from 25 years of ranching in Colorado and Wyoming in the great North American steppe.[18]

The predation scenes that distinguish many of the belt plaques can be traced back to third-millennium BCE iconography that first evolved in the ancient Near East. These motifs were likely slowly transmitted by pastoral peoples (Bunker 1989). In the course of these processes, their beliefs and zoomorphic symbols were altered to reflect the local fauna of the various regional environments (So and Bunker 1995, 54–56). It is possible that the meanings of certain motifs were also transformed by contact with the shamanistic beliefs that often evolve among semi-mobile herding groups. Without recognizing the cultural relationships that evolved between the numerous pastoral groups inhabiting the greater Eurasian Steppe in antiquity, we will miss the subtleties and intricacies of past worldviews that together contributed to the creation of the modern world in which we live today.

---

18   Northwestern America is one of the four steppe regions in the world, along with those in southern Africa, South America, and Eurasia, see Bone 2015.

Chapter 3a
Inner Asian Artifacts from South-Central Inner Mongolia West of the Taihang Range

Lush green pastures abound south of the Yinshan in south-central Inner Mongolia, west of the Taihang range. This area produced rich grazing land that was excellent for stock breeding and did not require long-distance herding. Burials of the heads and hooves of horses, cattle, sheep, and goats in local tombs underscore pastoral lifeways and reflect the composition of the herds (Linduff 1997, 56–57).

Personal ornaments among the grave goods display cultural traditions very different from those practiced by groups living east of the Taihang. Burials west of the Taihang reveal the use of prominent belt elements, enhanced by predation references to indicate status, in contrast to the pectorals worn high on the chest that signified status and prestige in burials excavated east of the Taihang (see discussion in Chapters 2a and b, pp. 46–51 and 76–83).

The major site that has been excavated in south-central Inner Mongolia is Maoqinggou, in Liangcheng county, a cemetery site located near Hohhot on the south-facing slopes of the Manhanshan. Seventy-nine graves dated typologically from the seventh to the third centuries BCE have yielded numerous belt accessories with zoomorphic decoration. Twenty-eight graves contain belt plaques: twenty-four of these graves are male, and four are female (Höllmann and Kossack 1992; Linduff 1997, 55–61). Twenty-one plaques display stylized raptor heads and seven are tiger shaped (Höllmann and Kossack 1992; Kost 2014, pl. 110–13). The Maoqinggou belt plaques are all similar in style, with surface details represented by intaglio lines and curved angles. Higher status is indicated by tinning, a surface enrichment that preceded amalgam gilding during the first millennium BCE,[19] suggesting that many of the herders' ornaments were made by dynastic Chinese workmen rather than by local craftsmen. The alloy compositions of entries 38, 39, and 40, all of which represent the same artistic style, are not closely related, suggesting that production took place in many places, rather than at a single Chinese foundry specifically charged with making ornaments for their pastoral neighbors.

19   Bunker 1990b; Han Rubin and Bunker 1993; Han Rubin and Wang Dong-Ning 2018.

To date, there is almost no evidence for the use of gold among the local pastoral groups. A necklace described as being made of gold from Dianzixiang was mentioned by Wu En, but without a picture or any further details (Kost 2014, 43).

Belt Buckles Formed by Two Mirror-Image Plaques

A sequence of tiger-shaped belt plaques from Maoqinggou throws new light on the introduction of the characteristic belt buckle that subsequently became the most prestigious item in the "status kits" of the Inner Asian pastoralists living west of the Taihang. These buckles are formed by two mirror-image plaques distinguished by pertinent zoomorphic iconography used to fasten the owner's belt, which was worn over a hip-length jacket (caftan), transmitting specific information about the owner to those who saw him wearing it (Höllmann and Kossack 1992, pl. 31; Tian and Guo 1986).

Maoqinggou M5, dated approximately to the sixth or fifth century BCE, contains two identical flat plaques, each in the shape of a schematized tiger.[20] In the slightly later grave M55, a single plaque of a walking carnivore is pierced through the shoulder with a circular hole that is part of the fastening system.[21] This same feature marks a similar walking-carnivore-shaped plaque associated with the Tagar culture from Minusinsk in southern Siberia (Piotrovskij 1978, 90–91, no. 120; Simpson and Pankova 2017, 146, no. 83).

This close similarity to Tagar culture items suggests that the walking-carnivore plaque in Maoqinggou M55 represents exotica from the Minusinsk region, confirming that this particular buckle system consisting of two mirror-image plaques was imported into dynastic China's Inner Asian zone from much farther north (see entry 46 and fig. 14, blue dots). The walking posture, with all four legs showing, also occurs in the Altai with the image of a tiger carved onto the wooden coffin excavated at Bashadar, tomb 2, dating from the second half of the sixth to the first half of the fifth century BCE,[22] images that can ultimately be traced back to ancient Near Eastern traditions (Bunker et al. 1997, 216). The carved

---

20   Rawson and Bunker 1990, 295, fig. 1.4; Höllmann and Kossack 1992, pl. 5.12–13; Kost 2014, pl. 110.
21   Rawson and Bunker 1990, 295, fig. 1.5; Höllmann and Kossack 1992, pl. 26.11; Kost 2014, pl. 64.3.
22   Rudenko 1970, 268–69, fig. 136; Bunker et al. 1997, 215, fig. 156.1; 216; Menghin et al. 2007, 122, fig. 4a–b.

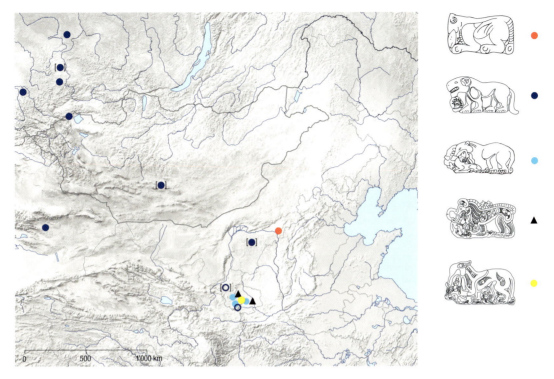

Fig. 14: Distribution of plaque types discussed in Chapter 3a: plaques similar to entry 38 ● and entry 46 ● and variants O – Distribution of plaque types discussed in Chapter 3c: plaques similar to entry 68 ●, entry 73 ▲, entry 74 and 75 ●. Mapped after Bogdanov 2006 and Kost 2014.

wooden eagle figures that adorn the saddles excavated from Bashadar, tomb 2,[23] also appear to be ancestral to the ubiquitous raptor-head-shaped plaques associated with Maoqinggou (see entry 39), suggesting continued contact with pastoral groups far to the northwest that are represented by the many artifacts from the Altai (Schiltz 1994, passim).

Rich archaeological treasures excavated from tombs in the High Altai at Pazyryk, now housed in the State Hermitage Museum in St. Petersburg, reveal extraordinary artifacts. They were preserved "because of the permanently frozen ground which formed under the stone cairns" in antiquity.[24] The finds include the remains of burial clothing, saddle pads, riding-horse gear, and personal adornments fashioned from a broad range of materials, including silk, felt, fur, wood,

---

23 Griaznov 1969, 142–43; Bunker et al. 1997, 9, fig. B5; Menghin et al. 2007, 123, fig. 5.
24 Piotrovskij 1978, 9; Rudenko 1970; Polos'mak 2001; Molodin et al. 2012; Törbat and Tséveéndorzh 2016.

leather, bone, bronze, and gold. Most of the artifacts are of local manufacture, but a significant number represent exotica in the form of silver plaques from the Achaemenid Persian world (Stark 2012, 116, fig. 77) and silk from dynastic China, which must have been acquired through exchange and perhaps intermarriage.[25] The extraordinary zoomorphic imagery that distinguishes the grave goods, especially the mythical creatures tattooed on the remains of skin from the frozen dead,[26] reappears in the iconography of the Inner Asian pastoralists living west of the Taihang, but apparently only on their artifacts and not their skin.

Daggers with Antenna-shaped Pommels

Another significant artifact found at Maoqinggou is a dagger distinguished by an antenna-shaped pommel that appears to have been exclusive to male burials (Höllmann and Kossack 1992, 28–29). Such dagger types can be traced back to the Tagar culture of the Minusinsk Basin area in southern Siberia (Piotrovskij 1978, 85, no. 109), along with certain belt plaques with predatory-tiger motifs, such as the belt plaque (entry 46) in the present chapter (Piotrovskij 1978, 90–91, no. 120). A special characteristic of such steppe daggers is that the hilt and blade are integrally cast (entry 45), whereas in dynastic China the hilt and blade were cast separately and then assembled.

Fanjiayaozi

Fanjiayaozi, a small burial site in Horinger county, yielded eight belt plaques with a predation scene, in which a stylized tiger is shown devouring a goat represented only by its head (entry 38). Plaques from another site, Guoxianyaozi in Liangcheng county, depict predation in the same way. The source for this particular motif may be seen on a deerstone in northern Mongolia from earlier periods.[27] The late-third-century BCE date proposed for Fanjiayaozi cannot be substantiated, since its predation plaques are related stylistically to certain Maoqinggou and Guoxianyaozi plaques and thus ought to be roughly contemporary. It should also be noted that the Fanjiayaozi burial was disturbed prior to discovery.[28]

---

25   Rudenko 1970, 175, fig. 89, pl. 178; Stark 2012, 107–38; Brosseder 2015.
26   Piotrovskij 1978, 47, no. 31; Menghin et al. 2007, 123, fig. 6; Simpson and Pankova 2017, 96–97, figs. 81–84.
27   Novgorodova 1980, 178; Linduff 1997, 59–60; Volkov 2002, 193, pl. 78; Törbat 2018b, 345, no. 1040.
28   Cheng Te-k'un 1963, 134; Linduff 1997, 59, fig. A79, Guoxianyaozi tomb 12; Kost 2014, 209.

Mold marks around the base of the attachment loops displayed on the backs of the Maoqinggou, Fanjiayaozi, and Guoxianyaozi belt plaques show clearly that the loops were integrally cast with the plaques in a multisection mold. Such a complex mold-casting tradition reflects the practices of the Jin state foundry in Houma in southern Shanxi province, according to studies of the vast amounts of casting debris and mold fragments recovered (Weber 1973, 232; Li Xiating et al. 1996).

The intaglio linear curves and angles that distinguish the flat surfaces of certain tiger- and raptor-head-shaped bronze belt plaques relate to patterns found on earlier dynastic Zhou carved jades (Shaanxi 1986, 63, fig. 27). They are also found on later dynastic Chinese vessels cast at Houma in present-day southern Shanxi, suggesting that the Jin state foundry there may have served a far wider market than has hitherto been realized. In essence, the flat tiger- and raptor-head-shaped plaques represent translations of Sinitic jade-carving techniques into bronze. Commercial connections between China and Inner Asia coincide with the exotic intrusion of predation motifs into the bronze decor of certain northern dynastic Chinese vessel iconography, such as that found on vessels from Hunyuan Liyu (Weber 1973, 232; So 1980, 267–68, no. 69). Herders in south-central Inner Mongolia seem to have relied on nearby dynastic Chinese foundries and itinerant Chinese metalsmiths to produce some of their artifacts, revealing commercial relationships and trade dynamics that are only just beginning to be investigated.[29] To date, there has been no mention of casting remains excavated locally that can be associated with the pastoral peoples.

Some of the bronze belt plaques found at Maoqinggou are tinned and are thereby indicative of status. Tinning was a surface enrichment practiced by dynastic-Chinese Zhou craftsmen, which produced a pleasing, silvery appearance used to enhance the surfaces of numerous Inner Asian artifacts, but only west of the Taihang range. It is not found on artifacts associated with groups living east of the Taihang (Bunker 1990b, 78–80; Han Rubin and Bunker 1993).

29   So and Bunker 1995; Li Xiating et al. 1996; Linduff et al. 2018.

Horse Gear

Although horse skulls are found among the sacrificial animal remains at Maoqinggou, there is no evidence of wheeled transport and few riding-horse items other than bits, suggesting that large-scale herding may not have been practiced and thus that long-distance transportation may not have been an important issue. Sheep and goat skulls were found in large numbers at Guoxianyaozi, another site in Liangcheng county (Neimenggu 1989). This is an indication of a more sedentary lifeway, as sheep and goats are not animals that can withstand being herded long distances, although they would be suitable herds for the rich, grassy environment of south-central Inner Mongolia. In antiquity, most herders would have travelled on foot, just as they do today, unless they have herds of horses that they need to tend on horseback.[30]

Sacrificial animal skulls in later-phase graves at Maoqinggou and Yinniugou dating to the fourth or third century BCE also include pigs, indicating a new cultural mixture among the inhabitants that stands in need of further clarification (Linduff 1997, 61). The presence of pigs indicates that some of region's inhabitants had a sedentary way of life, not because pigs cannot travel distances (Kost 2014, 45, no. 94), but because they do not herd. Grave goods also include S-shaped belt-hooks of a Central Plains type, suggesting the arrival of captives and farmers from the south (Linduff 1997, 61).

By comparison, the grave goods remaining from the pastoral peoples buried in south-central Inner Mongolia and northern Shanxi are different from the grave goods found further west in the greater Ordos region. Wu En, quoting the *Shiji*, insisted that the major population were the Loufan, but such so-called tribal names given to the various pastoral groups in the ancient dynastic-Chinese literature are not historically corroborated (Wu En 2007, 31).

30   Personal observations by Emma Bunker.

38 | Belt Plaque

South-central Inner Mongolia
5th century BCE

Height 3.5 cm
Width 5.7 cm
Weight 26.6 g

Cast bronze, alloy composition by J. Stenger: Cu 77%; Sn 17%; Pb 0.6%; As trace

This plaque is cast in the form of a stylized crouching tiger savaging a goat's head and is similar in design to eight plaques recovered from a fifth-century BCE burial at Fanjiayaozi, Horinger county, south-central Inner Mongolia (Li Yiyou 1959a, 79.5; Cheng Te-k'un 1963, 134; Linduff 1997, 59, fig. A77). The tiger and the goat head are represented in profile with their eyes indicated by an intaglio circular line. The tiger's pelt is marked by striated comma shapes, and intaglio lines accent certain bodily contours. The reverse of the plaque is flat and displays two vertical loops: one behind the haunch, the other behind the shoulder. Mold marks around the loop bases indicate that the plaque was cast integrally with loops in a multipiece mold. The Sackler Collection includes four other versions of this plaque design (Bunker et al. 1997, 206, no. 142) and the Thaw Collection has a mirror-image example (Bunker et al. 2002, 119–20, no. 90).

The motif of a carnivore attacking a vulnerable herbivore can be documented as early as the late fourth millennium BCE in the art of the ancient Near East and became far more common in the following millennium (Moortgat 1969, 11; pls. 15–16). The motif appeared in the art of the pastoralists of the Inner Asian Steppe during the first millennium BCE; then, as the motif was transmitted further eastward, the western Asiatic lion predator was replaced by various eastern Asiatic predators, including tigers, wolves, and leopards. The convention of representing the victim by means of its head alone was already anticipated on a deerstone from Uushgiĭn Övör, Khövsgöl aimag, northern Mongolia (Novgorodova 1980, 178). The animal-combat motif appears abruptly in the bronze vocabulary of the dynastic-Chinese state of Jin, as represented by foundry debris found at Liyu, Houma, the Jin state foundry in southern Shanxi, suggesting significant commercial relations between the pastoralists and their dynastic-Chinese neighbors (Li Xiating et al. 1996).

A plaque similar to the present plaque was discovered in M188, a female tomb in the Pingyang cemetery in Tailai county, southwestern Heilongjiang province, dated to about the fifth century BCE (Linduff and Sun 2004, 238; 246, fig. 9.6.2). Since plaques cast in this style belonged to pastoralists inhabiting south-central Inner Mongolia, the presence of such a plaque in a female tomb in Heilongjiang suggests that the woman was probably a foreigner married to a member of the local elite. Whether the Fanjiayaozi burial was female or not is unclear, since, due to its disturbed condition, the information obtained from the tomb was limited.

39 | Garment Plaque

South-central Inner Mongolia
5th century BCE

Height 2.6 cm
Width 3.8 cm
Weight 11.7 g

Cast bronze, alloy composition by J. Stenger: Cu 82%; Sn 6%; Pb 4%; As high

This small garment plaque cast in the shape of a stylized raptor head has excavated parallels that have been found throughout Liangcheng county in south-central Inner Mongolia, especially at Maoqinggou and Guoxianyaozi, and that date to the fifth century BCE (Höllmann and Kossack 1992, pl. 37B, grave 72; pl. 29.2, grave 59; pl. 11B4, fig. 16.8, grave 61). The back is flat with a substantial vertical loop that was piece-mold cast integrally with the plaque. Mold marks are visible along the edges and around the bases of the loop ends, indicating the use of a multi-piece mold. This plaque is stylistically related to the previous plaque (entry 38), and may have been cast in the same place. Almost identical examples have been excavated in Fanjiayaozi (Li Yiyou 1959a, 79, no. 5; Cheng Te-k'un 1963, 134). The Arthur M. Sackler Collections include several versions of this plaque cast from a high-tin bronze (Bunker et al. 1997, 212, no. 151). Numerous variations have also been published by Wu En (2008, 221, fig. 140).

On the present plaque, the emphasis relates to the head and the pattern made by the intaglio details. This is very characteristic both of dynastic-Chinese bird heads and of bird-of-prey heads represented in wood in the Altai region of southern Siberia, which may be distantly descended from images on Western Zhou vessels (Watson 1971, 147; Barkova 1987; Piotrosvkij 1978, 63, no. 64; 64, no. 67; Simpson and Pankova 2017, 112–13, no. 36). The presence of plaques of this shape in other burials in the northern frontier region is probably the result of exchange and marriage alliances, as plaques of this distinctive artistic style seem to be region specific.

40 | Belt Ornament

South-central Inner Mongolia
5th century BCE

Height 4.2 cm
Width 2.5 cm
Weight 13.5 g

Cast bronze, alloy composition by J. Stenger: Cu 65%; Sn 19%; Pb 7%

Two pairs of raptor heads, with each pair joined at the neck and facing outward, surround the central flat disk of this ornament. The heads have curved beaks, round eyes, and necks marked by parallel lines. A curious rounded protuberance with a central depression projects earlike from the back of each head. The reverse surface is flat, with a vertical loop behind the central boss.

Raptor heads of this type with round, bird-like eyes should not be confused with griffins, a mythical creature that is always represented with animal-shaped eyes. On the present plaque, the parallel lines marking the raptors' long necks suggest that the bird intended is probably a vulture, a major steppe scavenger that is often depicted with an elongated neck (see Chapter 2a, entry 14).

A plaque of the same design was excavated from tomb 22 at Maoqinggou, Liangcheng county, in south-central Inner Mongolia, west of the Taihang (Tian and Guo 1986, 275, fig. 42.5). These plaques were part of a series that distinguished a belt that was often closed by means of a simple buckle formed by a circle with a hook (Bunker et al. 1997, 210, no. 149; fig. 149.2). This plaque is multipiece cast integrally with the loop. A similar plaque in the Arthur M. Sackler Collections was inaccurately published on its side rather than vertically, which is how it was worn (Bunker et al. 1997, 213, no. 152).

41 | Belt Ornament Formed by Two Coiled Birds

South-central Inner Mongolia
5th century BCE

Height 3.7 cm
Width 2.4 cm
Weight 9.3 g

Cast bronze, alloy composition by J. Stenger: Cu 90%; Sn 2%; Pb 1%

A pair of stylized raptor heads with two coiled birds, with curving stylized bodies and feathered tails, form this belt plaque. A raised boss marks the juncture of their necks. The outer edges of the plaque have three scallops suggesting vestigial wings. The round eyes are raised and set off by an indented ring. The plaque has a vertical attachment loop behind the central boss. Mold marks in the plaque openings indicate piece-mold casting. A more stylized version of this plaque was recovered from grave 61 at Maoqinggou (Höllmann and Kossack 1992, pl. 32B3).

Similar coiled raptor-shaped ornaments have been collected from numerous non-Chinese burials in south-central Inner Mongolia west of the Taihang mountain range. The Arthur M. Sackler Collections have numerous versions of this type of belt ornament (Bunker et al. 1997, 220, no. 160), as does the Inner Mongolian Museum in Hohhot (Tian and Guo 1986, 115, fig. 81.2.4). A large variety of assorted plaques in stylistically related avian designs has been published by Wu En (2008, 177, fig. 109.3), revealing the popularity of such small personal avian-shaped ornaments, which may also have been associated with particular regions and clans. Similar zoomorphic plaques found in northern China have been considered earlier versions of the present plaque (Wu En 2008, 106, fig. 60.3.6).

Many plaques depicting a limited number of raptor and feline motifs, such as those discussed in this chapter, have long been associated with the Maoqinggou region, as a result of the discovery of many similar examples in burials in the region. Such ornaments must have been popular over a considerable period of time, as many are stylized versions of slightly earlier examples. The fact that some plaques are tinned suggests that Chinese craftsmen may have been involved in their production, as tinning does not appear to have been practiced by the local herding people. The many coiled avian motifs derive ultimately from earlier dynastic Chinese avian representations, such as that on a Western Zhou *zun* in the Sackler Collection (Delbanco 1983, no. 34).

42, 43 | A Tiny Plaque and Twelve Garment Ornaments

South-central Inner Mongolia, 6th–5th century BCE

42 | Tiny Plaque
Height 2.3 cm
Width 1.2 cm
Weight 2.5 g
Cast bronze, alloy composition by J. Stenger:
Cu 74%; Sn 13%; Pb 1%; As <1%

43 | Twelve Garment Ornaments
Height 2.5 cm
Width 1.5 cm
Weight 2.6–4.0 g
Cast bronze, alloy composition by J. Stenger:
bottom right:
Cu 62%; Sn 14%; Pb 1%; As <1%
bottom, second from the right:
Cu 53%; Sn 13%; Pb 7%; As trace
top right:
Cu 79%; Sn 13%; Pb 3%; As trace

The twelve tiny ornaments (no. 43) are each cast in the shape of a frontal animal head with circular pierced open eyes and ears. A vertical attachment strap on the concave back serves as an attachment device. Examination by Thomas Chase reveals that such pieces were cast with a vertical attachment loop from a high-tin bronze with a dark-gray patina (Bunker et al. 1997, 247, no. 205; Chase and Douglas 1997). Three of the ornaments were analyzed and show that they were also manufactured from a high-tin bronze. Numerous similar ornaments have been found in groups of multiples at various sites west of the Taihang, such as Taohongbala, Hanggin banner, among the personal belongings of a deceased Mongoloid male in tomb 1 (Tian Guangjin 1976, pl. 2.10, 136, fig. 6.6), and at sites in south-central Inner Mongolia, such as tombs M66 at Maoqinggou, Liangcheng county (Höllmann and Kossack 1992, pls. 2.5, 34B1, front and back views). More examples were also collected in the greater Ordos Desert region without any specific cultural context (Tian and Guo 1986, 211–12). Another small ornament known from a private collection is said to come from Övörkhangai aimag, Guchin-Us sum, in south-central Mongolia (Ėrdėnėchuluun 2011, 244, no. 258). In Tuva, similar plaques, albeit made of gold, are known from burial chamber 9 in Suglug-Khem II that belongs to the Sagly-Bazhy period of the fifth to third centuries BCE (Semenov 2003, 152, pl. 64.12–17; Parzinger 2006, 614).

Fig. 15: Ornaments found east of the Taihang, from the region of Khadain-sume. Stockholm, Östasiatiska museet (Joel Eriksson collection), acc. no. K-11281-023 (left) and K-11281-040 (right).

Tiny ornaments in the shape of frontal animal heads occur in numerous collections around the world, but, although similar in appearance, many of these tiny plaques are not constructed in the same way. For example, the tiny plaque with a frontal ass head (entry 42) that was mixed in with the twelve plaques (entry 43) does not have a vertical attachment loop on the back, and thus does not belong to the group. Instead, types similar to no. 42 have been associated with examples found east of the Taihang in the vicinity of Zhangbei in northern Hebei (fig. 15). This piece is more similar to entry 35, discussed in Chapter 2b, than to the group that it was associated with when acquired. No. 42 is included here as a caution.

44 | Personal Ornament

South-central Inner Mongolia
6th–5th century BCE

Height 2.3 cm
Width 4.2 cm
Weight 6.8 g

Cast bronze, alloy composition by J. Stenger: Cu 79%; Sn 9%; Pb 5%; As trace

This ornament is formed by two rosettes flanking a frontal animal head with eyes defined by circular open holes. The back of the ornament is slightly concave with a horizontal bar for attachment purposes. The piece appears to have been cast from a model on which the attachment bar was bent inwards (Bunker et al. 1997, 248, no. 206). The casting method description was provided by Lore L. Holmes and W. Thomas Chase.

Ornaments with this design exist in numerous Eurasian Steppe collections (Andersson 1932, pl. 29c–d), and have been found at sites west of the Taihang, such as Maoqinggou and Guoxianyaozi, Liangcheng county, south-central Inner Mongolia, where they adorned the belt of a deceased female (Höllmann and Kossack 1992, fig. 16.10, fig. 12.1, pl. 1C).

45 | Dagger

South-central Inner Mongolia
5th century BCE

Length 25.5 cm
Width 4.2 cm
Weight 159.1 g

Cast bronze, alloy composition by J. Stenger: Cu 83%; Sn 17%; Pb 14%; As <1%

This dagger is distinguished by an antenna-shaped pommel formed by two stylized inverted raptor heads that surmount a flat hilt marked by two longitudinal grooves. The hilt and the slender leaf-shaped blade are separated aesthetically by a guard formed by two additional back-to-back bird heads with round eyes and hooked beaks defined by raised lines. Traces of mold marks on the sides of the hilt indicate that the entire weapon, both hilt and blade, was integrally cast in one piece using a two-piece mold.

This dagger is similar to numerous examples found in graves of the pastoral peoples that lived west of the Taihang Mountains in northern China and south-central Inner Mongolia. The Inner Mongolian Museum in Hohhot has several examples in its collections (Tian and Guo 1986, pl. 29.1–3). The antenna shape of the present short-sword's pommel may derive from two bird heads joined at the neck, an example of which was found suspended from the belt of the deceased in tomb 58 at Maoqinggou, Liangcheng county, south-central Inner Mongolia (Höllmann and Kossack 1992, pl. 27.1).

The Maoqinggou pommel appears to be related to examples from the Tagar culture found in southern Siberia dated to the sixth century BCE (Zavitukhina 1983, nos. 198–202). Other than an antenna dagger excavated from a non-Chinese tomb at Beixinbao, Huailai county, northeast Hebei, such short swords with bird-head pommels do not appear to have been typical of the hunting peoples of northern Hebei (Hebei 1966, 231–42; Bunker et al. 1997, 204, no. 140). In some scholarly accounts, short swords have been referred to as *akinakes*, a Greek term for a small weapon used by the Scythians that was noted by Herodotus (4.70). "As we don't know what an *akinakes* looked like, the term is best avoided," cautions Roger Moorey (personal communication). Such small weapons originated somewhere in the Eurasian steppes and became one of the most characteristic steppe artifacts (Loehr 1949, 38). Known as a dagger in Western archaeological literature, such objects are often called *duan jian* (short sword) by Chinese archaeologists. It is doubtful that such small weapons were ever intended to be "battle-ready." Rather, they were personal male symbols of prestige and useful tools (see discussion in Chapter 3c).

46 | Walking Tiger-shaped Belt Plaque

Minusinsk Basin, Tuva, northern Mongolia; Xinjiang
Saragash phase of the Tagar-culture style
ca. 6th–4th century BCE

Height 4.8 cm
Width 9.1 cm
Weight 68.7 g

Cast bronze, alloy composition by J. Stenger:
Cu 89%; Sn 1%; Pb 3%; As 3%

Ex Dr. Jiro Sugiyama Collection, Tokyo

This bronze tiger-predation belt plaque was originally the proper left plaque of a mirror-image pair that together formed a complete belt buckle. The plaque is cast in the shape of a walking tiger with slightly open jaws savaging the remains of an argali (mountain ram) represented only by its horned head. The tiger's eye appears to be an elongated oval, but the rest of the plaque surface is so worn that many details are almost gone, suggesting that the plaque may have been in use for a long time.

The reverse displays three loops for attachment: one vertical loop behind the rump and two horizontal loops behind the tiger head and the argali head respectively. The perforation of the shoulder belongs to the fastening system that characterizes early mirror-image buckles.

The tiger image on the present plaque is similar to the exotic carnivore image from tomb 55 at Maoqinggou discussed earlier in this chapter (p. 116). Both this tiger and the Maoqinggou tiger look straight ahead, while the example from Fanijayaozi (discussed in entry 38) looks down, suggesting a mixture of steppe and dynastic sources for certain art-historically similar artifacts. Moreover, in the first two cases, the muzzles seem quite elongated for a tiger and may have been intended to represent a lupine carnivore.

Similar tiger-shaped plaques have been found throughout Inner Asia (fig. 14, p. 117, blue dots) reflecting the widespread cultural interaction typical of the latter half of the first millennium BCE (Salmony 1934, 8, fig. 11). The present example is said to have been found in Gansu. It belongs to a variant with tigers that have their prey tucked between their chin and their front paws. Such plaques have been ascribed to the Saragash phase of the Tagar culture and have been found in the Minusinsk Basin (Piotrovskij 1978, 90–91, fig. 120; Zavitukhina 1983, nos. 192–93; Mei Jianjun 2006, 141–42, fig. 11.8–9; Bogdanov 2006, 158, pl. 45.1–3), although one was found in the Altai (Bogdanov 2006, pl. 45.4). One such plaque has been excavated recently in northwestern Mongolia, in the Sagly valley, from a collective tomb of the Sagly culture (personal communication with Tsagaan Törbat, whom we thank for allowing us to use this information). A further plaque of this type is from Aidinghu in Xinjiang

(Mei Jianjun 2006, 141–42, fig. 11.7; Bogdanov 2006, pl. 47.5). Two other plaques which also depict a carnivore looking straight ahead, but with a whole mountain sheep in front of its mouth, are known from a private collection in Mongolia (Ėrdėnėchuluun 2011, 226–27, nos. 233–34). This variant of tiger-shaped plaques illustrates the connectedness of northern China and southern Siberia during the sixth to fourth centuries BCE. The walking pose itself is a foreign motif that originated in the ancient Near East and was transmitted to East Asia by the Eurasian pastoral peoples (Rawson and Bunker 1990, 295).

Chapter 3b
Artifacts Associated with the Ordos Region
of Southwestern Inner Mongolia, Shanxi,
and Shaanxi Provinces

In antiquity, the Loess Plateau of the Ordos Desert region in southwestern Inner Mongolia and northwestern China flourished with lush grass, bushes, and trees. Its dusty soil was abundantly watered by numerous rivers and streams, producing rich, open grazing lands. The remains of sacrificed horses and cattle among the grave goods found there suggest that the local pastoral peoples practiced a semi-mobile way of life, with some or all of the groups moving seasonally, whenever the land was incapable of sustaining large-scale, sedentary grazing.

In the past, the many zoomorphic artifacts associated with dynastic China's Inner Asian neighbors were collectively identified as "Ordos Bronzes," whether they came from the Ordos region or not, obscuring attempts to discern their original cultural contexts (Tian and Guo 1986).

More recently, artifacts of this kind have been described as belonging to the so-called "Taohongbala culture," named after a site in the Ordos region, the result of a vague perception of regional cultural regularity that cannot be confirmed archaeologically (Wu En 2007; Kost 2014, 48–49). These objects include small plaques credited to the Taohongbala culture by Wu En (Kost 2014, 51, fig. 10a.h), which, culturally speaking, seem to have belonged to non-Chinese cultures north of Beijing (Chapter 2b, entry 34) and Maoqinggou (Chapter 3a, entry 39) respectively.

Artifacts from the Ordos region have sometimes been attributed to various tribal groups mentioned in ancient Sinitic literature. For example, Kovalev (2009, 383) locates the Loufan in the Ordos region, while Wu En (2007, 318) locates the Loufan in the Maoqinggou region, although neither attribution can be properly substantiated. Such names are too "rich in cultural prejudices and political insinuations" to be accurate or illuminating (Pines 2005; Shelach 2009, 15–18).

Artifacts from the Ordos and adjacent regions do not form a coherent art-historical group. A brief survey points to the presence of various pastoral groups with diverse burial rituals related to Eurasian Steppe traditions, as well as the presence of traditional Chinese practices and artifacts, somctimes mixed together in the same grave.

*Artifacts Dating from the Seventh
and Sixth to the Fourth Century BCE*

The most characteristic and informative grave goods from the Ordos region are cast-bronze, animal-shaped fittings, primarily of wild ungulates, created to adorn wheeled vehicles and possibly canopies used in burial rituals (Tian and Guo 1986, pls. 102–6; 108–12). Such funerary paraphernalia were also used in burials by the Eastern Zhou state of Qin, whose ancestry is considered non-Chinese (So 1995, 230).

The present collection includes yoke ornaments that are piece-mold cast (entries 51 and 52) and similar to examples excavated at Sujigou (Gai Shanlin 1965, pls. 5; 6.2) and Yulongtai, both Jungar banner, in southwestern Inner Mongolia, with the remains of wheeled vehicles (Neimenggu and Neimenggu 1977, pl. 2.1; 3.3). The use of carts associated with elite funerary rituals can be traced back to burial customs that developed in the north Caucasus during the fourth millennium BCE (Shishlina et al. 2014, 378–94). Two finials surmounted by recumbent horses excavated in the Ordos-region burial at Sujigou, Jungar banner (Tian and Guo 1986, pl. 104; Cao Wei 2012, 145) are almost identical to those in the present collection (entry 48). Most finials were probably cast in sets of four or more in order to decorate the corners of funerary vehicles used in the burial rituals, a custom also practiced by the Scythian elite in western Asia (Cherednichenko and Fialko 1988, 163, fig. 8).

Ram-shaped finials adorned the corners of a burial canopy for the deceased at Arzhan 1 in Tuva dating to around 800 BCE (Griaznov 1984, pl. 25). Although to date there is no archaeological evidence for finials having had the same function in the Ordos, one of the finials in the present collection may well have been used in this way (entry 47). The custom is traceable to the fourth millennium BCE Maikop kurgans in the Caucasus (Phillips 1961, 320), suggesting that there may have been a later parallel use in the Ordos region.

The transmission routes of funerary finials and fittings from the western reaches of the Eurasian steppes to the eastern Inner Asian world have not been satisfactorily confirmed. Where the few Shang/Western Zhou-period finials published earlier fit culturally is unclear (Bunker et al. 1970, 88, nos. 57–60). A disparate group of finials published by Wu En (2008, 196–99) includes many examples without excavated provenance borrowed from other publications, with little attempt to relate them to excavated examples elsewhere, such as those found in the Ordos region or Arzhan 1 in Tuva.

Wheeled vehicles were apparently not found together with the three finials excavated in northwestern Hebei (Zheng Shaozong 1991, 22, nos. 110–12; Bunker et al. 1997, 177, no. 92). Those finials may therefore represent exotica acquired through exchange from other herding peoples in southwestern Inner Mongolia or southern Siberia.

Bronze Personal Adornments

Belt accessories appear to have been of little importance in the greater Ordos region between the sixth and late fourth centuries BCE, with the exception of a few simple buckles and small plaques with stylized zoomorphic designs of a type found in burials throughout the Inner Asian regions bordering northwestern China (Tian and Guo 1986, 117), suggesting that they may be Sinitic productions that were distributed within an expansive western Inner Asian commercial market.

Numerous stylistically related buckles and plaques with chains displaying felines with cowrie-shell collars, decorated haunches, body perforations, and pebbled textures (entries 54 through 57) similar to the surface decor also seen on mold fragments from the Jin state foundry in Houma, have been collected at various locations in Shaanxi and Shanxi.[31] Some of the examples have a fixed tongue, a fastening device of northern origin, suggesting that these personal ornaments were made by the Jin state at Houma for their herding neighbors. No foundry debris has yet been discovered in the greater Ordos region that can be associated with the local pastoral peoples, suggesting that the yoke ornaments and many metal grave goods were cast by the dynastic Chinese to trade for horses and other steppe desirables. This suggestion is supported by the casting complexities revealed by scientific examination of some of the present artifacts by Pieter Meyers, which will be referenced in the following entries.

Despite all of the prejudicial attitudes that differentiated the dynastic Chinese and their more pastoral, animal-oriented neighbors, the two culturally distinct peoples did interact and numerous innovations were adopted, adapted, and transformed so subtly that their steppe origins were often obscured in the Sinicizing process.[32]

31 So and Bunker 1995, 171–75, nos. 98–102; Li Xiating et al. 1996, 338, no. 740; 345, no. 764.
32 For an extensive discussion of this subject, see Shelach-Lavi 2015b, 25–27.

47 | Finial

Southwest Inner Mongolia
6th–4th century BCE

Height 16 cm
Width 8.3 cm
Weight 311.5 g

Bronze,
alloy composition
by E. Ferreira:
Cu 74.7%; Sn 10.2%;
Pb 7%; As 0.4%;
Fe 0.1%

This finial is surmounted by a standing ibex whose hooves extend slightly beyond the edges of the socket. The round eyes are pierced, its ribbed horns curve backwards to touch its back, the short tail curves up to touch the rump, and a slight beard depends from beneath the chin. The socket is elliptical in section, with a small ibex cast perpendicular and protruding from the proper left side. A hole perforates the front and back of the socket. The socket and the ibex figures are hollow.

"The object is cast by the piece mold process. In the shaft hole are remains of what may be original textile fragments. In the corrosion near the bottom edge on the inside of the shaft hole are pseudo morphs of a fibrous material, probably from a wooden shaft … The surface shows considerable wear" (P. Meyers, Technical Examination Report, April 23, 2006).

This finial may have once belonged to a set of four that decorated the four corners of a funerary vehicle or canopy, in the same way as the set discovered at Arzhan 1 in Tuva (Griaznov 1984, pl. 25). In the past, before it became known that such artifacts functioned as part of a set, they were sometimes separated, apparently for commercial reasons. For example, two finials, one in the Sackler Collections (Bunker et al. 1997, 230, no. 181) and one in the Werner Jannings Collection in the Gugong in Beijing (Loehr 1956, pl. 45.25) are visually identical. They have holes in their sockets that are not circular, but rather slightly triangular, suggesting that the two finials might once have belonged to the same set; perhaps they were all cast in the same foundry. As more finials that have been hidden away in collections for decades are published, we may be able to reassemble other sets.

48 | Pair of Finials

Southwest Inner Mongolia
6th–5th century BCE

48a | Finial (left)
Height 14.6 cm
Width 7.1 cm
Weight 316.7 g
Cast bronze,
alloy composition
from surface measurements by P. Meyers:
Side of cylinder: Cu 71%;
Sn 23%; Pb 5.2%;
Fe 0.7%; haunch of horse:
Cu 68%; Sn 26%;
Pb 5.3%; Fe 0.5%

48b | Finial (right)
Height 14.1 cm
Width 6.9 cm
Weight 361.1 g
Cast bronze,
alloy composition
not analyzed

These two finials are each formed of a cylindrical socket surmounted by a hollow recumbent horse. The lack of mold lines and any other evidence of piece-mold casting suggests that they were both probably lost-wax cast (P. Meyers, July 19, 2014). The sockets have a small hole on each of the two sides for the purposes of securing the finial to a support that was probably made of wood. The alloy composition can be characterized as a leaded tin bronze.

Such finials were probably cast in sets of four or more to decorate the corners of burial carts and canopies used during funerary rituals. Finials almost identical to the present examples have been excavated in Sujigou, Jungar banner, southwest Inner Mongolia (Tian and Guo 1986, pl. 11), from a burial that also included the remains of a two-wheeled vehicle (Gai Shanlin 1965, pl. 6.2). Two more finials surmounted by horses of this type were also excavated from a tomb at Yulongtai, Jungar banner in 1976, and published in an exhibition in Xi'an 36 years later (Cao Wei 2012, 145).

49 | Finial

Eastern Eurasian steppes
6th–5th century BCE

Height 21 cm
Width 9.7 cm
Weight 776.6 g

Cast bronze,
alloy composition
by E. Ferreira:
Cu 55.2%; Sn 23.9%;
Pb 3%; As 0.3%;
Fe 0.1%

This finial represents a ram with its legs draped over the edges of a hollow rectangular socket. Each of the longer socket sides has two attachment holes for attachment purposes. The ram's body is hollow and superbly cast, with two large diamond-shaped openwork cutouts on each side.

A bronze finial with very similar diamond-shaped body cutouts was illustrated by Wu En with a group of other finials from various collections, but with no serious cultural information given. His suggestion of a relationship with the Karasuk culture (Wu En 2008, 199, fig. 124.1, copied after Andersson 1933) cannot be substantiated; instead, finials made in a similar way are known from a hoard near Irkutsk (fig. 6, p. 47). To date, there is no analogous excavated example.

50 | Finial

Northwest China, Mongolia
ca. 6th century BCE

Height 9.1 cm
Width 6.1 cm
Weight 135.3 g

Bronze, alloy composition by E. Ferreira:
Cu 75.5%; Sn 10.3%; Pb 3.2%; As 0.3%; Fe 0.1%

Ex Eugene V. Thaw Collection, New York and Santa Fe

This handsome bronze finial depicts a small horse standing on the back of a larger horse. The object may have originally belonged to a set of five, used to distinguish the four corners and apex of a burial canopy covering the bier during elite burial rituals, such as those excavated from the huge kurgan at Arzhan 1 near Uyuk in Tuva, in the Western Sayan Mountains of southern Siberia (Griaznov 1984, fig. 25; Bokovenko 1995b, 271–72). Arzhan 1 is dated to the beginning of the eighth century BCE. Such burial customs using canopies and decorated funeral carts are known from earlier Maikop tombs of the third millennium BCE in southern Russia (Phillips 1961, 320).

A finial found by chance in Mongolia is very similar in shape and detail to the present finial (Volkov 1995, 323, fig. 2o), suggesting that they may belong to the same set. Both finials are pierced in the same way, front and back, for attachment purposes. The lack of any mold marks suggests that the present piece was hollow cast by the lost-wax process from a wax model formed of several separate elements.

51 | Yoke Ornament

Southwest Inner Mongolia
6th–5th century BCE

Height 8 cm
Width 18 cm
Weight 416.2g

Tinned bronze, alloy composition by J. Stenger:
Cu 83%; Sn 10%; Pb 9%; As trace

Ex Eugene V. Thaw Collection, New York and Santa Fe

This superb image of a recumbent ram forms an ornament that once belonged to a set of zoomorphic symbols that decorated the yoke of a burial cart used by the pastoral peoples who inhabited the greater Ordos region of southwestern Inner Mongolia around the sixth to fifth century BCE.

This yoke ornament was cast by the piece-mold technique. The mold join can be seen running longitudinally down the middle of the back and along the underside of the chin and neck. The impression of a rectangular, clay core extension can be seen on the interior and the center, as well as at the junction of neck and back. Casting-core material is still visible inside the head (examination by P. Meyers, December 26, 2014). The object's alloy is a leaded tin bronze; after casting, the entire surface was tinned, and shows significant wear.

The question of how the many hollow, bronze recumbent animals found in the greater Ordos region were used had long mystified scholars. The discovery of hollow animal-shaped ornaments that fit over the yoke of a wheeled vehicle excavated in a pre-dynastic Qin tomb at Bianjiazhuang, Long county, southwest Shaanxi province, provided the solution to the puzzle (Shaanxi and Baoji 1988, 16, fig. 3.39–42; 17, fig. 4). Such ornaments have been found extensively throughout the greater Ordos region. They all originally belonged to sets of four or six that were sometimes split up by people who did not understand their original function. This type of yoke ornament was ultimately discontinued by the third century BCE, as the horse itself, rather than the vehicle, increasingly became the symbol of status and prestige.

The ram's pose here, with its legs stiffly folded, appears to derive from Chinese conventions illustrated by a lacquer animal from the tomb of Duke Jing of Qin, near Xi'an, Shaanxi province, who died in 537 BCE, although the feature appears even earlier on Shang-period jades (Yinxu 1980, col. pl. 30.4). This pose is static and should not be confused with the bent-leg pose of certain cervid images that are not folded, thus suggesting movement (see discussion in Chapter 2a, entry 8). No foundry debris has yet been discovered in the greater Ordos region that can be associated with the local pastoral peoples, suggesting that yoke ornaments and other metal grave goods were cast by the Chinese to trade for horses and other steppe products. Some far-reaching contact with the West resulted in the appearance of cervids with the same pose on objects made in the Black Sea area (Chlenova 1963, passim).

52 | Shaft Terminal

Southwest Inner Mongolia
ca. 4th century BCE

Height 8.1 cm
Width 14.2 cm
Weight 423.5 g

Cast Bronze, alloy composition by J. Stenger:
Cu 86%; Sn 2%; Pb 7%

This naturalistic recumbent ram forms the terminal for the shaft of a cart used to transport the deceased to their final burial place. The ram is shown with its legs folded in the same pose as the previous cart ornament (entry 51). Its characteristic ribbed horns curl around the eyes, each represented by an intaglio circle framing a bulging pupil. The ram's hindquarters are open, forming a socket into which the shaft end of a cart could be fitted and then secured through numerous small holes in the bronze. Mold marks are visible under the head, indicating that the piece was cast in a two-piece mold. The present image is very similar to a ram-shaped shaft terminal found in the Arthur A. Sackler Collections, but is in much better condition (Bunker et al. 1997, 234, no. 186).

A highly similar shaft terminal has been excavated in Waertougou, southwest Inner Mongolia (Tian and Guo 1986, 166, fig. 114.7). Similar pole ends enhanced by ram images, which are associated with wheeled vehicles in numerous Ordos-region burials and chance finds (see So and Bunker 1995, 43–44; 55–56), suggest that sheep herding may have been a mainstay of the users' pastoral economy. The custom of adorning a wheeled vehicle for the funerary transport of the elite appears to have also been practiced by the Scythians in western Asia. For a decorated Scythian funerary carriage, see Cherednichenko and Fialko (1988, 163, fig. 8).

53 | Yoke Ornament

Southwest Inner Mongolia
5th – 4th century BCE

Height 14 cm
Width 10.5 cm
Weight 154.6 g

Cast Bronze,
alloy composition
by J. Stenger:
Cu 73%; Sn 8%;
Pb 5%; As trace

It is likely that this gangly hollow image of a fawn with overly long legs originally belonged to a set of ornaments that were created to fit over the yoke of a burial cart. Similar pieces have been collected throughout the Ordos region and grace numerous collections around the world. The present figure is very similar to an example in the Borowski Collection (Jäger and Kansteiner 2011, 101, no. 142, identified as a mule) and it is tempting to suggest the possibility that they were cast in the same place and are part of the same set.

The present figure is piece-mold cast, as indicated by a longitudinal mold mark down the center of the back. Similar seam lines are visible under the muzzle and along the center of the tail. During the casting process, the molten bronze apparently seeped between the two mold halves at the point where the front legs are conjoined.

54 | Belt Hook and Matching Plaque

Northwest China
5th century BCE

54a | Plaque with Hook
Length 10 cm
Height 5.4 cm
Weight 49.8 g
Cast bronze,
alloy composition
by J. Stenger:
Cu 66%; Sn 7%;
Pb 16%; As trace

54b | Plaque without Hook
Length 7 cm
Height 4.1 cm
Weight 36 g
Cast bronze,
alloy composition
by J. Stenger:
Cu 67%; Sn 12%;
Pb 13%; As trace
Ex C. T. Loo Collection,
Paris; Dr. Franco Vannotti
Collection, Lugano,
acquired 1948; Eskenazi
Ltd., London, 1989
Published:
Speiser 1953, no. 174;
Elisseeff 1954, no. 315;
Brinker 1975, no. 117;
Eskenazi 1989, no. 19

Both: Ex Therese and
Erwin Harris Collection,
Miami, Florida

Published:
So and Bunker 1995,
174–75, no. 101a and b

A crouching feline standing on a baseline formed by two serpents distinguishes this belt hook and matching plaque that together form a complete buckle. The pebbled texture, cowrie-shell motifs, and other surface decoration are all clues enabling these pieces to be associated with mold fragments found at Houma, the sixth- to fifth-century BCE Jin state foundry in southern Shanxi that may have produced metal items for the pastoral peoples along their northern borders. For an in-depth study of this buckle and technical details, see So and Bunker (1995, 174–75, no. 101; Li Xiating et al. 1996, 338, no. 740; 345, no. 764).

The felines are each represented with a cowrie-shell collar, suggesting that they may represent domesticated wild animals that have been trained to hunt. The heart-shaped ear derives from earlier Western Zhou tiger images, such as those found in a late Western Zhou burial in Yucun, Ning county, Gansu province (Xu Junchen and Liu Dezhen 1985, 349–52, pl. 5.1; So and Bunker 1995, 112, fig. 26.1), which is almost identical to a tiger-shaped plaque in the present collection (Chapter 3c, entry 93).

The loops that depend from the baseline of each buckle plaque were intended to hold linked chains, similar to the one hanging from the feline plaque in entry 55 below. A button for attachment purposes projects from behind the waist of each feline and is surrounded by a raised circular mold line, clearly indicating that each feline plaque was piece-mold cast. The personal ornaments discussed in the following entries display various surface markings that relate them to Houma and to the present piece, which, taken together, suggests that Sinitic productions were distributed within an extensive western Inner Asian commercial market.

Although the present two pieces form a complete buckle, the evidence of wear and zoomorphic details on them are not identical, raising the possibility that they were not originally made and used together. Instead, this archaeological pastiche was probably assembled by vendors and collectors to enhance their aesthetic appeal and value.

55 | Belt Plaque with Links

Northwest China, southern Shanxi region, Houma
ca. 5th century BCE

Height 9.8 cm including chain
Width 5.6 cm
Weight 44.8 g

Cast Bronze, alloy composition by J. Stenger:
Cu 71%; Sn 12%; Pb 16%; As trace

This feline-shaped plaque is the matching plaque to a belt hook from an assembly in which the two belt plaques were originally attached by a pair of chains, in a way reminiscent of another assembly in the Harris Collection (So and Bunker 1995, 175–76, no. 102). As in the previous buckle (entry 54), the feline represented is shown with a collar, suggesting the use of animals for hunting by humans. References abound in art and literature to trained falcons, dogs, leopards, and cheetahs (Andersson 1932, 304–6). The present plaque has a round stud protruding from the reverse behind the waist, with the remains of a chain suspended from the baseline.

Plaques with pendant chains belong to a group of personal ornaments that have long been stuck in archaeological limbo (Andersson 1932, pls. 13; 14). A few of these plaques are marked by semilunar perforations (Andersson 1932, pl. 13.3–4) that are now recognized as Jin-style artistic devices, an association confirmed by their presence on the body of a boar represented on a mold fragment excavated from the Jin state foundry at Houma, in southern Shanxi (Shanxi 1987, 76, fig. 13; 78, fig. 19). Some of the plaques have a fixed tongue—a characteristic steppe device—of the kind seen on the hook buckle in the present collection (entry 56).

56 | Fastener with Pendant Links

Northwest China
5th century BCE

Height 8.8 cm
Width 4.8 cm
Weight 46.5 g

Cast Bronze, alloy composition by J. Stenger: Cu 77%; Sn 7%; Pb 6%; As trace

This belt fastener is formed of an ungulate with a slim, elongated body, folded legs, and the tail raised over the rump. The animal is shown in profile, its head turned back, the eye and muzzle marked by circular cells—with slightly elliptical geometric cells at the shoulder and rump—and with worn triangular cells representing the hooves. The fastener plaque with a fixed hook was cast in a piece-mold, and the precast pendant links and attachment button on the reverse were cast on, the same production process used for the other belt items of a similar kind discussed in this chapter. A plaque resembling this example is held in the Arthur M. Sackler Collections (Bunker et al. 1997, 221, no. 163).

This belt-fastener plaque exhibits a mixture of styles that appears to have developed in northwestern dynastic China around the middle of the first millennium BCE. The fixed tongue is a device originating in the northern steppe, while the button has a dynastic-Chinese origin and was used on belt hooks. The chains on all of these belt assemblies were laboriously cast using the typical Chinese casting-on process, while the steppe chains were usually forged and then assembled mechanically, like the chain from Maoqinggou M5 (Höllmann and Kossack 1992, pl. 4.2). The stylistic relationships seem to suggest that those pieces that display a dual heritage were probably cast at a nearby foundry with a connection to Houma.

57 | Belt Elements and Chains

Northwest China
5th century BCE

Height 4.1 cm
Width 7.1 cm
(only belt elements, without chains)
Weight all 145.2 g

Cast bronze,
alloy composition
by J. Stenger:
Cu 77%; Sn 9%;
Pb 3%; As trace

These two belt elements, a fastener and plaque with two pendant linked chains, are the remains of a larger ensemble that belonged to the same stylistic group as the belt elements (entries 54–56). None of them are complete, but they all appear to derive stylistically from motifs and surface decoration found on casting debris associated with bronzes produced at the Jin state foundry in southern Shanxi (Li Xiating et al. 1996, passim). This group of belt elements with chains is represented in various collections around the world, but has received little scholarly attention. None of them have a precise excavated provenance, although a few pieces have been collected in the northern Shaanxi and Shanxi regions, for example, an animal-shaped hook with a similar chain collected at Xietuncun, Ansai district, of northern Shaanxi (Ji Naijun 1989, pl. 4.4, with chain, 72, fig. 1).

The zoomorphic design on the present fastener comprises two animals with long muzzles, and two highly conventionalized felines with shoulders, haunches, eyes, and paws indicated by circular cells Tangential loops are for the chains and projecting buttons on the reverse for attachment purposes. Ariadne Galleries has published a fastener and plaque similar to the present example, along with a matching plaque and a long chain intended to show how these belt elements may have been assembled, which may not be entirely correct (Ariadne Galleries 1998, 148–49, no. 166). A single plaque, whose casting is of far better quality than the present one clarifies the zoomorphic design, (Bunker 1981, 176, no. 916). In spite of the circular perforations that, to some, suggest a relationship to feline plaques found in northern Hebei, there is no evidence yet of any of these belt elements having been found there. Moreover, they all relate culturally to material found in what is now northwestern China.

The chains were laboriously cast using the piece-mold process, with precast rings attached to figure-eight-shaped connectors—one by one in multiple steps—through a process of casting on, which is characteristic of dynastic-Chinese workmanship (see description by So in So and Bunker 1995, 172–76). By contrast, the chains associated with the northern herders were formed by forged loops attached mechanically (see entry 56).

58 | Personal Adornment

Northwest China
5th century BCE

Height 2.7 cm
Width 6.1 cm
Weight 12 g

Cast bronze, alloy composition by J. Stenger: Cu 68%; Sn 21%; Pb 10%; As trace

This small plaque displays a highly stylized feline image in profile. The eye is marked by a circular cell and the ear by a triangular cell, resembling distinguishing features on the plaque in entry 56, as does the curving tail that turns up at the tip. The feet are indicated by circular perforations in the paws. The reverse displays the remains of two tiny vertical loops behind the neck and the waist. The body is marked by curved geometric perforations similar to those accenting a clay model of a sow with piglet recovered from among the foundry debris at Houma in southern Shanxi, in the heart of Jin territory (Shanxi 1987, 76, 78, figs. 13 and 19; Li Xiating et al. 1996, 101, no. 764 and 345, no. 764).

Although superficially similar to earlier bronze feline images from northern Hebei, such as entry 23 in Chapter 2b, the present plaque was cast from a different alloy, according to the analyses of Jens Stenger and Pieter Meyers. The present piece was very crudely cast in a two-piece mold that left flashing along the edges.

59 | Personal Adornment

Northwest China
5th century BCE

Height 2.8 cm
Width 5.8 cm
Weight 20.9 g

Cast gold,
alloy composition
by P. Meyers:
Au 88%; Ag 7.2%;
Cu 4.1%; Sn ca. 1.5%

A tiny feline, probably a tiger, adorns this personal ornament made of gold. The eye is a circular perforation and the paws are defined by circular cells, all features found on a buckle (So and Bunker 1995, 172–73, no. 99) that is stylistically related to the previously discussed belt ornaments with chains in this chapter (see entries 55–57). To date, nothing similar has been found in an archaeological context. The image shows considerable wear in some of the perforations, but otherwise much of the original figure is still intact. The reverse reveals the remains of two tiny, worn-off loops.

This gold tiger comes from an old European collection and displays heavy wear, suggesting considerable use in antiquity. The plaque is visually similar to the previously discussed bronze plaque (entry 58), but was produced by the lost-wax casting method. It is therefore doubtful that it was cast at Houma, since pieces at Houma were not cast by the lost-wax process. Analyses by XRF reveal a typical alloy for a fifth-century BCE artifact that was probably cast at some northern, dynastic-Chinese foundry specifically for one of its pastoral neighbors (P. Meyers).

60, 61, 62, 63 | Four Personal Ornaments

Northwest China and southwest Inner Mongolia
5th–4th century BCE

60 | Personal Ornament
Height 4.1 cm
Width 1.2 cm
Weight 5 g
Cast Bronze,
alloy composition
by J. Stenger:
Cu 71%; Sn 7%;
Pb 16%; As trace

61 | Personal Ornament
Height 3.5 cm
Width 4.8 cm
Weight 10.5 g
Cast bronze,
alloy composition
by J. Stenger:
Cu 88%; Sn 7%;
Pb 4%; As trace

62 | Personal Ornament
Height 7.8 cm
Width 7 cm
Weight 65.3 g
Bronze,
alloy composition
by J. Stenger:
Cu 99%; As very high

63 | Personal Ornament
Height 6.4 cm
Width 5.4 cm
Weight 34 g
Gold, alloy composition
by P. Meyers (2013):
Front, side 1: Au 94%;
Ag 5.6%; Cu 0.15%
Front, side 2: Au 94%;
Ag 5.7%; Cu trace

The elongated, S-shaped bronze plaque no. 60 features, at each end, the profile forequarters of a carnivore with a clawed paw. A tiny attachment loop appears behind each carnivore's head.

Bronze plaque no. 61 displays three tangent rings surmounted by a standing carnivore in profile, with its head shown frontally grasping the head of a herbivore and two tiny carnivore heads on top of the main carnivore's body. No loops appear on the reverse, which is hollow.

No. 62 is a bronze plaque formed by a horse represented in profile surmounting two profile ram heads. A horizontal attachment loop or button appears behind the horse on the flat back of the plaque.

Gold plaque no. 63 is cast in the shape of two profile carnivores with open jaws, flanking the profile figure of a doe with folded legs. No loops appear on the hollow reverse.

These four ornaments, all cast in the same style, belong to a group of tiny plaques that have traditionally been associated with the northwestern part of the frontier region and dated to the fifth century BCE (Bunker et al. 1997, 226–29). A hook buckle cast in the same style was collected in Yulin Fu in northwestern Shaanxi close to the Ordos Desert (Bunker et al. 1997, 227, no. 174), but no artifacts cast in this style have been excavated scientifically. Numerous similar examples are included in many collections around the world, but with only limited scholarly data.

The bronze plaques here were each piece-mold cast, leaving flashings in the design openings while the gold plaque was cast using the lost-wax method.

60

61

62

64 | Garment Hook

A circular body with a hook shaped like a raptor head projecting from one side and an attachment loop formed by a doe's head on the opposite side forms the small buckle. The ears have raised rims and a row of raised dots decorates the main body of the buckle. The buckle was piece-mold cast. Hook buckles were ubiquitous throughout dynastic China's Inner Asian regions.

An almost identical example has been associated stylistically with southwestern Inner Mongolia (Bunker et al. 1997, 228–29, no. 177) at sites both in the Jundushan (He Yong and Liu Jianzhong 1993, fig. 13.9) and in the Ordos region, such as Yulongtai, Jungar banner (Neimenggu and Neimenggu 1977, pl. 2.5). Buckles of this type appear to have been used to fasten belts, as well as horse gear, and they also appear in the early first millennium BCE in Iran. For a discussion of the development of this type of hook buckle see Bunker et al. 1997, 210–11, no. 149; Bunker et al. 2002, 95–96, no. 61.

North China and southwest Inner Mongolia
5th century BCE

Height 5.5 cm
Width 3.1 cm
Weight 13.7 g

Cast Bronze, alloy composition by J. Stenger:
Cu 60%; Sn 10%; Pb 18%; As trace

65 | Harness Plaque

**Northwest China
ca. 4th century BCE**

Height 10 cm
Width 14.9 cm
Depth 5.4 cm
Weight 527.2 g

Cast Bronze, alloy composition by J. Stenger: Cu 73%; Sn 3%; Pb 6%; As <1%

Ex David David-Weill Collection, Paris, DW 35/63; Sotheby's Paris, 16 December 2015, lot 1

Published: Trésors de la Chine ancienne 2015, 22–23, no. 1

A tiger with bared teeth and spiral-shaped ears, walking over a contorted deer, forms a predation composition represented earlier on the Bashadar kurgan 2 coffin in the Altai (Menghin et al. 2007, 122, fig. 4; Mir kochevnikov 2013, 54–55, cat. 158).

The surface pattern imitates heavy cord appliqué (Ackerman 1946, 61–62). Two flat slits designed to receive a strap appear on the reverse. The frontally facing head still retains its casting core. The body is concave, with one vertical loop that extends from the upper edge behind the neck and a second that extends from the upper edge behind the haunch. The eyes are both tear-shaped with an oval pupil. The jaws are open revealing teeth and fangs. The tiger's ear is defined by a spiral similar to the ear of a bronze Tagar-culture tiger from Minusinsk, which in turn resembles the tigers carved into the coffin lid from Bashadar kurgan 2 in the Altai (Schiltz 1975, 191, no. 176).

A pattern of ribbed units in infrequent occurrence distinguishes the present tiger's pelt, relating it visually to a bronze-tiger yoke ornament with a similar ribbed treatment of its pelt in the Sackler Museum at Harvard University Art Museums, Grenville L. Winthrop Bequest, 1943.52.98 (So and Bunker 1995, 116, fig. 30.2). The paws of both tigers are depicted in the same way, with the emphasis on four prominent claws that curve in one direction and dewclaws that curve in the opposite direction. Similar ribbing marks the pelts of two silver, mirror-image, tiger-shaped plaques from Nalin'gaotu, Shenmu county, northern Shaanxi, at the edge of the Ordos Desert region (Bunker 1993, 41, fig. 17.12–13).

These tigers were all originally cast in pairs and are very heavy. They appear to have been used to adorn a horse's breast-strap, which would explain the two heavy attachment loops on the back. A complete pair of plaques, similar to the plaque here, are housed in the collection of the Nelson-Atkins Gallery in Kansas City (Bunker et al. 1970, 115, no. 84; 140, no. 84); another single plaque is known from the Cernuschi Museum in Paris (Art animalier 2012, 134–35, no. 125). A mirror-image example collected in Suiyuan belonging to the Inner Mongolian Museum in Hohhot (Kost 2014, pl. 71, no. 6) might possibly be the mate of the

present plaque, as the details and dimensions are almost the same (Zheng Shaozong 1991, 16 drawing). Bunker suggests that two similar plaques from the Leon Levy and Shelby White Collection were used as harness ornaments (So and Bunker 1995, 115–16, no. 30).

The close similarity between the tiger image tattooed on the left shoulder of the man buried in Pazyryk kurgan 5, noted by Barkova and Pankova (2005, 51, fig. 4), and the tigers carved into the coffin from Bashadar kurgan 2, reveals the extensive cultural interconnections that appear to have existed throughout northwestern dynastic China, southwestern Inner Mongolia, and the Altai during the latter half of the first millennium BCE. Were these tattooed people buried in Pazyryk shamanic practitioners? And were these sacred symbols transmitted by their travel?

66 | Garment Plaque

This small plaque is cast in the form of a walking wild boar with all four legs shown. The reverse is flat and displays two vertical loops that are each formed by a flat strip on two posts. The boar's body is defined by a series of low ribs that relate the piece stylistically to the previous David-Weill plaque (entry 65), which exhibits units of curvilinear forms that represent a stylized version of the earlier incised zigzag lines that provide texture for the walking tigers carved into the coffin lid from Bashadar kurgan 2 (Menghin et al. 2007, 122, no. 4a–b).

Northwest China, southwest Inner Mongolia
ca. 4th century BCE

Height 3 cm
Width 5.2 cm
Weight 18.4 g

Cast Bronze,
alloy composition
by J. Stenger:
Cu 81%; Sn 11%;
Pb 20%; As trace

Ex Dr. Paul Singer Collection, Summit, New Jersey

67 | Openwork Belt Hook

South-central Inner Mongolia

Height 5.4 cm
Width 7.8 cm
Weight 39.3 g

Bronze, alloy composition by J. Stenger: Cu 78%; Sn 9%; Pb 11%; As trace

Openwork belt hook, with a hook protruding from a frame bent outward, followed by a square body consisting of two rows of stacked crouching felines with their heads turned backwards. The rear end has a small loop.

No exact analogies are known, but this item belongs to a family of hook buckles associated with south-central Inner Mongolia (Rawson and Bunker 1990, 320–21, no. 202). Another, far simpler round buckle is known from the Sackler Collection (Bunker et al. 1997, 190, no. 114).

Chapter 3c
Southern Ningxia Hui Autonomous Region, the Qingyang Plateau of Southeastern Gansu, and Parts of the Xinjiang Uyghur Autonomous Region

The Transformations in Iconography and Metallurgy during the First Millennium BCE

The first millennium BCE was a period of great cultural change for the elite dynastic-Chinese world and its pastoral trading partners. After the conquest of the Western Zhou homeland by mounted warriors from beyond China's northern frontiers, and the subsequent flight of the royal Zhou to their eastern capital located in present-day Luoyang, the northwestern territory was entrusted to the Qin to restore and manage. Archaeological evidence documents striking cultural changes in northwestern China during the first millennium BCE, but the historical information is limited and the exotic cultural contacts suggested are often confusing, leading Gideon Shelach-Lavi to astutely describe the circumstances as "fuzzy" (Shelach-Lavi 2015a, 237). Analysis of materials from traditional dynastic Chinese regions dated to this period reveal unprecedented contact with the outside world, as well as receptivity to new customs and artifactual types.

Recent research suggests a need to reconsider the interconnectivity of certain regional pastoral groups in order to shift emphasis away from thinking about "cultural" interaction to sharing regionally within "social fields" (Linduff 2015). This essay will consider material culture associated with Inner Asia that documents the interaction and exchange of ideas, technology, the types of objects and images adopted and adapted, as well as the appropriation of actual goods as markers of this interaction across what were sometimes vast territories and over considerable lengths of time.

Certain items among the grave goods in the region display visual markers and traits that come from diverse traditions associated with both the dynastic Zhou and the Eurasian pastoral world, which may be seen as exotic or foreign and which became significant status markers. Culturally hybrid artifacts form a special category of interpretation that reflects intrusive characteristics introduced through exchange or marriage with foreigners. Archaeological studies reveal that the "presence of gold as an elite status symbol became one of the pre-imperial Qin's distinguishing features. The first major discovery that highlighted this trait is the looted burial of an unnamed Qin nobleman at Dabuzishan, Li Xian, in southern Gansu province" (So 2014, 195).[33] Four of the objects taken from that burial are large bird-shaped plaques (height 42 cm) made from gold sheet worked in repoussé, with openwork holes produced by chisel cutting.[34] An in-depth reconstruction of the cultural contacts that fueled the appearance of gold during this period is beyond the scope of this publication, since it would involve the piecing together of seemingly disparate pieces of information into a hypothetical jigsaw puzzle for which many of the key pieces are still missing. The majority of gold from Dabuzishan consists of repoussé gold sheets worked by technological borrowings from beyond the foundry tradition of early dynastic China, since shaping and decorating metal objects in dynastic China was traditionally accomplished by casting (So 2014). The issue here is not just the adoption of a broader usage of gold, but also an understanding of the metallurgical technologies used to work it.

Exotica among Eastern Zhou Grave Goods in Northwest China

Grave goods belonging to certain elites in Eastern Zhou states located in the Yellow River basin reveal a surprising taste for ostentatious displays, through accouterments which were frequently fashioned in gold. Such objects of display have not been commonly associated with ancient dynastic-Chinese traditions (Keightley 1990, 50–51). In death, the dynastic-Chinese elite from earlier periods were surrounded by, or covered with, cast bronze and jade, but in the Eastern Zhou context personal adornments made of gold, which were previously unknown in the area, were included and often took precedence (So and Bunker 1995, 22), in part, at least, because of gold's luster and rather dramatic, unfamiliar appearance which never tarnished or corroded.

The Eastern Zhou-period interest in personal adornment and the preference for gold among elites has been identified with recently excavated grave goods

---

33 Some of the looted material, in the form of gold plaques, was presented to the Musée Guimet (Han and Deydier 2001, 23–32). Later, these plaques were reclaimed by China and published in a celebratory volume marking their return (Guojia wenwu 2015).
34 Microscopic examination reveals the presence of minuscule inclusions of osmium-iridium-ruthenium, "heavy metals found in natural, unrefined (perhaps panned alluvial) gold that was not melted down in the casting process." The production process described here is based on P. Meyers' examination of several similar gold bird-shaped plaques.

that highlight personal status. Elaborate belts formed of gold plaques strung on cloth or leather found in several early Eastern Zhou tombs indicate the adoption of a foreign, Eurasian steppe custom of wearing elaborate belts as a form of social expression and a sign of status (So 1997, 71). However, it must be noted that the decorative belt plaques were adapted to local dynastic-Chinese taste through the addition of traditional Zhou dragon motifs displayed on their surfaces (Shanghai Museum 2012, 164–65).

A "set of fifteen cast-gold belt ornaments decorated with traditional dynastic Zhou dragon motifs" was discovered in an eighth-century BCE Jin state tomb at Tianma-Qucun, in southern Shanxi province (Shanxi and Beijing 1994, 17, fig. 20). The Guo state cemetery at Shangcunling, near Sanmenxia in western Henan province, yielded a similar group of gold belt ornaments (Bunker 1993, 38, fig. 6), some of which are identical in design to the mentioned examples found at Tianma-Qucun. Recently, additional gold belt plaques have been discovered in a Rui-state tomb belonging to an elite male, M27, in a cemetery at Liangdaicun near Hancheng, Shaanxi province, along with a cast-gold openwork scabbard containing a superb jade dagger (Shanghai Museum 2012, 156, no. 76; Rawson 2015a, 91, fig. 17).

Gold Artifacts in the Rui Lord's Tomb (M27)[35]

The Rui Lord's tomb contained a gold scabbard (18.7 × 4 × 1.5 cm), found near the waist on the left hip, with a jade dagger (29 × 3.8 cm) outside the scabbard lying across the right side of the body. Below the right hand, two gold archer's thumb rings were found, thirteen dragon belt rings at the waist (diameter 6.9 × 0.25 / 5.4 × 0.15 cm) and two triangular plaques (height 8.7 cm) to the center right of the waist. Furthermore, ten gold mask ornaments and ring holders, two gold dragons at the left and right shoulders, and a folded-gold shoulder ornament at the right shoulder were also included among the gold artifacts in his tomb.

A jade dagger in a gold scabbard would have been an unusual accouterment for an Eastern Zhou lord and should not be taken as an indication of battle prowess or warlike ambitions on the part of the owner. Instead, the gold scabbard in the

---

35   The following brief descriptions of the gold artifacts from Rui M27 are taken from the archaeological publication (Shanghai Museum 2012) and a photograph of the pieces *in situ* kindly provided by Jenny F. So.

Rui Lord's tomb was intended to serve as a status symbol during his lifetime. The jade dagger may then have been considered to be imbued with mythological power to quell the supernatural demons known to lurk in the afterlife (Rawson 2015b, 35). Worn with a long robe, the gold belt plaques, flashy gold garment ornaments, and gold openwork scabbard must have lent the Rui Lord a deeply impressive appearance. The presence of an ornate cast-gold sheath and cast-gold personal ornaments in an Eastern Zhou grave are surprising in a dynastic-Chinese context.

Who was this Rui lord? His grave goods, which—besides the unusual gold scabbard and jade dagger—include the usual set of ritual bronze vessels, suggest that he was a member of the Qin elite. The grave goods of the woman in tomb M26, by contrast, include several interesting bronze vessels with special lids with loops designed to enable them to be sealed shut, possibly to accommodate a more mobile lifeway than that of the Zhou (Shanghai Museum 2012, figs. 102; 104). There are also bronze boxes with openwork panels that are technically similar to the openwork design of the Rui Lord's scabbard in M27 (Shanghai Museum 2012, figs. 100; 106). A jade pig-dragon among the grave goods in M26 appears to be an ancient example from northeastern China's Hongshan culture (Shanghai Museum 2012, fig. 117), suggesting that the woman who became the Rui Lord's consort may have come from the northeastern frontier region. This might explain the similarity between the design of the gold openwork sheath in the Rui Lord's tomb and the cast-bronze openwork dagger sheaths associated with the ancient hunting peoples who inhabited the Jundushan north of Beijing (Bunker et al. 1997, 196–97, figs. 130.1.3), which may have inspired the Rui Lord's gold scabbard.

Dagger Symbolism in the Ancient Near East and the Eastern Eurasian Steppe

The ritual and societal role of a dagger can be traced back to traditions from the third millennium BCE in the ancient Near East. For example, excavations at the royal cemetery of Ur in Mesopotamia, ca. 2500 BCE, yielded a dagger with a lapis lazuli hilt, a gold blade, and an openwork gold scabbard with a design made by cutting motifs out of gold sheet (Amiet 1980, 369, fig. 320; Eluère 1989, 171); the Temple of the Obelisks in Byblos, dating to the second millennium BCE, yielded a gold dagger (Aruz et al. 2008, 54, no. 24); and the Egyptian boy-king

Tutankhamun was buried along with an impressive dagger in an ornate gold sheath to mark his elite status in the royal hierarchy.[36] None of these artifacts were created for use in battle, but they may have served as visual symbols of elite authority and power. At Persepolis, an ornate dagger in an elaborate sheath hangs from a Saka man's belt in a tribute scene on the Apadana steps, which is often identified as an *akinakes*, the legendary personal weapon worn by the Saka elite. A Saka burial at Berel' in Kazakhstan has yielded a similar dagger with a lavish guard in the shape of a gold heart.[37] Daggers are also shown hanging from belts on carved deerstones in Mongolia (ca. 1200–700 BCE) that are considered to be representations of warriors (Fitzhugh 2009; Törbat 2018a; 2018b). Furthermore, the spectacular, undisturbed burial 5 at Arzhan kurgan 2 in the Republic of Tuva in Siberia, dating to the seventh century BCE, revealed a royal couple accompanied in death by more than 5,700 gold items (Čugunov et al. 2010, 29, fig. 37). Each of the deceased had a superbly fashioned dagger composed of a forged iron blade and a hilt surmounted by an ornate pommel, glistening with gold and silver inlays (Čugunov et al. 2006, pl. 19; Čugunov et al. 2010, 29, fig. 37), a dagger-production method that is atypical for the steppe world, where the blade and the hilt were usually integrally cast together in one piece.

Goldsmith Techniques of the Metallurgical World of the Eastern Eurasian Steppes

An examination of the gold grave goods from burial 5 at Arzhan 2 reveals an amazing range of goldsmith techniques. Almost every known ancient goldworking technique is represented, although to date, no evidence of any early Scythian goldsmith workshops has been found (Armbruster 2009, 188). Suggestions concerning the furnaces and the specialized tools necessary for creating a plethora of gold treasures have been formulated on the basis of an examination of the artifacts themselves, as well as ethnographic observations (Armbruster 2009).

---

36 Aruz et al. 2008, 54, 300. "Recent scientific examination by X-ray fluorescence spectrometry found that the blade's composition of iron, nickel and cobalt was an approximate match for a meteorite that landed in northern Egypt… [that] strongly suggests an extraterrestrial origin;" this was referenced as "iron from the sky" by ancient Egyptians (Walsh 2016, A7).

37 Chang and Guroff 2007, 93, no. 3. Francfort, Ligabue, and Samashev date the site by dendrochronological results to 294 BCE (Francfort et al. 2006, 126). The dagger is identified as an *akinakes*. According to P. R. S. Moorey, *akinakes* is a mythical name for a historical item of which we do not have knowledge (see Chapter 3a, entry 45).

Archaeological research and a few ancient literary texts reveal that an enormous amount of gold, together with specific goldsmith techniques, circulated in antiquity, probably accompanied by the movement of technological know-how that was passed along by transient metal-workers. The existence of an extensive exchange network operating throughout the Eurasian steppe world that dispersed a surprising range of artifacts from distant origins is illustrated by artifacts from Pazyryk: The silver belt plaques from barrow 2 are Achaemenid heirlooms dating from the sixth to fourth century BCE, while the tin-bronze mirror with ox-horn handle, also from barrow 2, is a product of ancient India (Stark 2012, 116; 130).

The procurement of ore, and the many ways in which it was worked, need to be considered when studying ancient gold (Eluère 1989, 225–31). "The different fine metal working techniques used in the manufacture of the gold and iron artifacts from Arzhan 2 were not new inventions … but previously known in other regions, such as the Near East, as well as China, before the 7th century BCE. … Lost wax casting, soldering, filigree, granulation, and polychrome metal inlay were also in use in Anatolia and Mesopotamia, as well as Iron Age Europe" (Armbruster 2009, 191). Contemporary scholars investigating the surprising enthusiasm for gold scabbards in the Qin context suggest distant contact with Siberia, whereas some goldsmith techniques may have been in use at an earlier date in dynastic China. As more gold is uncovered from burials throughout China and the eastern Eurasian steppe world, earlier theories concerning the manufacture and spread of the use of precious metals may need to be updated (Bunker 1988, 222–27; Bunker 1993; Bunker 1994c).

Dagger Transmission into the Eastern Zhou Sphere

Dagger types were transmitted throughout the Eurasian steppes via ancient herding and exchange networks that had probably been in use for millennia. As is the case today, such personal weapons may have had individual significance. The transmission of their various types, as well as their adoption and regional adaptation, stand as an example of the extended life of such objects across the Eurasian steppe world and into eastern Asia. Some daggers were accompanied by scabbards, while others were not, depending on who carried them and whether the daggers were intended to mark status or to be used for more practical purposes (Rawson 2015a, 87, fig. 4; 92, fig. 21). Some scabbards were made of metal, while others were made of organic materials, such as leather or fabric, that have not survived.

By the time daggers began to appear among the grave goods in the dynastic-Chinese world, a process of fusion may have taken place, in which the idea of a royal dagger and a pastoralist's tool became conflated, resulting in personal weapons that varied in length and style from place to place (Jettmar 1967, 49–50; So and Bunker 1995, 47, fig. 15). According to Loehr (1949, 38) this type of dagger was probably introduced into the dynastic-Chinese sphere through contact with mobile horse-riding traders arriving in the Ordos or further north in Siberia. Watson (1971, 104–5) believed that these daggers had a Eurasian Steppe heritage. Karlgren (1945, 101–44), however, argued the opposite.

A few daggers excavated from sites east of the Taihang have scabbards made of bronze. For example, a dagger with a bronze scabbard was excavated from an Upper Xiajiadian grave in Nanshan'gen, Ningcheng county, southeastern Inner Mongolia in 1958 (Xiajiadian 2007, 146–47). This was probably the result of contact with the far northwest, via the northern Fur Route that ran eastward, through the vicinity of the Lake Baikal region, before turning southward down the Amur Valley. This is, of course, a northern route of contact through the borderlands of northeastern dynastic China.

In light of recent archaeological research, it now seems that such daggers—or even the simple idea of such daggers—originated in the west, before being slowly defused eastward via numerous Eurasian Steppe roads during the second and first millennium BCE. An examination of the many daggers depicted on deerstones found throughout Mongolia and southern Siberia may reflect such a transmission (Wu En 2003; Pan Ling 2008).

As inferred by Chlenova, the origins of certain components from the eastern Eurasian steppe world ultimately hark "back to ancient cultures of the middle East and Iran where their prototypes had been formed and from where they spread eastwards to more northern regions" (Chlenova 1994, 518–19, figs. 14–16). The fact that many daggers may have similar utilitarian and ritual connotations "testifies to the similarity of the cult and religious beliefs," which were often altered in minor ways to accommodate the specific ecologies inhabited by the various regional hunting and herding groups (Chlenova 1994), as well as to accommodate local ideas about burial rites.

The Source of the Rui Lord's Gold Scabbard

The Rui openwork gold scabbard in M27 is decorated with a distinctly dynastic-Chinese dragon design, but relates typologically and stylistically to several bronze examples with openwork zoomorphic images associated with the peoples inhabiting the Jundushan, north of Beijing, around the seventh century BCE.[38] Two similar bronze scabbards with bronze short swords dated to the seventh century BCE by Watson (1971, 104–5), and two other scabbards, dated circa sixth century BCE by Loehr—based on the presence of zoomorphic designs resembling framed animal designs on plaques found at Jundushan sites, such as entry 34 (Chapter 2b)—can be associated with the hunting peoples inhabiting the mountainous regions north of Beijing (Loehr 1949, 46–47; 82–83; Bunker et al. 1997, 197). Daggers and scabbards of this type were probably cast by the dynastic Chinese living in southern Hebei for their hunting neighbors, who represented important sources for fur and leather. Maps published by Rawson indicate two possible routes through which steppe-cultural elements were introduced into northern dynastic China, one via the Hexi corridor and the other via the northern Fur Route (Rawson 2015a, 92, fig. 21). Her suggested route along the Yellow River would have entailed crossing the Ordos and the Gobi deserts, which would have been treacherous but feasible (Rawson 2015a, 94, fig. 23).[39]

Carnelian Beads[40]

Identifying exotica in dynastic-Chinese tombs and pinpointing their origins is often challenging, as can be seen from recent speculations concerning carnelian beads. According to Rawson, brilliant red carnelian beads, "whose origin was almost certainly Western Asia" (Rawson 2010, 3, 9), were often strung with jade beads to form pendants and necklaces to adorn the dead in Zhou tombs, including Rui tomb M27. As there are no sources of carnelian in the Chinese heartland, Rawson deduced that the unusual presence of this stone represented evidence of distant West Asian contacts with dynastic China (Rawson 2010, 4), although we

---

38   Tsunoda 1954, pl. 12; Bunker et al. 1997, 196–97, figs. 130.1.3; Bunker et al. 2002, 89–90.
39   Cast-bronze scabbard ornaments excavated from the tenth-century BCE Yu tombs at Baoji, Shaanxi, are often referred to as precursors to the Rui gold scabbard. However, the Yu examples are not actual scabbards, but rather appliqués used to decorate a basic scabbard form made of lacquered wood. So and Bunker 1995, 124; Rawson 2013, 23; Rawson 2015b, 32, fig. 6.
40   Many thanks to Deborah Noel Adams and Huang Tsuimei for their advice in researching carnelian.

may not have to go quite so far to find sources for these semiprecious materials. In a more recent article, Rawson points out that "the case for a western source for carnelian beads is less cut and dried" because examples have been found in the Hexi Corridor from sites of the Siba culture of the early second millennium BCE (Rawson 2013, 64; 51, fig. 36). The popularity of faience, carnelian, and agate beads for colorful display among the Zhou seems to have been introduced from their Inner Asian neighbors (Rawson 2013, 67). This is not surprising, since the latter traditionally expressed their personal identity through their dress and personal adornment, whereas the ancient dynastic Chinese represented themselves by means of jades and ritual bronzes.

Carnelian and agate are found in the Xinjiang Autonomous Region (Mo Jiangping et al. 1997, 7–12), which is considerably closer to ancient dynastic China than well-known sources such as Rajpipa and Ratanpur in Gujarat, India (Pearl 1967), or the Khur agate field in central Iran (Nazari 2005). Significant deposits of nephrite jade, as well as turquoise, also occur in Xinjiang (Tang Yanling 2005). It is not possible to match the many chalcedonies used in the ancient world with specific geological sources. However, as the nephrite beads in Zhou tombs could not have been imported from the West, it is possible that all of these minerals originated from the western borders of what is now China. Comparison of the drilling techniques used on these carnelian and nephrite beads might reveal whether they were produced in the same workshops, but a sufficient technical examination has yet to be conducted.[41]

Other Exotic Artifacts

Other exotic artifacts have been discovered among the grave goods of several small Eastern Zhou polities, providing evidence of down-the-line socioeconomic exchange networks located on an arc embracing the Central Plains. For example, the remains of leather riding pants created somewhere in ancient Xinjiang

---

41 Confounding the research on carnelian is the use of conflicting terminology. In the Chinese version of Rawson's book, *Ancestors and Eternity—Essays on Chinese Archaeology and Art*, carnelian is translated as *hong manao zhu* (red agate) (Rawson 2011). In English, the terms carnelian and agate are used to describe two types of chalcedony, itself a variety of microcrystalline or cryptocrystalline quartz (SiO_2). Gem-quality carnelian is translucent and bright reddish orange in color, colored by the presence of hydrous iron oxide. In contrast, agates are banded chalcedonies, appearing in a wide range of colors. As early as the third millennium BCE in India, agates and carnelians of poorer color were heat-treated to concentrate the iron oxides, thereby enhancing their color. So-called "exotica" are not always so exotic after all.

territory have been found in the eighth- to seventh-century BCE Guo state cemetery (Beck et al. 2014), along with a bronze mirror with raised-thread relief, cast somewhere beyond dynastic China's northern borders. One mirror example shows unexpected evidence of contact with distant Eurasian cultures, probably via Central Asia and the Gansu Corridor (O'Donoghue 1990). The extremely complicated cultural relationships not only among the peoples in Central Asia, but also between them and their better-documented neighbors to the south, east, and west, has resulted in scholars of ancient dynastic China suggesting Eurasia as the source of anything exotic in the culture they are researching. A clear understanding of the transmission routes and the way in which certain cultural characteristics were introduced into northwestern dynastic China has not yet been established, although a map recently published by Rawson suggests the similarity of dagger shapes across the Eurasian Steppe (Rawson 2017, 381, fig. 4).

New Artifact Types and Iconography in the Northwest Border Region during the First Millennium BCE[42]

There were certain pivotal periods in Inner Asia when significant changes in the character of local grave goods, iconography, and burial practices can be observed. It is imperative that we re-evaluate what we have said in the past about the artifacts found among pastoral Ordos grave goods in view of the similar artifacts made of precious metals, bronze, and carved wood that have recently been excavated from graves in Kazakhstan, Afghanistan, Mongolia, Russia, Siberia, and the Black Sea region. These similarities are not always mentioned in archaeological literature devoted to Inner Asian material.

Eurasian steppe artifacts of the first millennium BCE and the iconographic motifs that distinguish them were produced and used by regional pastoral groups with similar economies. Inner Asian artifacts from the first millennium BCE is distinguished by specific imagery derived from an ancient globalized heritage that appears to have been adapted by each of the various pastoral groups, in order to reflect their specific, regional ecosystem and belief system. Artifact types that became prominent in the northwestern Chinese frontier regions may have been

---

42 Although the archaeological sites discussed here will be referenced by their modern geographical names, it should be remembered that such political divisions did not exist in antiquity, when grazing lands extended uninterrupted for hundreds of kilometers, from the Ordos region south through Shaanxi into Ningxia, northwestern Gansu, and beyond (see Rawson and Bunker 1990, 289).

inspired by contact with Central Asian traditions. Achaemenid campaigns had displaced numerous herding peoples. In 530 BCE, the great Achaemenid Persian ruler, Cyrus, was killed fighting the horse-riding Massagetae, who were based east of the Caspian Sea, according to the Greek historian Herodotus (So and Bunker 1995, 54; Aruz et al. 2000, 44). In 517 BCE, Darius I, another Achaemenid ruler, fought with horse-riding groups from the Eurasian Steppe, such as the Saka, and chose to depict them on the walls of Persepolis, his great architectural monument near present-day Shiraz. Sculpted animal-combat motifs between a lion and a bull displayed on the walls of Persepolis have seasonal connotations (Stark and Rubinson 2012, 125, fig. 718) and may be precursors of the animal predation and combat scenes that enrich many metal artifacts from the Eurasian steppes.

By the fifth to fourth century BCE, the grave goods associated with the herding and hunting peoples in northwestern dynastic China, especially in the regions of Ordos, Ningxia, and northeastern Gansu, began to display zoomorphic predation scenes (entries 68 and 69), often with exotic-looking, raptor-head-shaped terminates on the tips of the predators' tails and crestlike manes, such as those found in the present collection (entries 73, 74, 75, 76).

Yanglang culture burials in present-day Ningxia have revealed tomb (catacomb) and artifact types, as well as an iconography, not previously found in the region. Such displays suggest more contact with the Eurasian steppe peoples via the Hexi Corridor and Gansu (Bunker 1992b, 100, fig. 1; 105, fig. 13; Luo Feng and Han Kongle 1990, 413, fig. 12.2–3). Belt plaques depicting animal-predation motifs (entries 68, 69, 73, 74, 75, 76) and bridle fittings featuring pendant volutes with raptor-headed terminates (entries 77 and 78) are similar to artifacts excavated at the Zhangjiecun cemetery in Pengyang county, Ningxia, grave 2.[43] Some examples are tinned (entry 77), a bronze-surface enrichment used to indicate a higher status than a plain bronze artifact (entry 78). Some of these artifacts display raised curls, striations, and pseudo-granulation, surface markings distinctive of Qin artifacts excavated from sites located in Shaanxi province (entries 68, 77, 79), visually revealing a symbiotic artistic relationship that must have developed between the Qin and their pastoral frontier neighbors (Bunker 1991b; Liu Yang 2013).

---

43   Ningxia 2002, 21, fig. 11; Liu Dezhen and Xu Junchen 1988, 420, fig. 7-3; Kost 2014, pl. 133A.B.

One immediate source for the designs of some of those artifacts can be traced back to examples of carved wood recovered from ancient kurgans in the Altai. Examples from Tuekta barrow 1, dated approximately to the late sixth or fifth century BCE (Piotrovskij 1978, 69, no. 79), display designs similar to the examples in the present collection. A tinned-bronze plaque (entry 72) cast in the shape of a recumbent horse is also very similar in concept to a carved-bone example excavated from Sagly-Bazhy II in Western Tuva (Piotrovskij 1978, 78–79, no. 101), which displays surface markings related to those on Qin artifacts (Liu Yang 2013). From studying the artifacts associated with the local pastoral peoples adjacent to the Qin world, it would appear that the surface decoration of their artifacts consisting of striated marks and raised curls are related to designs stamped on Altaic leather and carved in wood. These were combined with Qin-style granulation in the production of metal artifacts for pastoral consumption. However, "it is hard to determine who influenced whom … the similarity between the two forms is suggestive of an affinity, thus supporting a case for the presence of active exchange between the workshop of the Qin and steppe tribes" (Liu Yang 2013, 121). The entries for the various belt plaques in the present collection associated with Ningxia and Gansu will supply additional information about the extraordinary iconography, which displays raptor-head-shaped terminates on the tips of the predators' tails and crestlike manes.[44] The discovery of a Qin metalworker's tomb at Beikang, Xi'an, Shaanxi province, well within Qin territory, along with clay models for making mother molds and a few foundry tools make it clear that the Qin were casting metal ornaments and equipment for their herding neighbors (Liu Yang 2013, 123, fig. 10–11). The excavators date the tomb to the late fourth century BCE, but a few of the clay models exhibit designs representing zoomorphic scenes related to Inner Asian motifs that may not date to before the early third century BCE, such as the ungulate with raptor-headed appendages and its body twisted 180 degrees (Linduff 2009, 91, fig. 3, lower right). The latest casting model in the tomb dates to the third to second century BCE, suggesting that the deceased may have belonged to a metalworking family, and thus owned older, as well as more recent models and equipment.

The interconnections between the Qin and their pastoral neighbors begin to explain the amazing cultural hybridity found among the rich grave goods

---

44 For example entry 73 and entry 76. See also Bunker 1992b, 101–2, figs. 3–6.

discovered in the Majiayuan cemetery in Gansu.[45] Lindruff and Wu 2005 discussed these types of culturally mixed polities. Bodies adorned with cast-gold pectorals and hammered-gold belt plaques suggest that some members of the elite were probably of mixed dynastic-Chinese and Eurasian Steppe ancestry (So 2014; Xirong Yizhen 2014, 41; 49; 59).

Changes in Artifact Types, Technology, and Visual Symbolism in the Fourth to Third Century BCE

Significant changes also began to appear in graves of the late fourth to third century BCE in the greater Ordos region, possibly connected with the unrest brought about by the Eurasian campaigns of Alexander the Great of Macedonia (356–323 BCE). In addition to new technology, new imagery, and impressive iconographic exotica—such as gold headdresses and plaques distinguished with even more flamboyant antler tines ending in raptor heads— appeared among the grave goods in elite burial sites in the greater Ordos Desert region, such as at Aluchaideng, Nalin'gaotu, and Xigoupan.

In this period, wheeled burial vehicles were of much less importance in the region than they had been in the past, and the few yoke ornaments among the grave goods are of inferior quality (entry 83). The graves also contain a new type of bridle ornament (entry 84), which is not associated with the driving harness used earlier (Bunker et al. 1997, 236, nos. 187, 189).

Raptor-headed appendages are now more numerous and complex. The flamboyant gold-horned ungulate surmounting the remains of a headdress found at Nalin'gaotu, Shenmu county, northern Shaanxi province, has been considered part of a headdress belonging to a member of the elite (fig. 16). The body of the Nalin'gaotu gold ungulate is formed of two hollow, hammered pieces bisected longitudinally, while the surface is covered with cloud designs in repoussé (Michaelson 1999, 26). The horns were created separately and attached mechanically. The numerous repoussé gold plaques, especially those from Xigoupan, Jungar banner, western Inner Mongolia (Tian and Guo 1986, 356), were also formed by hammering and may possibly have been made by the pastoral peoples themselves. One of the plaques in the present collection, made from a thin gold sheet hammered over a raised model, depicts a prominent raptor head in repoussé

---

45 See Wu Xiaolong 2013 for an extensive discussion of this site.

Fig. 16: Headdress ornament excavated at Nalin'gaotu, Shenmu county, northern Shaanxi; third century BCE. Shaanxi History Museum.

at each of its four corners (entry 80), an example that uses a typical Eurasian hammered technique rather than the piece-mold cast characteristic of dynastic China.

One plaque from Xigoupan depicts a stag with a crest terminating in a raptor head, an iconographic detail that also marks the stag images depicted on gold belt plaques from a Saka site at Issyk near Almaty, eastern Kazakhstan (Bunker 1992b, 107, figs. 17.3 and 18; Aruz et al. 2000, 7, figs. 4–5). This symbolism is discussed below in more detail.

Bronze plaques depicting camels with riders from fourth- to third-century BCE burials in Pengyang county, Guyuan, in southern Ningxia (Yang Ningguo and Qi Yuezhang 1999, 29, fig. 1.1; pl. 6.5), support the suggestion that, during this period, contact between the Eurasian steppe world and northwestern dynastic China came from Xinjiang and Central Asia via the Gansu Corridor (entries 89 and 90). Camels were far more suitable than horses for travel with heavy loads, as this region is not ecologically uniform, containing not only vast areas for grazing and agriculturally sustainable land, but also arid, sandy deserts, as in Xinjiang, where more navigable routes to the Tuva and Altai regions branched off.

The camels depicted on plaques were of the Bactrian type, characterized by two humps between which the rider sits. A large number of camel images published by Korolkova—several of which are similar to examples in the present collection (e.g., entry 90; Chapter 4, entry 119)—demonstrates their widespread popularity (Korolkova 2006). From this time onward, the camel became a significant component of the artistic vocabulary of dynastic China's frontier.

In this period, tinned bronze seems to no longer have been popular as a major status marker. Instead, status was primarily indicated by precious metals and gilding. Gold and silver ornaments were either hammered or cast, frequently using the "lost-wax and lost-textile" method, in which a wax model was supported by a piece of textile, so that the finished gold plaque displayed a positive image of a woven textile pattern on the reverse side that was integral to the metal surface. This unusual technique was developed to produce luxury belt plaques of precious metals. It reduced the amount of ore used, reflecting contemporary Chinese practices in the production of luxury goods for their herding neighbors (Bunker 1988; Bunker 1994a). Among the most important examples cast by this technique are some of the gold belt plaques in the State Hermitage in St. Petersburg (Bunker 1992a, 201–22; Aruz et al. 2000, 277–79), and plaques associated with examples found at Yanxiadu in Yi county, the southern capital of Yan from 311 until its conquest by Qin in 222 BCE (Bunker 1993, 45–46). The details of the "lost-wax and lost-textile" casting method are often misidentified in scholarly publications. The visible pattern is not an impression, but rather a positive image reproducing the fabric that backed the wax model used in this specific casting method (Bunker 1994a, 41–42).[46]

In the past, any artistic innovations discovered in the Ordos region were traditionally associated with the Xiongnu in Chinese scholarly literature, an attribution that today appears historically incorrect (Bunker 1992b, 111–12). According

---

46 Unfortunately, the publication of the recent exhibition by the British Museum, *Scythians, Warriors of Ancient Siberia*, depicts several gold belt plaques in the Peter the Great Treasure, but describes the fabric pattern on the backs as an impression (Simpson and Pankova 2017, nos. 17, 18, 23, 240). In an article by Linduff and Rubinson, it is stated that some of the steppe-style objects were cast using the lost-wax and lost-textile process and "have the cast imprint of a textile on their reverse" (Linduff and Rubinson 2014, 111; 113). This is incorrect, unless the object being described is actually a fake plaque on the contemporary art market, whose production method the faker misunderstood. For a discussion of current fakes of this kind, see Bunker 1994b, 90. The lost-wax and lost-textile process was also incorrectly described as involving the imprint of a textile on the plaque's reverse side in Aruz et al. 2000, no. 210.

to Sima Qian, the great Western Han historian, the Xiongnu were initially subordinated to the Yuezhi (Rouzhi), Indo-European-speaking pastoralists who controlled parts of southwestern Inner Mongolia, Xinjiang, and Kazakhstan during the fourth to third century BCE. Then, in the second century BCE, the Yuezhi were defeated by the Xiongnu,[47] and a portion of the Yuezhi population (may be just the elite) were subsequently expelled from the region around 162 BCE, while others may have been absorbed into the Xiongnu confederation. The dating of this famous power exchange and final expulsion of the Yuezhi may suggest that the grave goods distinguished by raptor-headed appendages found in the Ordos region are associated with the Yuezhi, a suggestion that is further corroborated by the fact that plaques with this distinctive iconography disappeared during the later second century BCE, after the Yuezhi fled west.

Symbolism with Raptor-Headed Appendages and Its Cultural References

Zoomorphic symbols with raptor-headed appendages begin to appear in Ningxia and Gansu burials by the late fourth century BCE, and slightly later in the Ordos region, suggesting that this iconography entered dynastic China's northwestern Inner Eurasian frontier world via the Gansu Corridor from somewhere in Central Asia (Bunker et al. 2002, 25–28). Contact with Siberia and the Altai through Inner Mongolia was random and may have already been considered less practical by the second millennium BCE (Linduff 2015). This iconography occurs slightly earlier among the tattoos that distinguish the bodies of the elite preserved by permafrost in the Altaic kurgans. Examples include the Mongolian man in kurgan 2 in Pazyryk, radiocarbon dated to the late fourth century BCE, the man in tomb 3 at Verkh-Kaldzhin 2, and the woman in the kurgan at Ak-Alakha 3 on the high plateau of the Altai Mountains (see Polos'mak 1994). It is interesting to note that garments of the Pazyryk culture are similar to examples recovered from the later burials in Shanpula, Khotan (Xinjiang). These include the borders on long gathered skirts, which date approximately from the second century BCE to the second century CE. Surprisingly, some of the stags on the Shanpula textiles are shown with raptor-headed appendages (Shanpula 2001, 216, fig. 411; Bunker 2001, 17–18, figs. 13–15; Schorta 2001, 79, fig. 80).

---

47 Bunker 1992b, 111–12; Aruz et al. 2000, XIII; Golden 2011, 27–29.

This extraordinary symbolic system is characterized by the transformation of the antlers, horns, manes, crests, and tails of wild animals into a multiplicity of raptor-headed appendages. Without indigenous texts written by the pastoral peoples themselves, the significance and heritage of this iconography has long been challenging for scholars to explain. One of the first to research the various Eurasian variations of this iconography was Esther Jacobson, who suggests a distant origin among the myths of the archaic Evenk of Siberia, an ancient tradition that slowly changed over time to accommodate the needs of herding groups inhabiting different regional Eurasian environments (Jacobson 1984, 113–80; Jacobson 2006a, 63–70). By contrast, John Boardman's study of belt-plaque designs discusses only Chinese and Greek elements. His observations concerning the variations in belt-plaque design may ultimately help place the plaques chronologically, but offer little information about their sacred significance in their owners' lives and beliefs (Boardman 2010). Lin Yun refers to images with raptor-headed appendages as "horned spirit beasts," without further comment (Pan Ling 2015, 96–97). Since the creatures represented probably reflect the local fauna and help us understand where an artifact might have been made and for whom, it is important to identify the basic species correctly.[48]

The earliest-known representation of this symbolic system was previously thought to be a gold plaque from the seventh- to sixth-century BCE Saka grave at Chilikty (Shilikty) in eastern Kazakhstan (Bunker 1992b, 102, fig. 6), and the latest example was thought to be a first-century CE iron-backed gold belt buckle excavated at Zaporozh'e near the Dniepr River in Russia (Bunker 1992b, 103, fig. 7).

In light of recent discoveries of additional Eurasian material, it is now clear that this iconographic system had a much wider distribution and began much earlier throughout the ancient Eurasian steppe world. In other words, the pastoral world was far more interconnected than previously thought. For example, the mounted hunter with drawn bow on a gold mount for a fourth-century BCE bowl from Filippovka (Windfuhr 2006, 53, fig. 7a) is almost identical in design

---

48   For example, Francfort identifies the crouching carnivores from Aluchaideng, Hanggin banner, southwest Inner Mongolia, as antlered tigers, when in fact they are wolves, zoologically identifiable by their lupine-shaped snouts and long, curvy ears (Francfort 2012, 97, fig. 17). The carnivores on a plaque similar to an example in the present collection (Chapter 4, entry 104) are described by Davis-Kimball as two bears, when in fact one is a wolf and the other is a bear (Davis-Kimball 2006, 96, fig. 6).

to the mounted hunter with drawn bow on a tapestry skirt band from Shanpula in Xinjiang (Bunker 2001a, 20, fig. 8), demonstrating the long-distance interconnected relationships that existed at the time. Shanpula yielded tapestry bands that also represent deer with raptor-headed appendages (Bunker 2001a, 25, fig. 15). The graceful linear renditions of the various creatures with raptor-headed appendages in Altaic tattoos suggest a much-earlier, long-forgotten source. It is interesting to note that no raptor heads occur among the zoomorphic images from Arzhan 1 and 2 in Tuva, which suggests that the system probably did not emerge in Siberia. Years ago, Jettmar suggested that the Central Asian herding groups may have painted their bodies with graceful strokes that, over time, led to more permanent tattoos (Jettmar 1994, passim).

A survey of the many Eurasian Steppe artifacts associated with the pastoral peoples with an ancient Iranian cultural heritage reveals certain similarities in subject matter and style that cannot be coincidental. The subject matter encompasses the same cast of zoomorphic characters with specific regional variations: carnivores, ungulates, boars, hedgehogs, and raptors, sometimes replaced with griffins by the Greeks in western Eurasia. Such zoomorphic motifs are sometimes shown naturally and are at other times conflated, resulting in composite monsters such as the deer with a carnivore's mouth and antlers terminating in raptor heads from Filippovka (Windfuhr 2006, 50, fig. 2; 56; 61).

The various Eurasian zoomorphic images probably had totemistic protective functions, and may have also reflected a mystical bond between the hunter and the hunted. Hunting peoples "consider animals as givers of life … so their spirits are the objects of belief" and veneration (Turner 1941, 107). Windfuhr's brilliant and complex account of Eurasian Steppe iconography suggests the existence of a widespread globalized Iranian culture "in which aspects of solar and seasonal connotations dependent on constellations and zodiac symbolism have been splendidly integrated" (Windfuhr 2006, 78).

A multiplicity of heads is an archaic way of suggesting omnipotence and occurs in the symbolic systems of numerous peoples of Indo-European heritage, including the Saka of Central Eurasia and the Scythians of northwestern Eurasia. A study of the spectacular gold-covered wooden stags from kurgans near the village of Filippovka in the southern Urals has recently thrown new light on the development of the iconography of the first millennium BCE, enhanced by raptor-headed appendages, and provided suggestion about what it all might mean (Windfuhr

2006, passim). Windfuhr's literary observations, combined with Jacobson's interpretation of the visual material, suggest the need to reconceptualize Eurasia as an interlinked historical and geographic configuration connecting western Asia to eastern Asia via Inner Asia over the course of millennia, albeit only intermittently.

The conceptual missing link in all these recent studies is an understanding of the roles of mobile pastoralists. The globalization of their belief system was fueled by groups, including the Saka and Scythians, who inhabited the greater Inner Eurasian steppe world during the second and first millennia BCE. Pastoral peoples on the move developed belief systems that enabled them to structure their lives and to be economically productive. The pastoralists depended on the natural world they lived in, and interpreted it in zoomorphic terms in order to explain and guide their mobile lives.

The traditional ways of life in Inner Asia, which had depended for millennia on trade, barter, and animal-oriented economies, were shattered forever by the impact of Communism (Turner 1941). Any serious anthropological research today should be based on the work of past scholars, in an attempt to reconstruct first-hand experiences for regions where the original economies have not been practiced for some 75 years, according to observations and photographs made by Wulsin on his expedition to Chinese Inner Asia in 1923 (Fletcher and Alonso 1979, 59; 65; 84–85).

68 | Belt Plaque

This bronze belt plaque is cast in the shape of a standing tiger attacking a fallen ram, shown with folded legs. The tiger is represented in profile, with all four legs shown and four large claws on each paw. The tiger holds the ram's muzzle firmly between its open jaws, while pressing down on the ram's body with its right forepaw. The tiger's ear is described by a raised spiral that begins at the outside base, while the eye is indicated by an intaglio circle.

The plaque is a perfect blend of Qin and steppe traditions. A striding carnivore attacking a doomed herbivore is a well-known power theme from the Eurasian Steppe that originated in the art of southwestern Asia and was later transmitted eastward by the pastoral peoples. Similar tigers are carved on the wooden coffin from Bashadar in the Altai Mountains of southern Siberia (Jettmar 1967, fig. 98; Menghin et al. 2007, 122, fig. 4a–b) and shown on a silver plaque excavated at Shihuigou, Yijinhuoluo banner, in western Inner Mongolia Autonomous Region (Yikezhaomeng 1992, 92, figs. 1–5). The placement of the ram's muzzle within the tiger's jaws is a typical motif, which is also found on a wood carving from Pazyryk barrow 4 (So and Bunker 1995, 134, fig. 52.2).

The plaque was originally the left-hand plaque of a mirror-image pair that formed a single complete belt buckle, just like the pair discovered in Guyuan county, southern Ningxia Hui Autonomous Region dated to around the late fourth century BCE (Luo Feng and Han Kongle 1990,

Northwest China, Guyuan, Ningxia
4th century BCE

Height 3.9 cm
Width 8 cm
Weight 46.2 g

Tinned cast bronze, alloy composition by J. Stenger:
Cu 77%; Sn 5%; Pb 10%; As trace

Ex Therese and Erwin Harris Collection, Miami, Florida

Published:
Rawson and Bunker 1990, 324, no. 206; So and Bunker 1995, 133–34, no. 52

Fig. 17: Plaque similar to entry 68. E'erduosi, Ordos Museum.

413, fig. 12.2.3; Bunker 1992b, 101, fig. 3). Similar plaques come from Ningxia and the Qingyang area of Gansu province (Kost 2014, pl. 66.1; 65.3).

The reverse of the present plaque displays a round button that projects from the surface behind the tiger's haunch; the loop that once extended from the tiger's head had a hook projecting from the front that has since broken off, resulting in the loss of an essential part of the fastening system. An example in the Ordos Museum that still retains its hook section demonstrates how the plaque once looked. The image in E'erduosi Qingtongqi (2006, 175) indicates that the reconstruction drawing in So and Bunker (1995, 133, fig. 52.1) is not entirely accurate. The example from the Ordos Museum also has the remains of another carnivore on the hook area (fig. 17).

The front surface of the plaque has been enhanced by being wiped with molten tin in order to produce a shiny, silvery surface, now partially rubbed off by the wear of time. The presence of metal flashes around the openings in the design and mold join marks at the edges suggest that the piece was cast from a wax model formed in a mold (So and Bunker 1995, 133–34).

69 | Personal Ornament

Northwest China and eastern Inner Asia
5th–4th century BCE

Height 4.5 cm
Width 9.1 cm
Weight 45.9 cm

Tinned cast bronze, alloy composition by J. Stenger: Cu 71%; Sn 9%; Pb 4%; As trace

This handsome plaque is cast in the shape of a wolf-like carnivore attacking a fallen stag, all shown in profile. The carnivore has an almond-shaped eye, and an ear formed by a spiral-like volute that begins at the inner base of the ear. The surface of the plaque has a dull, silvery color, the result of intentional surface tinning. The plaque was cast by the lost-wax method from a wax model formed in a mold, according to the technical examination conducted by Pieter Meyers in June 2013. The openings in the design were pushed through the wax model from the front. Two small vertical loops appear on the reverse behind the head and rump respectively.

No identical examples of this plaque have been excavated, the best-known analogue is the silver example found at Shihuigou, Yijinhuoluo banner, in the Ordos region (Zhongguo 1993, no. 104; Kost 2014, pl. 80.1). Other similar pieces have been discovered in Ningxia, in northwestern China (Kost 2014, pls. 60.3; 71.2). A careful examination of the present plaque reveals rounded teeth and sharp fangs, and paws with four prominent claws, all characteristics that derive from a wood-carving tradition, such as the predation scenes on the Bashadar coffin from the Altai region of southern Siberia (Jettmar 1967, 135, fig. 98; Menghin et al. 2007, 122, fig. 4a–b).

70 | Belt Plaque

Northwest China, Ningxia region
ca. 5th–4th century BCE

Height 4.3 cm
Width 9.1 cm
Weight 56.1 g

Cast tinned bronze, alloy composition by J. Stenger: Cu 68%; Sn 7%; Pb 5%; As high

This belt plaque represents a standing wolf-like predator with an elongated ear formed by a raised spiral line beginning at the inner base, and a long muzzle with slightly open jaws revealing fangs and teeth. All four of the predator's legs are shown, with paws that each contain four prominent claws. The reverse displays a vertical loop behind the haunch. A hook projecting from the proper right front edge of the plaque and a vertical loop behind the haunch on the reverse serve as attachment devices. The surface was intentionally tinned after the plaque was cast.

Originally, the plaque was one half of a pair of mirror-image plaques that together constituted a complete buckle. A plaque depicting a similar wolf-like predator was excavated from tomb 2 at Zhangjiecun, Pengyang county in Ningxia (Ningxia 2002; Kost 2014, pl. 133B). We must remember that the territory from the Ordos south to Ningxia and beyond was all open grassland in antiquity, and culturally associated with the Inner Eurasian steppe world.

71 | Openwork Garment Plaque

Northwest China, Ningxia region
4th–3rd century BCE

Height 5.5 cm
Width 10.6 cm
Weight 63.1 g

Cast bronze with traces of tinning on the front, alloy composition by J. Stenger: Cu 73%; Sn 9%; Pb 5%

Ex Dr. and Mrs. Fritz W. Bilfinger Collection, Zurich and Sherborn, Massachusetts; Michael Ward, Inc., New York, 1990; Therese and Erwin Harris Collection, Miami, Florida; Christie's New York, 16 March 2017, lot 840

Published: Harris Collection 2017, 46, no. 840

This plaque depicts two recumbent wolves with their heads turned back that share a single convex body, with one inverted over the other to form a rectangular shape. The reverse has a small vertical loop behind the shoulder of each wolf. Mold marks are visible around each loop, suggesting that the loops were integrally cast in a multipiece mold. Each wolf is portrayed with elongated jaws and a small, pointed spiral ear.

The present plaque is a superb example of a little-known group of plaques that depict inverted carnivore designs that appear to have developed from an earlier complex design into this more simplified, stylized example in the Guyuan region of Ningxia (Kost 2014, pl. 35.1–5). A less well-cast example was excavated at Hechuan, Guyuan, Ningxia (Cao Wei 2012, 58). Another smaller example can be found in the Ordos Museum (E'erduosi Qingtongqi 2006, 231). Two more plaques with this design were included in the C. T. Loo Collection (Salmony 1933, pl. 14.3–4). The elongated jaws of the wolves' heads and their small spiral ears seen on the present plaque may derive from carved wooden examples, such as those excavated from kurgan 6 at Ulandryk 1 in southern Siberia (Kubarev 1987, 7, pl. 14.10), evidence for a far greater degree of connectivity between the pastoral peoples in northwestern China and the Altai in antiquity than has yet been acknowledged. The presence of tinning may suggest that they were produced by the Qin to exchange for brides, horses, fur, and leather.

72 | Belt Plaque

Northwest China, Ningxia region
5th–4th century BCE

Height 5.7 cm
Width 11.3 cm
Weight 43.1 g

Cast tinned bronze, alloy composition by J. Stenger: Cu 79%; Sn 9%; Pb 3%; As trace

Ex Dr. and Mrs. Fritz W. Bilfinger Collection, Zurich and Sherborn, Massachusetts; Sotheby's New York, 28 November 1994, lot 215; Therese and Erwin Harris Collection, Miami, Florida

Published: Sotheby's 1994, no. 215; So and Bunker 1995, 138–39, no. 57

The tinned-bronze belt plaque is cast in the shape of a recumbent horse with its legs folded in such a way that the soles of the front hooves face upwards and those of the back hooves face downwards. The body of the horse is decorated with indented lines that derive from patterns on stamped leather, carved wood, and carved bone artifacts found in southern Siberia. The surface of the plaque has been deliberately tinned to give it a shiny, silvery appearance. The circular hole piercing the shoulder suggests that the plaque was the proper left plaque of a pair of mirror-image plaques that together formed a single belt buckle. Felt may have been originally placed behind the plaque in order to lend color to the buckle, an effect which was usually achieved by colored inlays. There are no loops or buttons on the plaque's reverse; presumably it was attached by means of the holes in the piece.

The present plaque is very similar to a carved-bone plaque excavated from the tomb of Sagly-Bazhy II in western Tuva, southern Siberia, dated to the fifth to fourth century BCE (Griaznov 1969, 51–52; Piotrovskij 1978, 77, no. 101). The specific species of horse represented on both the present plaque and the Sagly-Bazhy plaque is a Przewalski's horse, a wild Asian horse that inhabited the Eurasian Steppe in antiquity and is named after Col. Nikolai Przhewal'ski, a Russian explorer of Polish descent who first identified it in the Gobi desert in 1879. For a discussion of *Equus przewalskii*, see So and Bunker (1995, 139).

73 | Belt Plaque

Northwest China, Ningxia region
5th–4th century BCE

Height 6.1 cm
Width 10.1 cm
Weight 61.6 g

Cast Bronze with traces of tinning, alloy composition by J. Stenger:
Cu 85%; Sn 5%; Pb 6%; As trace

Ex Calon da Collection

Published: Rawson and Bunker 1990, 326–27, no. 207; Bunker 1992b, 102, fig. 5a; So and Bunker 1995, 131–32, no. 50

This plaque represents a very graphic scene of a standing wolf, depicted in the act of dispatching a fallen doe, which is held fast by the wolf's raised forepaw. The doe's head appears under the wolf's open jaws, which reveal four rounded teeth and two fangs about to sink into the doe's flesh. The doe's hindquarters are twisted 180 degrees, an artistic convention for representing the victim also employed by craftsmen in Bashadar and Pazyryk in the Altai (Rudenko 1970, pl. 139.1, 268–69, fig. 136; Bunker et al. 2002, 122–23, no. 94). A tiny, crouching wolf cub can be seen on the ground line between the wolf's front and hind legs.

The wolf's elongated ear has a distinctive comma shape, and its pelt is marked by a variety of linear patterns that include braided bands, scrolls, dots, and scales; these lend a texture to the pelt that relates both to carved designs found on bone artifacts from the Guyuan region in Ningxia (Luo Feng and Han Kongle 1990, 413, fig. 12.1; So and Bunker 1995, 138, fig. 56.1) and to appliqué work found in the Pazyryk frozen tombs in the Altai (Rudenko 1970, passim). Both the wolf's crest and tail terminate in eared raptor heads, representing the symbolic system exhibited by the tattoos that distinguish some of the bodies buried in Pazyryk tombs (Piotrovskij 1978, 47, no. 31; So and Bunker 1995, 58, figs. 21; 22).

The present plaque was originally the right plaque of a mirror-image pair that constituted a complete belt buckle. The reverse displays a loop behind the head and a projecting button behind the haunch of the present plaque for fastening and attachment purposes. The back of the missing matching plaque would have probably looked like the back of no. 76, and the back of an extremely similar belt plaque in the Thaw Collection in the Metropolitan Museum of Art (Bunker et al. 2002, 122, no. 94).

The wolf is similar to several plaques discovered at various sites on the Qingyang plateau in southeastern Gansu, which are decorated with the same pseudo-granulation and surface designs (Liu Dezhen and Xu Junchen 1988, 420, fig. 17.3, pl. 4.3; 421, fig. 18.5, pl. 4.1). Another plaque cast in this style, held in the Ashmolean Museum at Oxford (Bunker 1990b, 79, fig. 3), is also tinned (Bunker et al. 1997, 244, no. 200).

74 | Belt Plaque

Northwest China
Ningxia region
ca. 4th century BCE

Height 5.6 cm
Width 7.9 cm
Weight 40.3 g

Cast bronze with traces of tinning, alloy composition by J. Stenger: Cu 92%; Sn 3%; Pb 2%

Ex Therese and Erwin Harris Collection, Miami, Florida

Published:
So and Bunker 1995, 133, no. 51; Kost 2014, pl. 61.2

This plaque shows a standing wolf menacing a fallen gazelle, whose body lies underneath the wolf's raised left paw. A tiny carnivore with three small, clawed paws is at risk of being trampled under the large wolf's hind leg, as it attacks another, much-smaller doe. The hindquarters of both cervid victims on the plaque are twisted 180 degrees, an artistic convention adapted to express the victim's impending demise, a device frequently found on artifacts of the Pazyryk culture (Piotrovskij 1978, 59, no. 56). The larger wolf's body is enhanced by linear patterns similar to those on the previous belt plaque (entry 73). The wolf's elongated ear is described by a raised outline that begins with a spiral at the outer edge. The wolf's crest and tail both end in raptor heads, linking the piece to the iconographic system that appears to have developed among the pastoral groups of the Eurasian Steppe with an Indo-European heritage, which spread to the people buried in the frozen tombs of Pazyryk and ultimately to the border pastoralists of northwestern China (Bunker 1992b, 102, fig. 5b).

Wolves did not play an important role in dynastic-Chinese iconography, but they certainly did in the neighboring herding societies, where there was an ever-present danger from predators. These Ningxia tombs have been attributed to the Xirong, which simply means "western warriors" and is a term that is no longer sufficient, as we have no idea what these people called themselves.

This plaque once belonged to a mirror-image pair that formed a single belt buckle. The reverse displays two vertical loops, one behind the wolf's head and one behind the haunch for attachment and closure purposes. The surface has been intentionally tinned, a surface enrichment used to indicate the owner's status and that was superseded by amalgam gilding by the third century BCE.

75 | Belt Plaque

Northwest China, Ningxia region
4th century BCE

Height 4.8 cm
Width 7.8 cm
Weight 37 g

Cast bronze, alloy composition by J. Stenger: Cu 80%; Sn 3%; Pb 1%

Ex Dr. Ping Yiu Tam Collection, Hong Kong; J. J. Lally & Co., New York, 1993; Therese and Erwin Harris Collection, Miami, Florida; Christie's New York, 16 March 2017, lot 833

Published: Harris Collection 2017, 39, no. 833

This belt plaque is almost identical to the belt plaque discussed in the previous entry 74, and is extremely similar to belt plaques excavated from a male tomb M2 in the Zhangjiecun cemetery at Caomiao township in Pengyang county, Ningxia (fig. 18; Kost 2014, pl. 61.1; 133A). Visually the two plaques in this collection appear to be almost identical, but the reverses are different: The vertical loop behind the wolf's head on no. 74 is placed before the open space, while the one on no. 75 is placed behind the vertical open space. Moreover, their alloy compositions are not identical. The two plaques were probably cast in the Qin state for its pastoral clients, but in two small, local foundries rather than in a major state foundry.

Fig. 18: Belt plaque from grave M2 at Zhangjiecun, Pengyang county, Ningxia.

76 | Belt Plaque with Hook

Northwest China, Ningxia region
4th century BCE

Height 4.3 cm
Width 9.1 cm
Weight 37.8 g

Cast bronze with traces of tinning, alloy composition by E. Ferreira:
Cu 89.7%; Sn 5%; Pb 5.3%; As 0.3%; Fe 0.3%

Ex David David-Weill Collection, Paris; Drouot Paris, 28 June 1972, lot 56; Therese and Erwin Harris Collection, Miami, Florida

Published: David-Weill Sale 1972, no. 56; Rawson and Bunker 1990, 328–29, no. 208; So and Bunker 1995, 165–66, no. 90

This belt plaque displays a slightly later version of the three preceding plaques (entries 73, 74, and 75). The wolf's static but aggressive pose is the same, but the victim here is an argali ram, shown with its legs folded underneath its body, in a stereotypical pose that lacks the drama expressed by the contorted poses of the victims on the slightly earlier plaque examples. The animal combat between the wolf's feet on the plaque in entry 74 has been reduced to a series of meaningless scalloped forms, suggesting that the artist did not understand the earlier design details. The surface patterning here has been tightened up into much smaller units than those found on the plaques in entries 74 and 75.

The present plaque was originally one part of a mirror-image pair that together formed a single belt buckle. It would have been the proper left plaque, since it has a loop with hook that is tangent to the wolf's head, as well as a loop on the back of the plaque behind the haunch to complete the fastening process. The tips of the tail and crest appear to terminate in raptor heads, although both are extremely worn. This iconographical identification relates the plaque to the artistic traditions that the pastoral groups acquired from further west, traditions which were driven eastward by Alexander's Central Asian campaigns in the late fourth century BCE.

77 | Harness Decoration

Northwest China,
Ningxia region
4th century BCE

Height 5.2 cm
Width 4 cm
Weight 19.8 g

Tinned cast bronze,
alloy composition
not analyzed

This harness decoration represents a round boss from which depend two volutes with stylized eared-raptor-head terminals. The ornament was intentionally tinned on the front and provided with a vertical loop behind the hollow boss. Mold marks along the edge indicate that it was piece-mold cast integrally with the loops. The surface pebbling indicated by pseudo-granulation on the volute reflects Qin workmanship, suggesting that it may have been made by the Qin specifically for their pastoral neighbors, with zoomorphic symbols used to appeal to Saka steppe taste. Such ornaments were made in sets of multiples that have sometimes been separated for commercial reasons in modern times.

A near-identical decoration is found in the Thaw Collection and may have once belonged to the same set as the present example (Bunker et al. 2002, 48, no. 11). Harness decorations similar to this example have also been excavated in the Guyuan region of southern Ningxia and date to the fifth to fourth century BCE (Tian and Guo 1986, 155, fig. 110i; Luo Feng and Han Kongle 1990, 415, fig. 14.10; Yan Shizong and Li Huairen 1992, 574, fig. 1.7; Kost 2014, pl. 133C–E). The actual shape and design of these ornaments derive from carved wooden examples, such as those recovered from Tuekta, Kurgan 1, in the Altai (Piotrovskij 1978, 69, no. 79).

78 | Harness Ornament

Northwest China,
Ningxia region
ca. 4th century BCE

Height 7.5 cm
Width 4.2 cm
Weight 20.7 g

Cast bronze,
alloy composition
not analyzed

This harness ornament is cast in the shape of a stylized owl's head with a pendant volute below its beak. The owl's bulging eyes are formed by a convex boss within a raised circular rim, emphasizing its typical physical characteristics, including its ruff, as indicated by the openwork scallops around the head. The owl intended may be the long-eared owl, which is widespread throughout Eurasia (Zhao Ji 1990, 87). The pendant volute echoes an earlier coiled bird motif such as that on the harness decoration previously discussed in entry 77.

The reverse of the present plaque displays a vertical loop behind the owl's head. Like the previous piece, the prototype for many of these harness decorations can be traced back to carved wooden examples, such as those found in Tuekta, barrow 1, in the Altai (Piotrovskij 1978, 69, no. 79; Mir kochevnikov 2013, 60–61, no. 177; 179; Bunker et al. 1997, 252, fig. 213) and those from the late fourth- to third-century site of Berel' in Kazakhstan (Stark and Rubinson 2012, 31–49; 168–75).

79 | Two Harness Ornaments

Northwest China, Ningxia region
4th–3rd century BCE

79a | Harness Ornament (left)
Height 5.5 cm
Width 5.4 cm
Weight 32.7 g
Tinned cast bronze, alloy composition by J. Stenger:
Cu 85%; Sn 8%; Pb 5%; As trace

79b | Harness Ornament (right)
Height 5.6 cm
Width 5.5 cm
Weight 37.9 g
Tinned cast bronze, alloy composition by J. Stenger:
Cu 71%; Sn 8%; Pb 12%; As trace

A lynx head with two pendant serpents, each biting a horned argali head, forms the design of these two cast-bronze harness ornaments. Pseudo-granulation marks the serpents' bodies, and intentional tinning lends the pieces a silvery appearance: Both of these metallurgical techniques indicate that these pieces were made by the Chinese for their pastoral neighbors, as these techniques were not practiced by the eastern Eurasian herders. The tinning of harness decorations in antiquity was also used to protect metal surfaces from horse sweat, which corrodes copper alloys. A wooden harness ornament excavated from Berel', kurgan 2, displays a carnivore mask with pendant raptor heads, a design that suggests a prototype for the designs of the present metal artifacts and a tentative fourth-century BCE date (Stark 2012, 125, fig. 7.19).

Harness ornaments were created in large sets that have been separated in modern times for commercial reasons by people who did not understand their original function. The reverse of each ornament displays a strong vertical loop that was soldered on behind each of the hollow lynx heads. According to Pieter Meyers, each ornament was cast from a positive wax model formed in a mold with a negative image of the piece. The loop was soldered onto the concave back of each of the cast plaques, behind the lynx head.

80 | Repoussé Gold Plaque

Northwest China,
Gansu region
4th–3rd century BCE

Height 5.9 cm
Width 5.6 cm
Weight 6.3 g

Gold sheet,
alloy composition
by P. Meyers
(May 4, 2013):
Au 90%; Ag 9.5%;
Cu 0.8%; Sn 1.5%

Four stylized raptor heads with circular eyes and tiny oval-shaped ears form the corners of this golden appliqué. Their long necks marked by overlapping scallops connect to a round boss in the middle of the plaque balancing the design. This plaque was manufactured from a thin gold sheet hammered over a mold. There is no evidence of tooling in the design, but the openwork was achieved by chisel-cutting the gold. There are holes punched in the corners to allow attachment to a support made of wood, textile, or leather. An x-ray fluorescence analysis suggests that the gold is probably unrefined natural gold, of which the silver and copper would be natural components.

Sets of identical gold plaques have been excavated from a disturbed tomb in Qingshui, Gansu province (Li Xiaoqing and Nan Baosheng 2003, 12, fig. 16; 16, fig. 252), tentatively dated to the late fourth century BCE. Such sets may have been broken up in modern times and sold as beautiful objects without concern for their cultural context. An example in the Barbier-Mueller Collection with the same four raptor heads was attributed to the Scythians when it was first published (Barbier 1996, 22, fig. 26; 39, no. 12). There are also four examples in a Belgian collection (Miniaev and Smolarski 2002, 56–57). Raptor images with similar elongated beaks carved in wood have been excavated from Ulandryk IV, kurgan 2 (Kubarev 1987, 273, pl. 72.4), suggesting close cultural contact between pastoral peoples in Gansu and those in the Altai in southern Siberia, Russia, due to commercial exchange and intermarriage.

81 | S-shaped Belt Ornament with Raptor-Head Terminals

Northwest China, Ningxia region
ca. 4th–3rd century BCE

Height 3.2 cm
Width 2 cm
Weight 8.1 g

Cast gold, alloy composition by P. Meyers (May 4, 2013): Au 80%; Ag 16%, Cu 0.2%

Two stylized raptor heads distinguish this small belt ornament. An indented line emphasizes the curve of their hooked beaks and raised circular bosses represent their eyes. A vertical attachment loop is placed behind the middle of the plaque.

A double-bird-head ornament identical to the present plaque was collected in the Guyuan region of southern Ningxia (Luo Feng and Han Kongle 1990, 414, fig. 13.8). Similar raptor heads also adorn numerous small plaques collected in the Ordos region, several examples of which are found in the Arthur M. Sackler Collections (Bunker et al. 1997, 220, no. 160).

As in the case of the previous plaque, similar images of raptor heads have also been found among the carved wooden grave goods excavated at Ulandryk, further confirming close cultural relations between the two regions around the late fourth century BCE.

82 | Fitting with Raptor Heads

Northwest China, southern Ningxia
ca. 5th–4th century BCE

Height 6.4 cm
Width 6.1 cm
Weight 30.4 g

Cast bronze with traces of tinning, alloy composition by J. Stenger: Cu 78%; Sn 9%; Pb 6%; As trace

Ex Paul Pelliot Collection, Paris; Therese and Erwin Harris Collection, Miami, Florida

Published: So and Bunker 1995, 130, no. 48

This bronze fitting is distinguished by four powerful raptor heads with circular, bulging eyes, elliptical ears, and long, hooked beaks. Their necks are marked with a series of tiny striated enclosures, while the eyes are indicated by raised bosses and the tiny ears are depicted by raised ovals with a striated interior. The back is flat and contains no loops. The piece appears to have been lost-wax cast from a model made in a mold and was then wiped with molten tin to give it a silvery surface. Recently, overzealous cleaning appears to have caused the loss of some of the tinned surface, with the result that it no longer has the original glowing, silvery appearance that it had when first published (So and Bunker 1995, 130, no. 48).

The piece is stylistically related to a bronze fitting excavated in the Guyuan region in southern Ningxia Hui Autonomous Region (see drawing in So and Bunker 1995, 130, fig. 47.2, based on Yan Shizong and Li Huairen 1992, 574, fig. 1.11). The same powerful raptor head appears on both the present piece and the Guyuan example, as well as on wooden harness gear from Ulandryk, kurgan 4 (Kubarev 1987, 273, pl. 272.4.9).

83 | Two Yoke Ornaments

Northwest China,
Shenmu, Shaanxi,
and Ningxia
late 4th century BCE

83a | Yoke Ornament
(left)
Height 6.4 cm
Width 6.6 cm
Weight 39.4 g
Cast bronze,
alloy composition
by J. Stenger:
Cu 89%; Sn 5%;
Pb 6%; As trace

83b | Yoke Ornament
(right)
Height 6.9 cm
Width 6.4 cm
Weight 36.8 g
Cast bronze,
alloy composition
by J. Stenger:
Cu 86%; Sn 8%;
Pb 7%; As trace

These two recumbent does are hollow cast, allowing them to fit over the rounded yoke of a two-wheeled vehicle primarily intended for burial purposes. Burial vehicles with zoomorphic decoration can be traced back to ancient customs in northwestern Eurasia dating back to the third millennium BCE. Such yoke ornaments were originally cast in sets of four or more, but have been split up by museums and collectors because their original function as enhancement for the yoke of a burial vehicle was misunderstood. Fifteen examples of this type were excavated at Shenmu, northern Shaanxi, archaeologically confirming that such artifacts were cast in sets of multiples in antiquity (Cao Wei 2012, 250.)

Several examples have also been found at Yulongtai, Jungar banner, in the Ordos region, with the remains of a wheeled vehicle that was probably used in funerary rituals to transport the dead (Neimenggu and Neimenggu 1977, pl. 2.1; 3.3). The present deer-shaped yoke ornaments are cast with open muzzles; such images have been misinterpreted as dogs by some archaeologists in the past (Ningxia and Ningxia 1993, 42, fig. 24.1–10). However, dogs do not fold their front legs under their bodies, whereas deer do, indicating the importance of zoological knowledge for scholars working on zoomorphic images from the Eurasian Steppe.

Yoke ornaments are peculiar to burials west of the Taihang Mountains, and appear to have been discontinued by the end of the third century BCE. With the increasing practice of mounted warfare, status became more closely associated with riding horses than driving them, a fact that also explains the poor quality of the present yoke ornaments in comparison to some earlier examples, such as entry 52 (Chapter 3b), which date from a time when wheeled vehicles were still important.

These two pieces are distinguished by complex mold marks. A longitudinal line runs up the muzzle and along both ears, to join at the back of the head in a single line that runs down the back and over the tail, bisecting the body. This indicates that the pieces were each cast in a multipiece section mold. A mold line also runs under the muzzle and down the neck to the chest, with the casting core remaining in the heads and necks.

The muzzle of each piece is a circular opening into the hollow head, a specific characteristic of doe-shaped yoke ornaments that have been excavated in Ningxia (Ningxia and Ningxia 1993, 42, fig. 24.1–10; Ningxia 1995, 94, fig. 15.6–7) and southeastern Gansu (Liu Dezhen and Xu Junchen 1988, 414, fig. 2.9); they are not characteristic of yoke ornaments found at Yulongtai in the greater Ordos region.

84 | Bridle Ornament

Northwest China
3rd century BCE

Height 5.7 cm
Width 3.3 cm
Weight 33.3 g

Cast gilded bronze, alloy composition by J. Stenger:
Cu 93%; Sn 3%;
Pb 1%; As trace

Ex Anthony J. Hardy Collection, Hong Kong; Therese and Erwin Harris Collection, Miami, Florida

Published:
Rawson and Bunker 1990, 334, no. 214;
So and Bunker 1995, 57, col. pl. 11; 136–37, no. 55;
Bunker et al. 1997, 236, no. 189

Two crouching wolves in profile, flanking a frontal ram head, distinguish this gilded bronze ornament intended for a bridle. Each wolf has an upturned snout, a long, attenuated comma-shaped ear, and four front claws with a dewclaw on the hind paw. A sturdy vertical loop for attachment is placed behind the hollow ram head. This ornament appears to have been cast using the lost-wax process and then heavily gilded on the front.

The basic shape of this bridle ornament derives from southern Siberian types seen among the wooden grave goods from Pazyryk in the Altai (Rudenko 1970, pl. 112G.H). Such bridle ornaments became popular among the herding peoples in the northwest after the introduction of riding astride and mounted warfare in the fourth century BCE. Silver examples with Chinese characters inscribed on them have been found at Xigoupan, Jungar banner, in western Inner Mongolia (Bunker 1992b, 105, fig. 11), and a similar gold ornament that features a non-Chinese human face has been excavated from tomb 30 at Xinzhuangtou, Yi county, Hebei province, the southern capital of the state of Yan (fig. 19). The human face has a prominent moustache and probably represents the steppe owner. A similar face with a mustache is also represented on small gilded plaques excavated from tomb 6 at Majiayuan in Gansu province (Wu Xiaolong 2013, 125, fig. 3a). This type of bridle ornament appears to have been made by Chinese craftsmen for steppe consumption, and to have fallen out of favor in the late third century BCE; it does not appear in burials attributed to the Xiongnu.

Fig. 19: Gold ornament from tomb 30 at Xinzhuangtou, Hebei; third century BCE.

85 | Owl-like Ornament

Northwest China
4th–3rd century BCE

Height 2.7 cm
Width 4.4 cm
Weight 25.8 g

Cast bronze, alloy composition by J. Stenger: Cu 97%; Sn 5%; Pb 2%; As trace; Ni high

Ex C. T. Loo Collection, Paris; Therese and Erwin Harris Collection, Miami, Florida

Published: Salmony 1933, pl. 11.22; So and Bunker 1995, 120, no. 36

This ornament presents a frontal view of an owl-like bird with a short hooked beak and large ears marked by an elongated spiral that begins at the lower inside of each ear. A vertical loop in the center of the back provides a means of attachment.

The image of a bird has been transformed into a fabulous mythological creature, about whose ancestry we can only speculate. The ears are spirals, as ears are drawn in Altaic art, while the ruff and the circular eyes are reminiscent of an owl. A suggestion that this beaked head depicts a griffin cannot be right, as the mythological griffin is always depicted with oval-shaped animal eyes, while this beaked head has circular bird eyes. To date, no plaques similar to the present example have been found in any archaeological excavation or any private collection, but there is a similarity between this plaque and entry 78, which is described in the present volume as having Altaic connections. Since so many plaques in worldwide collections were acquired years ago by missionaries and others without much by way of provenance, scholarly identification is often challenging, but hopefully the present volume will result in enlightening comparisons with objects in other unpublished collections.

86 | Decorated Disk

Xinjiang, Alagou, 3rd century BCE

Height 5.9 cm
Width 5.9 cm
Weight 77.2 g

Hammered gold sheet over iron, alloy composition by P. Meyers (May 4, 2013): Au 90%; Ag 7%; Cu 1.4%

A wonderfully playful tiger shown in profile decorates the top of this iron disc covered with gold sheet. The tiger's hindquarters are twisted 180 degrees, and each paw has prominent claws and a dewclaw in the typical style of the Eurasian Steppe. Four pieces like the present example, each with a diameter of 6 cm, have been excavated from a tomb at Alagou in the Xinjiang Uighur Autonomous Region (Xinjiang 1999, 163, no. 422; So and Bunker 1995, 72, fig. 31). The original function of the Alagou disks is unclear since the burial was disturbed and their placement unknown. The pose of the tiger on one these pieces can be associated with the pastoralists of the Eurasian Steppe, as can the repoussé method of working gold sheet. The curvilinear designs on the head and shoulder of the tiger image on the Alagou gold-covered iron disk are very similar to the body decoration of the tiger image tattooed on the shoulder of the man buried in Pazyryk, mound 5, in the Altai (fig. 20).

Fig. 20: Tattoo on the left shoulder of a male mummy from Pazyryk, kurgan 5.

87 | Personal Ornament with Griffin Images

Northwest China
late 4th–3rd century BCE

Height 8.3 cm
Width 7.4 cm
Weight 44.7 g

Cast bronze, alloy composition by J. Stenger: Cu 70%; Sn 10%; Pb 6%; As high

This openwork, cast-bronze hook buckle is distinguished by six griffin images with long, hooked beaks, long ears, and animal-shaped oval eyes that are represented in low relief surrounding a central raised boss. A hook is placed on the front of the right edge of the proper left plaque, opposite an elongated hole on the opposing proper right plaque to create a fastening system. This hook buckle is interesting for its iconography, but, to date, no other examples are known. The quality of the casting is rather poor, and the buckle was probably cast in a bivalve mold.

The griffin is a mythological creature with an impressive beak, long ears, and oval, animal-shaped eyes, a hybrid image that derives from the fantastic fauna that resulted from a mixture of western Asian and Greek artistic imagery in antiquity (Piotrovskij 1978, 100, no. 127; Mayor 1994, 52–58; Menghin et al. 2007, 131, fig. 15). Griffins may have been introduced into Scythian art in northwestern Eurasia, when the Greeks began to produce luxury goods for their Scythian customers living in the greater Black Sea region. By the time such images appeared at the eastern end of the Eurasian steppes, Greek imagery had already become a part of their artistic heritage, and should not be taken to suggest a Greek continuum. Similar-shaped plain wooden buckles have also been found among the grave goods at Ak-Alakha 5 in the Altai.

88 | Mythological Elk-Head Plaque

Northwest China
4th–3rd century BCE

Height 5.4 cm
Width 7 cm
Weight 30.3 g

Cast bronze, traces of gilding on the front, alloy composition by J. Stenger: Cu 91%; As high

An elk head with antlers transformed by griffin heads distinguishes this cast bronze openwork plaque. The piece shows signs of longtime wear, but traces of gilding are still visible here and there. The plaque once had a horizontal attachment loop of which only the stubs remain. Two tiny holes, made after the loop was lost, facilitate attachment: One hole is located under the eye and the other is just above the tip of the ear. To date there is no published example of a similar piece, but the way in which the head is conceived is similar to an animal-head image from Ak-Alakha 5 in the Altai, kurgan 1 (Polos'mak 2001, 217, fig. 143). This similarity helps to highlight the strong cultural connections that appear to have existed between the pastoral groups in northwestern China and the Altai, but the presence of amalgam gilding points to Chinese workmanship for non-Chinese consumption.

89 | Belt Plaque Depicting a Camel and Rider

Northwest China, Ningxia, Guyuan region
5th–4th century BCE

Height 4.2 cm
Width 5.3 cm
Weight 19.4 g

Tinned cast bronze, alloy composition by J. Stenger:
Cu 69%; Sn 9%; Pb 6%; As trace

Ex C. T. Loo Collection, Paris; David David-Weill Collection, Paris, DW 3074; Paris Drouot, 28 June 1972, lot 36; Therese and Erwin Harris Collection, Miami, Florida

Published: Salmony 1933, pl. 29.3; Janse 1935, pl. 9.36; David-Weill Sale 1972, no. 36; So and Bunker 1995, 164, no. 88

This small plaque displays an image of a man sitting between the two humps of a kneeling Bactrian camel. A hook projects from the camel's neck on the front of the plaque, and a vertical loop is placed on the back of the plaque, behind the camel's rump. Scattered, shiny, silver-colored patches indicate that the front of the plaque may have originally been tinned. The existence of similar plaques with the camel facing in the opposite direction and without a hook projecting from the front suggests that the present piece may once have been paired with a matching plaque to form a complete buckle (e.g., Kost 2014, pl. 86.3–4). As late as the twentieth century, herds of wild camels still roamed Ningxia in the vicinity of Edsin (Ejin) gol (Schafer 1950, 176–77).

Camels are so tall that they are trained to kneel, so that a rider can mount them. This resulted in a whole hierarchy of camel specialists charged with taming and handling them (Schafer 1950, 176–77). The present plaque is badly worn, making any discussion of the rider's costume difficult, but presumably he was outfitted with the same sort of jacket and trousers worn by the man riding a standing camel on the following plaque.

90 | Belt Plaque in the Shape of a Standing Camel and Rider

Northwest China, Ningxia
5th–4th century BCE

Height 5 cm
Width 5.5 cm
Weight 29.6 g

Tinned cast bronze, alloy composition by J. Stenger: Cu 70%; Sn 13%; Pb 3%; As trace

Ex Therese and Erwin Harris Collection, Miami, Florida

Published: So and Bunker 1995, 92–93, no. 5; Knauer 1998, 36, pl. 14

Dressed in a belted jacket worn over trousers, the rider of this standing Bactrian camel is shown holding a goad in his left hand, with his right hand placed high on the camel's neck. A hook projects from the ground line that extends up to the camel's muzzle on the front of the plaque, and a vertical loop is placed on the back of the plaque behind the camel's rump. As with the previous plaque (entry 89), silvery traces indicate that this plaque was originally completely tinned.

The two-humped Bactrian camel was native to Central Asia, while the habitat of the single-humped dromedary was the Arabian Peninsula and North Africa (Knauer 1998, 16). The Bactrian camel made trans-Asian travel possible. With their large, padded feet camels could walk on sand and safely cross deserts (Schafer 1950).

The artisans who designed plaques representing camels and riders must have been familiar with camels, as the details are all correct. Camels grind and regurgitate their food, making it impossible to place a bit in their mouths as one would with a horse; correspondingly, no bridle is represented. Instead, a plug is inserted into one nostril, with a single rein attached to it, by means of which the camel is led or guided. Camels are notoriously uncooperative and must be encouraged to move with a goad, which the rider on the present plaque is holding in his left hand. Camel riders and drivers were all foreigners to the Chinese and are recognizable by their prominent noses, a non-Chinese characteristic (Schafer 1963, 71).

91 | Belt Hook

Northwest China
late 4th–3rd century BCE

Height 5.8 cm
Width 12.5 cm
Weight 102.1 g

Cast bronze, alloy composition by J. Stenger: Cu 84%; Sn 8 %; Pb 7 %; As trace

Ex Adolphe Stoclet Collection, Brussels

Published: van Goidsenhoven 1956, 54–55

This belt hook and the next one (entry 92) are similarly shaped. A long hook extending from the proper left side of the plaque terminates in a snake head, with a button projecting from the back completing the fastening system. A predation scene, with a tiger and a gazelle, occupies the rectangular part. Since the hindquarters of both animals are twisted 180 degrees, it is necessary to count the paws and legs in order to be able to get a clear read on what is happening. The tiger is biting one of the gazelle's legs, while holding down the gazelle's other leg with its left paw. The terrified gazelle is shown above the tiger.

The apparent source for this scene is found on a rectangular wooden belt plaque worn by the ruler buried in a frozen tomb at Berel' II in the Kazakhstan Altai (Francfort et al. 2006, 120, fig. 10). Both the protagonists of the present scene and those on the Berel' plaque "are represented with twisted hindquarters, a typical stylistic motif occurring over a vast area centered on the Altai-Siberia region" (Francfort et al. 2006, 120–21). Dendrochronological results for the burial at Berel' provide a date of 294 BCE, twenty or thirty years after the fall of the Achaemenid empire (Francfort et al. 2006, 126), suggesting that the local artistic tradition had already been enriched by much earlier cultural contacts with the Achaemenid world.

The hybrid artistic style exhibited here throws new light on the extravagant decoration of a lavish, late-Warring States belt hook in the Arthur M. Sackler Gallery that displays two twisted does hanging upside down from the claws of a raptor among its sinicized steppe decor (So and Bunker 1995, 153–54, no. 75). The wooden frontlet for a Berel' horse displays two horned lions hanging upside down from a feline head (Francfort et al. 2006, 124, fig. 17), a perfect parallel for the transmission of artistic motifs.

92 | Belt Hook

Northwest China
late 4th–3rd century BCE

Height 5.7 cm
Width 13.5 cm
Weight 81.7 g

Cast bronze, alloy composition by J. Stenger:
Cu 77%; Sn 8%; Pb 4%; As trace

Ex Therese and Erwin Harris Collection, Miami, Florida, by 1990; Christie's New York, 16 March 2017, lot 815

Published:
Harris Collection 2017, 25, no. 815

This extraordinary belt hook depicts a fleeing stag being attacked from behind by a wolf which is biting its haunch. The long hook extending from the proper left side of the plaque terminates in a snake head, and there is a button projecting from the back.

This belt hook and the one discussed before (entry 91), combine Iranian, Saka, and Chinese elements. Several belt hooks exist with openwork animal-combat scenes that are similar to these two, but none have yet been found in an archaeological context. Art-historical comparison suggests that they may all have been produced in the same region, combining a dynastic Chinese buckle shape with a steppe combat scene and button attachment device, similar to a belt hook in the Thaw Collection (Bunker et al. 2002, 148, no. 124).

93 | Garment Plaque

Northwest China, Gansu province
ca. 8th century BCE

Height 2.6 cm
Width 6.1 cm
Weight 16.7 g

Cast bronze, alloy composition by E. Ferreira: Cu 70.5%; Sn 12.4%; Pb 0.8%; As 0.3%; Fe 0.2% by J. Stenger: Cu 86%; Sn 9%; Pb 2%; As <1%

Ex Therese and Erwin Harris Collection, Miami, Florida

Published:
So and Bunker 1995, 111–12, no. 26

This small, crouching tiger is depicted in profile with two legs ending in comma-shaped claws and a long, drooping tail. Intaglio spirals mark the shoulder and haunch, and scallop shapes suggest a striped pelt. The ear is an inverted heart shape. The slightly concave reverse displays a vertical attachment loop. Fabric impressions that remain on the surface incrustation near the shoulder and haunch suggest that such plaques were originally attached to articles of clothing.

Two virtually identical examples were excavated from a burial in Yucun, Ning county, Gansu province, with Western Zhou bronzes (Xu Junchen and Liu Dezhen 1985, 350, fig. 3.4–6, So and Bunker 1995, 112, fig. 26.1). Crouching feline images continued to appear on later dynastic-Chinese bronzes, and became particularly popular among the northern pastoral peoples, such as the gold example excavated at Jundushan, Yanqing county, just north of Beijing (see Chapter 2b).

There is a clear difference between the Gansu examples and those associated with the various pastoral peoples. The felines in the Gansu examples look straight ahead, while the northern images look down. It is tempting to consider that a crouching-tiger image became an important single icon during the Western Zhou period, and was introduced through various means of exchange to the northern pastoral peoples. The pastoral peoples may have adopted it to illustrate their animal-combat scenes, a motif not known to the Western Zhou, but which ultimately appears as an exotic motif on Eastern Zhou ritual bronzes, such as those found at Liyu, Hunyuan county, in northern Shanxi (Weber 1973, 232). The Liyu bronze vessels were cast during the fifth century at Houma, the Jin state foundry in southern Shanxi, illustrating the cultural interconnectivity that was in place during the first millennium BCE (So 1980, 267–68, no. 69).

94 | Dagger

Northwest China, Gansu province
8th–6th century BCE

Length 27.3 cm
Weight 142.8 g

Cast bronze, alloy composition by J. Stenger: Cu 70%; Sn 10%; Pb 7%; As trace

Ex Christie's New York, 1 December 1988, lot 140; Therese and Erwin Harris Collection, Miami, Florida; Christie's New York, 16 March 2017, lot 837

Published: Christie's 1988, no. 140; So 1995, 38, fig. 4; So and Bunker 1995, 126–27, no. 43, and 49, col. pl. 10; Harris Collection 2017, 42–43, no. 837

This dagger has a hollow hilt and a tapering double-edged blade that is strengthened by a raised midrib. The piece was cast in one piece using a two-part mold. The hilt is composed of a stacked column of profile dragon-like heads cast in relief on both sides. Each head has a rolled muzzle, an occasional crest, and a deep, round socket for an eye that may have once been accented by turquoise or some other semiprecious gemstone. The spirals of crest and muzzle line the edges of the hilt, marking its straight profile. A pronounced shoulder, accentuated by a mask-like guard with spirals at the sides, marks the transition from the ornate hilt to the blade. The hole beneath the twisted band that pierces the end of the hilt would have served to suspend the piece.

Similar daggers are found in the Baron von der Heydt Collection and in the Rietberg Museum, Zurich (Griessmaier 1936, no. 138, present location unknown; Brinker 1975, no. 75). Excavations from western China provide a possible provenance for this dagger. An example with a less sophisticated, more irregular, hilt design was found among the burial goods recovered from Yucun, Ning county, Gansu province, apparently wrapped in hemp or some similar kind of coarse fabric (Xu Junchen and Liu Dezhen 1985, pl. 5.2, 350, fig. 3.1). Another, with a hilt that closely resembles the present dagger, came from a seventh-century burial at Baqitun, Fengxiang county, in Shaanxi province, located in the heart of predynastic Qin territory (Shaanxi 1980, 84, fig. 23.2).

Daggers with rhombic blades, raised mid-ribs, and the blades integrally cast with the hilts originated earlier among the northern pastoral peoples (Loehr 1949, 38). However, daggers with ornate hilts that include a Chinese *taotie* mask in the artistic vocabulary, such as one that distinguishes the guard on the present dagger, are probably luxury items made by the Qin to exchange or trade with the neighboring pastoral peoples,

such as the bronze dagger and jade dagger in the Fogg Museum (Loehr 1975, no. 372). Qin workshops seem to have been active trading centers serving both their own markets and the northern peoples throughout the first millennium BCE (So in So and Bunker 1995, 126–27). Both the present dagger and the crouching feline (entry 93), are slightly earlier than similar examples found in non-Chinese burials in the Jundushan (see Chapter 2b; Bunker 1991b).

Chapter 3d
Ancient Chinese and Eurasian Cultural Connectivity

Acknowledging that cultural connectivity developed very early throughout the ancient world is essential to recognizing the exotic heritage of many characteristics long considered to be essentially dynastic Chinese. Suggesting that a certain motif has a "Scytho-Siberian" lineage is neither acceptable nor accurate.[49] For example, it would appear that certain early elements of landscape representation in art and the knowledge of plucked stringed instruments, ancestral to the *qin*- and *se*-zithers, were introduced into ancient China via contact with the Eurasian steppe world long before they became major hallmarks of Confucianism.[50]

Displays of majesty, such as hunting parks and the lavish, festive entertainment of guests with food, drink, and music were West Asian practices introduced into dynastic China by the Western Zhou during the first millennium BCE, replacing the formal rites and gestures of the earlier Shang dynasty (Turner 1941, 420, mentioned in the *Yili* [Book of Etiquette]).

The Introduction of Landscape Representation

According to Michael Sullivan, Alexander Soper "stated unequivocally that the introduction of Landscape representation into Chinese art … is due to foreign influences" (Sullivan 1953, 55). Soper attributed early Chinese landscape images to borrowings from a West Asian source, such as a "lost Achaemenid chase" (Soper 1941, 147). Sullivan added artifactual evidence for an even earlier possible source: a Mesopotamian cylinder seal dated by Henri Frankfort to circa 2500 BCE that shows bowmen in pursuit of a lion, which is in turn pursuing an antelope over precipitous peaks (Sullivan 1953, 56, note 7). Sullivan also cited other possible ancient West Asian examples (Pope 1938, pls. 204–5; 218; 228; 231). Soper's insightful suggestions, made long before any actual physical evidence for his theories had been excavated—such as the stylized, hammered-gold mountain images that distinguish the headdress of the "Golden Warrior" from Issyk, the fifth- to fourth-century BCE site in Kazakhstan discovered in 1969 (Chang and

---

49 The term has long been considered obsolete, as it has no historical or archaeological basis. For a discussion of such obsolete terms, see Bunker et al. 1997, 7–8; Bunker et al. 2002, 4; 8.
50 The focus here on early cultural connectivity is inspired by Allsen 2006.

Guroff 2007, 112; 117–18)—seemed almost clairvoyant, and continue to provide support for some scholarly observations made today.

Since mountains with wild animals among their peaks did not seem to reflect typical Chinese taste, early painting scholars associated these early attempts to depict landscapes to contact with their Eurasian pastoral neighbors, with whom they had interacted for centuries. "On tomb tiles, pottery vessels, and inlaid bronzes, the typical Han landscape is often presented as a setting for human and animal figures in violent action," (Sullivan 1953, 55), thus highlighting its non-Confucian characteristics. Sullivan was so impressed by Soper's conclusions that he made the following statement: "It is in the lesser service of decoration that landscape enters the art of the Han period, and under the strongest suspicion of foreign influence" (Sullivan 1953, 55–56; Soper 1941, 147).

Max Loehr, on the other hand, considered that Chinese ornament, "a language of symbolic forms based on abstract linear rhythms," created by "nameless artisans from the late Neolithic, Bronze and Iron Ages," to have been the earliest element in the development of Chinese landscape representation, citing the "exquisiteness and originality of its designs" (Loehr 1967–68, 8).

Loehr's prescient recognition of native elements in the development of landscape representation is echoed by both Sullivan and Soper when they allude to "an inherently Chinese quality that is common to all Chinese pictorial art," (Sullivan 1953, 59; 63) imbuing it with a cosmic vitality, referred to as *ch'i* (*qi*). Unlike Loehr, they did not understand its source. China's extraordinary ability to adopt, adapt, and Sinicize exotic objects or motifs was often so powerful that the actual non-Chinese origins were obscured. For example, the "mounted-archer motif" that distinguishes many Han-dynasty (206 BCE–220 CE) and post-Han artifacts does not always appear foreign, despite its non-Han origins (Wallace 2018, passim). Instead, the mounted-archer motif may have been transmitted eastwards as a textile design, such as an example (98QZM131:1-3) from the Zaghunluq site, in the Xinjiang Uyghur Autonomous Region (Zaghunluq 2016, 367–68).

The Beginnings of Plucked Stringed Instruments: The Qin- and Se-zithers

The exciting discovery in 1977 of the undisturbed burial of Marquis Yi of Zeng in Leigudun, Suizhou, Hubei province, "pushed the history of [Chinese] music back to the fifth century BCE" (So 2000b, 26). An inscription on one bell among the large set of 65 bells in the "court" ensemble in the central chamber confirmed the bell as a "funerary gift presented in 433 BCE to the Marquis by the Chu ruler Xiongzhang, his neighbor and overlord" (So 2000b, 27), giving the burial a precise date.

The eastern chamber of the burial complex represented the space for the marquis' intimate, personal life, containing his coffin along with eight smaller coffins for eight young women and the remains of five plucked stringed instruments: a ten-stringed *qin*-zither (fig. 21 top), a five-stringed zither (fig. 21 bottom), and three 25-stringed *se*-zithers (fig. 21 middle); So 2000b, 27–28, figs. 4; 6–7; Lawergren 2003a, 103, fig. 6). These three types of string instrument, buried with Marquis Yi, represent the earliest excavated evidence for plucked stringed instruments in ancient China.[51]

The rich contents of the marquis's tomb reveal his lavish personal lifestyle imbued with the spirit of "wine, women, and song," accompanied by music played on special plucked stringed instruments that were more soothing and melodious in intimate settings than the loud clanging of bronze bells buried in the main burial chamber. Such elite revelry is described in the *Chu Ci* (Elegies of Chu), written in the fourth- to third-century BCE:

> Before the dainties have left the tables,
> Girl musicians take up their places … sing the latest songs …
> Bells clash in their swaying frames:
> The catalpa-wood zithers' strings are swept …
> Then they sing songs of Wu and ballads of Cai
> And play the Dalü music.
> Men and women now sit together,
> Mingling freely without distinction:
> Hat-strings and fastenings come untied:
> The revel turns to wild disorder.[52]

The descriptions of some zithers in the *Elegies of Chu* as made of catalpa wood suggests that such instruments may have been made locally, since catalpa trees grow abundantly in regions along the Yangzi river, and their relatively soft wood was considered to have exceptional resonance. The Zeng Hou Yi excavation

---

51 See Hubei 1989, pl. 48, 167, fig. 78; So 2000b, 28–29, figs. 4; 6–7; Lawergren 2000, 70, fig. 3.4a; 72–73, fig. 3.6; Lawergren 2003b.
52 *Zhao Hun*, I: 106–23, quoted from Major and So 2000.

report also describes one *se*-zither as made of catalpa wood and another made of *jumu* (southern elm) (Hubei 1989, vol. 1, 155; 157).

The Horizontal Angular Harp and the Qin-Zither

Research by Bo Lawergren suggests that certain features associated with exotic horizontal angular harps found in non-Chinese burials throughout Inner Eurasia may have stimulated the development of the Chinese *qin*- and *se*-zithers recovered from the marquis's tomb, that would become the classical Confucian musical instrument *par excellence* for the Chinese literati (Lawergren 2003a, passim; 2003b; in present volume pp. 458–73). The horizontal angular harp is a plucked string instrument with an ancient West Asian heritage ultimately traceable to third millennium BCE chordophones found in the royal cemetery of Ur in Mesopotamia (Lawergren 2003a, 102, fig. 3b; 107, fig. 12). In Chinese archaeological literature, a horizontal angular harp is called a *wo konghou* to distinguish it from a vertical angular harp called a *shu konghou*, which is also a plucked stringed instrument but which does not occur in Chinese musical circles until the later Eastern Han period (Xie Jin 2005, passim). Similar horizontal angular harps have been found in first millennium BCE burials throughout Eurasia, such as Olbia on the northern shore of the Black Sea, Pazyryk culture burials in the Altai Mountains, and in non-Chinese burials in the Xinjiang Uyghur Autonomous Region (Lawergren 2003a, 107, fig. 11, a, b, c, f). This extensive similarity between the harps highlights the musical connectivity that appears to have existed throughout Eurasia during the first millennium BCE, leading Lawergren to call them "Steppe" harps to highlight their importance in the transmission and evolution of the plucked string harps of ancient Ur to Central Asia, and perhaps even to dynastic China, albeit in a vastly modified form.

The Pazyryk harp in kurgan 2, an early third-century BCE burial in the Altai Mountains of southern Siberia (Rudenko 1970, pl. 146), had strings made from animal sinew (Lawergren 1990, pl. 58b; Lawergren 2003a, 89; 107, fig. 11f). Fragments of a Steppe harp were also found in a fifth- to fourth-century BCE kurgan at Bashadar (Lawergren 1990, pl. 57.2). These Altaic dates are much more recent than those proposed years ago by Sergei Rudenko (Rudenko 1970), because they are based on more recent radiocarbon and dendrochronological testing (Stepanova 2006, 104, table 1). There is also the possibility that the two harps found in the Altaic kurgans were actually imports from Xinjiang, a theory that remains unconfirmed.[53]

The Olbia burial is Scythian, but the harp found among the grave goods (see fig. 50 d, p. 470) resembles the horizontal angular harp represented in the Assyrian relief of 860 BCE from Nimrud, Iran, on display in the British Museum (see fig. 51, p. 471). Mounted Scythian archers serving as mercenaries in Assyrian armies may have stimulated the transmission of the Assyrian harp into Central Asia, where it slowly lost its military associations as it evolved into what Lawergren has christened a "Steppe harp" that was smaller, lighter, and easier to carry and play, especially on horseback (Lawergren 2003a, 90–91).

Burial Details of Steppe Harps Excavated in the Xinjiang Uyghur Autonomous Region

Steppe harps discovered in the Xinjiang Uyghur Autonomous Region provide important archaeological evidence for the transmission of ancient Mesopotamian culture eastwards. The Xinjiang Steppe harps, made from local Euphrates poplar and tamarisk woods, have been called *konghou* by Chinese archaeologists (Wang Bo and Lu Lipeng 2016, 77). Scholarly interest in the grave goods has been primarily focused on textiles, resulting in a serious neglect of more informative details about the burial that are critical to the present study. For example, burial descriptions indicate that harps were often intentionally placed in particular ways in the graves and associated with certain corpses, suggesting the existence of cultural beliefs and rituals that previously went unrecognized and that are only now beginning to be revealed, albeit still fragmentarily.

Zaghunluq cemetery in Xinjiang is located near an oasis in Qiemo county, ca. 600 kilometers west of present-day Hetian (Khotan), an urban center on the southern rim of the Tarim Basin that, in antiquity, had extensive long-distance contacts with southern dynastic China.[54] One of the most interesting burials in the Zaghunluq cemetery is grave 14 (96QZIM14) that was excavated during the fall of 1996. Grave 14, situated on the *Gobi* terrace, about two kilometers west of Zaghunluq village, contained nineteen bodies and two Steppe harps (Wang Bo 2003b). The best-preserved harp (96QZIM14:20) had been placed across the

---

53   I am grateful to Sergei Miniaev for this information about the two Altaic harps. To date, their woods remain unidentified.
54   Lawergren 2003a, 106, fig. 10b, map; Bunker 2008; Zhagunluq 2016.

chests of two corpses: a child and a middle-aged woman wearing a pointed, black felt hat of the kind associated with steppe peoples or those from even farther west; the second harp (96QZIM14:27) was placed at the woman's left side (Wang Bo 2003a, fig. 13 nos. 1, 6).

The first Steppe harp mentioned has a sound box and a neck carved out of diversiform-leaved poplar that looks like half of a gourd, as well as a stick made of Chinese tamarisk wood, both locally available woods (Wang Bo 2003b, 57, fig. 2). The exterior of the sound box has a smooth, polished surface with traces of a cover made of skin that had been attached with glue. There are obvious trace marks of three strings on the stick (Xie Jin 2005). The second Steppe harp in grave 14 had a well-preserved neck and stick, but the trapezoidal-shaped sound box had become somewhat deformed. There were also traces of a skin cover on the outside of the sound box, and 24 pins used to attach it. Grave 14 has been radiocarbon dated to 761 BCE ± 61 (Zaghunluq 2016, 69).

A rescue excavation at Zaghunluq in 1989 by He Dexiu unearthed another grave with four mummified bodies: a disintegrated infant, a one-year-old male child with light-brown hair, a young woman about twenty years old, and an old woman with white hair who was presumably the main occupant (89QZM2). The bodies were not intentionally mummified, as corpses were in ancient Egyptian culture, but were the result of having "died in early winter, flash-freezing and freeze-drying over the next few months, whereas other dead bodies decomposed" (Barber 2014, 35). Descriptions of the mummified bodies led the excavator to believe that the young woman and child had been buried alive (He Dexiu 1998, passim). Many of the dead are described as European-looking (or Caucasoid) with reddish, blondish hair, and occasional minor local characteristics (He Dexiu 1998, 174). Hence, to call their culture and their grave goods "Chinese" is misleading and inaccurate.

A careful cleaning of the old lady's skin revealed amazing, tattooed body decoration. Semi-lunar tattoos adorned the upper eyelids, while bold bluish-green patterns enhanced the left arm and long, graceful fingers (He Dexiu 1998, 172, figs. 4–5; 173, fig. 6). Similar body decoration has been identified on some of the Pazyryk-culture bodies excavated from kurgans in the Altai (Barkova and Pankova 2005, 55, figs. 11, 13), revealing important cultural connections. Material from several Zaghunluq graves was submitted for radiocarbon dating, which resulted in a range of dates from 3200 to 2700 yBP, roughly equivalent to

1000–500 BCE, or the Western Zhou and the Spring and Autumn periods in Chinese history (He Dexiu 1998, 174; Zaghunluq 2016, 69).

The people buried in the Zaghunluq cemetery appear to have been settled pastoralists, with an economy dominated by animal husbandry, especially sheep. This situation led to the development of local expertise in weaving and dyeing, which enabled them to create beautiful woven woolen fabrics valued by the dynastic Chinese, with whom they had major down-the-line trade contact (He Dexiu 1998).

The Yanghai cemetery in Shanshan located on the northern rim of the Turpan Basin in the Xinjiang Uyghur Autonomous Region, is roughly contemporary with the Zaghunluq cemetery (Xie Jin 2005). It contained Steppe harps, European-looking mummified bodies, as well as a well-preserved supply of ancient cannabis, a fact that has drawn considerable attention (Xinjiang Wenwu 2004). The harps in the Yanghai tombs are varied in size, have strings made of ox tendons, and may actually be much earlier than the fifth-century BCE date proposed by Chinese archaeologists in the past (Xie Jin 2005). According to Xie Jin, the skeleton of a 45-year-old male lying on a slightly raised bier with his harp next to his right side (grave I M90; Xinjiang Tulufanxue 2011, fig. 16) has been identified as a shaman. In death, he was supplied with a substantial cache of cannabis that is still viable (Xie Jin 2005). The discovery of cannabis in the shaman's tomb attracted scholarly interest (e.g., Jian et al. 2006), but also caused a sensation, just like a recent discovery in westernmost Xinjiang[55] that resulted in an article in *Science* (June 12, 2019) entitled "Oldest evidence of marijuana use discovered in 2500-year-old cemetery in peaks of western China." If one considers how long drugs and alcohol have been used as mind-altering substances in world history, the excitement over the discovery of ancient cannabis is hardly warranted.

The complexities resulting from extremely long-distance, trans-Eurasian exchange, which frequently referenced the use of psychotropic plant products in the search for ways to communicate with ancestors and the afterlife in numerous ancient cultures around the world, provide significant cultural information that is seldom mentioned (Sherratt 2007, passim). When these burial details are considered in a wider archaeological context, they begin to reveal information

---

55 Jirzankal (Ji'erzankale) burial ground, Tashkurgan. Remarkably enough, the same graves also yielded horizontal harps, cf. Shen et al. 2015.

concerning the significant role played by the ever-changing populations of Inner Eurasia, contributing to the ongoing "center versus periphery" debate in antiquity concerning various Central Asian pastoral groups and the major civilizations to their east and west (Renfrew 1998, passim).

The cultural connectivity reflected by the spread of plucked stringed instruments from ancient Ur to Xinjiang sites over the course of some two millennia appears to be more the result of herders searching for better pasture and exchange networks than cultural diffusion associated with the spread of Indo-European languages. This fixation on a minor linguistic distraction tends to cause a more rational explanation for the transmission of certain cultural characteristics to be overlooked, especially given that we do not know what language the now-mummified Xinjiang individuals spoke. I prefer to heed Denis Sinor's cautionary exhortation: "when it comes to determining what language the mummies might have spoken, the mummies are 'mum'" (Kohl 2014, 93).

It is possible that modified versions of horizontal Steppe harps, such as those from Olbia, Pazyryk, and Xinjiang, spread eastwards into the northwestern Chinese cultural sphere, where they were sinicized and ultimately assimilated into native Chinese life (Lawergren 2003a, 89–90). Knowledge of harps in dynastic China appears to date back to the Spring and Autumn period (771–475 BCE), according to mentions in the *Shiben* (Book of Origins), an important early Chinese encyclopedia of imperial genealogies and accomplishments, which was not written down until the second century BCE (Xie Jin 2005).

The Invention of Qin Tuning Keys (qin zhen yao) and Se String-Anchors (se rui)

The marquis Yi's *qin*-zither included a wooden sound box with ten wooden tuning pegs (only four of which have survived) around which a string was wrapped, indicating that tuning the instrument was accomplished by turning each peg (So and Bunker 1995, 148–50; see fig. 43, p. 460). The four surviving tuning pegs were misplaced after excavation, and the tuning pegs shown in the 2000 exhibition catalogue are reproductions of the excavated examples based on the carefully recorded drawings and descriptions from the excavation report (So 2000a, 29, fig. 7).

On a modern *qin*, players can turn the pegs with their fingers because the pegs protrude from the sound board that forms the bottom of the instrument. On the ancient *qin*, the tuning pegs were inset deep into the sound box and spaced too closely together to accommodate fingers. This necessitated the invention of a tuning key with a narrow shaft terminating in a square socket that fit over each of the pegs to facilitate their turning (Lawergren 2007, 50, fig. 3). Since the same tuning key fits over every peg, only one tuning key is needed for each *qin*. Curiously, no tuning keys were found in the marquis's tomb. Most other Chinese plucked stringed zithers (the *se*, the *zheng*, and the *zhu*) are bridge-tuned, i.e., they are tuned by moving a bridge under each string to adjust the length of the string for vibration, so no tuning pegs or keys are needed (Lawergren 2000, 65–83).

Bronze tuning keys have been found at several northern Chinese sites, but not in association with *qin*-zithers, with the result that their tuning function went unrecognized. They were simply described as finials surmounted by charming zoomorphic imagery that seemed to be related to the art of the Eurasian steppe world. Their real function was finally confirmed by the excavation of Nanyue Wang's undisturbed second-century BCE tomb in Guangzhou, Guangdong province that revealed tuning keys and pegs together.[56] According to the archaeological monograph, the king of Nanyue's tomb contained a total of 48 bronze *qin* tuning pegs, and more in ivory and bone. Since the number of strings on a single instrument can range from five to ten, the exact number of instruments remains unclear. Only three bronze tuning keys were found (for three *qin* players?), but all of the instruments had already disintegrated.[57]

A discussion of five *qin* tuning keys in the present collection (entries 95–99) reveals the confusing cultural complexities that arise when one culture borrows an artifact from another culture. However, their descriptions here begin to reveal how and why tuning keys were created, and why the figurative motifs on the earliest examples resemble imagery primarily associated with the pastoral people inhabiting the northeastern Eurasian steppes on dynastic China's northwestern borders. Such motifs have nothing to do with Confucian culture, to which Chinese and many Western scholars have attributed the origins of the classic *qin*-zithers.

56 Guangzhou et al. 1991, pl. 47.1; 93, fig. 62.1; So and Bunker 1995, 148–49, no. 70; Bunker et al. 1997, 293, no. 267; Lawergren 1997, 47 and 51; Lawergren 2003a.
57 A recent tally of string instruments in the Nanyue tomb concluding that, based on the number of pegs, it contained five *qin*-zithers is misleading (Furniss 2008, 291), since no actual *qin*-zithers were found (Furniss 2008, note 606).

Where Were the First Qin-Zithers Made and Why?

Why would the rulers of the Jin, Qin, or Guo states of the Eastern Zhou period, to mention only a few, not welcome a beautiful young woman with blondish to reddish hair to warm their beds, play music for them, and perhaps sing sweet songs? Evidence, both literary and physical, has confirmed the existence of exogamic marriages and the taking of foreign concubines in dynastic China, a practice highlighted in So (2019). If the women came from the steppe world, they may have brought small harps with them that could be held in the arms and played by plucking the strings. Certainly, striking bronze bells was hardly soothing or romantic. Mention is made in numerous state texts of foreign wives and concubines taken by various rulers, a custom practiced already during the Shang period. Foreign ways and exotic objects have always been popular among the rich and powerful—and still are today—such that in China plucked string instruments came to be embraced by those who had time for music and leisure.

As will be seen from the following entries, all of the tuning keys are designed with a narrow shaft enhanced by a small figurative sculpture on the top and a square socket that fits over a tuning peg at the bottom. Although consistent in design, each tuning key also has its own individual characteristics indicating its date and cultural traits. The earliest keys have the shorter shafts to accommodate early *qin*, whose pegs are contained in shallower sound boxes, while the later keys have longer shafts to reach pegs in later instruments with different constructions and shapes. The varieties of animal sculptures can also reveal their individual heritage. In other words, both the shaft lengths and decorative imagery are important elements for the study of tuning keys, ones that seem, however, to have been overlooked. It is also tempting to suggest that these small, portable *qin*-zither tuning keys were personal items belonging to the musicians who played the instruments and wished to have them handy whenever or wherever they were expected to play, just as violinists today often travel with a special violin bow. The choice of sculptural decor probably had a personal meaning connected with the owner's heritage. The five tuning keys discussed below are presented in chronological order, making it abundantly clear that their most important characteristics are the imagery they display and the lengths of their shafts.

These keys were not all cast by the same process, suggesting that they were probably produced at various small regional foundries, an observation also made by Donna Strahan in her recent study of the tuning keys in the National

Museums of Asian Art, Smithsonian, previously known as the Freer/Sackler (Strahan, this volume).

Lawergren believes that the classical *qin*-zither emerged through a slow metamorphosis that unfolded over a period stretching from the end of the Han period until 500 CE (Lawergren 2003a, passim). By the end of the late Western Han period, the *qin* had increased in size, its clumsy early design improved, and tuning keys became obsolete. Our new observations give additional substance to Lawergren's pioneering research on the transmission of plucked string instruments from West Asia to Central and East Asia and help to further corroborate his research that has suggested an ancient West Asian heritage for the classical Chinese *qin* (see fig. 44, p. 462).

Fig. 21: Three types of plucked string instrument from the tomb of Marquis Yi of Zeng in Leigudun, Suizhou, Hubei; fifth century BCE. Hubei Provincial Museum. Top: Ten-stringed *qin*-zither. Middle: 25-stringed *se*-zither. Bottom: Five-stringed *zhu*-zither.

95 | Tuning Key Adorned with a Human-headed Argali Ram Held Aloft by a Small, Crouching Monkey-like Figure

Northwest China
ca. 6th–4th century BCE

Height 9.15 cm
Width 1.5 cm
Depth 4.3 cm
Socket:
Exterior 1.1 × 1.1 cm
Weight 102.8 g

Tin leaded bronze, alloy composition by P. Meyers (surface XRF):
Side: Cu 57%; Sn 30%; Pb 9.4%; Sb 0.21%
Monkey: Cu 49%; Sn 32%; Pb 18 %; Sb 0.32 %
Key, bottom: Cu 42%; Sn 37%; Pb 17%; Sb 0.27%.

Ex John Kasmin Collection, London

Published:
Lawergren 2003a, fig. 14i; Lawergren 2007, 51, fig. 4J; 53, fig. 5J (drawing)

This tuning key is surmounted by a composite crouching human-headed beast with the body of an Argali ram held aloft by a crouching monkey-like figure. Although visually similar to a later tuning key adorned with a goat-man figure (entry 98), "the casting technique of this tuning key is a sophisticated application of piece-mold casting." It is essentially a solid casting using a piece-mold system that is sufficiently different from that used to produce key no. 98, which is hollow-cast using an unrelated piece-mold system, pointing to different manufacturing histories in two different workshops (P. Meyers, April 26, 2009).

Such conflated human and animal forms do not appear to represent any specific iconographic system associated with dynastic China, but similar hybrid creatures are ubiquitous in Greek, Scythian, and ancient West Asian art, especially on seals and gems, highly portable items that have been found at caravan sites all over Central Asia. The chances of discovering close parallels or specific models for the imagery that distinguishes this tuning key are slim, considering the mass of small items that remain from the many cultures that were filtered through Central Asian markets by caravans with monks, travelers, and traders, not to mention the numerous mobile pastoral peoples, mercenaries for hire, and soldiers associated with periodic invasions by Iranian rulers, such as Cyrus and Darius, followed by the Macedonian Greek Alexander. Any artisan casting a tuning key for a stringed instrument with a West Asian heritage had a vast choice of conflated animal and human images from which to choose. Where the present tuning key was cast is not known, but it is worth noting that the alloy used to produce it is a leaded tin bronze with minor traces of antimony, a slightly different bronze from the leaded tin bronze used to cast three of the other tuning keys in the present collection.

96 | Tuning Key Surmounted by a Flying Raptor with a Bear Cub in Its Talons

Northwest China
ca. 5th–4th century BCE

Height 8.1 cm
Shaft height 3.4 cm
Width 4.4 cm
Socket:
Exterior 1.4 × 1.3 cm
Interior 0.9 × 0.9 cm
Tapering depth 1.1 cm
Weight 68 g

Leaded tin bronze, alloy composition by J. Stenger:
Cu 67%; Sn 10%; Pb 4%; As <1%

Ex Estate of Stevenson Burke, item #64; Therese and Erwin Harris Collection, Miami, Florida

Published:
So and Bunker 1995, 148–49, no. 70; Nadia White, *Casper Star-Tribune*, Casper, Wyoming, November 27, 1995, A1, A8; Lawergren 2000, 78, fig. 3.9.3d; Lawergren 2003a, fig. 14g; Lawergren 2007, 51, fig. 4.H; 56, fig. 1 2.H; Furniss 2008, 70, fig. 4.4; Lawergren 2019a, fig. 5 H.

A raptor with spread wings and a bear cub held in its talons surmounts the top of the square shaft of this *qin* tuning key, which terminates in a square socket that tapers inside to fit over a tuning peg. The scene enhancing this key is a local dynastic-Chinese variation of a steppe animal-combat theme that distinguishes certain artifacts from the fifth to fourth centuries BCE. This motif supplies visual evidence of cultural contacts between northern dynastic Chinese and the pastoral peoples beyond their northwestern borders (So and Bunker 1995, 148–49, no. 70).

An iconography depicting a raptor carrying off a defenseless animal is more typical of the dramatic scenes found in the Altaic cultures of southern Siberia than of artifacts associated with the pastoral groups along the northwestern borders of dynastic China. For example, the remains of a leather cutout appliqué from Pazyryk barrow 2, depicting a griffin with a mountain goat in its claws (Rudenko 1970, pl. 139L), is very similar to the griffin clutching an ibex in its claws found on a splendid gold ornament in the Hermitage in St. Petersburg (Jettmar 1967, 186, pl. 37).

Such scenes may also reference falconry, a hunting technique documented as early as the third millennium BCE in Anatolia, West Asia, which then spread to northeastern Asia, where it is still practiced today, especially in northwestern China, Mongolia, and Central Asia (Linduff 1997, 80 fig. A115, and 273–74; Bunker et al. 2002, 25; Wallace 2012).

The raptor on this tuning key is visually very similar to a carved, wooden raptor image found in kurgan 2, at Ulandryk 4, a fourth-century BCE site some 150–200 km east of Pazyryk, located on the Mongolian border with Russia (Kubarev 1987, 276, pl. 75.33). The Ulandryk 4 motif would have been meaningful throughout the Eurasian steppe world, as were most Eurasian zoomorphic images. At the same time, such similarities call out for a more thorough consideration of how and why they occurred. The

possibility of exogamic marriages may account for such cultural interconnectivity. Foreign brides from the Altaic world acquired by male pastoral groups bordering northwestern dynastic China, as well as by families from Eastern Zhou states, such as the Jin and Qin, likely brought exotic goods with them that were then copied by local dynastic bronze casters. The present tuning key is solid cast using a leaded tin bronze (see X-ray).

X-ray image of tuning key entry 96 showing that the top figure is solid cast.
Left 96-1: 150 kV, 5 mA, 90 sec. Right 96-2: 150 kV, 5 mA, 180 sec.

97 | Tuning Key Surmounted by a Crouching Bear

Northwest China, Shanxi province, style associated with the Houma foundry
5th century BCE

Height 7.2 cm
Shaft height 4.4 cm
Width 3.5 cm
Socket:
Exterior 1.3 × 1.3 cm
Interior 0.9 × 1.0 cm
Tapering depth 1.1 cm
Weight 44.1 g

Bronze,
alloy composition by J. Stenger:
Cu 65%; Sn 14%;
Pb 4%; As <1%

Ex Eugene V. Thaw Collection, New York and Santa Fe; Christie's New York, 24 March 2004, lot 112

Published:
Li Xueqin 2000, no. 94; Christie's 2004, 92, no. 122

This handsome *qin* tuning key is surmounted by a crouching bear with a tiny cub peering out from under its haunches. The shaft is distinguished by a tangle of four serpents represented in relief on the sides, terminating with a square socket that fits over a tuning peg. A circular hole piercing the back of the bear suggests that some small, unidentified element may be missing, but the hole would not be able to accommodate a flick knife, a tool used to cut the silk strings of a *qin* when they snapped and needed to be repaired (e.g., Bunker et al. 2002, 187–88, no. 178). For the intricate method employed for casting a tuning key with a flick knife, see Strahan (this volume, pp. 480–81).

The bear's pelt is marked by striated circles similar to those on certain bronze artifacts cast by the Jin state foundry located in what is now Houma in southern Shanxi province (So and Bunker 1995, 113, no. 28; Bunker et al. 2002, 165, no. 147). A longitudinal mold mark indicates that the piece was cast with a clay core and using section-molds, as is typical of artifacts associated with the Houma foundry (Li Xiating et al. 1996, 341, no. 751). X-ray images reveal that the top figure is cast hollow.

X-ray image of tuning key entry 97 showing the hollow top figure.
Left 97-1: 150 kV, 5 mA, 90 sec.
Right 97-2: 150 kV, 5 mA, 180 sec.

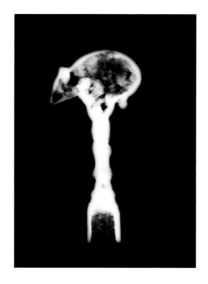
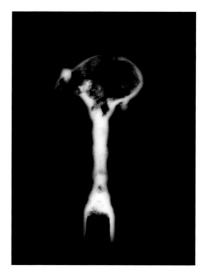

98 | Tuning Key Surmounted by a Recumbent Goat-Man

Central Eurasia
ca. 3rd century BCE

Height 10.9 cm
Socket:
Exterior 1.3 × 1.2 cm
Interior 0.9 × 0.8 cm
Tapering depth 0.6 cm
Weight 87.8 g

Leaded tin bronze with gold inlay decoration on the shaft,
alloy composition by P. Meyers (2017, surface XRF):
Cheek: Cu 43%; Sn 29%; Pb 24%; As 0.38%
Key: Cu 67%; Sn 21%; Pb 12%; Sb 0.28%

Ex Therese and Erwin Harris Collection, Miami, Florida, acquired 1981 in Hong Kong

Published:
So and Bunker 1995, 149–50 no. 71; Lawergren 2000, 78 fig. 3.9.3e; Bunker 2001a, 29, fig. 24; Lawergren 2003a, fig. 14h; Lawergren 2007, 51, fig. 4 I; 53,fig.5 I; Furniss 2008, 70, fig. 4.4.

This ancient bronze tuning key was made to tune a *qin*-zither, but the art that adorns it is not at all Chinese. Instead, the key is surmounted by a recumbent winged goat-man distinguished by a lavish beard and a horned headdress. Such hybrid images can be traced back to ancient West Asian imagery of the fourth millennium BCE, which continued to be represented in Assyrian and Achaemenid art during the first millennium BCE, especially the "long head, full lips, long beard and droopy mustache." They frequently appear as gate guardians (Amiet 1980, Neo-Sumerian, 381, figs. 400, 401, 403; and Assyrian, 276–77; 511, fig. 909). Conflated human and animal forms were also ubiquitous on Greek, Scythian, and ancient West Asian seals and gems, as well as in descriptions given by Aesop in his fables.

It is interesting to note that a skirt fragment from Shanpula, Cemetery III, a circa third-century BCE site near Hetian (ancient Khotan) in southwestern Xinjiang, depicts a mounted hunter pursuing a goat-man figure (fig. 22). Recent finds from Issyk, a circa fifth- to fourth-century BCE site in Kazakhstan, yielded two silver plaques each adorned with a human-headed winged animal that has been misidentified as a sphinx image (Chang and Guroff 2007, 110, no. 35). Instead, the Issyk head with its long beard and horned cap is strikingly similar to the head of our goat-man

Fig. 22: Tapestry band with hunting scene depicting a goat-man figure, from Shanpula, Xinjiang; first to second century CE. Riggisberg, Switzerland, Abegg-Stiftung collection, inv. no. 5138.

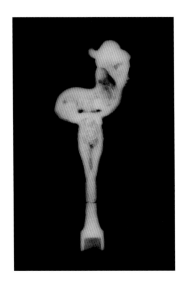

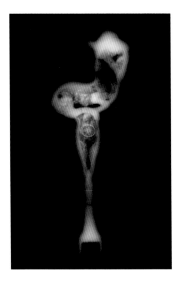

X-ray image of tuning key entry 98 showing that the top figure is hollow cast. Top 98-1: 150 kV, 5 mA, 90 sec. Bottom 98-2: 150 kV, 5 mA, 180 sec.

here, supporting the third-century BCE date given in *Traders and Raiders* (So and Bunker 1995, 149–50).

Pieter Meyers writes this of entry 98: "This tuning key is hollow cast. Based upon the empty space that can be seen through the open slits behind the beard, the casting core appears to have been removed. Because of the extensive corrosion and mineralization of the bronze, some of the finer surface details may have been obscured, making it difficult to observe the subtle surface marking. The X-ray radiographs and the CT scan (see images in Appendix 1, pp. 474–78) show the object to be hollow, including the head, the body, continuing down nearly halfway into the shaft. The lower border of the casting core space is at 4.5 cm from the bottom edge. The outline of the core space follows more or less the shape of the object indicating the use of a 'modeled' core. There are round gold inlays on the bronze shaft. Recessed rings between the large and small gold rings may also have held inlays, now lost. There is a break in the shaft just above the key socket that has been reattached." Meyers further remarks that since the analyses were carried out on the corroded bronze surfaces, the actual composition of the copper alloy may be considerably different. The alloy appears to be a leaded tin bronze with traces of antimony (P. Meyers, Technical Examination Report, December 11, 2017).

Where and when the goat-man tuning key was cast remains unclear, but the possible presence of itinerant craftsman from Central Asia or beyond fits well with Meyers' observations. This scenario would explain the fact that most of the tuning keys are cast from a similar leaded tin bronze alloy, but using a range of casting methods.

99 | Tuning Key Surmounted by a Coiled Dragon Image

South China
3rd–2nd century BCE

Height 16.9 cm
Width 4.2 cm
Socket: Exterior (round) diameter 1.5 cm
Interior 0.8 × 0.9 cm
Weight 142.6 g

Leaded tin bronze, alloy composition by J. Stenger: Cu 75%; Sn 10%; Pb 8 %

A fantastic, coiled animal adorns the handle of this tuning key. The body is openwork cast and appears to be hollow inside (see X-ray). Long ears flanking a long, vertical, curvy horn distinguish its lupine head, while curling marks lend texture to its pelt. A very similar coiled animal cast in openwork surmounts the circular shaft of a tuning key found in the Western Han tomb of the second king of Nanyue, in Guangdong province (Guangzhou et al. 1991, I, 93, fig. 62:1; II, pl. 47:2). The shaft appears to have been broken and repaired just below the circular ball that marks the transition between the jaws and the square shaft. The external socket is circular, but the internal socket is square.

The imagery is based on Chinese dragons that abounded during the Western Han period (206 BCE to 9 CE), but it should be remembered that the prevailing Han dragon image at that time was a Sinicized version of a lupine-headed creature ultimately derived from earlier Eurasian steppe imagery (Rudenko 1958, 119–21). This is another instance where a motif of Eurasian heritage became a Chinese icon, in the form of the elongated, lupine dragon so popular in Han China (Bunker et al. 2002, 274–75, no. 242).

X-ray image of tuning key entry 99 showing that the top figure is hollow cast. Left 99-1: 180 kV, 5 mA, 270 sec. Right 99-2: 150 kV, 5 mA, 180 sec.

100 | String Anchor (*se rui*)

North China
2nd–1st century BCE

Height 5.1 cm
Socket:
External: 1.8 × 1.7 cm
Internal: 1.4 × 1.3 cm

Gilded cast bronze, alloy composition by J. Stenger:
Cu 79%; Sn 6%; Pb 3%; As trace

Ex Jay C. Leff Collection, Pittsburgh; Sotheby Parke-Bernet New York, 25 October 1975, lot 90; Therese and Erwin Harris Collection, Miami, Florida; Christie's New York, 16 March 2017, lot 852

Published:
Haskins 1965, 37; Sotheby 1975, no. 90; So and Bunker 1995, 150–51, no. 72; Furniss 2008, 91, fig. 90; Harris Collection 2017, 57, no. 852

The compact body of a seated bear forms the domed top of this string anchor, likely for a *se*-zither. A square socket, around which the *se*-strings were wrapped, extends from the underside of the domed top. Another Han-period string anchor exquisitely inlaid with agate and turquoise reveals how ornate such *se*-string anchors became during the Western Han dynasty (Jiao Tianlong 2018, no. 96), this example has been incorrectly identified as a tuning key, but based on its shape, it is actually a string anchor.

Similar bear images occur on ornaments found in Xiongnu burials (e.g., Miniaev 1998, pl. 83.32–33; Ėrėgzėn et al. 2016, 169, fig. 12), and on another circular ornament discussed in this volume (entry 150).

According to their placement on ancient excavated *se*-zithers, such string anchors were cast in sets of four (see So and Bunker 1995, 151, fig. 72.1). The strings were gathered into bundles and wound around one of the four anchors. Several string anchors in the Museum of Far Eastern Antiquities in Stockholm still retain traces of these strings (Karlbeck 1955, 105–6, pls. 41.1–6). If the strings were on a Chinese instrument, they would have been silk, while strings on instruments in the pastoral world were always sinew. Few such *se*-zithers have survived from the last quarter of the first millennium BCE, but their popularity is evidenced by the large number of bronze string anchors found in tombs (So and Bunker 1995, 150–51). *Se*-zither string anchors adorned with images of bears provide further support for a northwestern Eurasian element in the development of early plucked string instruments in ancient dynastic China, as do the string anchors adorned with solid lost-wax cast three-dimensional mountain forms inhabited by animals (Bunker et al. 2002, 188–89, no. 179). Similar inhabited mountain forms can be seen on innumerable Western Han-era censors and jars. A set of four string anchors, each in the form of a three-dimensional mountain, enhances the set (*se rui*) excavated from Nanyue Wang's tomb in Guangdong province (Guangzhou et al. 1991, I, 46, figs. 30.2–30.3; 93, fig. 62:3; Furniss 2008, 266, fig. 9.3). Inhabited mountain scenes are also represented on a few rectangular belt plaques dated to the late Western Han period, such as those discussed below

(Chapter 4, entries 112 and 113). The mountain-shaped string anchors are superb tiny sculptures that are solid cast integrally with their square sockets (Bunker et al. 2002, 188, no. 179). Alexander Soper has insightfully pointed out that the subject matter of inhabited landscapes ultimately derived from ancient West Asia via Central Asia (Soper 1941, 148). The Cosmic Mountain motif has played a fundamental role in shamanism, an ancient nature-oriented belief system adhered to by most of the herding and hunting peoples scattered throughout northern Eurasia (Eliade 1964, passim; Bunker et al. 2002, 188–89, no. 179). In the present day, it remains a timeless concept, which, in certain parts of the world, is believed to connect the heavens, the earth, and the underworld.

Chapter 4

Belt Plaques from Inner Asia and China, Third Century BCE to First Century CE

By the end of the first millennium BCE, belt plaques were widely used in Eurasia to express status and rank (e.g., Linduff 2008; Brosseder 2011; Kost 2014). Especially during the Xiongnu period in Inner Asia, from the third century BCE to the first century CE, as well as in the more remote western regions of Eurasia, belts adorned with figuratively decorated plaques were widespread and popular. Belt plaques have long been studied, resulting in an abundant literature (Dèvlet 1980; Brosseder 2011; Kost 2014). While we cannot provide a comprehensive account of belt plaques in this chapter, we intend to bring together the available data from southern Siberia, Mongolia and northern China in order to provide context for the plaques in this collection, drawing heavily on previous studies (Brosseder 2011; Kost 2014). The metallurgical aspects of the belt plaques are discussed in Chapter 10.

The plaques treated here date from the third to first centuries BCE. They can be grouped in several ways, either by manufacturing process, by fastening and attachment method, or by decor motifs. Although each aspect provides a different perspective on this group of artifacts, there are significant overlaps.

One large group comprises plaques cast using the lost-wax, lost-textile method, while the other plaques were cast using "only" the lost-wax method. Furthermore, while the majority of plaques in the first group are solid cast belt plaques, those in the second group are generally openwork plaques. Moreover, one can also group the plaques according to the way they are attached to the belt. Among the plaques that are solid cast, there are a small number (entries 101, 102, and 116) that have three massive loops on the back: two horizontal loops at the outer end of the plaque and one vertical loop at the inner end, where the belt is closed. Most often, however, the solid plaques are attached to the belt with two vertical loops only. The circular or slender oval hole on the wearer's left-hand plaque is used to close the belt.

The openwork cast plaques, by contrast, for the most part have no loops on the back, as they can be sewn directly onto the belt fabric. The findings from burial 107 of Dyrestui (Miniaev 1998, pl. 87–88), in the Transbaikal area, as well as a plaque from the Sackler Collection (Bunker et al. 1997, 266, no. 233), show that those openwork bronze plaques were fixed onto a wooden frame. It is possible that this was the normal method for attaching the plaques to the belt, but because of the unfavorable preservation conditions for wood, the wooden backing has survived only in a few instances. Belts with openwork plaques usually have a stud on the wearer's left-hand plaque that is used to close the belt. Pairs of such belt plaques are usually worn by mature women of the Xiongnu confederation (Brosseder 2007; Linduff 2008). While these two general groups—solid plaques and openwork belt plaques—can be identified, some belt plaques exhibit features of both groups.

The presentation of the belt plaques in this chapter roughly mirrors the division into two large groups. The first entries of the first group (nos. 101–118) comprise those plaques which are solid cast using the lost-wax, lost-textile method. The following entries (119–124) contain belt plaques which are cast using the lost-wax method, some of them solid, others openwork, but which, from their design, can be attributed to the Ordos area. Mapping the types of belt plaques that have been found during excavations gives us a rough idea where the plaques from this collection might have come from (figs. 23 and 24). While the solid-cast rectangular plaques with various motifs are found between Liaoning province and southern China (fig. 23), the bovine-shaped plaques are known from a more restricted central area and are not known from Liaoning province or southern China, (fig. 24). Most of the solid plaques are also cast with a tin-leaded bronze, an aspect that will be further explored in Chapter 10.

The second group (entries 125–134) comprises the group of openwork plaques and small appliqué plaques (entry 135) attributed to the Xiongnu. If we map the plaques of these types contained in the collection, it reveals that they are known predominantly in the area stretching from southern Siberia, to Mongolia, to the regions of China north and west of the Taihang Mountains (figs. 25 and 26). Although they are also cast by the lost-wax method, one notices a variety of metallurgical recipes that were used, even for the same type of plaque, another aspect that will be discussed further in Chapter 10. The openwork plaques overlap with the previous group of belt plaques in Manchuria, Liaoning province, and in the Ordos region.

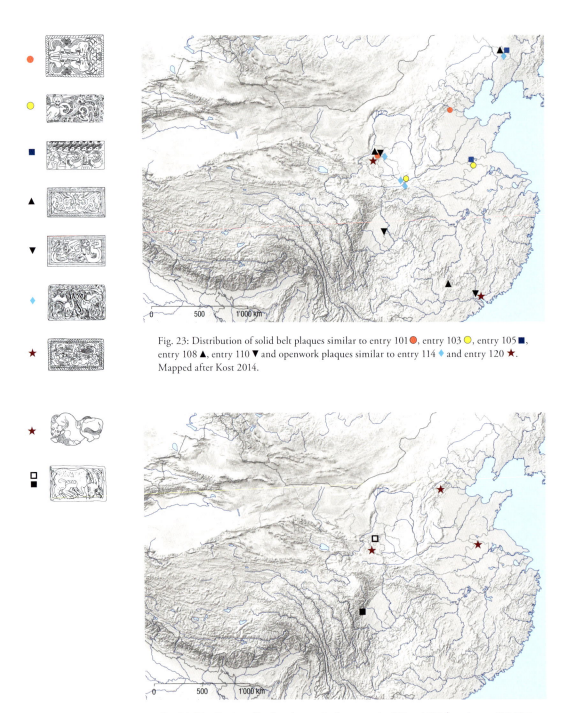

Fig. 23: Distribution of solid belt plaques similar to entry 101 ●, entry 103 ●, entry 105 ■, entry 108 ▲, entry 110 ▼ and openwork plaques similar to entry 114 ♦ and entry 120 ★. Mapped after Kost 2014.

Fig. 24: Distribution of bovine plaques similar to entries 116 and 117 ★ and entry 123 □ ■. Mapped after Kost 2014.

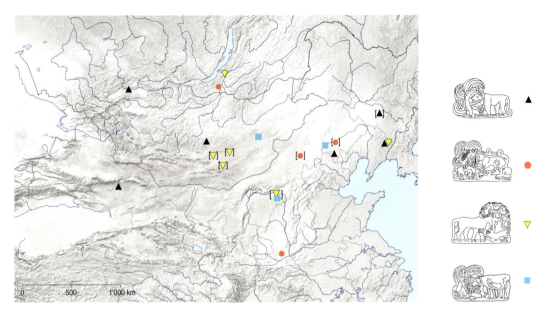

Fig. 25: Distribution of different types of P-shaped plaques similar to entry 125 ▲, entry 127 ●, entry 128 ▽ as well as one type that is not represented in this collection ■. Mapped after Brosseder 2011, 380–83, figs. 30; 31; 33, lists 6a–d.

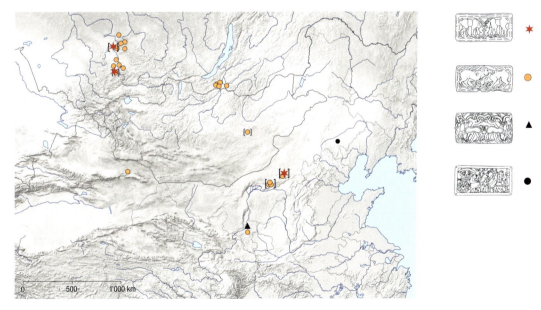

Fig. 26: Distribution of different types of rectangular openwork belt plaques similar to entry 129 ✱, entry 130 ●, entry 132 ▲ and entry 121 ●. Mapped after Brosseder 2011, 365, fig. 13, list 2a and after Kost 2014.

Chapter 4 | Han and Xiongnu Belt Plaques   285

101 | Pair of Belt Plaques with Tigers and Ungulates

Southwest Ordos and north China, east of the Taihang Mountains (Hebei province)
3rd–2nd century BCE

101a | Belt Plaque (left)
Height 7.5 cm
Width 10.6 cm
Weight 145.9 g
Cast bronze, alloy composition by E. Ferreira:
Cu 80.3%; Sn 4.1%; Pb 12.2%; As 0.5%; Fe 0.2%

101b | Belt Plaque (right)
Height 7.5 cm
Width 10.7 cm
Weight 157.4 g

Cast bronze, traces of silver foil, alloy composition by E. Ferreira:
Cu 76.9%; Sn 4.8%; Pb 16.4%; As 0.7%; Fe 0.1%

Both: Ex Therese and Erwin Harris Collection, Miami, Florida

Published:
So and Bunker 1995, 137–38, no. 56; 61, col. pl. 13

A pair of solid bronze plaques manufactured using the lost-wax, lost-textile method. They show two tigers attacking two recumbent ungulates with eared raptor-headed tails and horns opposite each other horizontally (Kost 2014, motif 26b1, pl. 46). The ungulate's bodies are marked by striated enclosures. The scene is bordered with a rope pattern. Plaque 101a has three loops on the back: Two are horizontal, while the third is placed vertically. Instead of the vertical loop, plaque 101b has a vertical opening. Under the microscope traces of silver foil and lead to fix the foil can be detected, indicating that the plaques were once covered with silver foil (So and Bunker 1995, 138).

The design of these bronze plaques and the manufacturing technique are similar to plaques from tomb 30 at Xinzhuangtou, Hebei province (Kost 2014 pl. 45.3; pl. 131A–D; 222, cat. 49) and from Daodunzi, tomb 5 in Ningxia province (Bunker et al. 1997, 84, fig. A124; Kost 2014, cat. 10.7–8; pl. 45.1–2). They provide a date between the late Warring State period and the late second century BCE. The plaques closest to them in terms of design are housed in the British Museum (Bunker et al. 1970, 128; 143, no. 109) and the Los Angeles County Museum of Art (Bunker 1981, 157, no. 836); however, the latter specimen turned out to be a fake, as an analysis by Pieter Meyers showed high zinc content.

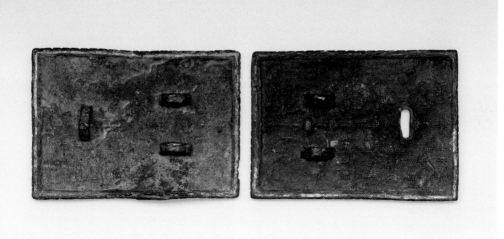

102 | Pair of Massive Belt Plaques

North China
3rd–2nd century BCE

102a | Belt Plaque (left)
Height 5.6 cm
Width 11.1 cm
Weight 114.6 g
Gilded cast bronze,
alloy composition
by E. Ferreira:
Cu 90.3%; Sn 1.4%;
As 0.1%

102b | Belt Plaque (right)
Height 5.5 cm
Width 11.1 cm
Weight 130.1 g
Gilded cast bronze,
alloy composition
by E. Ferreira:
Cu 80.6%; Sn 0.8%;
As 0.1%

This pair of heavy plaques, manufactured by the lost-wax, lost-textile method, depicts an attack scene, which is hard to identify because the bodies are heavily dismembered. A gazelle is being attacked by a wolf and a tiger; the animals are intertwined and their body parts inverted. Raptor-headed appendages are visible. The whole scene is fitted into the rectangular space of the plaque without a border. This borderless design and the way in which the animals are depicted compare favorably with the plaques in entry 103. The back reveals not only a comparatively thick frame but also three massive rectangular loops for attachment (see also entry 101). To our knowledge, no plaque of this type has been excavated.

103, 104 | Belt Plaques Depicting Ungulate, Wolf, and Bear

Central Plains and
north China
late 3rd–2nd century BCE

103a | Belt Plaque
Height 5.3 cm
Width 11.4 cm
Weight 69.5 g
Gilded cast bronze, alloy composition by J. Stenger:
Cu 80%; Sn 8%; Pb 3%; As trace

103b | Belt Plaque
Height 5.4 cm
Width 11.2 cm
Weight 66.6 g
Gilded cast bronze, alloy composition by E. Ferreira:
Cu 84.5%; Sn 9.3%; Pb 1.1%; As 0.2%; Fe 0.2%

104 | Belt Plaque
Height 5.9 cm
Width 12.2 cm
Weight 85.7 g
Gilded cast bronze, alloy composition by E. Ferreira:
Cu 91.9%; Sn 4.5%; Pb 1.1%; As 0.2%; Fe 0.2%

All three massive plaques are produced using the lost-wax, lost-textile process with remains of copper corrosion. All have two delicate vertical rectangular loops on the back side. This type has been treated in detail (Bunker 1989; Brosseder 2011, 355–57; list 1; Kost 2014, pl. 51–53.1–2; motif 28). The motif shows a fallen mythical ungulate with raptor-head appendages being attacked by a wolf and a bear. Plaques 103a and b form a pair: 103b is the wearer's left-hand plaque, which has a hole that has been punched through the wax model from the front, while 103a is the wearer's right-hand plaque. On the front bottom of plaque 104, remains of textile are visible, which represent the original piece of textile it was covered with and which has been replaced by copper-corrosion products.

Two similar plaques have been found in the burial of King Liu Wu, who reigned from 174 BCE until his death in 154 BCE, thus providing a reference date for these plaques. A plaque of this kind was also found in a burial in the southern Ural region, highlighting the interconnectedness of the steppe world during this time (Brosseder 2011, 356, fig. 3; 358, fig. 5; Brosseder and Miller 2018). A further pair belonged to the Therese and Erwin Harris Collection (So and Bunker 1995, 144, no. 64; Harris Collection 2017, 62–63, no. 857).

103 a 103 b

104

105, 106, 107 | Three Belt Plaques with Recumbent Wolf and Argali

Northeast China and Central Plains
3rd–2nd century BCE

105 | Belt Plaque (top)
Height 4.6 cm
Width 9.5 cm
Weight 64.8 g
Gilded cast bronze, alloy composition by E. Ferreira: Cu 78.0%; Sn 8.6%; Pb 8%; As 0.1%

106 | Belt Plaque (middle)
Height 4.5 cm
Width 9.5 cm
Weight 75.2 g
Gilded cast bronze, alloy composition by J. Stenger: Cu 66%; Sn 8%; Pb 10%; As trace
Ex Therese and Erwin Harris Collection, Miami, Florida, acquired in Paris, 1994; Christie's New York, 16 March 2017, lot 844
Published: So and Bunker 1995, 143, no. 63; Harris Collection 2017, 50, no. 844

107 | Belt Plaque (bottom)
Height 4.3 cm
Width 9 cm
Weight 58.2 g
Gilded cast bronze, alloy composition by J. Stenger: Cu 62%; Sn 9%; Pb 5%; As trace
Ex J. J. Lally & Co., New York, 3 October 1990; Therese and Erwin Harris Collection, Miami, Florida; Christie's, New York, 16 March 2017, lot 844
Published: So and Bunker 1995, 143, no. 63; Harris Collection 2017, 50, no. 844

All three plaques are of the same type. Although plaques 106 and 107 were both acquired from the Therese and Erwin Harris Collection and are both made of a similar alloy, they may not form an exact pair. Remarkably, plaque 107 was attached to the belt with two massive vertical loops, while the loops on plaques 106 and 105 are rather delicate. All three plaques display on the reverse an elevated rim and fabric imprints, the latter indicating that they were cast by the lost-wax, lost-textile method. Plaques 105 and 107 have a large circular hole, indicating that they are both the wearer's left-hand plaque, while plaque 106 is the wearer's right-hand plaque.

A recumbent wolf is depicted, with two coiled argali superimposed on its body. Above, we see a band of horned gazelle heads and a row of eared raptor heads. The whole scene is stylized and organized in design (Kost 2014, motif 7e). While most such plaques are known from collections (Andersson 1932, pl. 23.3; Ariadne Galleries 1998, 130–31; Bunker et al. 2002, 100, no. 67), one has been found in Xichagou, Liaoning province (Bunker et al. 1997, 78, fig. A110; Kost 2014, cat. 46.2). The motif is similarly depicted on a pair of golden plaques with a braided border from a kingly tomb in Bojishan, Jiangsu province, in the tomb of the marquis of Yi of Wanqu, who was the sixth son of the first king of Chu, thus providing us with a *terminus post quem* of 154 BCE (Kost 2014, 203, cat. 3.1–2, pl. 13.1–2). Their distribution is confined to the Central Plains and northeast China. Moreover, they all show a similar metallurgical composition of tin-leaded bronze.

108, 109 | Two Pairs of Belt Plaques with Symmetrically Arranged Ungulates

China, southern Ordos, Liaoning province
2nd century BCE

108a | Belt Plaque

Height 5.7 cm
Width 11 cm
Weight 62.9 g

Gilded cast bronze, alloy composition by E. Ferreira:
Cu 75.2%; Sn 11.9%; Pb 4.0%; As 0.3%; Fe 0.1%

The two pairs of gilded belt plaques are almost identical, but no. 108 has been produced using the lost-wax, lost-textile method, indicated by the textile structure visible on the back, while the manufacturing of no. 109 did not involve any textile. Each of them also has two delicate angular loops used to attach the plaques to the belt. Although the dimensions, shape, weight, alloy composition, and motif of nos. 108a and b are extremely similar, suggesting that they may have been produced as a pair, neither plaque has a hole for closing the belt. This raises the question of whether they were intended to constitute a pair. Nos. 109a and b have been produced and used as a pair, as one has such a fastening hole.

Two symmetrically arranged ungulates are depicted facing outward, with inverted hindlegs and raptor-headed appendages between them. Certain body parts are marked by striated curvilinear elements (Kost 2014, motif 18b; pl. 29–39). The scene is framed by a braided pattern. A similar pair of belt plaques is known from grave 19 at Daodunzi dating to the end of the second century BCE or the early first century BCE (Bunker et al. 1997, 83, fig. A122; Kost 2014, pl. 29.1–2; pl. 101). The motif also closely resembles those found on plaques from Xichagou (Kost 2014, pl. 28.4) and Yinshanling in Guangxi (Kost 2014, pl. 28.5); both plaques are, however, cast in higher relief. According to the few plaques that have been documented from excavations, such belt plaques are found in China, in the southern Ordos area, in Liaoning province, and as far south as Guangxi province (fig. 22; Kost 2014, 253, map 12, motif 18).

108 a

China, southern Ordos, Liaoning province
2nd century BCE

108b | Belt Plaque
Height 5.7 cm
Width 10.9 cm
Weight 59.7 g
Gilded cast bronze, alloy composition by E. Ferreira:
Cu 71.9%; Sn 9.6%; Pb 1.6%; As 0.2%; Fe 0.2%

109a | Belt Plaque
Height 5.5 cm
Width 10.9 cm
Weight 72.7 g
Gilded cast bronze, alloy composition by J. Stenger:
Cu 81%; Sn 3%; Pb 1%; As trace

109b | Belt Plaque
Height 5.4 cm
Width 10.9 cm
Weight 69.5 g
Gilded cast bronze, alloy composition by J. Stenger:
Cu 94%; Sn 4%; Pb 1%; As trace

108 b

109a 109b

110, 111 | Belt Plaques and Gold Sheet with Tiger Attacking Ram

Southwest Ordos to
Guangdong province
2nd century BCE

110a | Belt Plaque
Height 4.9 cm
Width 10.2 cm
Weight 93.8 g
Cast bronze,
alloy composition
by E. Ferreira:
Cu 73.8%; Sn 12%;
Pb 7.7%; As 0.5%;
Fe 0.2%

110b | Belt Plaque
Height 4.9 cm
Width 10 cm
Weight 91.9 g
Cast bronze,
alloy composition
by E. Ferreira:
Cu 76.4%; Sn 12.1%;
Pb 11.2%; As 0.2%;
Fe 0.2%

111 | Gold Repoussé Sheet
Height 4.2 cm
Width 9.2 cm
Weight 8.5 g
Gold, alloy composition
by P. Meyers:
Au 94%; Cu 1%; Ag 4.8%

The pair of belt plaques 110 are cast by the lost-wax, lost-textile method. Each has an elevated rim on the back and two thick, round attachment loops arranged vertically. The orientation of the design is not mirrored, but rather identical, raising the question of whether they had been cast to form an exact pair. No. 110b has a large, round hole and constitutes the wearer's left-hand plaque. The gold repoussé sheet (no. 111) was created to fit over a bronze plaque. The four corners each have two small holes for attachment punched through the gold from the front. It is adorned with the same combat scene as plaques 110, in which a horned ram is being attacked by a tiger with a heart-shaped ear, which is biting the ram in the back (Kost 2014, motif 27, 254, map 14). Both animals have tails that terminate in a raptor's head and hindquarters inverted 180 degrees. Striated curvilinear designs that mark the body derive from wood-carving or leather-working traditions traceable to the Altai and/or related cultures. Plaques of this kind are found in Daodunzi in Ningxia province, grave 19 (Ningxia et al. 1988, 344, fig. 9.12), as well as in the grave of the king of Nanyue in Guangzhou, who died in 122 BCE (Huang Zhanyue 1996, 55–60, fig. 1) and grave 3 in Xiufengcun in Sichuan (Kost 2014, cat. 50; pl. 128.2; 129). Several similar pieces, either gilded or bronze, are known from different collections (e.g., Bunker et al. 2002, 131, no. 103). A similar gold repoussé example was published by Miniaev and Smolarski (2002, 74, no. 59) with no specific provenance.

110 a　　　　　　　　110 b

111

112, 113 | Belt Plaques Depicting Animals in Mountainous Landscape

Central Plains and South China
late 2nd century BCE

112 | Belt Plaque

Height 6.2 cm
Width 12.5 cm
Weight 100.5 g

Gilded cast bronze, alloy composition by E. Ferreira:
Cu 76%; Sn 12.9%; Pb 2%; As 0.1%; Fe 0.2%

A complex, mountainous landscape populated with animals and birds distinguishes these two gilded-bronze belt plaques from the previously discussed examples and appears to represent a favorite *xiangrui* design. Asian elm trees growing along the peaks of stylized mountains provide an idyllic setting for a variety of non-threatening wildlife. A bear facing inward stands at each of the plaque's upper corners, while a tiger and a wild boar appear below the mountains at the bottom of the plaque. This may indicate that the origins of Chinese landscape painting, a subject that came to define "Chineseness," owes a curious debt to dynastic China's pastoral neighbors, whose mountainous world populated with wild animals was referenced in their art and constituted their material means of survival, but was not yet a typical subject matter. See also Chapter 3d, pp. 255–65, on the development of the *qin*-zither (Jacobson 1985; So and Bunker 1995, 72–74).

Although almost identical in design, these two plaques may not form a functional set, as they are slightly different in size and one is considerably heavier than the other. The reverse of each plaque displays two vertical attachment loops and has the characteristic woven pattern produced by the lost-wax, lost-textile casting process. Plaque 112 reveals two pairs of tiny holes in the middle that were probably used to repair the break visible on the back (stabilized today with nylon web and adhesive).

The scene on these ornaments is highly unusual. If the plaques were made for a Chinese aristocrat with a taste for exotica, they might represent animals living in harmony with nature, a favorite *xiangrui* (auspicious) design typified by fantastic craggy landscape with wild animals (Sturman 1985b, 1–17; Sturman 1985c, 1–12). The braided borders are known all the way from southern China up to the southern Ordos area (Kost 2014, 262, map 29), pointing to Chinese production, while the subject matter reflects Western Han ideology. The "correlative thinking" characteristic of the early Han period was frequently expressed in terms of animals and mountains, as in the following passage from the *Shiji* (Records of the Grand Historian, of ca. 90 BCE): "As … wild beasts congregate in the most

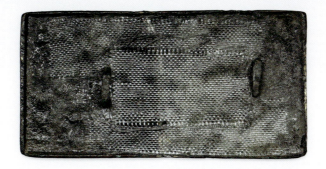

Central Plains and South China
late 2nd century BCE

113 | Belt Plaque

Height 6.1 cm
Width 12.2 cm
Weight 91.8 g

Gilded cast bronze, alloy composition by E. Ferreira: Cu 70.3%; Sn 16.2%; Pb 6.7%; As 0.3%; Fe 0.1%

secluded mountains, so benevolence and righteousness attach themselves to a man of wealth" (quoted by Sturman 1985b, 67). As Peter Sturman explains, "the beginnings of the description of landscape in China relied first upon a symbolic mode of representation. It was what the landscape was understood to be, a cultural perception, quite distinct from objective observation, that defined its representation in art" (Sturman 1985b, 67). Further zoomorphic *xiangrui* are mentioned in a second-century BCE *fu* (rhapsody), in which the author describes Han Wudi's magnificent Shanglin hunting park near present-day Xi'an (Sturman 1985a, 3–5).

A similar pair of plaques comes from the Borowski Collection (Jäger and Kansteiner 2011, 23–24, no. 14), but since no parallels are known from excavations, their cultural context remains unknown. A plaque with a less fluid landscape and more animals was excavated from a late Western Han tomb at Shuanggudui in Anhui province, central China (Kost 2014, pl. 37.1; pl. 124A). A source for the mountain design appears on a Han-dynasty Daoist silk textile excavated from Noyon Uul, northern Mongolia (Hermitage 2014, 59; 100, no. 4), and dated to the late Western Han period. The Noyon Uul textile includes an immortal on a winged horse galloping through swirling clouds, whereas the swirling forms on the plaques appear to be mountains, given the presence of trees.

114 | Openwork Belt Plaques with Symmetrically Arranged Camels

Southwest Ordos to Liaoning province
ca. 2nd century BCE

114a | Belt Plaque (left)
Height 4.4 cm
Width 9.1 cm
Weight 61.1 g
Gilded bronze, alloy composition by J. Stenger:
Cu 79%; Sn 6%; Pb 3%

114b | Belt Plaque (right)
Width 9.1 cm
Weight 65.6 g
Gilded bronze, alloy composition by J. Stenger:
Cu 88%; Sn 6%; Pb 6%; As trace

Ex J. J. Lally & Co., New York, 17 February 1990; Therese and Erwin Harris Collection, Miami, Florida; Christie's New York, March 16 2017, lot 859

Published:
Harris Collection 2017, 65, no. 859

A pair of openwork plaques manufactured by the lost-wax, lost-textile method, as indicated by faint traces of textile patterns on the reverse. Two thin, angular loops are arranged vertically on the backside. Both belt plaques have a round hole on one short side. Two confronting Bactrian camels are depicted, flanking and nibbling on an Asian elm tree (Bunker et al. 2002, 102, no. 79; Kost 2014, motif 15b–c). The camels are shown realistically in profile. The scene is framed with a braided-rope pattern. The closest parallel to this pair of plaques does not come from an excavation, but is rather part of the Eugene V. Thaw Collection of the Metropolitan Museum (acc. nos. 2002.201.104 and 105). It exhibits the same details in the depiction and is also gilded (Bunker et al. 2002, 109–10, no. 79). Simpler openwork plaques depicting a pair of camels facing each other are known from Xi'an, Xichagou, Dabaiyang and Daodunzi (Kost 2014, cat. 45.1; 46.4; 7.1; 11.3), stretching from Liaoning province in the northeast to the southwestern part of the Ordos (Kost 2014, map 11, motif 15).

115 | Belt Plaque with Kneeling Camel and Man

Western Inner Mongolia
3rd–1st century BCE

Height 5 cm
Width 8.3 cm
Weight 56.2 g

Cast gilded bronze, alloy composition by E. Ferreira:
Cu 66.4%; Sn 4.3%; Pb 3.2%; Fe 0.1%

This gilded belt plaque was cast by the lost-wax, lost-textile technique and has a single vertically arranged attachment loop on the reverse; the second one has broken off. This plaque is the wearer's left-hand plaque of a mirror-image pair of plaques. The motif shows a semi-kneeling Bactrian camel, with a man peering between the two humps while gripping them with his hands. The man has a round face and the camel's body is marked by striated enclosures. Such plaques are exclusively known from collections, such as the Nasli M. Heeramaneck Collection in the Los Angeles County Museum (Bunker 1981, 157, no. 837; So and Bunker 1995, 141–42, no. 61), from the Ariadne Galleries (1998, 132–33 no. 142), the National Museum Tokyo (Kokuritsu Hakubutsukan 2005, 151, no. TJ-5663), and the British Museum (unpublished). The tin-leaded bronze recipe is typically Chinese and the one in the Los Angeles County Museum is also made of a tin-lead bronze, as Pieter Meyers has established.

116 | Bovine-shaped Massive Plaque

East of Taihang Mountains, southwest Ordos and Central Plains
3rd–2nd century BCE

Height 7 cm
Width 12 cm
Weight 127 g

Cast gilded bronze, alloy composition by E. Ferreira: Cu 73%; Sn 10%; Pb 10.8%; As 0.5%

Ex Therese and Erwin Harris Collection, Miami, Florida

Published: So and Bunker 1995, 140–41, no. 59a

This yak-shaped plaque was manufactured using the lost-wax, lost-textile method. On the reverse there are three massive round loops: two near the rump of the animal, arranged horizontally, and one at the head, attached vertically. This system of attachment is the same as that found on the massive belt plaques in entries 101 and 102 of this chapter. It seems that this fastening system is restricted to the Central Plains and the southern Ordos area. Depicted is a bovine animal, probably a yak with the tail and other hair represented by fine lines. Most such plaques are known from collections, but one very similar plaque has been found near Shijiazhuang in Hebei province, which could potentially be the missing mirror plaque (So and Bunker 1995, 140; Kost 2014, motif 1b2).

117, 118 | Three Bovine-shaped Plaques

East Taihang range, southwest Ordos, Central Plains
3rd–2nd century BCE

117 | Bovine-shaped Plaque
Height 5.8 cm
Width 9.9 cm
Weight 97.3 g
Gilded cast bronze,
alloy composition
by E. Ferreira:
Cu 87.6%; Sn 5.0%;
Pb 0.7%; As 0.2%; Fe 0.2%

118a | Bovine-shaped Plaque
Height 5.2 cm
Width 9.4 cm
Weight 82.1 g
Gilded cast bronze,
alloy composition
by E. Ferreira:
Cu 66.5%; Sn 6.0%;
Pb 3.9%; As 0.2%; Fe 0.1%

118b | Bovine-shaped Plaque
Height 5.1 cm
Width 9.3 cm
Weight 86.8 g
Gilded cast bronze,
alloy composition
by E. Ferreira:
Cu 71.2%; Sn 8.8%;
Pb 7.3%; As 0.3%; Fe 0.2%

The three plaques are very similar. Each shows a bovine with its head turned downward and slightly back toward the rump. The facial features are represented naturalistically, the body of each bovine is marked by ridges and emphasized by means of striated curvilinear elements (Kost 2014, motif 1b2; pl. 3.2–5.2). On the back, two delicate, vertical rounded thin loops aid attachment. While the first one (no. 117) is cast with the lost-wax method and a lower amount of lead, the pair (nos. 118a and b) are manufactured using the lost-wax, lost-textile method. Plaque 118a is the wearer's left-hand plaque, with a larger fastening hole than the other two plaques. Plaque 117 is very similar to those found in Subao, Ningxia province, and Shouzhou, Anhui province (So and Bunker 1995, 140, no. 59b; Kost 2014, 219, cat. 4; pl. 3.2). Numerous similar belt plaques are known from various collections and museums, for example from the Museum of Far Eastern Antiquities in Stockholm (Karlbeck 1955, 97, pl. 32.1–2) and from the Eugene V. Thaw Collection of the Metropolitan Museum (Bunker et al. 2002, 98–99, no. 65). All bovine-shaped plaques have been found either in the Central Plains or in the south of the Ordos bend.

117

118a 118b

119 | Openwork Belt Plaque with Camel

North China
2nd–1st century BCE

Height 5.5 cm
Width 8.9 cm
Weight 89.3 g

Cast bronze, alloy composition by E. Ferreira: Cu 86.4%; Sn 6%; Pb 14.4%; As 0.5%

A Bactrian camel is shown in half-crouching position within a rectangular frame which appears to be decorated with a rope pattern. The reverse is flat with a single vertical round loop behind the rump of the camel and an elongated opening for fastening the belt below the camel's head. A similar example, albeit gilded, is known from the Eugene V. Thaw Collection (Bunker et al. 2002, 138, no. 111) which shows many more details that can be linked to Western Han elite tombs in Hebei and Guangdong provinces (Bunker et al. 2002, 138). To our knowledge, no such plaque is known from archaeological contexts. Depictions of camels on belt plaques are common in northern China (Kost 2014, 258, map 22), Central Asia, and the Black Sea (Korolkova 2006; Brosseder 2011, 385, fig. 35). The metal composition is a high leaded tin bronze with a small amount of arsenic.

120 | Openwork Belt Plaques with Two Tortoises

Southwest Ordos,
Guangdong province
2nd century BCE

120a | Belt Plaque (left)
Height 4.7 cm
Width 8.9 cm
Weight 60.1 g
Gilded bronze,
alloy composition
not analyzed

120b | Belt Plaque (right)
Height 4.7 cm
Width 8.9 cm
Weight 53.3 g
Gilded bronze,
alloy composition
not analyzed

The design displays a large dragon with a figure-eight-shaped body wrapped around two tortoises (So and Bunker 1995, 158, no. 80; Bunker et al. 2002, 130, no. 102; Kost 2014, motif 22; 254, map 13; pl. 36). The dragon has a lupine head seen in profile which is depicted in a similar manner as seen on the plaques in entry 133. The workmanship is exquisite, with all of the details finely represented. This is the finest pair of this type known so far. Neither of the plaques exhibits a stud on the front functioning as a hook. The two plaques are identical, with a small hole on the left side for fastening, as if they were cast from the same mold. Thus, they are not mirror images. On the flat back is a thick rim and two round vertical loops, in order to attach the plaques to the belt.

From excavations, such belt plaques have been found in grave 14 of Daodunzi in Ningxia province (Kost 2014, cat. 10.17–18; pl. 100) and in the grave of the king of Nanyue in Guangdong province (Kost 2014, cat. 16; pl. 103–4). Belt plaques depicting tortoises have never been found farther north and are unknown from the north loop of the Huanghe, west of the Taihang Mountains, Mongolia, or the Transbaikal region. The depiction of the serpentine-bodied dragon either fighting with another dragon or being attacked by a tiger is, however, well known farther north, from Xiongnu-period burials (Brosseder 2011, 379, fig. 28).

121 | Openwork Plaque with Scene of Cart and Men

Northeast China
2nd–1st century BCE

Height 5.8 cm
Width 11.2 cm
Weight 62.6 g

Bronze, alloy composition by E. Ferreira: Cu 78.6%; Sn 3.7%; Pb 3.6%; As 11%; Fe 3.7%

Ex Eugene V. Thaw Collection, New York and Santa Fe

This belt plaque depicts a northeast-Asian pastoral family on the move. A man dressed in a belted jacket worn over loose trousers tucked into boots is walking ahead of a wheeled cart. The outdoor setting is established by the stylized leafy tree branches behind the man and the cart. The cart has spoked wheels and is drawn by one or two horses and driven by a person seated in the cart. There are two horse heads visible but only four legs, which makes it impossible to determine the number of horses. This is not only true for the piece in this collection, but also for the one found in the Los Angeles County Museum (Bunker 1981, 186, no. 886), as well as for the plaque from the Liu Collection (Miniaev and Smolarski 2002, 84–85, no. 69–70). The cart is covered and described by some as having people inside, but the casting is too blurred to make out such details (So and Bunker 1995, 91, no. 3; Miniaev and Smolarski 2002, 84–85, no. 69–70). The present plaque was originally the proper right-hand plaque of a pair, in which the left-hand plaque carried the projecting hook used to close the buckle. The present plaque once belonged to the Eugene V. Thaw Collection and was separated in 2004 from its matching plaque, which is in the Metropolitan Museum, because its function was not understood by those involved. The way in which the cart is harnessed to the horse looks suspicious, but the metallurgy of a tin-leaded bronze with arsenic is typical for Inner Asian belt plaques (see Chapter 10).

One such plaque comes from Paozi, Ongniud banner, Inner Mongolia, northeast China, but no excavation report is published (Kost 2014, cat. 31; pl. 84.1–2). The high arsenic content of the otherwise tin-leaded copper alloy is noteworthy, as is the flat back without a rim. Such flat backs are also seen on plaques in the following entries (123 and 124).

122 | Belt Plaque with Combat between Feline and Carnivore

Probably western Inner Mongolia
3rd century BCE

Height 3.7 cm
Width 6.3 cm
Weight 38.7 g

Cast bronze, alloy composition by E. Ferreira: Cu 70.8%; Sn 4.1%; Pb 22.8%; As 0.5%; Fe 0.1%

This left-hand openwork belt plaque has a stud projecting from one short edge in front. On the uneven backside is a thick rim and only a single massive angular loop. The casting process left raised borders around the openwork holes on the backside. Depicted is a combat between a beak-headed feline and horned carnivore head. The border is a coarse braided pattern. A plaque of this kind is known from the Nasli M. Heeramaneck Collection of the Los Angeles County Museum (Bunker 1981, 157, no. 839; Kost 2014, pl. 48.5). A mirror-image plaque, the wearer's right-hand plaque, was published by Ariadne Galleries (1998, 136, no. 146). The coarse depiction resembles a small, solid plaque in the Metropolitan Museum (Bunker et al. 2002, no. 100). While similar plaques have not been recovered from excavated contexts, the coarse depiction is reminiscent of wood carvings of the Pazyryk culture, such as the coarse braided pattern employed for belt plaques from Olon-Guriin gol 10, gr. 1 (Parzinger et al. 2009, 208, fig. 11; 213, fig. 17; Molodin et al. 2012, 478, fig. 48; 485, fig. 55). The leaded tin bronze with low levels of arsenic and the fastening stud point to a steppe production.

123 | Small Rectangular Bovine Plaques

North China
3rd–2nd century BCE

123a | Belt Plaque (left)
Height 4.5 cm
Width 7.7 cm
Weight 82.9 g
Cast bronze,
alloy composition
by E. Ferreira:
Cu 86.7%; Sn 4.4%;
Pb 1%; As 0.1%; Fe 0.2%

123b | Belt Plaque (right)
Height 4.4 cm
Width 7.5 cm
Weight 82.2 g
Cast bronze,
alloy composition
by E. Ferreira:
Cu 85.9%; Sn 5.9%;
Pb 2.6%; As 0.2%;
Fe 0.1%

This pair of small, rectangular massive belt plaques is cast using the lost-wax method. It was attached to the belt with two round loops. The backside is flat, without an elevated rim and this differentiates these plaques from other massive plaques that often display an elevated rim on the back. Plaque 123b, the wearer's left-hand plaque, has a small circular hole. On each plaque, a bovine head is turned full frontal, while one front leg is folded, in a posture just like that of the shaped bovine plaques discussed earlier (entries 116–118), while the rectangular form recalls the small openwork plaques depicting standing oxen (e.g., Bunker et al. 2002, 99, no. 66; Kost 2014, pl. 1–2). A pair similar in size to no. 123 have been excavated at Shiyang in Sichuan (Kost 2014, pl. 2.7–8; cat. 36). Coins from this site include the earliest Qin-dynasty *banliang* coins, thus providing a *terminus post quem* of 122 BCE (Kost 2014, 217, cat. 36). Another pair with the same image is associated with Inner Mongolia (Miniaev and Smolarski 2002, 94, no. 82). Apart from the plaques in Sichuan, bovine plaques are known from the southwestern Ordos region, from Hebei province, as well as from central China (see entries 116–118).

124 | Small Plaques with Beak-headed Ungulate

North China
3rd–2nd century BCE

124a | Belt Plaque (left)
Height 5 cm
Width 7.8 cm
Weight 85.8 g
Gilded cast bronze,
alloy composition
by E. Ferreira:
Cu 95.1%, Sn 1.9%;
Fe 0.2%

124b | Belt Plaque (right)
Height 5 cm
Width 7.8 cm
Weight 73.9 g
Cast gilded bronze,
alloy composition
by J. Stenger:
Cu 95%, Sn 2%, Pb <1%

This pair of small rectangular gilded bronze plaques is cast by the lost-wax method. The reverse is completely flat, just like the reverse of the previously discussed plaques. No. 124b is the wearer's left-hand plaque, with a circular hole for fastening the belt. It was attached by means of two vertical, round loops. The back of plaque 124a displays only one loop; the second one has broken off. Instead, two small holes were punched through the front to allow the plaque to be fastened to the belt fabric.

Depicted is a beak-headed ungulate with bird-headed tail and antler, as well as cloven hooves. The posture with the front legs bent down is similar to the camel's on the plaque in entry 119. A similar design is seen on one of the casting models from a bronze caster's tomb found near Beikang village, in the northern suburbs of Xi'an, Shaanxi province, dated to late fourth and third century BCE (Shaanxi 2003, 6, fig. 5; 8, fig. 10.1).

125, 126 | P-Shaped Plaques with Combat between Griffin and Feline

Northeast China,
Mongolia, Tuva
2nd – early 1st century
BCE

125a | Belt Plaque (left)
Height 7.6 cm
Width 11.8 cm
Weight 86 g
Bronze,
alloy composition
by E. Ferreira:
Cu 75.2%; Sn 6.9%;
Pb 11.1%; As 0.8%;
Fe 0.2%

125b | Belt Plaque (right)
Height 7.6 cm
Width 11.9 cm
Weight 95.2 g
Bronze,
alloy composition
by E. Ferreira:
Cu 82.6%; Sn 6.2%;
Pb 10.7%; As 0.8%;
Fe 0.2%

These two pairs of belt plaques depict a battle between a griffin and a feline (Kost 2014, motif 24a, Brosseder 2011, 380, fig. 30; 421–22, list 6a). All four paws are visible and placed in a row along the baseline, one after the other, in a way reminiscent of the feline on plaque 46. The body parts of the animals, such as the mouth, eyes, and wings are represented by low ribs, with the ears depicted by a circle. Plaques 126a and b have a much higher arsenic content in the alloy. They are also more massively cast than 125a and b, which have a higher lead content. A plaque of this type has been excavated in Urbiun III in Tuva with a copper-tin-arsenic alloy (Brosseder 2011, 380, fig. 29). In China, such plaques have been excavated in Chifeng city and Xichagou, in Liaoning province.

Northeast China, Mongolia, Tuva
2nd – early 1st century BCE

126a | Belt Plaque
Height 7.6 cm
Width 12.3 cm
Weight 65.3 g
Cast bronze, alloy composition by J. Stenger:
Cu 58%; Sn 9%; Pb 3%; As high

126b | Belt Plaque
Height 7.8 cm
Width 12.2 cm
Weight 79.1 g
Cast bronze, alloy composition by J. Stenger:
Cu 63%; Sn 11%; Pb 2%; As high

Ex Christie's London, 10 December 1990, lot 14; Therese and Erwin Harris Collection, Miami, Florida: Christie's New York, 16 March 2017, lot 842

Published: Christie's 1990, 22–23, no. 14; Harris Collection 2017, 48, no. 842

126a

126b

127 | P-Shaped Plaque with Tiger, Griffin, and Ungulate

Transbaikal area, northeast China, Ordos
2nd–1st century BCE

Height 6.6 cm
Width 10.6 cm
Weight 71.7 g

Cast bronze, alloy composition by E. Ferreira: Cu 88.9%; Sn 3.1%; Pb 3.1%; As 0.6%; Fe 0.1%

Ex Therese and Erwin Harris Collection, Miami, Florida

Published: So and Bunker 1995, 166–67, no. 91

This bronze P-shaped plaque has a stud on the front, at the center of the short edge near the tip of the griffin's wing, and is therefore the wearer's left-hand plaque. It depicts a scene of animal combat involving three animals: a winged griffin and a tiger with a raptor-head mane attack their fallen prey, an ungulate with a long horn (Kost 2014, motif 24c; Brosseder 2011, 381, fig. 31; list 6c). A pair of similar plaques have been excavated from grave 7 at the Xiongnu cemetery, Dyrestui, in the Transbaikal region, dating to the second to first half of the first century BCE (Miniaev 1998, pl. 2.16.17; Davydova and Miniaev 2008, 52–53).

128 | P-shaped Plaque with Ungulate and Carnivore

Transbaikal area, Mongolia, northeast China
late 2nd – first half 1st century BCE

Height 7.6 cm
Width 11.5 cm
Weight 93 g

Cast bronze, alloy composition by E. Ferreira: Cu 103.1%; Sn 2.4%; Pb 2,5%; As 0.8%; Fe 0,2%

Cast using the lost-wax method, this plaque shows a fantastic ungulate with a beak and stylized antlers decorated with raptor heads. A small carnivore bites the chest (Kost 2014, motif 33). A small stud above the carnivore's tail indicates that it constitutes the wearer's left-hand plaque. The reverse is flat. An almost-identical plaque was discovered at Xichagou (Kost 2014, pl. 57.1); although no context is known for this cemetery, the *wuzhu* coins indicate a rough timeframe of the later second to first century BCE. The design is very similar to the Verkhneudinsk gold plaque in the Hermitage Museum which is cast using the lost-wax, lost-textile method (Rudenko 1966, pl. 27.1; Bunker 1992a). These plaques are found mainly in Mongolia, in northeast China, and in the Transbaikal area (Brosseder 2011, 382–83, fig. 33; list 6d).

129 | Rectangular Openwork Belt Plaque with Two Horses

Minusinsk Basin, north China
2nd–1st century BCE

Height 4.9 cm
Width 10.7 cm
Weight 69.5 g

Bronze, alloy composition by E. Ferreira:
Cu 85.9%; Sn 2.3%; Pb 5.7%; As 0.6%; Fe 0.2%

Ex Therese and Erwin Harris Collection, Miami, Florida

A rectangular, bronze, openwork belt plaque depicts two grazing horses in mirror-image arrangement within a rectangular frame punctuated by small rectangular indentations. The back displays a flat rim, with the bodies of the horses as depressions. The present plaque was originally the proper right-hand plaque of a matched pair forming a complete buckle. Similar plaques are housed in collections worldwide (e.g., Bunker et al. 1970, 136, no. 126; Bunker 1981, 169, no. 884; Jäger and Kansteiner 2011, 36, no. 36). Apart from these single finds without context, we know that two plaques of this type have been found in southern Siberia, in the Minusinsk Basin, for one we even know the site where it was found (Dévlet 1980, 43, nos. 20–22; Bunker et al. 1997, 270, no. 237). Rectangular indentations on the border are typical for openwork plaques from that area as well (Dévlet 1980, pl. 1–10; Brosseder 2011, 370, fig. 18). All of this points to the present plaque having an origin in southern Siberia. The metal composition of the plaque from this collection is a tin-lead-arsenic alloy which is typical of Xiongnu plaques. The plaque in the Sackler collection is, however, cast with a tin-lead alloy (Chase and Douglas 1997, 314, chapter 8B, acc. no. V-7025). Where this piece was produced cannot be determined with certainty.

130 | Rectangular Openwork Plaque with Two Fighting Stallions

Mongolia
2nd–1st century BCE

Height 6.3 cm
Width 11.5 cm
Weight 93.3 g

Bronze, alloy composition by E. Ferreira:
Cu 87.3%; Sn 3.6%; Pb 4.2%; As 0.6%; Fe 0.1%

This plaque represents a fight between two stallions under a leafy tree, within a rectangular frame punctuated by small rectangular and oval indentations. The present plaque has a projecting hook on the front, indicating that it was the proper left-hand plaque of a pair. The closest analogy to this design was found in eastern Mongolia and looks like the mirror-image plaque corresponding to this piece (Bunker et al. 1997, 261, fig. 224.1). Generally, plaques depicting two fighting horses are found widely throughout the Minusinsk Basin and the Transbaikal region. They are less typical for the Ordos area, and one plaque comes from eastern Xinjiang (Brosseder 2011, 364–70; 365, fig. 13). One belt buckle consisting of two mirror-image plaques displaying the same scene comes from graves 107 and 102 in the Dyrestui cemetery in the Transbaikal region (Davydova and Miniaev 2008, 73–80; Brosseder 2011, 366–67, figs. 14–15). The plaque from Dyrestui grave 107 had a wooden back, which suggests that a colored textile, perhaps felt, was inserted behind it to imitate inlay (Miniaev 1998, pl. 88). The bronze alloy with tin, lead, and arsenic is typical for the Xiongnu.

131 | Small Openwork Plaques with Fighting Stallions

Transbaikal area, Mongolia, Ordos
2nd–1st century BCE

131a | Belt Plaque (left)
Height 3.3 cm
Width 5.3 cm
Weight 17.4 g
Cast gilded bronze, alloy composition by J. Stenger:
Cu 92%; Sn 1%; Pb 7%; As trace

131b | Belt Plaque (right)
Height 3.3 cm
Width 5.2 cm
Weight 17.4 g
Cast gilded bronze, alloy composition by J. Stenger:
Cu 97%; Sn 1%; Pb 10%; As high

Ex Therese and Erwin Harris Collection, Miami, Florida, by 1995; Christie's New York, 16 March 2017, lot 858

Published: So and Bunker 1995, 95, no. 8; Harris Collection 2017, 64, no. 858

Each of the gilded openwork plaque depicts two fighting stallions with leaves on the top and bottom visible, indicating an outdoor setting. One horse bites the other on the back, while his opponent snaps at his leg. All four legs of each of the horses are shown. These plaques are about half the size of the other openwork belt plaques and they do not form a typical pair with one having a hook in the front. Instead, both plaques appear identical and may have been cast from the same model by the lost-wax process (So and Bunker 1995, 95, no. 8). A similar, but ungilded openwork plaque is known from the Sackler Collections (Bunker et al. 1997, 263, no. 226).

Large plaques with two fighting stallions without the gilding have been found in the Minusinsk Basin, in the Transbaikal area, and in Mongolia. A few pieces also come from the Ordos area (Brosseder 2011, 365, fig. 13; list 2a). Openwork plaques of this kind with various animal-combat scenes are characteristic of the later second and first century BCE in Inner Asia. They mostly adorn the belts of mature women (Brosseder 2007; Linduff 2008). The smaller openwork plaques adorn the belt alongside the large plaques at the front (see Leus 2011, 534, fig. 17). Only rarely were these plaques gilded, but we know of one such example from grave 102 at Dyrestui (Brosseder 2011, 366–67, figs. 14–15). Openwork plaques of this kind were produced using various copper alloys, with copper-arsenic alloys predominating in the Minusinsk Basin, while a recipe containing tin, lead, and arsenic predominated in the Transbaikal region and in Mongolia.

132 | Rectangular Openwork Belt Plaque with Two Rams

Southwest Ordos
late 2nd–1st century BCE

Height 6.3 cm
Width 11.8 cm
Weight 107.4 g

Cast bronze, alloy composition by E. Ferreira: Cu 76.6%; Sn 5.3%; Pb 11.4%; As 0.6%; Fe 0.2%

This plaque is the wearer's right-hand plaque of what was originally a mirror-image pair. It depicts two rams in a naturalistic setting, as indicated by a leafy tree behind each ram (Kost 2014, motif 12b; pl. 19.2–3; 20). These animals have been traditionally called caprids (goat images distinguished by a beard), but since we see no evidence of beards, they are now labelled rams (horned sheep). The border is marked on three sides by leaf-like indentations. It was cast using the lost-wax method from a model formed in a mold (Bunker et al. 1997, 205). One example was collected in Ningxia, near the excavation of a tomb at Lijiataozi, Tongxin county in Ningxia province, together with *wuzhu* coins that were not minted before 118 BCE (Ningxia 1988; Beifang 1995, 39; 86 no. 122; Kost 2014, pl. 19.2). Numerous similar plaques are found in collections worldwide, such as in the Sackler Collections (Bunker et al. 1997, 265, no. 231b), Ariadne Galleries (1998, 88, no. 91), the Borowski Collection (Jäger and Kansteiner 2011, 35–36, no. 33–34), the Tokyo National Museum (Kokuritsu Hakubutsukan 2005, 153, no. 8–9) and the Los Angeles County Museum of Art (Bunker 1981, 164–65, no. 875). A variant of this type exhibits the same composition, with a third animal in frontal view between the two rams (e.g., Bunker et al. 2002, 136, no. 108). The metal of this plaque is a lead-tin-arsenic alloy typical of the Xiongnu in Inner Asia.

133 | Openwork Plaques with Dragon-shaped Creature

Transbaikal area,
Mongolia,
northeast China
2nd–1st century BCE

133a | Belt Plaque (left)
Height 5.9 cm
Width 11.3 cm
Weight 73.2 g
Bronze,
alloy composition
by E. Ferreira:
Cu 89.9%; Sn 2.4%;
Pb 1.6%; As 5.8%;
Fe 0.2%

133b | Belt Plaque (right)
Height 5.8 cm
Width 11.3 cm
Weight 76 g
Bronze,
alloy composition
by E. Ferreira:
Cu 45.4%; Sn 1.8%;
Pb 1.4%; As 3.9%;
Fe 0.1%

Each of these plaques depicts two fantastic creatures with serpentine bodies, clawed limbs, and horned, lupine heads biting each other's tails. This pair of plaques is unique and no exact analogies are known to us. The arsenic-tin-lead-copper alloy is typical for belt plaques of the Xiongnu and suggests that they were produced in the Transbaikal region or in Mongolia.

Plaques depicting similar confronted dragons biting each other have been found in tomb 118 in the Dyrestui cemetery of Buryatia (Davydova and Miniaev 2008, 95–96). Similar belt plaques are also known from Zorgol-I in eastern Transbaikal area, as well as in Daodunzi (Brosseder 2011, 379, fig. 28, green dots) and Toupaizi (Kost, 2014, cat. 42.1, pl. 34.3). A version of this plaque's design that has to a large extent disintegrated is seen on a plaque found in a Xianbei context collected in the region of Erlanhugou, Chayouhou banner, Inner Mongolia (Wu En 1997, 302, fig. W7).

134 | D-shaped Openwork Plaque with Raptor

Transbaikal area
1st century BCE –
1st century CE

134a | Plaque (left)
Height 8.4 cm
Width 5.3 cm
Weight 47.2 g
Cast bronze,
alloy composition
by E. Ferreira:
Cu 91%; Sn 1.5%;
Pb 7.2%; As 0.6%;
Fe 0.2%

134b | Plaque (right)
Height 8.4 cm
(8.7 cm with stud)
Width 5.2 cm
Weight 45.5 g
Cast bronze,
alloy composition
by E. Ferreira:
Cu 85.2%; Sn 1.4%;
Pb 6.1%; As 0.5%;
Fe 0.1%

Each of these unusual plaques depicts a raptor in full flight grasping a wild animal in its talons, while its prey collapses under the attack, all within a rectangular frame, one of whose short ends is rounded. The frame is adorned with rectangular indentations, the back is flat, and the borders are only slightly raised. No. 134b, which has a stud at the curved end, is the wearer's left-hand plaque. The prey may possibly be a *kulan* (wild donkey?), but the details are difficult to make out. No close analogy is known to us, but plaques with similar shapes and subject matter have been associated with the Transbaikal region of Buryatia (Bunker et al. 1997, 271–72, fig. 238; Brosseder 2011, 392–98). Chronologically, they may be somewhat later than the previously discussed rectangular and P-shaped openwork belt plaques (Brosseder 2011, 392–98).

135, 136, 137 | Four Small Appliqué Plaques for the Belt

Transbaikal area, Mongolia, north China
2nd–1st century BCE

135 | Plaque
Height 2.8 cm
Width 3.9 cm
Weight 12.8 g
Cast bronze, alloy composition by J. Stenger:
Cu 79%; Sn 8%; Pb 2%

136 | Plaque
Height 3.5 cm
Width 4.1 cm
Weight 8.7 g
Cast bronze, alloy composition by E. Ferreira:
Cu 77.9%; Sn 7.1%, Pb 1.7%; As 3%; Sb 9.5%

137a | Plaque
Height 3.8 cm
Width 3.7 cm
Weight 11.5 g
Bronze, alloy composition by J. Stenger:
Cu 90%; Sn 2%; Pb 8%; As high

137b | Plaque
Height 3.7 cm
Width 4.2 cm
Weight 12.9 g
Bronze, alloy composition by E. Ferreira:
Cu 34.9 %; Sn 2.8%; Pb 31.6%; As 4%; Sb 5.3%

All four small plaques are lost-wax cast, according to an examination by Pieter Meyers on July 19, 2014. Nos. 135 and 136 depict a grazing argali mountain ram, while the pair 137a and b depicts female and male grazing gazelles. The animals are standing on a straight base, as is typical for these small plaques from burials of the Xiongnu period in the Transbaikal area (Bunker et al. 1997, 276–77). They may adorn the rest of the belt and are usually either combined with the large openwork belt plaques, such as in Dyrestui, grave 107 (Miniaev 1998, pl. 87–90), or appear without the large belt plaques, such as in grave 38 of Dyrestui (Miniaev 1998, pl. 38). Small, rectangular appliqué plaques, albeit with different motifs, are also known from the Xiongnu-period cemetery of Terezin in Tuva (Leus 2011, 530, fig. 11.3) and from Daodunzi in Ningxia province (Pan Ling 2011, 465, fig. 3.14).

135

136

137a   137b

138 | Small Appliqué Horse Plaque

North China
4th–2nd century BCE (?)

Height 2.5 cm
Width 4.5 cm
Weight 18.8 g

Cast bronze,
alloy composition
by J. Stenger:
Cu 76%; Sn 12%; Pb 8%

This horse plaque, with a bent-leg pose described as galloping by Miniaev, is very similar to a plaque in a Belgian collection (Miniaev and Smolarski 2002, 82, no. 67). It is also made of a lead-tin bronze. Both plaques have a strong horizontal attachment loop on the reverse. Two circular openings mark the shoulder and rump, resembling those that held inlay on animals in northern Hebei—although none of the Hebei plaques have thick, horizontal loops on the reverse. In the Transbaikal area, in Dyrestui, a similar horse plaque, but with a strong vertical loop has been excavated (Miniaev 1998, pl. 103.3). Two horse plaques with attached rings seem to be related; they also display a thick, horizontal attachment loop, which Wagner and Butz attribute to the sixth to fourth centuries BCE (Wagner and Butz 2007, 4–5, no. 2).

Chapter 5

Xianbei

By the end of the first century CE, the Xianbei had succeeded the Xiongnu as masters of the eastern Eurasian steppe world. In the second century BCE, they had been one of the groups of pastoral peoples defeated by the rising Xiongnu that subsequently fled to the Xianbei Mountains in far northern Inner Mongolia, from which they took their name.[58] The Xianbei spoke an Altaic language, thought by Edwin Pulleyblank to be proto-Mongol (Pulleyblank 1983, 452–54).

By the third century CE, the Xianbei had expanded southwards to Inner Mongolia, ultimately taking control of northern China, where they established the Northern Wei dynasty in 386 CE. According to the Weishu (History of the Wei Dynasty), a "heavenly beast in the shape of a horse" led the Xianbei chiefdom's southward migration, an origin myth that may be commemorated by the winged-horse symbols depicted on many of their belt ornaments (Kessler 1993, 75, fig. 46; Su Bai 1977, 46, fig. 6).

Although much of Xianbei material culture, including both mortuary practices and burial goods, is similar to that of the Xiongnu, there are clear differences (Wu En 1987). Xianbei burials commonly contain a number of bodies in individual graves, while the Xiongnu favored single burials. Sacrificial animal bones, a prominent feature of Xiongnu burials, are less common in Xianbei burials.[59] Xianbei iconography is also different from its Xiongnu counterpart, although the shapes are often superficially similar. Besides the deer motif, the major mythological animal featured in Xianbei imagery is a fantastic winged horse, referencing the legendary history of the Xianbei's origins recounted in the *Weishu*. For the Xianbei, who were mostly pastoralists, hunting was probably important, a fact which is reflected in the design of a cast-gold, openwork plaque

---

[58] For the history of the Xianbei, see Bunker et al. 1997, 279–83; Wu En 1997; Wei Jian 2004; Miller 2016.

[59] Wu En 1997, 300–305 for a discussion of the many known burials; Wei Jian 2004; Sun Wei 2007.

depicting three standing stags excavated at Sandaowan, Qahar Youyi Hou banner, Ulanqab league, in southeastern Inner Mongolia (Li Yiyou and Wei Jian 1994, 419, fig. 14.5). Xianbei plaques appear to have been made of either gold or bronze, depending on the owner's status. It is doubtful whether the bronze examples from early Western collections described as mercury gilded are, in fact, authentic, since the Xianbei do not appear to have used the technique and no examples have been found in burial contexts.

139 | Belt Plaque

Northeast China
1st–2nd century CE

Height 2.7 cm
Width 3.7 cm
Weight 23.3 g

Cast gold,
alloy composition
by P. Meyers
(June 22, 2013):
Au 77%; Ag 16%;
Cu 6.4%

This openwork plaque shows two confronted rams within a rectangular frame and wheel-shaped forms that fill the space beneath and between the two animals. On the reverse, the animals' bodies are concave and the border areas flat. The plaque is lost-wax cast, and its worn appearance testifies to its lengthy use. The reverse carries two vertical attachment loops that have been soldered on, and thus may not have been attached to the piece when it was first made. Few Xianbei plaques seem to display loops, suggesting that they were attached using the pierced areas of the design (see Bunker et al. 1997, 282 for a discussion of its function). A similar gold example was found at a Xianbei site in Tianmiliang, eastern Inner Mongolia (Qi Dongfang 1999, 241, fig. 2-84), and bronze examples are held in public and private collections (Salmony 1933, pl. 28.4; Barbier 1996, pl. 55).

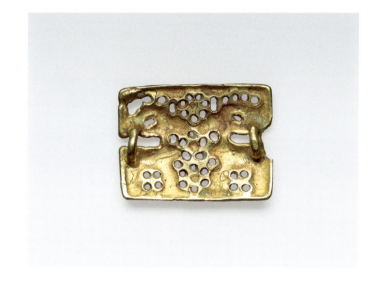

140 | Garment Plaque

North China
1st–2nd century CE

Height 2.5 cm
Width 3.5 cm
Weight 5.5 g

Cast bronze,
alloy composition
by J. Stenger:
Cu 83%; Sn 5%; Pb 7%;
As trace

This small, bronze plaque shows a small horse on the back of a larger horse, each with a fan-shaped forelock. The bottom horse's legs are so abstract that they are fused into a ground line that continues up the tail. The reverse of the plaque is slightly concave and does not contain any loops. Similar examples have been excavated at a Xianbei cemetery in Houbaoshi, Da'an, Jilin (Guo Min 1997, 6, fig. 1.1–4).

Numerous bronze examples depicting similar horses have been found throughout northern China and are associated with the Xianbei peoples (Feng Zhou 1983, 104; Psarras 1994, 66–67; Bunker et al. 1997, 283; Wu En 1997, 300–303; Bunker et al. 2002, 168, no. 153). A gold example unearthed in 1984 in Keerqin Zuoyi Zhong banner, Zhelimu League, which is less stylized than the present piece, shows the horse kneeling, demonstrating that the legs should be understood to be folded (Kessler 1993, 76).

Chapter 6

Artifacts with Exotic Overtones in the Arts of Dynastic China and the Neighboring Pastoral World during the Latter Half of the First Millennium BCE

Strange and exotic zoomorphic images, which are foreign to the traditional artistic vocabulary of dynastic China, occur frequently on artifacts traditionally considered Chinese during the latter half of the first millennium BCE. Numerous luxury artifacts in the present collection reveal exotic imagery on objects associated with the northwestern pastoral world (e.g., entry 141), highlighting the complexities that emerge when one culture borrows from another culture's artistic vocabulary. At the same time, tantalizing evidence exists for regional production centers with surprisingly extensive markets. Their existence is a product of encounters between diverse cultures about which little is yet understood.

Luxury Goods with Adopted Foreign Motifs or Xiangrui

Other artifacts in the present collection exhibit extraordinary zoomorphic images cast in hybrid styles (entries 144–147) that were probably inspired by the myriad fantastic creatures described in Warring States texts, especially the *Shanhaijing* (Classic of Mountains and Seas). Such images were not borrowed indiscriminately to decorate dynastic Chinese objects because they were novel. Instead, they fit into a form of thinking called *xiangrui* (good omen) that figured prominently in the art and literature of dynastic China of the time. We suggest that entries 148–150 are examples of this. Their appearance in the art of dynastic China was thought to indicate the approval of Heaven (Wu Hung 1986; So and Bunker 1995, 70–73).

141 | Bronze Socketed Axe, *Ge*

North China,
Shanxi, Houma
6th–5th century BCE

Height 6.5 cm
Width 11 cm
Weight 116.2 g

Cast bronze,
alloy composition
by J. Stenger:
Cu 63%; Sn 15%; Pb 10%;
As <1%

This small axe (*ge*) has a blunt, rectangular blade without a cutting edge, which issues from the mouth of a mythical feline, which is entangled with serpents and which holds a small feline head with a rounded mushroom-shaped hammer in its mouth, all raised on a hollow socket of oval cross-section. A longitudinal line that bisects the piece indicates that it was cast in a two-part mold. The socket is pierced on both sides, enabling it to be attached to an upright element, presumably made of wood.

Such tiny axes appear to have been status symbols representing elite regalia meant for ceremonial display during the late Spring and Autumn (770–475 BCE) and early Warring States (475–221 BCE) periods. A similar axe has been unearthed from the sixth- to fifth-century BCE Changzhi Fenshuiling tomb 269 in Shanxi province (Li Xiating et al. 1996, 37, fig. 3.2), a site that has yielded bronzes associated with the ancient foundries at Houma, in Shanxi province, which are associated with the Jin and the successor states of Han, Zhao, and Wei (Xu 1996). Several similar examples are known from numerous other Jin-state tombs (Rawson and Bunker 1990, 178–79, no. 83, note 1).

The imagery on the present axe-head exhibits exotic intrusions into the artistic vocabulary of dynastic China, due to cultural contact with the pastoral peoples beyond China's northwestern borders, as suggested by Xu (1996, 84). Since this tiny axe has no defensive characteristics, it falls into the category of a luxury item with exotic overtones signifying status.

142 | Harness Ornament

Northwest China
5th–4th century BCE

Height 3.8 cm
Width 8 cm
Weight 51.3 g

Cast bronze with gold sheet overlay on the eyes, alloy composition by J. Stenger: Cu 74%; Sn 11%; Pb 9%; As <1%.

P. Meyers noted that "the eyes have gold sheet inlays, but it is not certain that the gold inlays are original [...]."

Both this ornament and the following one (entry 143) are similar to harness ornaments associated with burials in the Guyuan region of the southern Ningxia Hui Autonomous Region, such as those discussed in entries 77 and 78 (Chapter 3c), but their production methods and concepts are quite different. These differences suggest that the Qin may have used exotic imagery borrowed from their pastoral neighbors in order to enrich artifacts made for their own use. Whether these two ornaments were also used as harness ornaments is unclear.

A lupine carnivore protome with almond-shaped eyes, clawed paws, and a curled serpentine body terminating in an eared raptor head cast in the round represents the most prominent element of this ornament. Another coiled serpentine body, with a beaked head and elk-shaped antlers, is shown tangentially in profile, thus providing the ungulate symbol necessary to complete the iconographical requirements. The body surfaces appear to have been tinned, while the almond-shaped eyes are enhanced by gold foil. The piece has been cast in a multipiece mold with a vertical attachment loop on the back that has been cut off (examination by P. Meyers, 2011).

The decoration of this harness ornament transforms realistic zoomorphic forms into fantastic creatures rendered in graceful linear designs that relate stylistically to those from the frozen burials in the Altai (Piotrovskij 1978, 60–70), especially those tattooed on male and female corpses (Barkova and Pankova 2005, 48–59). A bronze ornament in the Musée Guimet resembling the present ornament was first published with a Six Dynasties-era date (Mostra d'Arte Cinese 1954, 54, no. 156), but was later recognized as being much earlier due to its similarity to artifacts found in the Altai (Bunker et al. 1970, 127, fig. 106, based on Rudenko 1960, pl. 94).

The present harness ornament is stylistically related to other harness ornaments in this collection (Chapter 3c, entries 77 and 78), but is far more expertly cast. The fragile nature of the gold-foil overlay of the eyes suggests that it may have been primarily intended for funerary purposes, rather than for practical use.

143 | Harness Ornament

Northwest China
ca. 5th–4th century BCE

Height 6.1 cm
Width 3.8 cm
Weight 32.4 g

Cast bronze, inlaid, alloy composition by J. Stenger: Cu 77%; Sn 11%; Pb 4%; As <1%

A beaked carnivore head with almond-shaped eyes and spiral ears cast in the round on a circular suspension ring is tangential to a raptor head with a serpentine, volute-shaped body that terminates in an ungulate head with a round bird's eye, animal's nostril, and elk-like horns. Once again, visual references to a carnivore, a bird, and an ungulate completes the northern iconography, but the execution and decorative style of the piece are dynastic Chinese. Substantial wear is visible on the suspension loop.

144 | Silver Annular Ornament

North China
4th–3rd century BCE

Diameter 5.7 cm
Weight 35.9 g

Cast silver,
alloy composition
not analyzed

This circular ornament is decorated on only one side with two pairs of confronted lupine carnivore images. Each carnivore is shown in profile with open jaws and its hindquarters twisted 180 degrees, with its tail curled around its hindfeet, a distinctly steppe-like way of rendering certain animals with a distant Eurasian heritage. The eyes are almond-shaped, the snouts are curled up, and the bodies are defined by curvy, raised lines in striated enclosures against a recessed, unpolished, black-tarnished background.

Silver and gold artifacts with a surface decoration consisting of curvilinear lines and striations have been associated with Xiadu, the capital of the state of Yan in modern-day Hebei (Hebei 1996) and Xinzhuangtou, near Yi county, Hebei, the southern capital of Yan during the late fourth and third centuries BCE (Li Xueqin 1985, 335, fig. 150). This surface texturing descends from earlier Altaic wood-carving traditions, such as the coffin from Bashadar (Piotrovskij 1978, 63, no. 64; Menghin et al. 2007, 123, fig. 5), and from bone carving (So and Bunker 1995, 138, fig. 56.1; Bunker et al. 2002, 172, no. 159–60).

145 | Two Annular Gold Ornaments

Northwest China
4th–3rd century BCE

145a | Gold Ornament
Diameter 4.7 cm
Weight 4.6 g

145b | Gold Ornament
Diameter 4.8 cm
Weight 4.9 g

Both: hammered gold, alloy composition not analyzed

Each of these two artifacts is decorated in repoussé, with four pairs of confronted lupine heads with slightly open jaws shown in profile. These ornaments were acquired years ago with the gold-repoussé plaque (Chapter 3c, entry 80) which has a counterpart that was excavated at Qingshui in Gansu; other similar examples were also excavated there. The shape of each ornament was created by chisel-cutting the sheet gold, while the decoration was produced by hammering the gold over a mold (P. Meyers, July 16, 2012). The turned-over edges suggest that each of these two pieces may have been attached to an unknown object.

145 a   145 b

146 | Four Silver Roundels

North China
4th–3rd century BCE

Diameter 3.8 cm
Weight 16.6 g, 15.4 g, 14.8 g, 14.0 g

Cast silver, alloy composition not analyzed

Produced using the lost-wax, lost-textile process. A goat is depicted, with inverted hindquarters slung over its head. The body is accentuated by striated, curvilinear elements. A similar piece is known from the Therese and Erwin Harris Collection (So and Bunker 1995, 139, no. 58). Several golden pieces are known from tomb 30 at Xinzhuangtou in Hebei province (Hebei 1996; Kost 2014, pl. 131G-K).

147 | Garment or Accessory Hook

North China
3rd–2nd century BCE

Height 4.6 cm
Width 2.9 cm
Weight 25.6 g

Gilded cast bronze with turquoise inlay, alloy composition by J. Stenger: Cu 85%; Sn 10%; Pb 2%; As trace

Ex Therese and Erwin Harris Collection, Miami, Florida, by 1995; Christie's New York, 16 March 2017, lot 854

Published: So and Bunker 1995, 171, no. 97; 82; Harris Collection 2017, 59, no. 854

This superb, small hook is cast in an ingenious openwork design of a camel, whose serpentine body is wrapped around itself, with its neck and head set at an angle to form the hook. The reverse displays a silver-colored button almost the size of the camel. This piece represents a wondrous fantasy created for some member of the Han elite. For an in-depth discussion of this piece, see Jenny So (So and Bunker 1995, 171, no. 97).

148 | Ornamental Appliqué

North China
2nd century BCE

Height 8.1 cm
Width 3.2 cm
Weight 24 g

Gilded cast bronze, alloy composition by E. Ferreira:
Cu 73.3%; Sn 8.3%; Pb 6.3%; As 0.2 %; Fe 0.1%

Ex Edgar and Hedwig Worch Collection, Paris and New York; Christie's New York, 2 June 1994, lot 57; Therese and Erwin Harris Collection, Miami, Florida

Published: Christie's 1994, 28–29, no. 57; So and Bunker 1995, 156, no. 78; 73, col. pl. 17

This delightful image of a gazelle is shown with its hindquarters rotated 180 degrees and its horns together terminating in tiny raptor heads. The gazelle exhibits a markedly hybrid style, combining the best of Han workmanship with an animal image derived from traditions inspired by the pastoral world to the northwest and introduced into dynastic China under the guise of exotica and *xiangrui* (auspicious omens) during the last quarter of the first millennium BCE.

Two projecting pins on the flat back suggest that the piece may have originally adorned a larger object, which is now lost. A plaque from a collection in Hong Kong is, with minor differences, the mirror image of the present example, as is a plaque in the Metropolitan Museum of Art (Hearn 1987, 61, no. 87), suggesting that such appliqués may have been popular during the Western Han period. Similar painted images enliven the décor of the famous lacquer Mawangdui coffin from the Han era (Bunker 1991b, 580–81, figs. 13 and 14).

149 | Belt Hook

North China,
Western Han
ca. 2nd century BCE

Height 3.2 cm
Width 12.8 cm
Weight 116.8 g

Cast gilded bronze with surface details accomplished using hatched lines, alloy composition not analyzed

Ex J. J. Lally & Co., New York, by 1996; Dr. Susan Beningson Collection, New York

Published:
Lally & Co. 1996, no. 37

This elegant belt hook is cast in the form of a tiger stealthily striding forward with head lowered and the body close to the ground. The tiger's long tail streams out behind it, looping back to form a serpentine-headed hook. The tiger's head and body are extensively gilded and finely decorated with wavy double-line stripes, ring circles, and finely hatched lines depicting fur. The tiger's reverse reveals a domed button in the center for attachment purposes. A bronze belt hook formed by a similar tiger is in the collection of the British Museum, but lacks the gilding and the elegance of the present belt hook (Watson 1962, no. 80b).

150 | Ornament Adorned with a Crouching Bear Image

North China
2nd–1st century BCE

Diameter 4.2 cm
Weight 22.8 g

Cast gilded bronze, alloy composition by E. Ferreira: Cu 76.5%; Sn 7.5%; Pb 6.5%; As 0.3%

A superb image of a foreshortened crouching bear with all four paws shown distinguishes this domed, gilded-bronze roundel. A careful examination reveals the remains of textile embedded in the back, indicating that it was likely used for personal adornment. The reverse has no viable loop, providing no indication how the ornament was attached or functioned.

Bears traditionally signified rebirth, since they hibernate in the winter before reemerging each spring. Rebirth and immortality were fundamental Daoist concerns during the Western Han period, which may account for the popularity of bear motifs (Bunker 1993).

The present bear's ruff continues as an outward spiral at each end describing an ear, a stylistic feature that has been considered typical of Western Han representations. This stylistic convention occurs earlier on carved wooden images found in the Altai, such as the faces of animals on the legs of a table from Pazyryk, kurgan 2 (Rudenko 1970, pl. 50 B).

The Sackler Collections contain five circular artifacts adorned with similar foreshortened, squatting bears shown frontally (Bunker et al. 1997, 263, no. 228). Such images of foreshortened, squatting bears appear to have been popular decorations on both steppe and dynastic-Chinese harness and belt ornaments. Two plain, bronze ornaments enhanced by sitting bear-images were recently excavated from a Xiongnu-period grave in Mongolia (Ėrėgzėn et al. 2016, 169), and similar ones are known from other Xiongnu burials, such as those in the Dyrestui cemetery (Miniaev 1998, pl. 83.32–33; 101.3; Davydova and Miniaev 2008, 81, fig. 80).

Chapter 7

Beyond Inner Asia: Artifacts Relating Visually to Inner Asian Materials

The present collection includes numerous artifacts belonging to the many horse-riding pastoralist cultures located throughout greater Central and West Eurasia during the first millennium BCE. The similarities between these artifacts and those associated specifically with dynastic China's northern pastoral neighbors demonstrate how culturally interconnected the whole of the Eurasian steppe world had become by the first millennium BCE.

7a Central Asia, Pamir Mountain Regions (entries 151–154)

Several bronze plaques in the present collection are similar to artifacts found in seventh- to fourth-century BCE burials in the Pamirs, eastern Tajikistan, which have been associated with the Saka peoples (Yablonsky 1995b, 236, fig. 102; Lebedynsky 2006, 212). Today, the Pamirs extend into the following countries: Tajikistan, Pakistan, Afghanistan, China, and Kyrgyzstan (Yablonsky 1995b), making comparative studies of artifactual material challenging (Litvinskiĭ 1972).

The Saka are often mentioned by ancient historians, such as Herodotus and Ctesias (Yablonsky 1995a, 194–95), and are specifically depicted in the fifth-century BCE reliefs at Persepolis bringing riding trousers as tribute to the Achaemenid Empire (Schiltz 1994, 349, fig. 252); the trousers were probably made of leather rather than fabric. A piece of leather attached to a Saka bronze plaque may be the remains of clothing worn by the deceased Saka owner (Yablonsky 1995b, 235), suggesting that the following plaques may have adorned some ancient Saka pastoralists in both life and death.

Where the bronze plaques associated with the Pamir Saka discussed in this chapter were cast cannot be determined from the limited evidence available, but they all exhibit the same iconography and artistic style. More importantly, they are characterized by the same fastening system of raised attachment buttons on the backs. The similar bronze alloy, with a high tin content and only minimal amounts of lead, found in three of the four plaques (entries 151, 153, 154) also suggests a similar area of production.

The antlers, horns, and body parts of some of the animals portrayed on the plaques are transformed into raptor heads, revealing a connection to an iconography that has been identified among other pastoral peoples, whose artifacts have been found in the Altai mountains of Siberia and the Ordos region of northwestern China (see Chapters 3b and 3c, pp. 141–254). Most of the Saka bronze plaques in this chapter come from various old collections and appear to be cast by the same lost-wax process using a wax model that may have been formed in a mold. Even the gold plaque in the al-Sabah Collection in Kuwait is cast in the same style, although it is not noted as having a connection to Central Asia or Saka (Freeman 2013, 109, no. 53).

7b Kazakhstan, Lower Syr Darya Region (entry 155)

According to written sources, the Saka were the eastern neighbors of the Scythians and are generally associated with the Early Iron Age remains found east of Lake Aral, in the lower Syr Darya region. The constant relocation of riverbeds has had long-lasting effects on the history of this region. The two burial-grounds, Uĭgarak and Tagisken-South, are characteristic of the Early Iron Age. Small burial mounds covering a central pit, with the deceased in supine position, are typical and mark an abrupt cultural change in this area, which is associated with the arrival of a new population (Parzinger 2006, 668).

7c Kazakhstan, Almaty Region (entry 156)

Many kurgans associated with the Saka peoples have been discovered in the Almaty region of Kazakhstan, revealing the immense wealth often interred in their elite burials, such as that of the so-called "Golden Man" buried in the Issyk kurgan, located fifty kilometers east of Almaty (Akishev 1978; Akishev 2006, 57–62).

7d Northwest Caucasus, Maikop, Kuban Region (entries 157–160)

Flat bronze artifacts with chased decoration and design details similar to those found on the first two plaques in this chapter (entries 157 and 158) are known from an area to the northwest of the Caucasus (Schiltz 2001, 87–89, no. 18;

Leskov 1990, pl. 84, no. 70). The Kuban was an influential region, serving as an international crossroads throughout antiquity. Consequently, the so-called Maikop treasure includes many stylistically disparate artifacts that were acquired without any specific cultural context, resulting in innumerable "archaeological orphans," for which we have almost no information regarding their past or place of production (Leskov 2008, vii; 1–13). A few examples in the present collection can be attributed to this area.

7e Olbia, Black Sea Region (entry 161)

Numerous bronze and gold artifacts associated with the Scythians have been discovered in the Black Sea region in southern Russia. The Scythians were horse-riding peoples who lived north of the Black Sea and are discussed extensively by Herodotus, the Greek historian. In antiquity, the Greeks were known to have produced many of the Scythians' lavish artifacts. Hence, Herodotus may have learned about their customs and culture from the tales told by travelers and merchants.

7f Bulgaria, Thracian Period, Sixth to Fourth Century BCE (entry 162)

The Thracians were Indo-European-speaking peoples living in southeastern Europe, who appear to have been culturally related to the Scythians and other Inner Asian horse-riding groups. The belt was a particularly important item in Thracian mythology and was associated with the Thracian ideology of kingship (Marazov 1998, 32–71).

7g Western Iran, Luristan, First Half of the First Millennium BCE (entry 163)

The majority of bronzes associated with Luristan are well cast and of extremely high quality. To date, they have not been found in any scientifically controlled excavations, so their precise cultural contexts remain unclear. Their identification as harness ornaments is based on the importance of horses among the peoples in Luristan and is no more than an educated guess. For a discussion of the so-called Luristan bronzes, see Moorey (1981, 14–19; 36–50).

7h Eastern Iran, Fourth to Third Century BCE (entry 164)

Zoomorphic motifs in Iranian art that are similar to zoomorphic motifs seen on many Inner Eurasian steppe artifacts indicate the vast globalization process characterizing Eurasian art during the first millennium BCE. Bold raptor and griffin heads are especially popular on artifacts found among the various pastoral groups living between dynastic China in the east and the Black Sea in the west, discussed elsewhere in the present volume.

7i Southern Chinese Borderlands (entries 165–167)

According to the Shiji, written by the Han-dynasty historian Sima Qian, the southwestern borderlands of dynastic China were inhabited by non-Han peoples sometimes described as "southern barbarians." Ancient cemeteries in present-day Guizhou, the Lake Dian region of Yunnan, and the mountainous areas of western Sichuan have long been tentatively associated with "southern barbarians" by Chinese archaeologists, based on the presence of non-Han artifacts among the grave goods exhibiting an extraordinary range of zoomorphic images.

A few scholars have even suggested that the emphasis on animal motifs in these grave goods might represent an exotic cultural intrusion from the northern Eurasian steppe world. Without indicating how such cultural transferences might have occurred, we can say that any long-distance cultural contact, if actually provable, will be immensely more complex than has been acknowledged. A study of two non-Han artifacts in the present collection (entries 165 and 166) will discuss the possible cultural connections with the Inner Asian steppe world.

151 | Garment Plaque

Pamir Mountains, Tajikistan
ca. 7th–4th century BCE

Height 5.9 cm
Width 7.6 cm
Weight 52.6 g

Cast bronze, alloy composition by E. Ferreira: Cu 91.2%; Sn 2.7%; As 1.9%

A recumbent doe surmounted by two opposing raptors, all with their eyes depicted as circles with raised rims and intaglio centers, form this elegant garment plaque. The plaque was cast using the lost-wax process, and two attachment buttons supported on stems project from the plaque's slightly concave back. The pointed muzzle, the rounded loop of the ungulate's front legs, the profile raptor images, and the two buttons appear to be characteristic of plaques associated with the Saka located in the Pamirs, such as those excavated in present-day east Tajikistan (Litvinskiĭ 1972, 63–64, pl. 22.1; 23.8; Yablonsky 1995b, 236, fig. 102i). The raptors on the present plaque have prominent, elongated beaks and are shown hunched over their ungulate victim, features which suggest that the raptors intended are vultures, a major bird of prey on the steppe. Such predation scenes were popular among Pamir herding groups where survival depended on guarding their specific grazing and water rights from being infringed on by other groups. The bronze hilt of a dagger from Akbeit in eastern Tajikistan is enhanced by the profile image of a similar ungulate, with looped and folded front legs and circular marks on the hip and shoulder, typical characteristics of the Pamir Saka (Bunker 1970 et al., 62, fig. 8; Litvinskiĭ 1972, 112, pl. 40.4; 113, photo 20).

152 | Garment Plaque

Pamir Mountains, Tajikistan
ca. 7th–4th century BCE

Height 3.4 cm
Width 4.6 cm
Weight 18 g

Cast bronze, alloy composition by J. Stenger: Cu 85%; Sn 1%; Pb 1%; As high; Ni high

A graceful, mythological deer with raptor-headed antler tines and folded legs is depicted on this garment plaque. The deer has a pointed muzzle and only a single attachment button, which projects from the back of the plaque. Similar examples are known from burials in the eastern Pamir Mountains (Litvinskiĭ 1972, 63, pl. 22.3; 64, pl. 23.16). The transformation of horns and antlers into raptor heads is an iconographic phenomenon that first developed among the Eurasian pastoral peoples during the first millennium BCE. The earliest known example was discovered in a late seventh-century BCE grave at Shilikty (Chilikty) in eastern Kazakhstan. From there, this iconography was transmitted westwards to the Black Sea region and eastwards to southern Siberia and the borders of northwestern China (Bunker 1989, 53). The deer's hooves and tail are also transformed into raptor heads, a rare rendition of this symbolism.

153 | Garment Plaque

Pamir Mountains, Tajikistan
ca. 7th–4th century BCE

Height 5.6 cm
Width 8.4 cm
Weight 72.5 g

Bronze, alloy composition by E. Ferreira: Cu 86.3%; Sn 12.7%; Pb 0.6%; As 1%; Zn 0.2%

Two horses joined at the midsection form this plaque. Like the previously discussed deer image (entry 152), they display slightly pointed muzzles. The eyes are once again indicated by rimmed circles with intaglio centers. The shoulders are each marked by rimmed circles. The reverse of the plaque has two projecting attachment buttons on stems, one circular and the other diamond shaped.

154 | Garment Plaque

Pamir Mountains, Tajikistan
ca. 7th–4th century BCE

Height 5.5 cm
Width 8.5 cm
Weight 69.1 g

Cast bronze, alloy composition by J. Stenger:
Cu 68%; Sn 15%; Pb 0.5%

A final garment plaque represents a crouching wild boar, identified by its bristly mane described by striated lines. Once again, attachment is accomplished by means of two buttons on stems projecting from the back of the plaque: one button is circular, while the other is diamond shaped, like the buttons on the previous plaque.

155 | Girth Ring

Lower Syr Darya
6th–4th century BCE

Height 8.7 cm
Width 6.1 cm
Weight 56.5 g

Cast bronze,
alloy composition
by J. Stenger:
Cu 95%; Sn 2%; Pb 2%

This circular ring is surmounted by a crouching carnivore devouring the remains of its prey. Certain artistic conventions, such as the circular eye, circular depressions marking the shoulder and haunch, and the elongated ear suggest a stylistic relationship to other Saka plaques discussed in the present chapter. The reverse displays two heavy vertical loops that exhibit substantial wear and were integrally cast with the plaque using the piece-mold method from an alloy containing a very high amount of copper. The possibility that this artifact served as a girth ring is based on a general similarity of its shape to two other objects described as girth rings from Tagisken-South and Uĭgarak (Itina and Iablonskiĭ 1997, 126, fig. 30.3–4; Yablonsky 1995b, 221, fig. 63; Stöllner and Samašev 2013, 623, fig. 4.2–3; 635, fig. 5b). However, these rings are fastened by means of a button on the reverse and not by loops, as in the present piece. The shoulder and hip markings relate the plaque stylistically to a plaque in the Eugene V. Thaw Collection that also has a loop on the reverse (Bunker et al. 2002, 185, no. 174).

156 | Scabbard Guard

Northeast Kazakhstan
5th–4th century BCE

Height 4.6 cm
Width 13 cm
Weight 139.1 g

Cast gold,
alloy composition
by J. Stenger:
Test 1: Au 83%;
Ag 13%; Cu 0.93%
Test 2: Au 69%;
Ag 25%; Cu 2%

According to the examination conducted by Pieter Meyers on December 17, 2001 the piece "was produced by lost-wax casting. The design was made entirely in the wax as there is no evidence of chasing or tooling in any of the design elements. It is significant that the interior contains the remains of wood from which the scabbard element may have been fashioned, as well as the presence of roots and root marks."

An openwork design of two confronted mythical elk with raptor-headed crests, their bodies twisted 180 degrees, distinguishes this gold scabbard ornament. The elk heads on the present piece are similar to those that distinguish several artifacts excavated in Berel' located in northeastern Kazakhstan (Chang and Guroff, 2007, 129, no. 74). The Berel' ungulates, misidentified as moose, are actually elk, since moose live only in North America. This ornament may have once enclosed the top of a wooden scabbard for a lavish burial, such as that of the young adult male in the Issyk kurgan near Almaty in Kazakhstan (Akishev 1978, 106, pl. 25; Popescu et al. 1998, 175, no. 270; 184, fig. 320; Chang and Guroff 2007, 112, fig. 39). Jacobson (2006a, 64) maintains that the plethora of gold artifacts in the rich Issyk burial "reflects the dominant warrior-theocracy of the Saka culture."

157 | Plaque

Kuban, Maikop region
5th–4th century BCE

Height 7.1 cm
Width 15.1 cm
Weight 140.7 g

Bronze,
alloy composition
by J. Stenger:
Cu 73%; Sn 15%; Pb 2%;
As trace

The feline head on this flat plaque has a heart-shaped ear and a curled muzzle. A male figure in the round shooting an arrow at an antlered deer head, also in the round, projects outward from the front of the plaque, cleverly depicting an abbreviated three-dimensional hunting scene. The figure of the hunter is missing its head, but otherwise the figure has remained intact. Both images, that of the hunter and that of the deer head, were cast separately and then soldered on. An attachment loop on the reverse was also cast separately and soldered on (P. Meyers, examination 2014). The design of this plaque is extraordinary and as yet unmatched in any other collection.

158 | Plaque

Northern Caucasus, Maikop region
4th century BCE

Height 8.2 cm
Width 14.6 cm
Weight 85 g

Bronze, alloy composition by J. Stenger:
handle: Cu 71%; Sn 18%; Pb 6%; As trace
head: Cu 95%; Sn 20%; Pb 7%; As trace
backside: Cu 77%; Sn 19%; As high

A recumbent feline with a returned head forms this flat plaque. Anatomical details are revealed by fluid lines chased on the front surface. The feline's open jaws appear to hold the long beak of an inverted bird head. A vulture head with a prominent curved beak shown in the round appears to have been cast separately and then soldered onto the front. A horizontal attachment loop on the reverse of the plaque was also precast and soldered on. This plaque and the previous plaque (entry 157) appear to be stylistically related and may have been produced in the same place.

159 | Two Plaques

Caucasus
4th century BCE

159a | Plaque (left)
Height 8.5 cm
Width 8.3 cm
Weight 101.4 g
Bronze,
alloy composition
by P. Meyers:
Front: Cu 81%/82%;
Sn 7.1%/8.1%;
Pb 7.7%/9.9%
Back: Cu 77%/64%;
Sn 9.9%/12%;
Pb 10%/24%

159b | Plaque (right)
Height 8 cm
Width 8.1 cm
Weight 101 g
Bronze,
alloy composition
by P. Meyers:
Front: Cu 70%/70%;
Sn 10%/13%;
Pb 16%/18%
Back: Cu 70%/72%;
Sn 11%/12%; Pb 15%/15%

Published:
Barbier-Mueller 2013,
227, fig. 16

These two plaques present a curious problem. They were apparently intended to represent a pair of mirror-image, stylized recumbent deer with flamboyant antlers, but instead the antler tips, as well as the ear of one of the deer, are completely missing. One's first thought is that the plaque with these missing details was cast more recently than its mate by someone who wanted a pair and did not understand the original ancient design, but that is not the case. Instead, an examination by Pieter Meyers (July 16, 2015) has revealed that the plaque with missing details must have been cast without the antler tips, as there is no evidence that they ever broke off. The two plaques were cast by the lost-wax process from a leaded tin bronze. Both plaques have similar alloy compositions and "the presence of a well-developed red cuprite and green copper corrosion on both front and back of the plaques … strongly support the antiquity of … both plaques" (Meyers ibid.). Barbier-Mueller (2013, 227) believes this pair to come from the Don area. Another, similar pair of mirror-image plaques in an old German collection, described as harness fittings, has also been attributed to the Black Sea region (Eisenberg 2006).

160 | Belt Plaque

Transcaucasia
1st–3rd century CE

Height 9.4 cm
Width 10.3 cm
Weight 221.9 g

Bronze, alloy composition by J. Stenger: Cu 75%; Sn 10%; Pb 5%; As trace

This belt plaque presents an openwork design of a mythological ungulate being attacked by dogs within a wide, striated square frame with large bosses at each corner. The zoomorphic images are highly stylized, almost beyond recognition. The ungulate has antlers, a plump body pinched in at the waist, and a long tail terminating in a spiral. The reverse displays the remains of a turned-back hook and a horizontal attachment loop. Many buckles similar to the present example have been excavated in present-day Georgia, with the center of their distribution being located in the regions of Imereti and Western Kartli (Curtis 1978, 119, pl. 3), few are found in museum collections outside Georgia (Curtis 1978, 89; appendix 1; Bunker et al. 2002, 117, no. 87; Jäger and Kansteiner 2011, 142–43, no. 202–3; Art Animalier 2012, 111–14, cat. 110–11; Barbier-Mueller 2013, 227, fig. 15). They are mainly known from burials of the first to third century CE (Curtis 1978; Art Animalier 2012, 112) and were used to adorn the belt. They are made of bronze or brass (Craddock in Curtis 1978; Jäger and Kansteiner, 142, no. 202), the present example is a tin-leaded bronze and fits well with the alloys known from similar clasps in the British Museum (Craddock in Curtis 1978, 110). Farkas claims that, on such plaques, "the theme of a stag hunted by dogs had become an apparently meaningless decoration" (Farkas 1970, 46–47; 57, no. 32).

161 | Quiver Decoration

Black Sea region
6th–5th century BCE

Height 12.3 cm
Width 7.8 cm
Weight 137.8 g

Bronze,
alloy composition
by J. Stenger:
Cu 82%; Sn 10%; Pb 5%;
As trace; Ni trace

This cross-shaped decoration is adorned with zoomorphic motifs. The reverse shows two horizontal attachment loops, one at the top and one behind the center roundel. Such cross-shaped decorations are associated with the Scythians of western Eurasia and were used to decorate the quiver or as a clasp for the quiver lid (Il'iukov 2016). They are known from the Black Sea area as well as from southeastern Europe. Similar appliqués have been erroneously published upside down (Reeder 1999, no. 48; Jacobson 1995, 255, no. 121).

A coiled panther image, shown in the center roundel on the present frontlet, is surrounded by three dynamic raptor heads, all shown in profile, symbols that also adorn an example from Olbia (Schiltz 1994, 120, no. 90; Alekseev et al. 2001, 51, no. 32). The rest of the plaque displays two standing ungulates with returned heads in the center panel, flanked by two recumbent animals and a standing carnivore at the top. Similar zoomorphic images adorn artifacts associated with numerous horse-riding pastoralists throughout the Eurasian steppe lands between the sixth and third century BCE, suggesting a common belief system that was illustrated regionally by zoomorphic images reflecting the local fauna.

162 | Wolf-shaped Belt Buckle

Bulgaria, Thracian period
5th century BCE

Height 3.8 cm
Width 8.8 cm
Weight 44.3 g

Cast bronze, alloy composition by J. Stenger: Cu 79%; Sn 17%; Pb 5%

Ex Four Corporations, New York; Mathias Komor, New York; Eugene V. Thaw Collection, New York and Santa Fe

Published: Bunker et al. 2002, 95, no. 60

This Thracian plaque is cast in the shape of a crouching wolf. The reverse is flat, displaying a horizontal hook behind the head and a tiny horizontal loop behind the rump. The buckle was lost-wax cast integrally with the fastening devices.

Several similar hooks are known from the lower Danube, Bulgaria, in the fifth century BCE (Kull 1997, 224, fig. 15.8–11; Marazov 1998, 62, fig. 17). A buckle of the same type is found in the Eugene V. Thaw Collection (Bunker et al. 2002, 95, no. 60). In ancient times, a young Thracian warrior was often rewarded with such a belt upon coming of age, as "a sign of his completed initiation" into manhood (Marazov 1998, 17).

163 | Harness Ring

Western Iran, Luristan
8th–7th century BCE

Height 7.7 cm
Width 8.1 cm
Weight 84.8 g

Cast bronze, alloy composition not analyzed

Ex Mathias Komor, New York, 12 September 1955; Howard and Saretta Barnet Collection, New York; Sotheby's New York, 14 May 2018, lot 28

Published: Shape of Beauty 2018, 142–43, no. 28

This handsome horse-harness ornament is a typical example of many such artifacts associated with the equestrian peoples inhabiting the Luristan Mountains in western Persia during the first half of the first millennium BCE. The piece is surmounted by the head of a mouflon with great, arching horns being bitten by two predatory beasts. A suspension loop is provided on the reverse side behind the mouflon's head. The Nasli M. Heeramaneck Collection in the Los Angeles County Museum contains several similar examples topped with the same horned mouflon head, as does the Ashmolean Museum in Oxford (Moorey 1971, 128–30, cat. 135–39; Moorey 1981, 46–47) and the British Museum (Moorey 1974, pl. 8b). Although the alloy of the present piece has not been determined, it seems that such harness rings were cast with a tin-copper alloy (see Moorey 1971, 128–30, cat. 135–39). The metal analyses conducted on a similar harness ring in the Harvard Art Museums/Arthur M. Sackler Museum demonstrate that it is made of a tin-copper alloy, with a small amount of arsenic: Cu 88%; Sn 10%; As 0.4% (https://www.harvardartmuseums.org/collections?q=1931.3, inv. 1931.3).

It has been suggested that the design of a chariot fitting from the Western Zhou cemetery of Zhangjiapo at Chang'an district, Xi'an, Shaanxi province is similar to the design of a Luristan harness ring and may possibly provide evidence of contact between the Zhou of northwestern China and the herders of the Iranian Plateau (Rawson 2010, 2, figs. 2a.c). In Rawson's opinion, carnelian beads worn by the Zhou nobility might also have originated in West Asia. While we are convinced that early contacts between West Asia and China are possible, the case for the Luristan bronze is not very convincing.

164 | Harness Ornament

Eastern Iran
4th–3rd century BCE

Diameter 8.5 cm
Weight 67.4 g

Bronze,
alloy composition
by E. Ferreira:
Cu 78.5%; Sn 12%;
Pb 4%; As 0.1%; Fe 0.1%

An openwork design of four prominent, raptor-beaked heads arranged within a circular frame of hybrid Iranian/Hellenistic spiral ornamentation distinguishes this harness ornament. The beaked heads' eyes are almond-shaped, like those of an animal, indicating that these creatures are not birds, but rather mythological griffins, combining raptor beaks with animal-shaped, oval eyes. This ornament displays two crossed strap loops on the reverse, a device typical of ornaments used on riding bridles and breastplates, which are not seen on harness equipment produced in eastern Eurasia or ancient dynastic China, but only further to the west.

When this bronze roundel was acquired, it was described as having a tinned surface and was associated with artifacts cast west of the Taihang Mountains, along the northern border of dynastic China, where tinning was a popular surface enrichment (Bunker 1990b). Subsequent examination has revealed that the ornament was never tinned; two very similar examples in the Borowski Collection (Jäger and Kansteiner, 2011, 159–60, no. 225) suggest that they may all have been made in eastern Iran. This confusion highlights the importance of establishing so far as possible an object's proper cultural context, before attempting to reconstruct its function and meaning. The inclusion of this ornament in the present collection is a warning that visual similarities in an object's imagery, shape, surface treatment, and function may be coincidental.

165 | Buckle in the Shape of a Bovine Head Surmounted by a Standing Horse

Guizhou, southwest China
1st century CE

Height 14.6 cm
Width 15.6 cm
Weight 179.2 g

Cast bronze, examination by J. Twilley (July 14, 2014): leaded-tin bronze

This sculptured frontal bovine head with long, slender, rising horns is surmounted by a small stocky horse standing in profile. The presence of a button and a horizontal, rounded hook on the back suggests that it served as some kind of personal ornament. The alloy is a leaded tin bronze that was lost-wax cast in a single pour. The present piece was once associated with the Dian culture of Yunnan (Ariadne Galleries 1998, 172, no. 194), but further research indicates that its hook shape and design are significantly different from anything found in Yunnan (Rawson 1983, 150; 178–79; nos. 173; 210–11).

Instead, the present buckle is similar to an example excavated at Liyuan, in northwestern Guizhou province, a site that has been associated with the Yelang, a tribal group with whom the Dian interacted. Both buckles, the present one and the Guizhou example, are cast in the shape of a wild-yak head with long horns and have the same attachment system (Guizhou and Weining 1981, 230, fig. 12.13; pl. 9.2). I am grateful to TzeHuey Chiou-Peng for this reference.

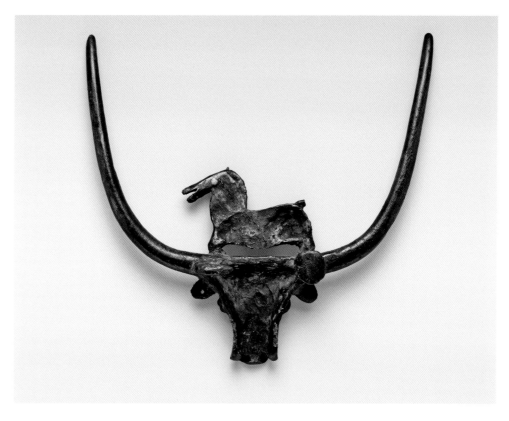

166 | Trapezoidal Plaque

Tibetan Plateau
ca. 4th–3rd century BCE

Height 14.5 cm
Width 15 cm
Weight 215.2 g

Cast high copper, alloy composition by J. Stenger: Cu 102%; Pb <1%; As 1%

This trapezoidal openwork arsenical high copper plaque displays four horizontal rows of zoomorphic images, separated by three rows of bosses within concentric circular raised rims. The top zoomorphic row depicts eight antelopes with spiraling horns shown in profile, the next row shows four horned wild yaks in profile facing in the opposite direction, the third row consists of three tigers with open jaws, also in profile, and the bottom row displays three S-shaped serpents seen from above.

Another trapezoidal plaque similar in design to the present one was excavated from tomb 1, Moutuo village in Mao county (Maoxian and Aba 1994, 30, fig. 49.4), located in the Aba Tibetan and Qiang Autonomous Prefecture of western Sichuan province. This plaque exhibits the same hybrid artistic style as the present plaque and is also made of a similar very high-copper alloy with a small amount of lead (Moutuo report 2012, 141, M1:65).

Von Falkenhausen (1996, 53–54) and Pirazzoli-t'Serstevens (2001, 47, fig. 7) date Moutuo tomb 1 to the middle or the second half of the first millennium BCE. Von Falkenhausen also stresses the visual similarities between the Moutuo zoomorphic images and those represented on Dian artifacts from Yunnan province, tentatively suggesting that they may ultimately be related to the zoomorphic imagery associated with the pastoral peoples of the Eurasian steppe world (von Falkenhausen 1996).

Although such similarities could be the result of parallel thinking in pastoral economies, there are other possibilities that should be taken into consideration. Contact through exchange networks, as well as possible marriage alliances with women from distant places introducing artifacts representing different belief systems, is always a possibility. It is also interesting to note that no representations of horses are identified and only one predation scene, omissions that beg for further study. Several similar trapezoidal bronze plaques are known from the Tibetan plateau and have been discussed extensively by Bellezza (2010, fig. 10; 2016a, figs. 1–6). Another plaque is known by Lally & Co (2011, cat. 22). The zoomorphic images on these plaques appear to continue petroglyphic zoomorphic renditions found throughout the Himalayas (Bellezza 2004; Linrothe 2016). Little is

known about the origins and functions of all these trapezoidal plaques, as they were random discoveries made by herders and farmers throughout the Tibetan Plateau, a region that was never dominated by a single culture, but was occupied by many diverse groups that spoke diverse Tibetan dialects.

What we do know is that the known trapezoidal plaques appear to have been cast by the piece-mold technique and are distinguished by multiple rows of zoomorphic images. The designs of these artifacts probably reflect the beliefs of some local early culture with a special symbolic system that governed the choice of species and how they were to be portrayed. The creatures represented include rabbits, antelope, wild yaks, wild asses (*kulan*), bears, snow leopards, tigers, wolves, cranes, and certain snakes that apparently had auspicious meanings in local iconography. One openwork plaque shows an animal-predation scene of two tigers attacking a *kulan* (wild ass) (Bellezza 2016a, fig. 1). A similar rendition of the tiger is also found on deerstones in Mongolia (Novgorodova 1984, 99, fig. 37; Francfort et al. 1992, 176, fig. 26).

A careful examination reveals that each of the known trapezoidal plaques originally had a small pendant tang that could have been inserted into a support for display. On some plaques the tangs have broken off, but their remains are recognizable. The backs of the plaques are also equipped with various tiny attachment rings.

According to the site report, the Moutuo tomb 1 example was cast from an arsenic, high-copper alloy using the piece-mold technique (Moutuo report 2012, 141; 146). Whether the arsenic was already contained in the copper when it was mined or whether it was intentionally added has not been determined, but a small amount of lead was certainly added by the artisans doing the casting to ensure that the metal would flow smoothly into the molds, which must have been fairly elaborate. Analyses of fifty metal objects from Moutuo that appear to have been made locally confirm that they are all made of a tin-lead copper, reinforcing the exotic nature of this trapezoidal plaque from the collection, which is made almost exclusively of copper.

The earliest-known trapezoidal plaque is flat with complex raised curvilinear forms on the body and a row of tigers in the round on the top, three moving to the right and three to the left. The reverse displays a multitude of loops for unknown attachment purposes, three loops below the tiger row, and numerous smaller loops along the edges of the lower two sides and along the bottom edges.

The other plaques have several rows of openwork rows of zoomorphic images. The Moutuo tomb with an openwork example has been given a tentative date in the fourth century BCE (von Falkenhausen 1996, 53–54). The recent suggestion that some of the images represented on some trapezoidal plaques may, in fact, resemble certain zoomorphic images found on several deerstones dating to the early first millennium BCE suggests that the earliest trapezoidal plaque could be much earlier in date than the fourth century BCE.

This brief discussion provides tantalizing evidence for the existence of a Bronze/Iron Age culture located in the Tibetan Plateau region that has yet to be properly identified and defined. This topic is the subject of Bellezza 2020 (see also Bellezza 2016a and 2016b). We thank John Vincent Bellezza for graciously sharing his research with Emma Bunker.

Fig. 27: A trapezoidal openwork copper alloy plaque, Tibet. Collection of David Salmon, UK.

167 | Plaque

Tibet
early first millennium BCE

Height 4.3 cm
Width 4.6 cm
Weight 14.7 g

Cast bronze,
alloy composition
by P. Meyers (July 2014):
Cu 77%; Sn 20%;
Pb 2.6%; Fe 0.1%

This small, crudely cast plaque portrays a humped bovine standing on the back of a tiger with open jaws. Irregular ridges on the tiger's body indicate stripes, and a worn circle indicates the tiger's eye. The back of the plaque is flat and displays no attachment loops. A technical examination confirms the antiquity of the plaque and that it was cast by the lost-wax process from a leaded tin bronze. An identical plaque is known from a collection of bronzes from Tibet (John 2006, 132, R-313), and similar feline plaques in the same ridged style are also known from the Ordos region and Siberia (Bruneau and Bellezza 2013, 143, fig. V.23; Bellezza 2004, fig. 3c; Salmony 1934, 9, fig. 12; Kovalev 1992, 85, pl. 51.8–9). The ribbed surface markings on the tiger's pelt are similar to those that distinguish the tigers that form the hilt of a dagger excavated at Nanshan'gen, tomb 101 (Linduff 1997, 69, fig. A103).

Depictions of similar felines with striped pelts are also known from rock art in Upper Tibet and Ladakh (Bellezza 2012; Bruneau and Bellezza 2013, 65–66; 142 fig. V.22) and from deerstones in Mongolia (Bruneau and Bellezza 2013, 53 fn. 184; Novgorodova 1984, 99, fig. 37; Törbat 2018a, 155, no. 161; 319, no. 458; Volkov 2002, 54, pl. 40-1; Törbat 2018b, 317, no. 1004; Törbat 2018b, 424, no. 1152). The Sackler Collections also include about seven tiger examples in the same ridged style, with an unconfirmed early-first-millennium BCE dating that may no longer be accurate (Bunker et al. 1997, 139, no. 31).

Such small plaques known throughout Tibet are called thokchas (*thog-lcags*) and considered a gift from the sky. Most of them are so worn that the styles are often unrecognizable. Therefore, we can at best guess—and probably inaccurately—where many of them were cast. There is no specific thokcha style, but they are surrounded by dense layers of myth and imagination.

Chapter 8

Individual Pieces beyond the Scope of the Guyuan Mizong Collection

Like many collections also the Guyuan Mizong Collection has a fiew pieces that fall outside its general focus—eastern Eurasia—and timeframe—late second millennium BCE to the first centuries CE. Although not forming a homogenous group they are interesting individual pieces that are assembled in this chapter. And like in other collections, we sometimes, because of our limited expertise, simply do not know where they belong but publish them for their aesthetics (see also Moorey 1981, 256–257).

The bear-shaped nephrite ornament (entry 170) was originally sold with the label "Ordos" which highlights the popularity of this label for the art market. The piece is in fact much closer to objects from the Liao–Jin Dynasty of the eleventh to twelfth century CE. The other outstanding piece, a bag fitting from the Old Turkic period (entry 169), is exceptional in its beauty and illustrates that once in a while artifacts surface that are previously best known from illustrations. We do not know where the repoussé sheet with a mountain scene with animals belongs (entry 168). It is our hope that its publication might change this.

168 | Repoussé Sheet, Mountain Scene with Animals

This silver sheet depicts a mountain scene with animals. An autopsy and surface XRF conducted by Pieter Meyers revealed that the silver had been exposed to a natural, long-term corrosion process and that the silver was alloyed with arsenical copper, as well as with small amounts of gold and lead. The style and general alloy composition is similar to early Bactrian silver objects (late third to early second millennium BCE). However, its copper content is much higher than is usually observed in Bactrian silver. We do not know of any analogue object and research suggests that there is no precedent for this. Although this repoussé sheet does not fit into the timeframe and area of this volume, it deserves publication in virtue of its unique appearance.

Height 10.7 cm
Width 13.3 cm
Weight 36 g

Silver sheet, alloy composition not analyzed

169 | Bag Fitting

Possibly western China
Ancient Turkic period,
mid-6th to
8th century CE

Height 7.2 cm
Width 8.2 cm
Weight 117.4 g

Gold foil, iron backing,
inlaid turquoise stones,
alloy composition
not analyzed

Published:
Cultural Exchange 2020,
106–7, 334

This beautiful piece of a bag fitting is made of gold foil over an iron backing and secured by folding the foil over the rim of the iron base. The buckle with movable pin is attached by three rivets. In the center, two argali are depicted in full run. The border is decorated with a scale pattern of inlaid turquoise stones. The same pattern, without inlays, is repeated in the center of the fitting where the strap would be fastened. The two symmetrically shaped ends are crafted as two opposing horse heads. They were made three-dimensionally, as the remains of the gold foil on the backside of one of the horse heads suggests.

We do not know of any analogue pieces, but the fitting was part of a pouch typical of the Old Turks, who wore pouches of this kind hanging from their belts. A very similar bag clasp is depicted on a figurine from Xianyang in Shaanxi province (Stark 2008, 571, fig. 105d), which shows the same outline as the fitting from the present collection. Similar belt clasps from bags are also shown on the murals on the western wall of Afrasiab in Uzbekistan (Stark 2008, 475, fig. 9d; 531, fig. 65d).

170 | Bear-shaped Nephrite Belt Ornament

North China
Liao–Jin dynasty,
11th–12th century

Height 3.2 cm
Width 6 cm
Weight 38.5 g

Siberian black nephrite

Ex Robert H. Ellsworth, New York; Eugene V. Thaw Collection, New York and Santa Fe, acquired in 1999

This charming crouching bear is carved from a dark-green nephrite and is well used as the result of extensive touching over a long period of time. The stone is nephrite of a type and color found in Mongolia and eastern Siberia, according to Janet Roberts from personal knowledge acquired while working in Irkutsk (Bunker et al. 1997, 134). The back of the bear reveals four pairs of drilled holes enabling the ornament to be attached to a belt. Although sold as an "Ordos" with a late-first-millennium BCE date, close comparison with another jade animal in the collection of Cissy and Robert Tang indicates that the present bear fits far better with a Liao–Jin, eleventh-century date (So and Xin 2015, 168–69).

Several jade ornaments in other collections have been given the label "Ordos," because of their similarity to certain zoomorphic images associated with the art of the northern pastoral peoples. One such example, a husky jade ox similar to entry 116 (Chapter 4), is encased in a gilded Han-period bronze frame with loops on the reverse (Bunker et al. 2002, 139, no. 114). This design is an image of an ox that may have been adopted as a *xiangrui* and then carefully Sinicized by enclosing it within a Han-period, gilded-bronze frame marked by sinuous Han felines.

Another so-called Ordos jade plaque (Bunker et al. 2002, 133, no. 105) displays an animal-combat scene almost identical to that found on a bronze belt plaque excavated from grave 100 in Ivolga, a second-century BCE Xiongnu burial in Transbaikalia (Davydova and Miniaev 2008, 101). Two semicircular cuts on either end of the jade version of the Ivolga bronze plaque may have facilitated attachment to some type of frame (Bunker et al. 2002, 134, no. 106).

These two so-called "Ordos ornaments" are shaped from a dark-green nephrite of a type found in Mongolia and eastern Siberia, suggesting they were made locally, rather than in China (Bunker et al. 2002, 134). It is doubtful whether the Xiongnu themselves had mastered the technique of shaping nephrite, but they were known to have always had Chinese artisans in their employ.

Hence, positing the existence of a category of "Ordos" or "steppe" jades is clearly misleading and unjustified, although some jades made for elite Chinese in antiquity were enhanced by zoomorphic iconography from the Eurasian Steppe.

Chapter 9
Forgeries and Modern Productions

In this chapter, we present those pieces that are considered modern forgeries. For any collection, whether private or in a museum, it is crucial to establish the authenticity of the pieces, since the archaeological context has been lost. In the case of the present collection, this has been achieved in many instances through stereomicroscopic examination, which provides insight into the corrosion process, and x-ray fluorescence (XRF) analyses, which show the alloy composition. Numerous pieces were examined by Pieter Meyers from the Conservation Center of the Los Angeles County Museum, whose reports are incorporated into the description of each piece.[60]

Those collections of Asian bronzes that have undergone systematic metallurgical testing, like the bronzes of the Sackler Collections (Bunker et al. 1997) or the Lloyd Cotsen Collection of Bronze Mirrors (Cahill 2009; von Falkenhausen 2011), have been shown to also contain forgeries. By publishing those pieces that we recognize as fakes, we aim to improve our evaluative standards for Inner Asian bronzes (see von Falkenhausen 2011, 31), as well as to provide data for expanding our knowledge about the context of forgery production.

While one might assume that unique pieces are more likely to be forgeries, the bronzes in this chapter are—apart from the pair of gilded bronze plaques (entry 176)—not exceptional or unique in any way.

A point of contention and ongoing research regarding the authenticity of copper-alloy objects is the zinc content (Craddock 2009, esp. 145–52).[61] Small amounts of zinc could, under specific circumstances, occur as an element in a copper alloy due to co-smelting of the ore (Craddock 2009, 146). However, zinc is highly volatile. Any object with more than trace amounts, that is older than 2000 years, and that lacks a secure excavation context should thus be regarded as highly suspicious.[62] In China, early brass artifacts are reported from the Late

---

60 For the procedures of the metallurgical testing, see Chapter 10, pp. 437–39.
61 We thank Dr. Yiu-Kang Hsu, Deutsches Bergbau-Museum Bochum, for his advice concerning the discussion on zinc.
62 Chase and Douglas 1997, 311; Craddock 2009, 147. For a review of the discussion on early brass objects see also Thornton et al. 2002.

Neolithic, but these early instances are only proof of experimental metallurgy (see Scott 2011, 203). Before the Tang period, there is no evidence for the use of zinc in China. Brass is, however, typical of the Roman world, as well as of northern India and Bactria (Craddock 2009, 147).

Sergei Miniaev reports that bronzes from the Zakamenka hoard from southern Siberia can reach 3–4% zinc content and that he has found minimal quantities of zinc—below 1%—in bronzes from the cemetery of Dyrestui in Transbaikalia (Miniaev 2002, 102). In northern Bactria, at least during the Kushan period, brass objects with a high zinc content are known (Bogdanova-Berezovskaia 1966). A brass, lyra-shaped plaque found in the Xiongnu elite burial from Noyon Uul in Mongolia was probably imported from there (Miniaev 1976). Furthermore, Miniaev suggests that multicomponent alloys with zinc are possibly the results of co-smelting a mixed copper-zinc ore or of re-smelting of objects (Miniaev 1976, Miniaev 2002, 102). During the recent excavations in Noyon Uul, bronzes were also recovered that had a high zinc content (Kuper et al. 2015, 76), possibly an import from Bactria as well.

In sum, while objects with a very low zinc content can theoretically occur in the Transbaikal area and Mongolia from the period between 200 BCE to 100 CE, such artifacts should be treated with suspicion, if they lack a proper archaeological context. In China, no zinc-containing object has yet been reported prior to the Tang period.

171 | Vulture Plaque

Height 3.6 cm
Width 5.1 cm
Weight 3.8 g

Cast bronze,
alloy composition
not analyzed

This small plaque is similar to entry 14 (Chapter 2a), which we believe comes from northeast China, 8th–7th century BCE.

It is cast, and the alloy of the piece was determined by means of a portable XRF on the surface conducted by Pieter Meyers on May 4, 2013. It shows that the metal contains Cu, Zn, Sn, Pb, and As. The proportion of zinc is estimated to be 5%. It is unlikely that the surface is covered with artificial corrosion, which would explain the high zinc content. Instead, it is likely that the zinc is part of the alloy and thus that this piece is a modern copy.

172 | Ibex Appliqué

Pieter Meyers' examination with a portable XRF on May 4, 2013 also indicated a high zinc content. Furthermore, the corrosion products were capable of being easily removed and appear to be artificial. Thus, this piece is also a modern forgery.

Height 5 cm
Width 5 cm
Weight 19.9 g

Leaded gunmetal, alloy composition by J. Stenger:
Cu 49%; Sn <1%; Pb 14%; Zn 5%

Chapter 9 | Modern Productions   423

173 | Belt Buckle with Lynx in a Tree

Height 10.8 cm
Width 7.3 cm
Weight 99.8 g

Leaded gunmetal, alloy composition by P. Meyers, by XRF on the surface (July 19, 2014): front, face: Cu 71%; Sn 10%; Pb 14%; Fe 0.9%; Zn 1.3% back: Cu 46%; Sn 10%; Pb 35%; Fe 4.1%; Zn 1% top loop: Cu 70%; Sn 10%; Pb 18%; Fe 0.6%; Zn 1.1% Alloy composition by J. Stenger: Cu 67%; Sn 9%; Pb 9; As <1%; Zn 2%

This openwork plaque depicts a lynx peeking above an argali with folded legs through a tree. Such plaques are known from the Xiongnu period in southern Siberia (see Brosseder 2011, 371–72, fig. 19–20; list 8b), such as Grave 128 in Dyrestui in the Transbaikal area (Miniaev 1998, pl. 118.1) or from the Minusinsk Basin (Dèvlet 1980, pl. 28.109.110). The Thaw Collection in the Metropolitan Museum contains an analogue pair of plaques (Bunker et al. 2002, 110, no. 80). The typical recipe for belt plaques from that region generally contains—in addition to copper, which serves as the base—tin, lead, and arsenic, which is also the case for one such plaque from the Minusinsk Basin (Miniaev 1980, 33, no. 58). The zinc content of the piece from this collection raises suspicions about its authenticity. Pieter Meyers (report May 4, 2013) furthermore observed under the stereomicroscope that the surface was covered with several layers of brown, green, and black paint. Depending on the extent of wear observable, one or more layers of paint had been removed. Additionally, an examination of the microstructure of the metal, by means of a small sample extracted using a jeweler's saw, did not show any evidence of a long-term natural corrosion process. Although the low zinc content is not unique, it is unusual, as is the absence of any arsenic in the alloy, which is typical for belt plaques from southern Siberia. Its technical characteristics, alloy composition, and surface appearance, as well as the lack of long-term natural corrosion, suggest that this piece is a modern fake.

174 | Plaque with Ibex Grazing

Height 3.7 cm
Width 5 cm
Weight 29.2 g

Cast leaded gunmetal, alloy composition by J. Stenger:
Cu 82%; Sn <1%; Pb 9%; Zn 8%

A previous examination by Pieter Meyers with a portable XRF (May 4, 2013) had also shown a high zinc content, estimated at 8%. This small plaque appears to imitate small belt appliqués characteristic of Xiongnu-period belts from the Transbaikal region, such as , which date to the last two centuries BCE. Such a high zinc content, however, indicates that this piece is a modern production.

175 | Plaque with Horse

This small plaque depicting a horse is similar to Xiongnu-period belt appliqués found, for example, in grave 107 of Dyrestui in Transbaikalia (Miniaev 1998, pl. 89.11–17) (see previous entry 174 and entry 135 [Chapter 4]).

The alloy-composition analysis conducted by Pieter Meyers using a portable XRF (May 4, 2013) showed a high zinc content, estimated at 7%, indicating that this piece is a modern production.

Height 3.8 cm
Width 4.9 cm
Weight 19.3 g

Cast leaded gunmetal, alloy composition by J. Stenger:
Cu 76%; Sn <1%; Pb 11%; Zn 7%

176 | Pair of Belt Buckles with Walking Wolves

176a | Belt Buckle (left)

Height 4.2 cm
Width 6.4 cm
Weight 44.6 g
Gilded brass,
alloy composition
by J. Stenger:
Cu 96%; Zn 3%

176b | Belt Buckle (right)

Height 4.2 cm
Width 6.4 cm
Weight 39.1 g
Gilded brass,
alloy composition
by J. Stenger:
Cu 94%; Zn 2%

This pair of openwork plaques each shows a predator-like composite animal. The context of very similar pair of gilded-bronze plaques is unknown (Kost 2014, pl. 15.2.3), while another bronze plaque comes from Shuoxian in Shanxi and belongs to the early Western Han dynasty of the second and first century BCE (see Kost 2014, cat. 39; pl. 125.2A).

A technical examination by Pieter Meyers (February 29, 2010) has shown that the two plaques are cast by the lost-wax casting process. On the reverse, two small, vertical loops were attached. The gilding was achieved by mercury-amalgam gilding. A stereomicroscopic examination reveals that the corrosion is superficial and appears to be applied. The pieces show little or no wear. When taken together with the amount of zinc measured, it is clear that this pair is a modern fake.

177 | Plaque with Two Confronting Rams and Wheels

Height 7.7 cm
Width 10 cm
Weight 102.2 g

Leaded gunmetal, alloy composition by E. Ferreira: Cu 79%; Sn 1.6%; Pb 1.4%; As 0.1%; Zn 11.5%

This openwork plaque shows two confronted rams in a double frame with indentations and three wheel-shaped forms that fill the space between the two animals. On the reverse, the animals' bodies are concave and the border areas are flat. This piece is similar to the gold plaque discussed in entry 139 (Chapter 5), which was attributed to the Xianbei period of northeastern China in the 1st and 2nd century CE. The extremely high amount of zinc is inconsistent with such a date and shows that this plaque is a modern fake.

178 | Harness Ornament with Bird's Head Terminals

Height 5 cm
Width 3.9 cm
Weight 19 g

Brass, alloy composition by J. Stenger: Cu 68%; Zn 36%

This harness decoration represents a round boss from which depend two volutes with stylized, eared, raptor-headed terminals. On the reverse, one finds a vertical loop behind the boss. This piece is extremely similar to entry 77 (Chapter 3c) and appears to form a pair with it. The very high zinc content, however, proves this piece to be a modern forgery, since this alloy is inconsistent with a provenance from China and a date in the 4th century BCE. In this case, one might wonder whether it was more profitable to sell pairs of objects, which would have created an incentive to produce a mirror-image forgery of an original item.

179 | Small Appliqué Horse Plaque

North China, Mongolia, southern Siberia (?)
2nd–1st century BCE (?)

Height 2.9 cm
Width 4.6 cm
Weight 13.1 g

Bronze, alloy composition by J. Stenger: Cu 93%; Pb 1%; Zn 1.5%

The plaque represents a horse with its legs folded in a recumbent pose. Three holes, two near the head and one at the tail, enable this small plaque to be fastened. A very similar, but broken, plaque has been excavated from a Xiongnu-period burial at Ala-Tey, in Tuva (Kilunovskaya and Leus 2018, 8, fig 27). Similar small horse appliqués, only gilded and without context, were published in the catalogue of the Ariadne Galleries (1998, 96, no. 102). The image is distantly related to a recumbent horse image found among the Xichagou grave goods and the larger horse plaques, such as those in the Thaw Collection in the Metropolitan Museum (Bunker et al. 2002, 128–29, no. 101). Very recently, a highly similar horse plaque, albeit made of bone, was found in a Xiongnu burial in Mongolia, confirming the date of these horse plaques (Ėnkhtör et al. 2020, 22, fig. 5). The measurement of 1.5% zinc in the plaque in the present collection raises suspicions concerning its authenticity, but it cannot be decided with certainty whether it is a fake, since Miniaev has reported zinc occurring, also at higher percentages, among bronzes from the Zakamenka hoard (see introduction to this chapter, pp. 420–21). However, since the archaeological context is missing, as a precaution the object is treated here.

Chapter 10

Production and Distribution of Belt Plaques in Inner Asia: Preliminary Insights from the Guyuan Mizong Collection

Ursula Brosseder and Yiu-Kang Hsu

Introduction

Working with materials from any collection, whether a museum collection or a private collection, usually brings with it the difficulty that the context of the artifact is lost. In the absence of essential information about the contextual inclusion of each piece, researchers must focus on the object itself. Objects can be studied with regards to their type and artistic expression, which has been the predominant approach chosen for bronze artifacts from Inner Asia. Another avenue of research is to investigate physical aspects of objects, in order to identify the production process that was employed. This primarily includes the study of the chemical and isotopic fingerprints used to trace the origin of the metals, but should also incorporate metallographic observations, in order to reveal the nature of the manufacturing process in combination with the qualities of the specific alloy used (Roberts and Thornton 2014). Such a holistic approach is beyond our capabilities and expertise, given that the present study is a first step towards understanding the general framework of Inner Asian bronzes.

Thankfully, in view of the importance and potential of metallurgical analysis, metallurgical testing of the Guyuan Mizong Collection was made possible. Our primary goal here is to characterize the alloy compositions (primarily tin, lead, and arsenic) of Inner Asian belt plaques in the collection. The outcomes, in combination with published legacy data, will allow us to paint a broad picture of alloy practices and their relationships between different regions of Inner Asia. More generally, the metallurgical data published here may serve as a data mine for future research and will provide a starting and reference point for many items for further investigation. In the following, we present an analysis of all of the published metallurgical data for belt plaques, as well as some thoughts about individual pieces from the collection.

The question of the origins of metallurgy and of the metals used in a given ancient community is no doubt important, when it comes to studying Xiongnu bronze production. However, the analysis in this chapter will not deal with this topic in detail for several reasons. The scientific analysis of the Xiongnu metals is still at an early stage, in which data concerning trace elements, rare-earth profiles, and isotopic ratios remain insufficient for an in-depth discussion. Moreover, a proper provenance study requires considerable archaeological excavation, geological fieldwork, and laboratory analysis in order to identify the time and place of ancient exploitation. This detailed work has never been done in core regions of the Xiongnu, such as Mongolia and Transbaikal, even though we are aware of abundant local copper-ore and tin deposits that could have met the need for bronze manufacture. Instead, the current analytical project focuses explicitly on the variability of copper-alloying traditions during the Xiongnu period, as the alloy practice contains evidence of human behavior that approaches metals in different ways (Pollard et al. 2018a). On the one hand, copper alloys could be deliberately made to manifest particular physical properties or the desired appearance of the finished object. On the other hand, the alloying process could be intentional or unintentional, as a result of which objects were derived from the recycling of mixed metals with different levels of alloying elements. As we shall demonstrate below, Xiongnu metallurgy is more similar to the second mode of production, which is indicative of dynamic political and social interactions with the outside world.

Method and Material

Most objects from the Guyuan Mizong Collection were tested. Those that were acquired from the Harris Collection in the most recent sale at Christie's, in 2017, and some single pieces were not examined.

The elemental composition of the Guyuan Mizong Collection was determined by the micro X-ray fluorescence spectroscopy (µXRF) at the Swiss Institute for Art Research (SIK-ISEA) in Zurich. Prior to measurements, a small spot, ca. 1 cm in diameter was cleaned by a conservator to expose fresh surface for the quantitative analysis. The measurements were conducted in two series:

The first was led by Ester Ferreira in 2015 and the second by Jens Stenger between 2016 and 2017. However, the change of analysts resulted in the instrument's being set up differently. While the series that was measured under the direction of Ferreira gives precise values for detectable elements (Cu, Sn, Pb, As, Ni, and Zn), elements reported by Stenger tend to be recorded in qualitative terms, as "high" or "trace." The values of the second series as they are reported here were not normalized. Thus, in particular instances the individual percentages may add up to more than 100%. Nevertheless, the data give a reliable overview of the alloy composition. However, for this reason, we do not include these data in our analyses or diagrams, but provide them in the body of the text.

The instrument used for the µXRF analysis was a Bruker AXS ARTAX 800 system equipped with a Rh target and polycapillary lens. The analytical conditions were set up as follows: generator voltage 50 kV, current 600 µA, helium atmosphere, spot size 70 µm, and acquisition time 100 seconds. Quantification was achieved by calibrating raw data against a series of the certified bronze and bass reference materials, using a linear regression. Each object was measured at three (1st series) or two different locations (2nd series) and the results were averaged.

Although the Guyuan Mizong Collection contains a variety of Inner Asian copper-based artifacts dated between the late second millennium BCE and the first centuries CE, this chapter will mainly focus on belt plaques, as they are one of most remarkable signature items from Inner Asia, especially between the third century BCE to the first century CE. Belt plaques from Inner Asia—i.e., from southern Siberia, Mongolia and Inner Mongolia—but also from other areas in present-day China are well known and have been studied intensively.[63] The typology of belt plaques is well established: For the vast majority of belt-plaque types, their general area of distribution is known and has been discussed in previous studies (Dévlet 1980; Brosseder 2011; Kost 2014).

Taking into consideration additional manufacturing details—e.g., whether they are solid plaques or openwork plaques, casting methods, such as the lost-wax, lost-textile method or only the lost-wax method—three larger zones in which belt plaques play a significant role can be identified: 1) the Minusinsk Basin, 2)

---

63   See Chapter 4 and Dévlet 1980; Bunker et al. 1997; Bunker et al. 2002; Brosseder 2011; Kost 2014, to name but a few works.

Mongolia, along with the Transbaikal area, Manchuria and Inner Mongolia, including the northern part of the Ordos region, and 3) China east of the Taihang range, from the southern Ordos region down to southern China. In our analyses and diagrams, we refer to the area between Transbaikalia and the northern Ordos as the "northern steppes." These zones are not strictly separated, and while some types exhibit a restriction in their geographical distribution, for example in the Minusinsk Basin (e.g., Dėvlet 1980, pl. 13–15; 19–27), others can be found in a larger geographical area stretching from the northern Ordos area, Mongolia, to the Transbaikal area (e.g., fig. 25, p. 285).

Belt plaques are, moreover, a good starting point for investigating bronzes more generally, as a more extensive series of compositional data has been published for them (Miniaev 1980). This series provides insight into the alloy composition of belt plaques from all over Inner Asia—from the Minusinsk Basin, the Transbaikal area, and Mongolia—and thus provides an excellent background for the data concerning the present collection.

Apart from metallurgical belt-plaque data, there also exist compositional data for other bronzes from different sites: from the cemetery of Dyrestui in the Transbaikal area (Miniaev 1977), Noyon Uul in northern Mongolia, which to our knowledge has only been published summarily (Miniaev 1981), and from the cache of bronzes found in the Kosogol hoard in the Minusinsk Basin (Miniaev 1978). More recently, data relating to bronzes from excavations in south-central Mongolia, in Baga Gazryn chuluu (Park et al. 2011) and from bronzes of chariots from the terrace tomb in Gol Mod 2 (Park et al. 2018) can be added, as well as data for bronzes from the Sackler Collection (Chase and Douglas 1997) and the Liu Collection (Miniaev and Smolarski 2002).

These series provide an insight into the circulation and occurrence of metal compositions of bronzes at different sites. Sergei Miniaev has summarized the state of knowledge in the 1980s on the basis of his series of Inner Asian data and highlighted the variety of alloy compositions used in Transbaikalia, the differences between sites, and other regional specifics (Miniaev 1983; 2016).[64]

---

64 This article was translated and republished in English in 2016, with an introduction by William Honeychurch (Miniaev 2016). Nadezhda Sergeeva has also published compositional data from burials in the Transbaikal area, including bronzes from Dyrestui (Sergeeva 1981). It remains unclear whether these constitute an additional series, alongside Miniaev's series (Miniaev 1977), or whether they concern the same objects.

*A Metallurgical View on the Belt Plaques
from the Guyuan Mizong Collection*

In Chapter 4, we outlined the geographic distribution of the belt plaques in the collection dating from the second century BCE to the first century CE, based on their typology and analogue finds from known archaeological contexts. The vast majority of belt plaques in the collection were attributed to northern China, specifically to regions east of the Taihang Mountains, the southern Ordos area, and the Central Plains (see figs. 23 and 24, p. 284). A smaller group of belt plaques in this collection belong to types typical of the northern part of the Ordos, Mongolia, the Transbaikal area, and the Minusinsk Basin (see figs. 25 and 26, p. 285).

Figure 28 presents a plot of compositional data from the belt plaques in the Guyuan Mizong Collection based on their tin, lead, and arsenic concentrations. These three elements have been widely recognized as the main constituents of prehistoric copper alloys. Tin and lead are correlated to each other in the late Early Iron Age in eastern Asia, meaning that it makes sense here to treat them as a combined element for belt plaques. The majority of the belt plaques are characterized by the alloying of tin and lead, with little or no arsenic (fig. 28). This alloy practice has been viewed as a signature of metal production in the regions of northern China since the beginning of the first millennium BCE (Hsu et al. 2016). It is remarkable to observe the huge variation in tin and lead in those plaques, ranging from 1% to 27%. This might suggest a variety of alloy practices adopted by archaeological communities in northern China, where each area—or even a single site—would have been able to organize its own network of metal supply or its own production method for belt plaques. Since we attribute the majority of belt plaques to northern China, we take these as a proxy for the baseline of the Chinese belt-plaque tradition (fig. 28, red dots). This is consistent with the analysis of their typology and distribution that shows that similar belt plaques are found in excavation contexts in central China, the southern Ordos area, and southern China (figs. 23 and 24, p. 284).

Among the Chinese plaques, it is interesting to note that plaques of the same type were not necessarily made using a standardized recipe, but that their alloy composition varies. The pair 103a and b (Chapter 4), depicting ungulate, wolf, and bear was manufactured using tin (around 8–9%) and some lead (1–3%); the other pair with the same motif (entry 102, Chapter 4) was manufactured with a much lower tin content (around 1%) and no lead at all. This shows that the craftsmen utilized different resources to produce plaques with the same motif.

Belt plaques that depict the same motif of a recumbent wolf and argali (Chapter 4, entries 105, 106, and 107), however, all show very similar amounts of alloying elements. The three plaques were alloyed with tin (around 8–9%) and lead (5–8%).

The homogeneity or heterogeneity of metal composition does not allow us to conclude whether plaques were produced in the same or in different workshops, since the workshops also depended on the availability of resources and we currently know very little about the organization of the production process (mining, smelting, and casting) in northern China.

Once the baseline for the Chinese plaques is established, we may consider those belt plaques that we attributed to the northern steppes based on their typology, but which fall either into the group of tin-lead alloys with little arsenic (see fig. 28, green dots) and the group of those that we were uncertain about (fig. 28, grey lozenges). Plaques 125a and b, 127, and 128 deserve a particularly close look. They all belong to the group of P-shaped plaques that are mainly found in northeastern China, Liaoning province, and Mongolia (see fig. 24, p. 284, and Chapter 4, entries 125 through 128).

The plot that differentiates between tin and lead (fig. 29) shows widely varying amounts of tin and lead. However, most plaques that were identified either as belonging to the northern steppes or as being uncertain tend to cluster with lower tin values. Too much should not be made of this pattern here, which only serves to highlight the complexity of the patterns that emerge when there is more data available. The forthcoming publication of the Xichagou material from Liaoning province will help to establish whether and how metallurgical practices in northeastern China possibly differ from other areas of China (Pan Ling forthcoming).

Another outlier in the plot fig. 28 is the pair of belt plaques 133a and b, which contain low levels of tin and lead, but a considerable amount of arsenic. The same is true for belt plaque no. 121. As we shall discuss below, arsenic is a diagnostic element for copper alloys produced in the Eurasian Steppe, especially in the Minusinsk Basin of southern Siberia, while an alloy that uses tin, lead, and arsenic is typical for bronzes found in Mongolia and in the Transbaikal area of the Xiongnu period. The presence of arsenic, tin, and lead in belt plaques may hint that they are made out of a mixed or recycled metal, as these three elements do

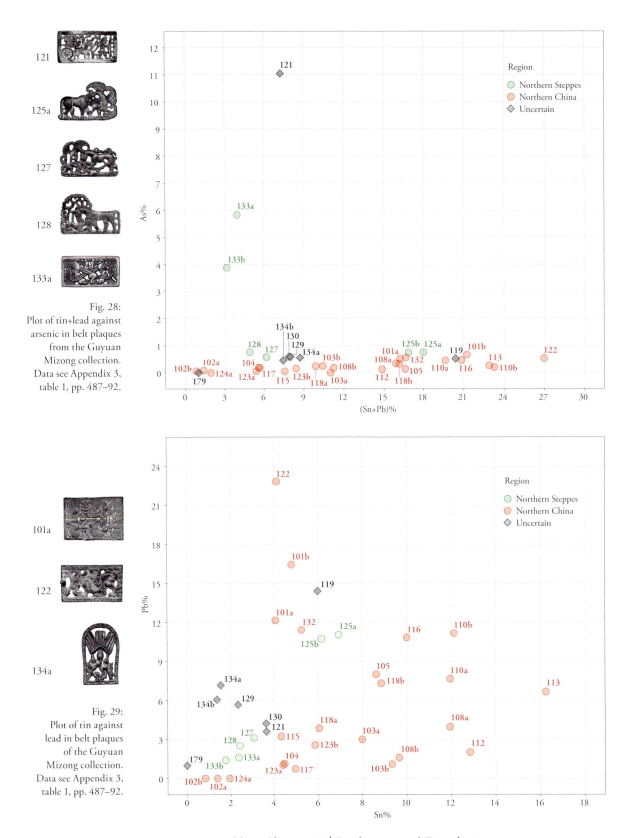

Fig. 28: Plot of tin+lead against arsenic in belt plaques from the Guyuan Mizong collection. Data see Appendix 3, table 1, pp. 487–92.

Fig. 29: Plot of tin against lead in belt plaques of the Guyuan Mizong collection. Data see Appendix 3, table 1, pp. 487–92.

442   Chapter 10 | Production and Distribution

not usually occur side by side in the primary alloy production. The presence of tin and lead in belt plaques that we attribute to the northern steppes may point to the recycling of metal from northern China. Likewise, we can further hypothesize about the group to which those belt plaques marked as "uncertain" belong: The pair of belt plaques 134a and b (Chapter 4), with higher amounts of lead, cluster more closely together with the belt plaques that we believe to have come from the northern steppes. Belt plaque 122 (Chapter 4) is also completely different, as it is the only one with such a high percentage of lead. Also of interest is the Chinese pair of belt plaques (entry 101a and b, Chapter 4) with a high leaded tin bronze, which is a type that may be slightly older than most of the other Chinese belt plaques. All of these plaques appear to cluster together in a region with low tin values, while most of the Chinese belt plaques (fig. 29, red dots) show higher percentages of tin.

Metallurgical Analyses of Belt Plaques in Inner Asia

Compositional analyses of the present collection provide a good reference point for outlining various metallurgical practices in Inner Asia during the Xiongnu period and early Western Han period in northern China. Figure 30 presents belt-plaque data from the Minusinsk Basin, Mongolia, and the Transbaikal area (northern steppes) for which we know the archaeological context or, in the case of old finds, the area of provenance.[65] It clearly highlights a sharp contrast between metal production in the Minusinsk Basin and that in northern China, since the former is dominated by arsenical copper and the latter by leaded tin bronze. Apart from these two main alloying patterns, belt plaques from Mongolia and Transbaikalia tend to have intermediate levels of arsenic, tin, and lead, a practice that makes use of all three of these common alloying elements.

The plot shows that various belt plaques that were classified as objects from the northern steppes were made with an alloy composition that is in line with the Chinese recipe (figs. 30 and 31), namely, two gilded plaques from Dyrestui, burial 10, and one from the Sackler Collections (Appendix 3, Table 2, nos. 3–4, 93), all of which belong to the same type depicting two fighting stallions. Furthermore,

---

65   The belt plaques from the Minusinsk Basin published by Dévlet 1980 are mostly finds without context.

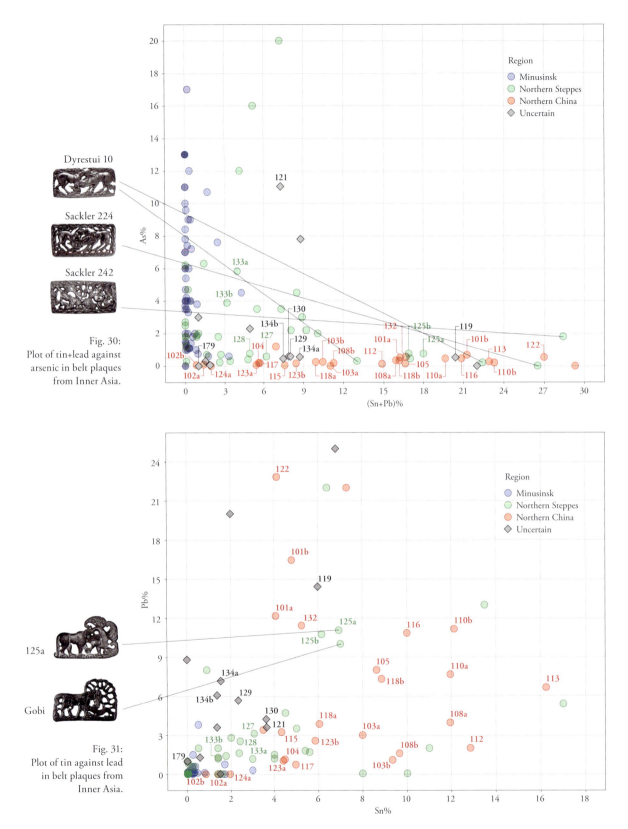

Fig. 30: Plot of tin+lead against arsenic in belt plaques from Inner Asia.

Fig. 31: Plot of tin against lead in belt plaques from Inner Asia.

444   Chapter 10 | Production and Distribution

the single plaque depicting a fight between a dragon and a tiger from the Sackler Collections falls into this group (Bunker et al. 1997, 274, no. 242, Appendix 3, Table 2, no. 88). The alloy of the P-shaped plaque from the Gobi (Appendix 3, Table 2, no. 16) is very similar to the pair 125a and b from this present collection (fig. 31). Since these plaques all fall into the group of Chinese plaques, they were most likely produced in China, and in the case of the pair from burial 10 in Dyrestui, distributed further north.

Some belt plaques attributed to the northern-steppes type (nos. 133a and b, 128, 64) tend to cluster in an area with low tin and lead, normally less than 3%. This can potentially be interpreted as a recycled alloy, where copper and leaded tin bronzes of different levels of tin and lead have been mixed together (Pollard et al. 2018b, 118–19). However, it is equally likely that the smelting of polymetallic ores could have produced such a low alloying pattern (Pernicka 2014, 256). The further study of trace elements and lead isotopes in the objects will hopefully shed more light on the origins of this alloy.

The results of our analysis also highlight that belt plaques of the same type were produced with different alloying compositions. In the following, the data available for specific types shall be discussed.

There are three types of openwork belt plaques that are mainly known from the Minusinsk Basin and are, as a rule, manufactured with an arsenic bronze: The first type represents openwork belt plaques that depict two confronting bulls. They are distributed only in the Minusinsk Basin: one specimen is known from Mongolia and another one from Xichagou, northeast China (Brosseder 2011, 370, fig. 18).[66] Only three plaques are known to also contain lead and tin.[67] This is also the case with belt plaques that depict geometric motives which also occur only in the Minusinsk Basin and in Tuva and are exclusively made of an arsenic bronze (Dèvlet 1980, pl. 13–18). The same holds true for D-shaped or semicircular openwork plaques that depict an animal with its tail around its head (Dèvlet 1980, pl. 19–27).

---

66   The compilation of those plaques that were found in China by Kost (2014, pl. 17–18.1–2) did not alter the distribution.

67   Utinka with 1.7% Sn, 0.76% Pb (see Appendix 3, Table 2, no. 23), Abakanskoe (Appendix 3, Table 2, no. 80) with 0.5% Sn and 3.8% Pb. A similar composition is also described for the specimen from the Thaw Collection (Bunker et al. 2002, 139, no. 113).

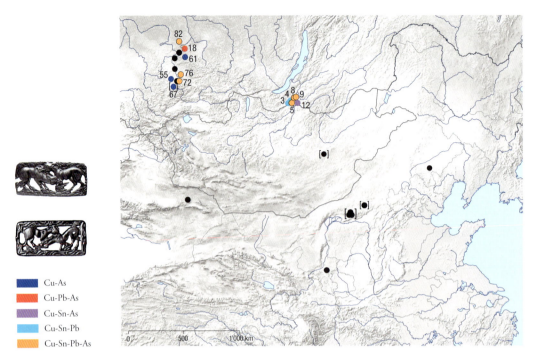

Fig. 32: Distribution of rectangular openwork belt plaques depicting two horses fighting and with different alloy compositions. Mapped after Brosseder 2011, 365, fig. 13; data see Appendix 3, table 2, pp. 493–96.

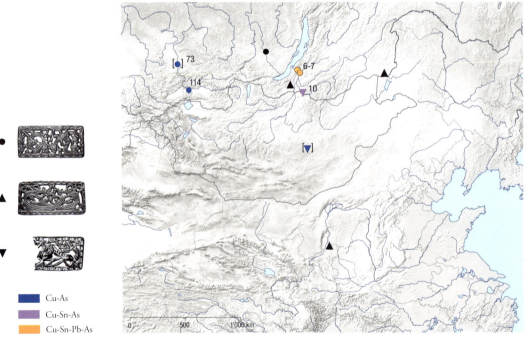

Fig. 33: Rectangular openwork belt plaques with dragon motifs and with different alloy compositions. Mapped after Brosseder 2011, 379, fig. 28; data see Appendix 3, table 2, pp. 493–96.

446   Chapter 10 | Production and Distribution

More interesting, however, are those types of belt plaques whose distribution is not restricted to the Minusinsk Basin alone, but spread across Mongolia and Transbaikalia, in addition to either the northern Ordos region or northeastern China (but usually not both).

One type, for which several analyses have been published, comprises the openwork belt plaque depicting two horses fighting which is known in two variants (fig. 32). If we take both variants together, we see that in the Minusinsk Basin this variant has been made from a copper-arsenic (Cu-As) alloy, while in Transbaikalia, alloy compositions containing lead, tin, and arsenic (Cu-Sn-Pb-As) predominate, apart from the pair from Dyrestui, burial 10, discussed above that follows a Chinese recipe.

The same is true for belt plaques depicting dragons and tigers (fig. 33): Those from the Minusinsk Basin and Tuva are—as expected—made of an arsenic-copper alloy.[68] The pair of plaques from Ivolga in Transbaikalia was made of an alloy containing tin, lead, and arsenic (Cu-Sn-Pb-As), the alloy composition typical for this region.[69] Two such plaques are also known from collections: The one from the Thaw Collection in the Metropolitan Museum was manufactured from almost pure copper with small quantities of lead and only a minimal amount of arsenic (Bunker et al. 2002, 133), while the one of the Sackler Foundation displays an extremely high amount of lead, but little tin and arsenic.[70]

The case of the semi-circular belt plaques depicting a wolf or plaques with a feline and a caprid is not as clear, as there are no analyses for the specimen from Transbaikalia and Mongolia. Such plaques are not known from the Ordos region, but only from northeastern China, Mongolia, and southern Siberia (fig. 34). However, we can state that the plaques from the Minusinsk Basin are made of an arsenic bronze (Cu-As). The specimen from the Thaw Collection is made of an arsenic bronze with traces of iron and antimony (Bunker et al. 2002, 103, no. 71).

The P-shaped plaques depicting animal combat between a griffin attacking an animal have been produced with different alloys as well (fig. 35): The one found in the northern Gobi is made of an arsenic bronze (Appendix 3, Table 2, no. 113), just like a plaque with a similar—though not identical—motif housed in

---

68   Plaque from the Minusinsk Basin (Appendix 3, Table 2, no. 73); from Terezin, Tuva (Appendix 3, Table2, no. 114).
69   Appendix 3, Table 2, nos. 6–7.
70   Appendix 3, Table 2, no. 88; Bunker et al. 1997, no. 242; Chase and Douglas 1997, 313, V-3925, lab no. 2787.

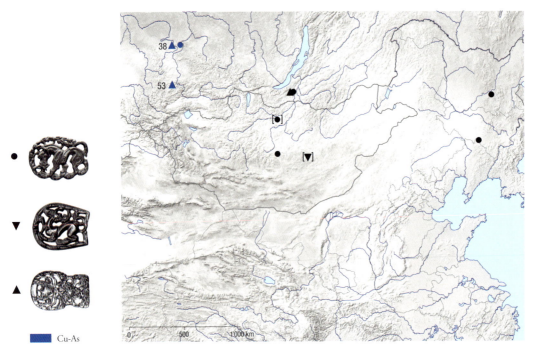

Fig. 34: Variants of D-shaped belt plaques with different alloy compositions. Mapped after Brosseder 2011, 371, fig. 19; data see Appendix 3, table 2, pp. 493–96.

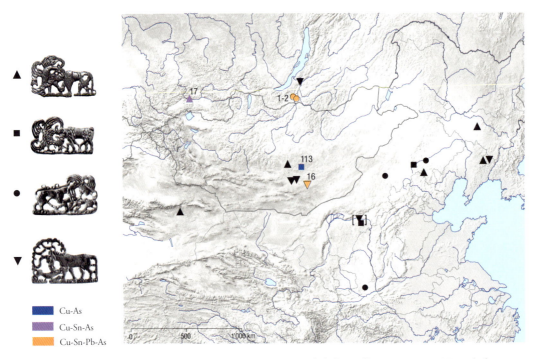

Fig. 35: Group of P-shaped belt plaques with different alloy compositions. Mapped after Brosseder 2011, 381, fig. 31; 383, fig. 33; data see Appendix 3, table 2, pp. 493–96.

448   Chapter 10 | Production and Distribution

the Metropolitan Museum (Bunker et al. 2002, 102–03, no. 70). The pair from Dyrestui in Transbaikalia and the one from the Gobi desert are made of an alloy with tin, lead and arsenic added to the copper base.

The distribution maps all show that the same type of belt plaque is not always made with the same alloy composition, but rather the alloy composition can vary within a single type or a single group of belt plaques. This is similar to what we have observed among the belt plaques from the Guyuan Mizong Collection which—despite the fact that they are almost identical with respect to their typology—are produced with different alloys.

A Site-based Analysis

In general, compositional data concerning ancient metal artifacts with well-defined archaeological contexts would allow us to identify a metallurgical province or center with an established supply network. In order to gain more insight into these processes, it is reasonable to perform a site-based analysis that highlights the presence of objects with different alloy compositions at a single site, thus helping us to identify site-specific metallurgical practices.

To illustrate this concept, figure 36 displays compositional data for bronzes from various sites in Inner Asia that belong to the same time period: the Xiongnu period and the early Western Han period. We also included the belt-plaque data from the present collection as a proxy for a Chinese recipe (fig. 36, red dots). Values are normalized to 100% (Sn+Pb+As) in order to display the relations between these three elements. The diagram appears to show three alloy practices that correspond to the different regions, respectively: Minusinsk, the northern steppes (Transbaikal area and Mongolia with Dyrestui, Baga Gazryn chuluu, Gol Mod), and northern China.

We have already discussed the belt-plaque data of the present collection, indicating that it represents a Chinese recipe. At the other extreme, we find the objects from the Kosogol'skii hoard in Minusinsk Basin (fig. 36, blue dots). Although we must assume that, in this hoard, objects were accumulated over a longer time span, we see that the alloying practice displayed is similar to the one used for the belt-plaque material from the Minusinsk Basin, i.e., it represents a bronze with arsenic as the main alloying element.

The bronzes from Dyrestui, Baga Gazryn chuluu, and Gol Mod, which are sites belonging to the Xiongnu empire, fall mainly between the two previously

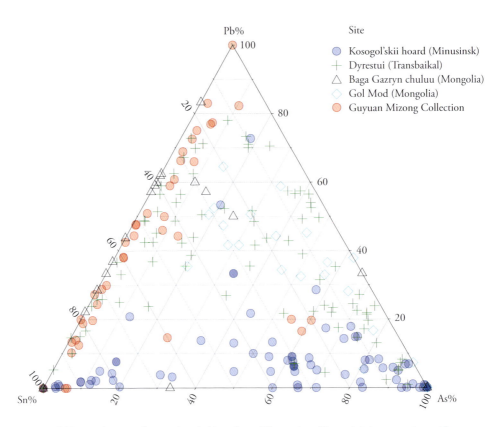

Fig. 36: Ternary diagram of copper-based objects from different sites of Inner Asia in comparison with the Guyuan Mizong collection. Data see Appendix 3, tables 1 and 2, pp. 487–96.

discussed poles in that the bronzes contain tin, lead, and arsenic as alloying elements. Some of the bronze artifacts from the Xiongnu sites follow a Chinese recipe, while others follow a recipe from the Minusinsk Basin and indicate the flow of artifacts in the Xiongnu empire. Although the bronzes from sites from Mongolia (Baga Gazryn chuluu and Gol Mod) and Transbaikalia (Dyrestui) have similar alloying patterns, subtle differences can be identified between the sites. Objects from Gol Mod are characterized by quaternary alloy (Cu+Sn+Pb+As) and none of the tested objects follows a Chinese recipe, while only a very few fall into the arsenic apex. The objects tested are flower petals, which were used to decorate chariots and were locally made (Park et al. 2018).

At Dyrestui, we find a variety bronzes with different alloying practices. While some objects are made of a tin-leaded bronze and thus follow a Chinese practice, most objects were manufactured making use of all alloys (fig. 37 a–b). We can also find objects made with different alloy compositions in one burial (fig. 37).

As one can see the tin-lead-arsenic alloy predominates (orange), but bronzes made with other alloying types occur. In burial 10, for example, the pair of belt plaques was made of a tin-lead alloy, while the pair of rings and bell pendants, which are also integral part of the fancy belt the woman wore, were made with different alloys (fig. 37). In burials 7 and 9, the belt plaques were made of an alloy with tin, lead, and arsenic, while the broad variety of small objects was made with different alloys. This may hint at different circumstances, times, or sources of acquisition.

By contrast, in Baga Gazryn chuluu, in the northern Gobi, we find more bronzes that follow a Chinese alloying recipe and fewer bronzes that employ tin, lead, and arsenic, or copper and arsenic alone (fig. 38; Park et al. 2011). Park and his colleagues identify two main alloy groups—copper-arsenic alloys and tin-lead bronzes—dismissing the objects with tin lead and arsenic as outliers (Park et al. 2011). While this specific alloy composition may be atypical for Baga Gazryn chuluu, all of the other metal assemblages in the diagram suggest that copper metal alloyed with tin, lead, and arsenic was the norm for the area of Mongolia and Transbaikalia ("northern steppes") in the Xiongnu period (fig. 36; see also Miniaev 1977; Miniaev 1980, 31, fig. 2). The outlier with respect to this specific alloy is a belt plaque made from arsenic copper (fig. 38, A.18), while the button and the spoon-shaped strap ends were made of a leaded tin bronze. In Baga Gazryn chuluu, we also see that Chinese artifacts, such as cross-bolt arrowheads, made with a leaded tin bronze and thus probably imported from China (Park et al. 2011, 809, table 1, no. 34–35), were also locally manufactured with an alloy of copper with tin, lead, and arsenic (fig. 38, C.2; Park et al. 2011, 809, table 1, no. 30). And while some or most of those bronzes with a Chinese recipe can be considered imports from China, the possibility of resmelting from Chinese metal cannot be excluded.

In order to illustrate the differences between sites within the Xiongnu empire, we have also taken into consideration the data summarily published Sergei Miniaev (Miniaev 1983; Miniaev 2016). In this, we follow his classification of alloy types: He simply organizes the data into groups according to the presence of various elements in the bronze (Miniaev 2016, 153, fig. 5).[71] We have also

---

71 Miniaev (1977, 44) suggests that an addition of more than 0.3% of arsenic speaks for a deliberate addition. Chase and Douglas (1997, 310–11) mention that low arsenic content ranging between 0% and 0.5% is also found in Chinese bronzes and is likely to have been introduced with other alloying components, such as copper.

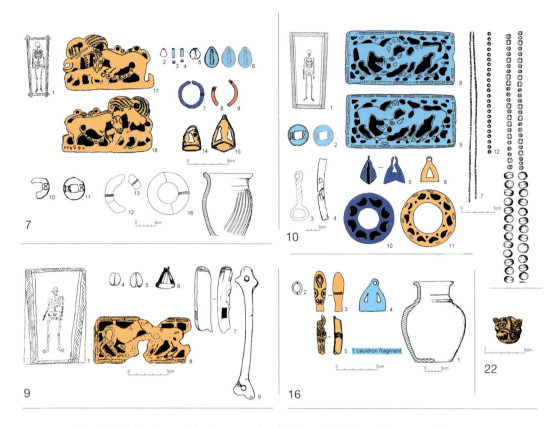

Fig. 37: Burials at Dyrestui showing copper-based artifacts with different alloy compositions. Light blue: copper-tin-lead; dark blue: arsenical copper; orange: copper-tin-lead-arsenic. Values based on Miniaev 1977, see Appendix 3, table 3, pp. 497–502.

amended the data, by combining the cemetery and the settlement data from Ivolga, while, for Dyrestui, we used the data Miniaev published in 1977, which explains different numbers. The pie-charts (fig. 39) highlight differences between single sites, as Miniaev has already stated (Miniaev 1983; Miniaev 2016).

The site located farthest north is Ivolga, which displays a great variety of alloy compositions and which also more arsenic bronze objects than any other site (fig. 39). While there may be many reasons why arsenic bronzes occur in Ivolga—for instance, different alloy mixing on the part of the artisan, the availability of supply, or the exchange of objects—it has also been proposed that, in some instances, we can suppose intermarriage from the Minusinsk Basin into the Ivolga community (Brosseder 2007).

In Dyrestui, the percentage of tin-lead-arsenic alloys (Cu+Sn+Pb+As) is much higher than in Ivolga; more than half of the bronzes were made with such a mixture. The share of arsenic-copper objects is furthermore lower than in Ivolga.

Also of interest is the summary data from Il'movaia Pad' and Noyon Uul (fig. 39). Both sites are cemeteries with terrace tombs that represent elite burials from the late first century BCE to the first century CE. At both sites, the percentage of bronzes with a tin-lead alloy are dominant and arsenic bronzes are absent (Miniaev 1981). Due to the complex political relationship between the Han Dynasty and the Xiongnu, with tribute being paid by the former to their northern neighbors and the marriage of Chinese princesses to the *Chanyu's* court, it is no surprise that we find a higher percentage of imported objects from China assembled in these elite contexts.[72]

In Baga Gazryn chuluu, by contrast (fig. 39), we find an equal proportion of objects that follow a Chinese recipe, despite the fact that this site is not an elite site. Here, the higher proportion may be explained by the greater proximity to China and/or a greater dependency on contacts to other sites in order to meet their need for bronzes.

The leaded tin bronze is also attested for the terrace tomb in Gol Mod 1, where a Chinese bronze vessel was made out of such an alloy (Pons and Lacoudre 2003, 144). A smaller group of objects in Il'movaia Pad' and Noyon Uul consists of a copper-lead (Cu-Pb) alloy or of pure copper (Cu) (Miniaev 1983). The recent compositional analyses of artifacts from kurgan 20 in Noyon Uul (Polos'mak et al. 2011, 161–63) show that most bronze objects analyzed were made of copper-lead (Cu-Pb) alloys, with the exception of a single cup containing only tin as the primary alloying element (Cu-Sn). However, from the list presented (Polos'mak et al. 2011, 163, chart 2.3), it remains again unclear which objects were analyzed. Conversely, while leaded-copper objects have not been found in Dyrestui and Baga Gazryn chuluu (BGC), one may ask whether this specific alloy was not a special mixture used for manufacturing objects for the elite. Furthermore, the otherwise typical tin, lead, and arsenic alloy (Cu-Sn-Pb-As) seems to be absent from these elite contexts. One needs to keep in mind that besides a potential difference in the social context, this could also indicate a temporal difference, given that all the above-mentioned elite contexts belong to a later phase of the Xiongnu

---

[72] The lyre-shaped buckles with movable tongue, one of which is from kurgan 6 in Noyon Uul, are made of brass, which seems to be typical for Kushan period in Central Asia (Elikhina and Miniaev 2014, 190) and thereby underlines the presence of foreign objects with a different alloy compositions in these elite tombs.

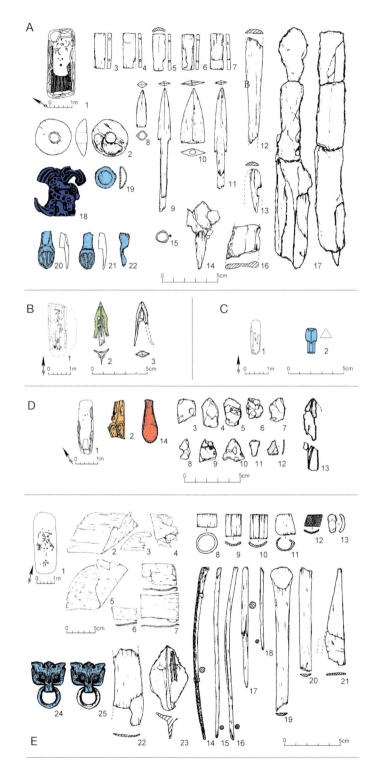

Fig. 38: Burials at Baga Gazryn chuluu showing copper-based artifacts with different alloy compositions. Light blue: copper-tin-lead; dark blue: arsenical copper; orange: copper-tin-lead-arsenic.

454   Chapter 10 | Production and Distribution

empire (late first century BCE to first century CE), while the sites at Ivolga and Dyrestui also yield data from the second and first century BCE.

Evidence for Primary Bronze Production in Inner Asia

Finally, let us turn to the existing evidence for primary bronze production in Xiongnu-period Inner Asia. Generally, detailed research on primary production (mining and smelting) for both the Early and Late Iron Ages in the region has not yet been conducted, and we have no direct evidence for the organization of bronze production. However, Mongolia is rich in mineral ores and, at least theoretically, copper, arsenic, tin, and lead are readily available. Research on ancient mining is, however, almost non-existent. This dearth of knowledge hampers any comprehensive evaluation of ancient bronze-working practices and the reconstruction of supply networks.

Evidence for local bronze casting is derived from findings of crucibles, as well as off-cast in the settlement of Ivolga alone (Miniaev 1983; Davydova 1995, 34; 52–54).[73] The crucibles were excavated in buildings and pits within the settlement. Moreover, at the open settlement of Dureny no workshop has been identified. In the disturbed surface layer, remains of casting channels and bronze ingots were found (Davydova and Miniaev 2003; Miniaev 2016, 153), while in the open settlement of Boroo, where only limited excavations have been conducted, no indications of local bronze working have come to light (Ramseyer and Pousaz 2013, 192).

Based on the spectrum of different alloy compositions and the occurrence of certain trace elements, Sergei Miniaev has suggested the existence of several distinct bronze-producing centers in the Transbaikal region: one in Ivolga, one around Dyrestui, and one around Dureny (Miniaev 1983, 10–11; Miniaev 1980, 29–31; Miniaev 2016, 154). More specifically, a higher amount of *indium* signifies

---

[73] According to Miniaev (1983, 73, fig. 10), it seems that the evidence for bronze production has accumulated at the southern fringe of the settled space of Ivolga, close to the surrounding wall-ditch system. However, if we examine the original publication (Davydova 1995), in order to reproduce and control the distribution of evidence for bronze working that Miniaev mapped, the picture looks more balanced. Another problem with the illustration provided by Miniaev is that there is no discussion of or information about the site formation (layering and taphonomy) that could have had a potential influence on the distribution of crucibles and cast-off that might contribute to the accumulation in the south. On the basis of the publication alone, this information cannot be retrieved and thus we should refrain from concluding that most bronze working is attested at the fringe of the settlement.

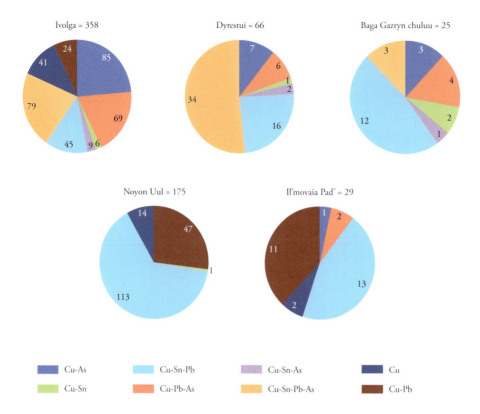

Fig. 39: Pie-charts of metal compositional data from different sites. Values after Miniaev 1983; for Dyrestui after Miniaev 1977.

bronzes from the Dyrestui area, which he calls the "Dzhida metallurgical center" (Miniaev 1977; Miniaev 1983, 11; Miniaev 2016, 153–54).

The discussion above has suggested that the character of Xiongnu bronze metallurgy in the northern steppes appears to be opportunistic, using whatever resources they have available to fabricate the final products. We also suspect that recycling was taking place with raw materials could have been leaded tin bronze from China and arsenical copper from the Minusinsk Basin. Local production by mixing the above two metal stocks could also have taken place.

The phenomenon and practices observed are not unique to the Xiongnu period, as we have envisaged such a practice in the preceding slab burials in the same geographic region (Hsu et al. 2020). The ternary diagram (fig. 40) clearly shows that some slab-burial artifacts exhibit a certain mixing character of chemical composition, similar to those Xiongnu metals, manifested by the mixture

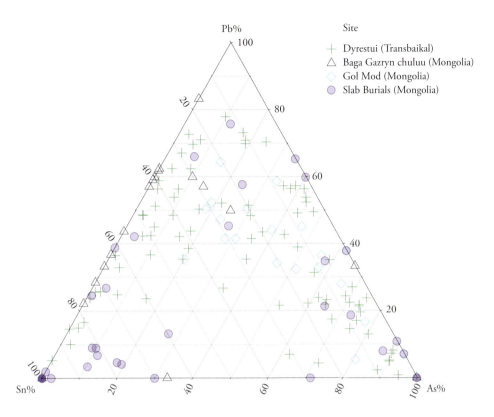

Fig. 40: Ternary diagram showing alloy composition of copper-based objects from Xiongnu sites (based on Appendix 3, table 3, nos. 1–109, 113–29) and those from the preceding slab burial culture in Mongolia (based on Hsu et al. 2020).

between copper-arsenic and copper-tin-lead alloys. It reveals to us the intriguing fact that, while the Xiongnu and slab-burial people are archaeological distinct groups in many ways, there seems to be a continuity of metallurgical practice among them. The long-standing tradition of using different sources for their metal stock might be due to the intermediary location of the northern steppes, as an important contact zone between the two substantial metallurgical centers of the Minusinsk Basin and China. Even so, the organization of bronze production in Mongolia and Transbaikalia should be characterized as decentralized, in which metal-producing communities had their own exchange links.

Chapter 11

Using Music Archaeological Methods to Establish a New History of Chinese Strings

Bo Lawergren

The Classic and Ancient Qin-Zither in China

The *qin* is a musical instrument invented in ancient China, and still largely confined to that country. For those who read English, the classic book on the *qin* is *The Lore of the Chinese Lute* by the Dutch diplomat Robert H. van Gulik.[74] In its present, classic form, it is an approximately 120 cm long wooden board, with seven strings stretched across its top surface. The player's left-hand fingers press down on the strings plucked by the right hand. Because it is a board across which strings are stretched, it is classified as a zither by musicologists. The strings vibrate and set the board into vibration, and this amplifies the sound. The *qin* board is more massive than the walls of violins. Consequently, it vibrates less vigorously than the board of the violin and makes a softer sound. For this reason, the *qin* is usually played in small rooms or intimate settings, whereas the violin functions well in concert halls.

The *qin* is formed by two pieces of wood glued together after their undersides have been scooped out to provide an internal resonating box, open to the outside through two sound-holes on the bottom piece. The opening near the left end is called the "phoenix pool," and the one on the right is the "dragon pond" (Wang Binlu 1983, 10–11). Sound holes appear on both Western and Eastern chordophones. On the former, the hole has an acoustic function, forming a Helmholtz resonator. But on the latter, it has a more symbolic purpose. Indeed, parts of the

---

74   First edition 1940, when the author made the error of calling the *qin* "a lute." His book concentrates on "*qin* lore"—a review of post-Zhou texts, but touches lightly on technical aspects of the *qin*, the focus of the present discussion.

qin form potent symbols rather than acoustic systems, and the Chinese names for *qin* parts reflect this reality, e.g., two spacers are inserted in the resonating cavity, the one near the left end is called "earth pillar" and the one on the right is "heaven pillar" (fig. 41).

The classic *qin* is also called *guqin*, meaning "ancient *qin*." The oldest surviving instruments date only from the Tang dynasty (618–907 CE). There was also unsubstantiated talk that it was much older, perhaps even earlier than the beginning of recorded Chinese history, a time when mythological heroes and sages populated the landscape. One hero, Shen Nong, was said to have "invented" the *qin*, but such a unique event is hardly credible. We know that the *qin* existed during the Zhou Dynasty, because its name is mentioned several times in the *Classic of Poetry* (*Shi Jing*), a compilation of folk songs, poetry, and hymns from the first half of the first millennium BCE, although nothing was known about its shape and characteristics.

This was the understanding of *qin* history before 1978, when the tomb of Marquis Yi of Zeng (Zeng Hou Yi) was discovered in Suizhou, Hubei province. The burial dates from 433 BCE, and contained a wealth of instruments—65 bronze bells, 30 stone chimes, 12 *se*-zithers, a *zhu*-zither, a ten-stringed *qin*-zither (figs. 41 and 45 a), a set of panpipes, and two transverse flutes.[75] Organologists concentrated on the bronze bells, which were inscribed with musical notation, and mostly ignored the *qin*-zither. The discovery had a significant impact on several topics in music archaeology, including—in addition to the tuning of bronze bells—drums, mouthorgans, and *zhu*- and *qin*-zithers. It also revealed for the first time the shapes of *qin*-zithers from the fifth century BCE. Before the discovery of the *qin*-like instrument in the fifth-century BCE tomb of Marquis Yi of Zeng in 1978, there was some reason for the name "*guqin*." It acknowledged that the *qin* had old roots, but after the 1978 discovery, it became plain that a much older, and well established, *qin* had existed centuries earlier. It is pointless to keep the expression "*guqin*," and I shall avoid it from now on.

---

75 See So 2000a, especially Lawergren 2000, the first study of ancient Chinese chordophones in a Western language. For the full archaeological report, see Hubei 1989.

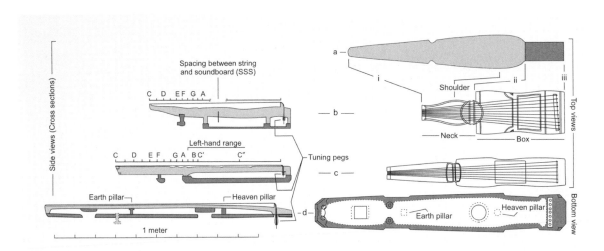

Fig. 41: Diagrams of ancient *qin*-zithers, side views (left) and top views (right). a) Proposed outline of Xi Kang's *qin* (see fig. 46 below). b) Ancient *qin* from the tomb of Marquis Yi of Zeng, 433 BCE, length: 67 cm. c) Ancient *qin* from Mawangdui, Changsha, Hunan, second century BCE, length 83 cm. d) Classical *qin* signed by Prince of Lu, 1633 CE, length: ca. 120 cm.

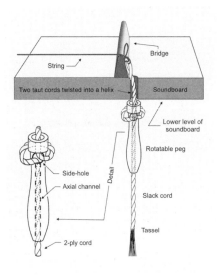

Fig. 42: Tuning mechanism of a modern *qin* with details of a tuning peg.

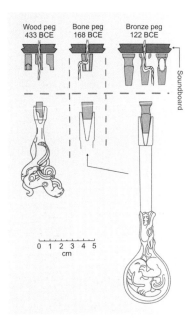

Fig. 43: Details of the tuning pegs of ancient *qin*, with ancient tuning keys. The cords' paths are drawn in a simplified manner.

The Tuning Mechanism of the Ancient and Classic Qin

What makes Marquis Yi's *qin* unique is its tuning mechanism. It is remarkably close to the mechanism on the modern *qin*, but differs significantly from that of the other ancient chordophones. Generally, the pitch of a string is determined by three parameters: length, mass per unit length (kilogram/meter), and tension. For an open string, if length and mass are fixed, tension alone is used to obtain proper pitch. On *qin*-zithers and violins, tuning pegs are used to regulate the tension. On violins, strings are wound around tuning pegs ("lateral pegs"). If we turn violin pegs around their axis, the string gets pulled, the tension changes, and the pitch rises. On the classic *qin*, the mechanism is different. Its strings are not wound directly around pegs, but tied to a loop formed by a thick cord pulled through a channel drilled through the length of the peg (fig. 41). When the peg is turned, it twists the cord and shortens it; this in turn pulls on the string, increases its tension, and causes the pitch to rise. The string was probably made of fairly rigid material (tightly twisted gut, treated sinew, or waxed silk) which is not easily twisted. This is the reason why a cord was introduced as the intermediary. The more flexible cord converts the rotary motion of the tuning peg to the pulling motion on the string.

This complex tuning mechanism is the main reason we call Marquis Yi's instrument a "*qin*." Both it and the classic *qin* have tuning pegs around which the string is wound. It implies the marquis' *qin* is the ancestor of the classic *qin*. The top of figure 43 shows three types of tuning pegs. The one dated to 433 BCE is a wooden peg; the others are made from bone (168 BCE) and bronze (122 BCE), but the material is apparently not correlated with the date of manufacture (Guangzhou et al. 1991). Among Chinese zithers of the first millennium BCE this "peg-tuning" mechanism is unique to the *qin* (Lawergren 1997). Other Chinese zithers also present in Marquis Yi's tomb—*se*, *zhu*, *zheng*—alter the pitch by leaving tension fixed but changing the string length by moving a bridge under it ("bridge-tuning").

By 2016, six additional ancient *qin*-zithers had been excavated, and like the marquis' *qin*, they were all tuned by pegs (figs. 42 and 43) (Yang Yuanzheng 2016; 2019). Some had more strings, but were less wide. Under their existing constructions, with the tuning pegs located inside a rectangular trough on the underside of the top board, it was difficult to reach the tuning pegs with one's

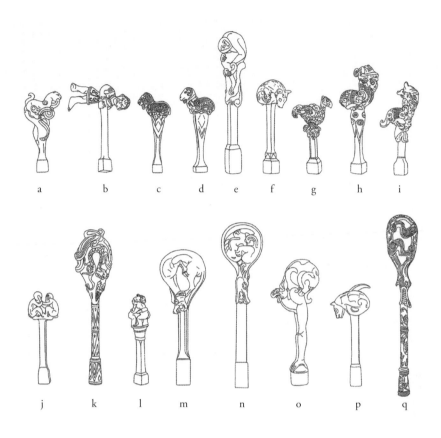

Fig. 44: Tuning keys, 500–100 BCE. All are made of bronze, except item q, made of silver inlaid with carnelian, agate, and turquoise. For item a) see Appendix 2, p. 482; for items g), h), and i) see entries 96, 98, and 95.

fingers, so tuning keys with narrow shafts were introduced to aid tuning. These were mostly made of bronze and date between ca. 500 and 110 BCE (fig. 44; see also Chapter 3d). The map (fig. 45) shows the geographical distribution of sites where metal tuning keys, evidence for the presence of wooden *qin*-zithers that have disintegrated in burials, dating to the first millennium BCE have been found (Lawergren 2019a, 110, fig. 8). Tuning keys (red circles) have mostly been found in northern China; their decorations depict animals that inhabit northern and northwestern China. The few surviving wooden zithers were all found in southern China (green circles), where special circumstances (i.e., anoxic environment inside the tombs preventing bacterial growth that destroys wood) allowed the wooden instruments to survive.

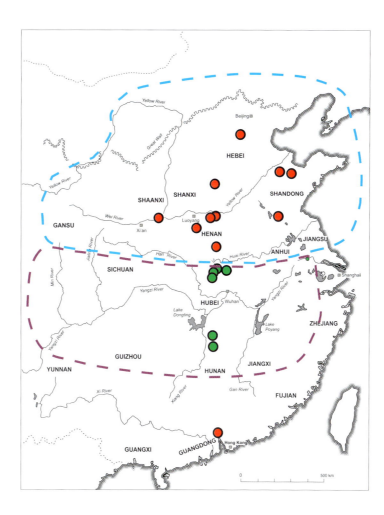

Fig. 45: Find spots of bronze tuning keys (red dots) and wooden *qin*-zithers (green dots). The blue and purple lines indicate the northern and southern heartland of China.

The Ancient Qin, the Story of Boya, and the Classic Qin

Could these *qin*-like instruments—evidence for whose existence is provided by their tuning keys—be predecessors of the classic *qin*? An affirmative answer is given by Han-dynasty bronze mirrors illustrating the famous story of Boya (伯牙) playing a *qin* that clearly has the same shape as the *qin*-zither discovered in Marquis Yi's tomb. The proportions and the structure are the same. The instrument displays the same narrow neck on the player's left side and the same wide body on his right side (Cahill 1994, 55; Lawergren 2003b, 32–33, fig. 8).

The story of Boya and his *qin* was first mentioned in *The Annals of Lü*, compiled around 240 BCE, a date contemporary with many of the tuning keys:

"Whenever Boya played the *qin*, Zhong Ziqi (鍾子期) would listen to him. Once when he was playing the *qin*, his thoughts turned to Mount Tai. Zhong

Fig. 46: *Qin* zithers. Two ancient excavated ones (a–b), six ancient ones shown on bronze mirrors (c, f–j), one ancient one shown on a stone relief (d), one on a terracotta figure (e), one painted on a lacquered bowl (k), one from an molded brick tile (l), and three recent extant ones (m–o).

Ziqi said, "How splendidly you play the *qin*! Lofty and majestic like Mount Tai." A short time later, when his thoughts turned to rolling waters, Zhong Ziqi said, "How splendidly you play the *qin*! Rolling and swelling like a rushing river." When Zhong Ziqi died, Boya smashed the *qin* and cut its strings. To the end of his life, he never played the *qin* again because he felt that there was no one in the world worth playing for..." (Lü Buwei 2000, 308; Lieh-Tzu 1990, 109–10).

Decoration on Han-dynasty bronze mirrors illustrate salient episodes from this story (fig. 46). We see Boya along with his bosom friend Zhong Ziqi, who is listening intently to his music and applauding. The mirrors are skillfully cast with details reminiscent of extant *qin*-zithers, such as their convex surface, or hints of *hui* pitch-markers along the front edge. His left-hand fingers press down on strings near the center of the *qin*'s top surface,[76] while his right-hand fingers pluck the strings on the right side. The same playing technique is still used today.

Advanced photographic technology allows sharp images of the *qin* from the side, top, and bottom of many bronze mirrors, revealing that the ancient *qin* had a consistent shape. Western Han mirrors show a *qin*-zither like that of Marquis Yi, while later mirrors have designs close to the *qin*-zithers of the Six Dynasties, Sui, and Tang periods. In figure 46 the first two zithers (figs. 46a–b) are extant, but most of the examples closely resembling them are pictured on mirrors (fig. 46c; Lawergren 2003b, 32, fig. 2). On these early *qin*-zithers the front-end of the strings were all gathered and tied to a string anchor under the instrument, which also serves as a foot for both the old and classic *qin*. In figure 46c, the *qin* body extends into the slim front-end with a prominent string anchor underneath, just like Marquis Yi's *qin* of 433 BCE (fig. 46a). Figure 46b excavated at Guodian, Jingmen, Hubei province (ca. 300 BCE), has similar features. The ancient *qin* forms a distinct class of instruments, different in shape, but related to the classic *qin*. These features all provide evidence for the continuous development of the *qin*—from Marquis Yi's *qin* of ca. 433 BCE to the classic Tang *qin* (figs. 46m–o)—an idea first proposed by me in 2000, but not accepted by *qin* scholars and players at the time.[77] However, several Chinese musicologists at Chinese universities, conservatories, and museums now largely agree with the interpretation given here.[78]

Before the discovery of the *qin* in Marquis Yi's tomb in 1978, musicologists thought that the earliest surviving *qin*-zithers dated from the Tang dynasty. Music archaeology took historical research on *qin*-zithers back to the time before

---

76   From the perspective of the player, the left side of the *qin* is a narrow, thin neck lifted up off the ground. This is why the fingers of the left hand cannot press on the neck, but only on the *qin*'s belly.
77   Lawergren 2000; 2003b. Traditional *qin* scholars argue that the ancient instruments were inferior, much smaller, and played only open strings (and not *glissandi* like the classic instrument).
78   See Yang Yuanzheng 2014; 2015a; 2015b; 2016; Lawergren 2016; Fang Jianjun 2009.

the Han dynasty (220 BCE–220 CE). The discovery brought to light a much-older *qin*, with an unusual tuning mechanism that required the use of tuning keys. Since all tuning keys for *qin*-zithers had disappeared by the Six Dynasties period (220–500 CE), the design-construction of post-Han *qin*-zithers probably had no use for such a tuning device (Lawergren 2019b). Around that time, too, *qin*-zithers had acquired their full length. The ancient *qin* had transformed into the classic *qin* by the Six Dynasties period. The lore about famous *qin* players like Boya and Confucius lent prestige to the instrument, even if we do not know what their *qin* looked like. Tuning keys, small sizes, and ten strings were all forgotten. The "accepted" history of the *qin* was formulated by the Tang dynasty.[79] After the Tang dynasty, there were practically no further developments.

Ancient China's Qin, the West and Central Asian Harp Connections

Archaeology is increasingly contributing to the study of music and related fields. We have seen this phenomenon in *qin* studies and we also find it in harp studies, which have been made especially relevant by recent discoveries from ancient Central Asia, contemporary with the appearance of the ancient *qin* in China.

Harps, lyres and lutes are the three basic types of chordophones recognized by musicologists.[80] Harps developed gradually over time in ancient West Asia. First came arched harps in Mesopotamia (3100–2000 BCE), frequently shown on Mesopotamian seals and representational art. This was then followed by angular harps (2000 BCE to 300 CE), which spread over a wide area, reaching as far as Spain, while arched harps declined. Frame harps, the third type, appeared much later in Europe (ca. 900 CE) and has now become the dominant harp in orchestras and folk music, especially in Europe.[81]

Angular harps had the longest lifespan by far, covering three millennia, but remained mainly on the Eurasian continent. Judging from the large collection of

---

79   DeWoskin 1982 thoroughly discusses early Chinese sources on the *qin*, but omits any mention of the *qin* in Zeng Hou Yi's grave (but see DeWoskin 1982, 25; 43; 45), and fails to notice the relevance of Han-dynasty bronze mirrors.

80   Studies and definitions of musical instruments can be found in *The New Grove Dictionary of Music and Musicians* 2001, second edition, London and New York. For lyres, see Lawergren 1993.

81   The Utrecht Psalter (second quarter of the 9th century CE) is among the first to show frame harps, especially in the illustrations accompanying Psalms 150 and 92 (Winternitz 1967, pl. 16).

Fig. 47: A horizontal and a vertical angular harp shown on terracotta plaques from Eshnunna. Old Babylonian date (2000–1600 BCE). Oriental Institute of the University of Chicago.

surviving representations, Mesopotamia may have been the center of harp playing between 3000 BCE and 300 CE. Most likely, there was a continuous presence of harps in Mesopotamia/Iran/Elam between 3000 BCE and the Hellenistic period (Lawergren 2018).

Around 2000 BCE, angular harps split into two versions in Mesopotamia / ancient Iran: vertical and horizontal angular harps, depending on the orientation of the strings and how they were played (von Hornbostel and Sachs 1914; 1961). Vertical harps, strings oriented vertically, are played by finger-plucking, never by plectra (fig. 47, right). All horizontal harps are played the same way: The harp body is held horizontally, with the strings projecting horizontally in front at the level of the player's navel. The fingers of the left hand press the strings, dampening most of them, allowing just a few to sound freely. The right hand holds a long, narrow stick, which is used to strike across all the strings from top to bottom (fig. 47, left). Not only do vertical and horizontal angular harps differ in string orientation, playing position, and technique, they also differ with respect to another important musical characteristic. Vertical harps had a much larger number of strings, typically 20–25 (fig. 48 E), while the horizontal harp

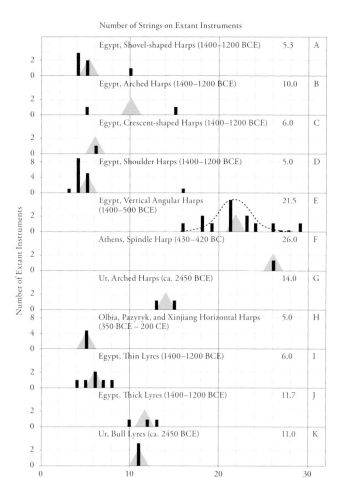

Fig. 48: Counting strings on ancient extant string instruments. Most examples come from pharaonic Egypt where the dry sand preserved wooden instruments. Generally, very early instruments have fewer strings than later ones. The most prominent exceptions are vertical angular harps, which may have up to 30 strings. The height of the black columns indicates the number of instruments extant; the columns' position on the horizontal axis corresponds to the instruments' number of strings. The gray triangles mark the average string counts for each category.

had fewer than ten (fig. 48 H).[82] Nine was the most common string count on horizontal harps in the ancient Near East. Although vertical harps enjoyed prolonged popularity from in the ancient Mediterranean regions, Iran, and across the Eurasian continent as far as China, Korea, and Japan, it is rather the horizontal harp, especially examples recently excavated from Central Asia, that present intriguing questions in connection to the history of the ancient Chinese *qin* (Lawergren 2008).[83]

82 Quantitative data on chordophone strings are difficult to find. Some scholars confuse string counts from representations and from extant instruments. Illustrations are often unreliable, especially if there are many strings. Only extant instruments are reliable. For antiquity, such data is available in Egypt (Lawergren 1994, fig. 2).
83 He Zhiliang, to be published in *The Galpin Society Journal*, 2021. Circa 22 new harps have been found in Xinjiang.

Fig. 49: Lion hunt; King Ashurbanipal pours a libation over his prey, four lions. Gypsum wall panel from the North Palace of Ashurbanipal; Nineveh, Northern Mesopotamia, 645–640 BCE. London, The Trustees of the British Museum, museum no. 124887.

Horizontal Angular Harps of Ancient Mesopotamia and Steppe Harps

The earliest horizontal harps are seen on West Asian images from Mesopotamia, Elam, and Iran.[84] Many horizontal harps have been found on Assyrian wall reliefs, now held in London and Paris (Rimmer 1969: 45, pls. 9; 13).

Horizontal harps dominated during the Neo-Babylonian and Neo-Assyrian periods and seem to have had a specific role in Neo-Assyrian rituals, often figuring in royal rites after a lion hunt. On the Balawat gate, King Shalmaneser III (858–824 BCE) is shown at such a ritual after a lion hunt (Schachner 2007). In such rituals, pairs of horizontal harps led the rites. Another scene shows King Ashurbanipal (ca. 645 BCE) pouring libation on dead lions while pairs of harps play music (fig. 49). Of the seven Assyrian depictions of horizontal harps at the British Museum, all are shown being played in pairs. No other types of harps are present, and a tangible sense of cultic music marks the scenes.

Isolated finds of horizontal harps from Pazyryk (Lawergren 1990) and Olbia (Bachmann 1994) have also been published. But recently, several horizontal harps have been found in Xinjiang, the westernmost province of China, in Central Asia. These date from 700 to 400 BCE (fig. 50). Two were excavated at Zaghunluq, Qiemo county on the Silk Road along the southern rim of the Tarim Basin

---

84   Lawergren 2001, 526–27, figs. 6 and 7; see also Spycket 1972 and Lawergren 2018.

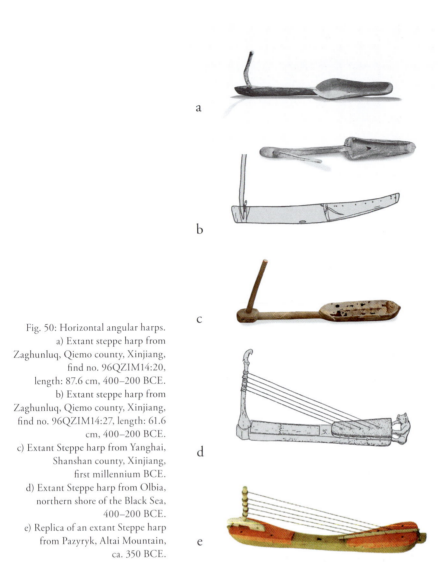

Fig. 50: Horizontal angular harps.
a) Extant steppe harp from Zaghunluq, Qiemo county, Xinjiang, find no. 96QZIM14:20, length: 87.6 cm, 400–200 BCE.
b) Extant steppe harp from Zaghunluq, Qiemo county, Xinjiang, find no. 96QZIM14:27, length: 61.6 cm, 400–200 BCE.
c) Extant Steppe harp from Yanghai, Shanshan county, Xinjiang, first millennium BCE.
d) Extant Steppe harp from Olbia, northern shore of the Black Sea, 400–200 BCE.
e) Replica of an extant Steppe harp from Pazyryk, Altai Mountain, ca. 350 BCE.

(Wang Bo 2003a, fig. 25: M14:20; M14:27; M2:105), and three were unearthed at Yanghai, Shanshan county on the northern rim of the Tarim Basin.[85] The latter harps had sound boxes at the back and a narrow solid spear at the front (figs. 50 a–c). The Yanghai site has just been published in detail and constitutes a rich source of Xinjiang harps. It has already given rise to secondary studies, as in this

---

85 Turpan et al. 2019. Horizontal Harps found were identified as M90:12; M63:1; and a partially preserved one as M48:2.

Fig. 51: Assyrian harp. Gypsum wall panel from the North West Palace of Ashurnasirpal II; Nimrud, Northern Mesopotamia, 875–860 BCE. London, The Trustees of the British Museum, museum no. 124533.

case of a harp tomb that has been observed to contain a stash of cannabis (Zhao et al. 2019) used both as medicine and as a shamanistic ritual aid.

About twenty more horizontal harps have been discovered in Xinjiang. Most are now kept in Ürümqi, the capital of Xinjiang Uyghur Autonomous Region, but have not yet been published. Desert-like conditions prevail across the region, in particular in the Taklamakan and Kumtag Deserts. Because of the extremely dry conditions, tombs have survived in an excellent condition and wooden objects (such as harps) have been preserved.

The discovery of large numbers of horizontal harps from Xinjiang was totally unexpected. Were the Xinjiang examples inspired by the Mesopotamian harps, or was it the other way around? The answer depends on the relative dates of the instruments from Mesopotamia and Xinjiang. We know the dates of Assyrian Palace reliefs (883–859, 858–824, 668–627 BCE), but the dating of Xinjiang tombs (750–400 BCE) is less precise. I had previously discussed the resemblance of these harps to Assyrian horizontal angular harps shown on Neo-Babylonian and Neo-Assyrian wall reliefs (Lawergren 2003a, esp. 89). Since these harps form a distinct class, I have named them "Steppe harps," which include the horizontal angular harps on the Neo-Assyrian Palace reliefs, the harps from Olbia and Pazyryk, and the recently excavated harps at Zaghunluq and Yanghai.

Since there are no images from Xinjiang to show how the harps were played, one cannot determine how it was held. But when we compare shapes, as well as function, a remarkable correspondence appears between the Steppe harps and the images on the Assyrian reliefs, whose geographic distribution spans about 4,000 kilometers, a not-inconceivable distance to traverse, even in ancient times:[86]

a. The Xinjiang harps were recovered in the tomb at the waist of the deceased, indicating clearly that they were horizontal angular harps (Wang Bo 2003a, fig. 25 M14:20; M14:27).

b. Based on their appearance alone, one suspects that the horizontal harps shown on Assyrian reliefs may have influenced (or been influenced by) the harps in the Zaghunluq tomb.

c. The presence of a pair of harps buried in Zaghunluq tomb M14 (400–200 BCE) indicate they were also played in pairs, like Assyrian horizontal harps.

d. Finally, tomb M90 at Yanghai contained a large stash of *Cannabis sativa*, stored in a leather purse near the head of the harpist, while the harp rested on the right side of the deceased (Zhao et al. 2019). Excavators concluded that the harpist had been a shaman who performed rituals that connected him to the spiritual (or magical) world. A similar spiritual gesture was enacted when the Assyrian king poured libations over the prone lions in the presence of harpists. The rituals, though different in detail, are connected through their spiritual intent. In Mesopotamia, the numinous manifests itself in the libation. In Xinjiang, it is the presence of marijuana that plays the same function.

---

86   The distance between Assyrian Palaces and Ürümqi is approximately 4,000 km. On horseback this distance could be covered in 80 days, riding possibly 50–60 km per day (Cunliffe 2015, 77).

Some Observations

As we have seen, the first millennium BCE brought to light a hitherto-unknown tuning mechanism for *qin*-zithers in China. By the middle of the millennium, the mechanisms had become sufficiently accurate to deal with fine details of tuning, offering empirical ways of estimating tensions. In 245 BCE, the book *Lüshi Chunqiu* appeared, presenting the mathematical forms for the steps of the major scale (Lü Buwei 2000, 157). The method is known to Chinese musicologists as the *Sanfen Sunyi-fa* 三分損益法 (von Falkenhausen 1993, 277–79). Tuning devices control string tensions. With accurate devices, one can turn one's attention to systematic observations, such as those required to formulate *Sanfen Sunyi-fa*. This virtually parallel development can hardly be coincidental.

At the same time, it appears that horizontal angular harps were developed in the Neo-Assyrian empire and in Xinjiang nearly simultaneously. The tuning mechanism differed between zithers and harps. On harps, collars were turned around a vertical round axis and the strings were attached to them. The dates of Neo-Assyrian harps are well known since they fit the Assyrian King List and the known dates of palace construction. In the Xinjiang region of China, many horizontal harps have just been unearthed, but the dates are less precise (700–500 BCE). It is hard to know which region, Assyria or Xinjiang, can claim precedence in the development of horizontal harps until more precise dates for Xinjiang become available. How these two developments in ancient harps and zithers relate to each other (or not) remains to be seen.

Appendix 1

CT-Scan Documentation of the Tuning Key with Recumbent Goat-Man

After X-ray imaging could not fully resolve all issues regarding the manufacturing of the goat-man *qin* tuning key (entry 98), and after extensive discussion whether this piece might actually be a pastiche, it was decided to additionally examine the tuning key with CT computed tomography scanning. The scans showed the key to be hollow cast in one piece.
The CT scans were made with the help of Jens Stenger at Empa Materials Science and Technology, Dübendorf (Switzerland).

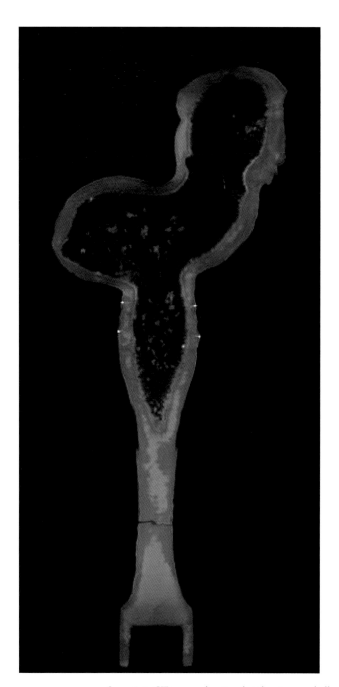 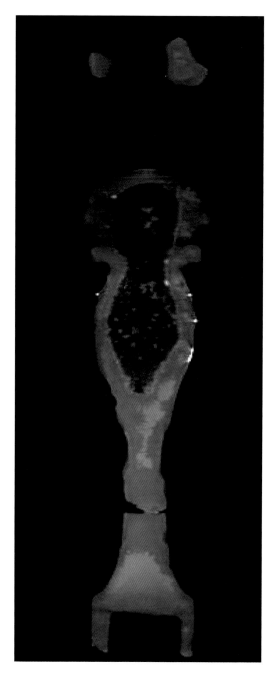

Scans 1–2. CT images showing that the piece was hollow-cast.

Appendix 1 | CT-Scan Documentation

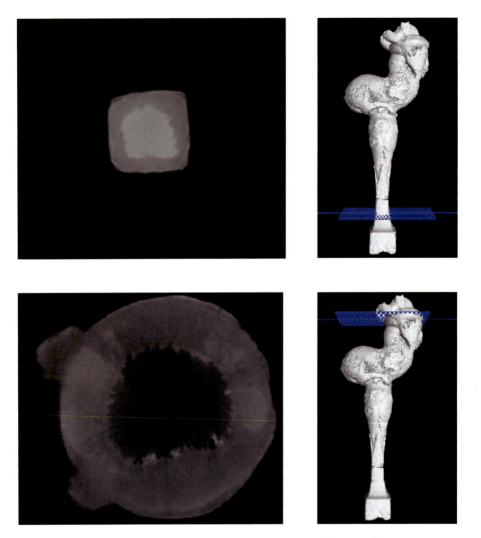

Scan 3. Cross-section of the solid foot and of the hollow head-section of the tuning key.

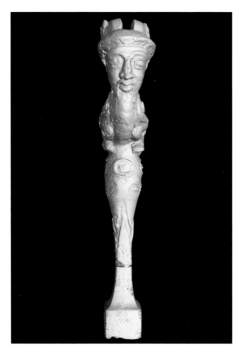

Scan 4a. Front view of the tuning key.

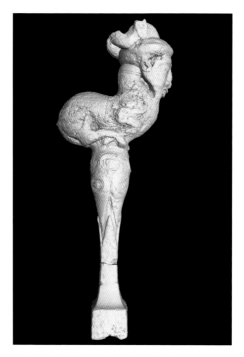

Scan 4b. Side-view from the right displaying the less well preserved side.

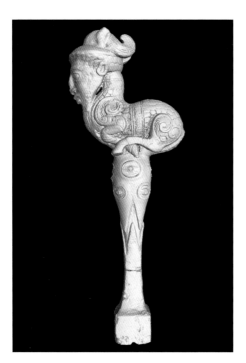

Scan 4c. Side-view from the left showing the details of the front and hind legs and their decoration.

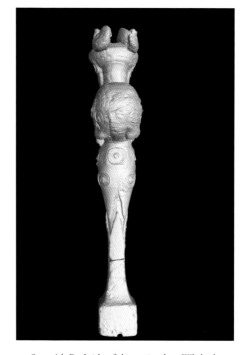

Scan 4d. Backside of the tuning key. While the stem is well preserved, the figure's back part is less clearly visible.

Appendix 1 | CT-Scan Documentation

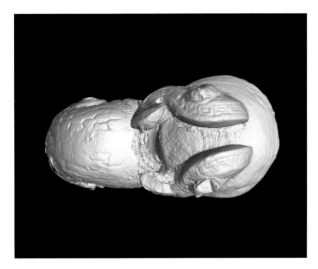

Scan 5a. Top-view showing the solid head and the well articulated horns, while the back of the goat-man is less well preserved.

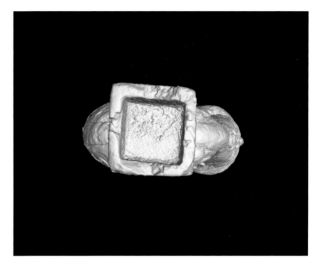

Scan 5b. Bottom view of the socket.

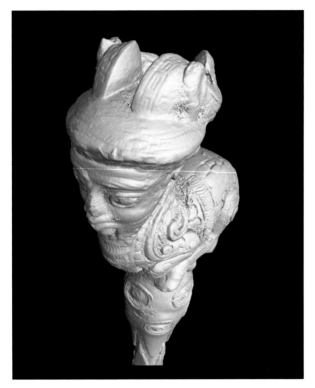

Scan 6a. Detail view from top left.

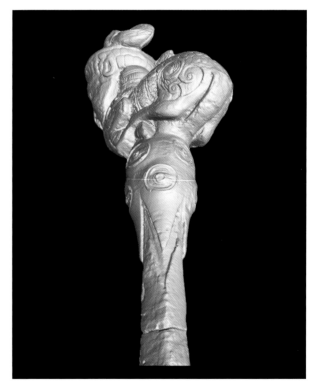

Scan 6b. Detail view from bottom left.

Appendix 2

Casting the Qin *Tuning Keys in the Freer and Sackler Collections*

Donna Strahan[87]

The Freer and Sackler Collections has four copper-alloy *qin* tuning keys. The tools were used to tune the strings on a *qin* (zither) instrument by placing the socket end over the instrument's wooden pegs and turning it. Each key in the collection was examined to determine how it was cast. They were examined under the binocular microscope, X-radiographed, surface analyzed by X-ray fluorescence, and photographed. While the height of each key is different, the socket shape and size for all four is nearly identical and the interior of all sockets taper. Interestingly, while their alloy compositions are similar, the casting method for each of them is somewhat different. Three were cast by the piece-mold method and the casting method of the fourth one is inconclusive at this time. The most sophisticated key is F1951.7b, with an internal knife blade. The simplest one is the solid Tiger key S2012.9.2692.

---

[87] Head of Department of Conservation and Scientific Research, Freer Gallery of Art and Arthur M. Sackler Gallery, the Smithsonian's National Museum of Asian Art, Washington, DC 20013.

Qin Tuning Key with Crouching Bear

Freer Gallery of Art, Smithsonian Institution, Washington, DC: Purchase—Charles Lang Freer Endowment, F1951.7b

China, Eastern Zhou period, 4th century BCE

Height 9.2 cm; socket: exterior 1.25 × 1.25 cm, interior 1.0 × 1.0 cm, tapering depth 1.4 cm

Leaded tin bronze

This qin tuning key consists of a crouching bear on top of a shaft that ends in a square socket. X-radiographs revealed that the bear is hollow and has a comma-shaped flick-knife blade running down the center of the bear's back. The blade slightly tapers as it runs down the back and is thinnest at the pointed end at the tail. Long-term burial in the ground has corroded the blade in place and it cannot be opened. There is no visual evidence of a hinge pin penetrating from the outside through the bear's body. X-radiographs reveal the shape of the flick knife and the presence of a rod running perpendicular through its larger rounded end. This would allow the blade to rotate up and down on the rod. Additionally, there is a U-shaped metal stop on the interior near the bear's tail, again visible only in the X-radiograph.

Both the internal rod and U-shaped stop were cast as part of the bear and shaft. The knife was opened at the bear's tail and swiveled upward on the rod parallel to the bear's body. When closed, the tip of the knife rests against the U-shaped stop that keeps the blade from going deeper into the bear's back. When closed, the blade fits so snugly that it is barely visible.

How was this small, complex bronze made? First, the blade was separately cast with a hole in the middle of the rounded end. It was then set into the core to form the bear's body. It was inserted such that the point (or thinnest part of the blade) was pointing upward, away from the opening in the back. This provided space for core and mold material to surround the blade and ensure it would remain free-moving once it was cast and the core material was removed. Core material lined the hole in the blade, but the middle was left open, so that molten metal running through it would not attach the blade to the newly formed rod. The bear with the shaft (and precast knife in place) were cast as one.

It is unclear whether this was piece-mold or lost-wax cast, but the area around Luoyang was in China's Central Plains where piece-mold casting was the norm. No seams from mold sections could be found. There are no core extensions, because the core had to be removed after casting to allow the blade to move. The opening in the back may have served as a core extension. There is no evidence of spacers, chaplets, or any other core pin.

Stylistically, the Freer tuning key probably came from the area of Luoyang, where a similar tuning key was excavated in 1934 (see White 1934, 99; 169). However, that one has a longer shaft with a small ball in the middle. It is not possible from the photos to determine whether it has a flick knife. Another crouching bear with a flick knife, whose construction is well illustrated, can be seen in Lawergren (2007, 60, fig. 21). There are two identifications of this object in the picture credits, of which the first one is incorrect: It is not from Christie's 2000, no. 175, which is the Metropolitan Museum of Art key 2002.201.150, but from Lally 2001. The Metropolitan key does have a flick blade extending out of its back. This bear is also similar to the piece-mold cast entry 97 (Chapter 3d), but that one does not have a flick blade.

 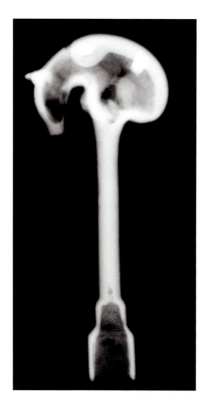

F1951.7b. Photo and computed radiograph.

Qin Tuning Key with Tiger and Snake

Freer Gallery of Art, Smithsonian Institution, Washington, DC: Gift of Charles Lang Freer, F1916.454

China, Eastern Zhou period, 4th century BCE

Height 8.2 cm; socket: exterior 1.3 × 1.3 cm, interior 0.9 × 0.9 cm, tapering depth 1.6 cm

Leaded tin bronze

This *qin* tuning key with entwined feline, bird, and snake was cast in one piece by the piece-mold method. Open spaces between the legs of the feline were the location of core extensions that held the core in place during casting. After casting, the core extensions between the legs were removed. The shaft supporting the feline contains an enclosed core that extends three-quarters of the way down the interior. X-radiographs reveal at least four pyramidal core extensions present on the enclosed core. These internal core extensions are similar to the Houma-foundry techniques and are found earlier in the legs of Shang-dynasty *ding*. For illustrations of core extensions in Houma, see Li et al. 1996, 485–87.

Four mold sections were used to cast the key. One front section included the face, the front of the ears, the shaft, and the socket front. One mold section for each side and a final mold section for the bottom that incorporated the pouring gate.

The bottom of the shaft ends in a square socket that was placed over a wooden peg wrapped with a silk or sinew string. Fiber pseudomorphs are present inside the socket.

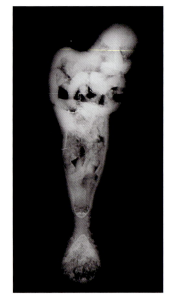

F1916.454, Photo and computed radiograph.

Qin Tuning Key with Tiger

This qin tuning key was solid cast by the piece-mold method. It was probably cast using three mold pieces. One for both sides and a third in the bottom of the socket. Mold lines are visible around the front of the neck, and in the openings between the legs and in the tail. All of the design was carved in model or mold, and no apparent surface work was done after casting. However, the surface is badly corroded obscuring surface details.

Arthur M. Sackler Gallery, Smithsonian Institution, Washington, DC: The Dr. Paul Singer Collection of Chinese Art of the Arthur M. Sackler Gallery, Smithsonian Institution; a joint gift of the Arthur M. Sackler Foundation, Paul Singer, the AMS Foundation for the Arts, Sciences, and Humanities, and the Children of Arthur M. Sackler, S2012.9.2692

Eastern Zhou dynasty, Warring States period, 3rd century BCE

Height 8.3 cm; socket: exterior 1.25 × 1.25 cm, interior 0.9 × 0.9 cm, tapering depth 1.3 cm

Leaded tin bronze

S2012.9.2692. Photo.

Qin Tuning Key with Crouching Bear

Arthur M. Sackler Gallery, Smithsonian Institution, Washington, DC: The Dr. Paul Singer Collection of Chinese Art of the Arthur M. Sackler Gallery, Smithsonian Institution; a joint gift of the Arthur M. Sackler Foundation, Paul Singer, the AMS Foundation for the Arts, Sciences, and Humanities, and the Children of Arthur M. Sackler, S2012.9.2694

China, Eastern Zhou period, 3rd century BCE

Height 12.4 cm; socket: exterior 1.3 × 1.3 cm, interior 0.9 × 0.9 cm, non-tapering depth 1.4 cm

Leaded tin bronze

This qin tuning key consists of a crouching bear on top of a shaft that ends in a square socket. It is the tallest of the four. It is simpler in design and lacks the depth and detail of F1951.7b. X-radiographs and viewing through an open slit in the back have revealed that the bear is hollow and empty. The long slit may originally have held a flick-knife blade in this gap. However, unlike F1951.7b, there is no internal rod to hold the blade in place and no stop bar to keep the blade from falling into the hollow. Neither is there evidence of a hinge pin being present. There is a lead-tin repair on the middle of the proper left side of the gap. This damage may have occurred when the blade broke off. The key was cast by

S2012.9.2694. Photo and computed radiograph.

the piece-mold method. A mold seam between the legs indicates that two mold sections bisected the bear. A third mold section was used for the socket interior.

While the alloy and socket size are nearly the same as the other tuning keys, the surface is very different. The dense brown surface of the tuning key may have developed during burial in an anoxic environment, such as a tomb or underwater. Or it has been chemically treated. There are re-deposited copper prills over the surface. Many have been dislodged, but others can still be found in the recesses and interior of the key.

Appendix 3

Alloy Compositional Data

Abbreviations

Baga Gazryn ch.	Baga Gazryn chuluu
British Mus.	British Museum
Cheremu. Pad'	Cheremukhovaia Pad'
Coll. Liu	Foundation Richard Liu, European Institute of Chinese Studies, Brussels
Minus.	Minusinsk
Mong.	Mongolia
Nov. Chernaia	Novaia Chernaia
Sackler Coll.	Arthur M. Sackler Collections
Transb.	Transbaikal area
OES	Optical emission spectroscopy
PIXE	Particle induced X-ray emission
SEM-EDS	Scanning electron microscopy coupled with energy-dispersive X-ray spectrometry
XRF	X-ray fluorescence
n.d.	not detected

Table 1

Overview over XRF metal compositional data of bronzes from the Guyuan Mizong Collection; compiled by Ursula Brosseder. Measurements by Pieter Meyers were taken on corroded surface, by Jens Stenger and Ester Ferreira on the surface after cleaning (for details and different measurement procedures see Chapter 10, pp. 437–38). Only the main elements are reported.

Entry	Cu	Sn	Pb	As	Zn	Ni	Analyst
1 knife	74	11	5	<1	n.d.		Stenger
2 dagger	70	7	12	<1	n.d.		Stenger
4 ornament	66	9	13	trace	n.d.	n.d.	Stenger
5 harness cheek-piece	75	12	2	trace	n.d.	n.d.	Stenger
6 harness cheek-piece	76	14	6	trace	n.d.	n.d.	Stenger
7 fitting	52	6	8	<1	n.d.		Stenger
8 fitting	61	11	11	high	n.d.	n.d.	Stenger
9 knife	85	3	3	<1	n.d.		Stenger
10 knife	89	3	3	trace	n.d.	n.d.	Stenger
11 knife	54	17	5	<1	n.d.		Stenger
12 knife	78	10	11	<1	n.d.		Stenger
13 knife	59.8	14.7	3.4	0.0	0.1		Ferreira
14 vulture-shaped garment plaque	88	9	1	high	n.d.	n.d.	Stenger
15a garment plaque	75	15	8	trace	n.d.	n.d.	Stenger
15b garment plaque	83	15	21	trace	n.d.	n.d.	Stenger
16 spoon-shaped pendant	70	5	18	<1	n.d.		Stenger
17 spoon-shaped pendant	84	6	13	high	n.d.	n.d.	Stenger
18 garment plaque	70.0	9.2	8.5	0.7	0.0		Ferreira
19 garment plaque	70	13	12	trace	n.d.	n.d.	Stenger
20 spoon-shaped pendant	98	2	5	n.d.	n.d.	n.d.	Stenger
23 pectoral plaque	59	15	13	trace	n.d.	trace	Stenger
25a round garment plaque	70	5	10	<1	n.d.		Stenger
25b round garment plaque	72	4	5	<1	n.d.		Stenger
26a garment plaque	57	1	9	n.d.	n.d.		Stenger
26b garment plaque	71	n.d.	21	n.d.	n.d.	n.d.	Stenger
27 fitting with coiled leopards	86.2	3.0	0.0	2.9	0.0		Ferreira
28a deer-shaped plaque	61	n.d.	20	n.d.	n.d.	n.d.	Stenger
28b deer-shaped plaque	77	3	13	n.d.	n.d.	n.d.	Stenger
29a deer-shaped ornament	87	3	trace	very high	n.d.	n.d.	Stenger
29b deer-shaped ornament	87	3	2	high	n.d.	n.d.	Stenger
31 deer-shaped ornament	80	3	<1	n.d.	n.d.		Stenger

Entry		Cu	Sn	Pb	As	Zn	Ni	Analyst
102a	gilded belt plaque	90.3	1.4	0.0	0.1	0.2		Ferreira
102b	gilded belt plaque	80.6	0.8	0.0	0.1	0.1		Ferreira
103a	gilded belt plaque	80	8	3	trace	n.d.	trace	Stenger
103b	gilded belt plaque	84.5	9.3	1.1	0.2	0.0		Ferreira
104	gilded belt plaque	91.9	4.5	1.1	0.2	0.0		Ferreira
105	gilded belt plaque	78.0	8.6	8.0	0.1	0.0		Ferreira
106	gilded belt plaque	66	8	10	trace	n.d.	trace	Stenger
107	belt plaque	62	9	5	trace	n.d.	trace	Stenger
108a	gilded belt plaque	75.2	11.9	4.0	0.3	0.0		Ferreira
108b	gilded belt plaque	71.9	9.6	1.6	0.2	0.0		Ferreira
109a	gilded belt plaque	81	3	1	trace	n.d.	trace	Stenger
109b	gilded belt plaque	94	4	1	trace	n.d.	trace	Stenger
110a	belt plaque	73.8	12.0	7.7	0.5	0.0		Ferreira
110b	belt plaque	76.4	12.1	11.2	0.2	0.0		Ferreira
112	gilded belt plaque	76.0	12.9	2.0	0.1	0.0		Ferreira
113	gilded belt plaque	70.3	16.2	6.7	0.3	0.0		Ferreira
114a	openwork belt plaque	79	6	3	n.d.	n.d.	trace	Stenger
114b	openwork belt plaque	88	6	6	trace	n.d.	trace	Stenger
115	gilded belt plaque	66.4	4.3	3.2	0.0	0.0		Ferreira
116	bovine belt plaque	73.0	10.0	10.8	0.5	0.0		Ferreira
117	bovine plaque	87.6	5.0	0.7	0.2	0.0		Ferreira
118a	bovine belt plaque	66.5	6.0	3.9	0.2	0.0		Ferreira
118b	bovine belt plaque	71.2	8.8	7.3	0.3	0.0		Ferreira
119	camel plaque	86.4	6.0	14.4	0.5	0.2		Ferreira
121	belt plaque	78.6	3.7	3.6	11.0	0.0		Ferreira
122	belt plaque	70.8	4.1	22.8	0.5	0.0		Ferreira
123a	gilded belt plaque	86.7	4.4	1.0	0.1	0.0		Ferreira
123b	gilded belt plaque	85.9	5.9	2.6	0.2	0.0		Ferreira
124a	gilded belt plaque	95.1	1.9	0.0	0.0	0.0		Ferreira
124b	gilded belt plaque	95	2	<1	n.d.	n.d.	high	Stenger
125a	openwork belt plaque	75.2	6.9	11.1	0.8	0.0		Ferreira
125b	openwork belt plaque	82.6	6.2	10.7	0.8	0.0		Ferreira
126a	openwork belt plaque	63	11	2	high	n.d.	n.d.	Stenger
126b	openwork belt plaque	58	9	3	high	n.d.	n.d.	Stenger
127	belt plaque	88.9	3.1	3.1	0.6	0.0		Ferreira
128	openwork belt plaque	103.1	2.4	2.5	0.8	0.0		Ferreira
129	belt plaque	85.9	2.3	5.7	0.6	0.0		Ferreira

Entry		Cu	Sn	Pb	As	Zn	Ni	Analyst
130	openwork belt plaque	87.3	3.6	4.2	0.6	0.0		Ferreira
131a	openwork belt plaque	92	1	7	trace	n.d.	trace	Stenger
131b	openwork belt plaque	97	1	10	high	n.d.	trace	Stenger
132	openwork belt plaque	76.6	5.3	11.4	0.6	0.0		Ferreira
133a	openwork belt plaque	89.9	2.4	1.6	5.8	0.0		Ferreira
133b	openwork belt plaque	45.4	1.8	1.4	3.9	0.0		Ferreira
134a	D-shaped openwork belt plaque	91.0	1.5	7.2	0.6	0.0		Ferreira
134b	D-shaped openwork belt plaque	85.2	1.4	6.1	0.5	0.0		Ferreira
135	belt ornament	79	8	2	n.d.	n.d.		Stenger
136	belt ornament	77.9	7.1	1.7	3.0	0.2		Ferreira
137a	appliqué plaque	90	2	8	high	n.d.	trace	Stenger
137b	appliqué plaque	34.9	2.8	31.6	4.0	0.0		Ferreira
138	appliqué plaque	76	12	8	n.d.	n.d.	n.d.	Stenger
140	garment plaque	83	5	7	trace	n.d.	trace	Stenger
141	socketed axe *ge*	63	15	10	<1	n.d.	trace	Stenger
142	harness ornament	74	11	9	<1	n.d.		Stenger
143	harness ornament	77	11	4	<1	n.d.		Stenger
147	belt hook	85	10	2	trace	n.d.	trace	Stenger
148	ornamental appliqué	73.3	8.3	6.3	0.2	0.0		Ferreira
150	round ornament	76.5	7.5	6.5	0.3	0.1		Ferreira
151	garment plaque	91.2	2.7	0.0	1.9	0.0		Ferreira
152	garment plaque	85	1	1	high	n.d.	high	Stenger
153	garment plaque	86.3	12.7	0.6	1.0	0.2		Ferreira
154	plaque	68	15	0.5	n.d.	n.d.	n.d.	Stenger
155	girth ring	95	2	2	n.d.	n.d.	trace	Stenger
157	plaque	73	15	2	trace	n.d.	n.d.	Stenger
158	plaque, back	77	19	n.d.	high	n.d.	n.d.	Stenger
158	plaque, handle	71	18	6	trace	n.d.	n.d.	Stenger
158	plaque, head	95	20	7	trace	n.d.	n.d.	Stenger
159a	plaque, back	77/64	9.9/12	10/24				Meyers
159a	plaque, front	81/82	7.1/8.1	7.7/9.9				Meyers
159b	plaque, back	70/72	11/12	15/15				Meyers
159b	plaque, front	70/70	10/13	16/18				Meyers
160	belt plaque	75	10	5	trace	n.d.	n.d.	Stenger
161	quiver decoration	82	10	5	trace	n.d.	trace	Stenger
162	wolf-shaped buckle	79	17	5	n.d.	n.d.	n.d.	Stenger
164	harness ornament	78.5	12.0	4.0	0.1	0.0		Ferreira

Entry		Cu	Sn	Pb	As	Zn	Ni	Analyst
166	trapezoidal shaped plaque	102	n.d.	<1	1	n.d.		Stenger
167	plaque	70	20	2.6				Meyers
171	forgery					5		Meyers
172	forgery	49	<1	14	n.d.	5		Stenger
173	forgery, back	46	10	35		1		Meyers
173	forgery, front	71	10	14		1.3		Meyers
173	forgery, loop	70	10	18		1.1		Meyers
173	forgery, belt plaque	67	9	9	<1	2		Stenger
174	forgery	82	<1	9	n.d.	8		Stenger
175	forgery	76	<1	11	n.d.	7		Stenger
176a	forgery	96	n.d.	n.d.	n.d.	3		Stenger
176b	forgery	94	n.d.	n.d.	n.d.	2		Stenger
177	forgery	79.0	1.6	1.4	0.1	11.5		Ferreira
178	forgery	68	n.d.	n.d.	n.d.	36	n.d.	Stenger
179	forgery	93	n.d.	1	n.d.	1.5	n.d.	Stenger

Table 2

Metal compositional data of belt plaques from Inner Asia as reported in the literature; compiled by Ursula Brosseder and Yiu-Kang Hsu.

No.	Site	Region	Cu	Sn	Pb	As	Method	Reference	Publ. ID
1	Dyrestui	Transb.	97.18	1.4	1.2	0.22	OES	Miniaev 1977	425
2	Dyrestui	Transb.	96.3	1.4	2	0.3	OES	Miniaev 1977	426
3	Dyrestui	Transb.	77.4	17	5.4	0.2	OES	Miniaev 1977	427
4	Dyrestui	Transb.	86.7	11	2	0.3	OES	Miniaev 1977	428
5	Dyrestui	Transb.	87	5	3.5	4.5	OES	Miniaev 1980	5
6	Ivolga	Transb.	89.2	5.6	1.7	3.5	OES	Miniaev 1980	6
7	Ivolga	Transb.	91	4	1.5	3.5	OES	Miniaev 1980	7
8	Polkanovo	Transb.	78.8	4	1.2	16	OES	Miniaev 1980	8
9	Polkanovo	Transb.	72.8	5.4	1.8	20	OES	Miniaev 1980	9
10	Sharagol	Transb.	97.673	1.6	0.027	0.7	OES	Miniaev 1980	10
11	Dureny	Transb.	98.184	0.005	0.011	1.8	OES	Miniaev 1980	11
12	Sava	Transb.	92.27	1.4	0.03	6.3	OES	Miniaev 1980	12
13	Transb.	Transb.	88.6	4.5	4.7	2.2	OES	Miniaev 1980	13
14	Mongolia	Mong.	99.644	0.02	0.056	0.28	OES	Miniaev 1980	14
15	Zavkhan	Mong.	88.1	0.9	8	3	OES	Miniaev 1980	15
16	Gobi	Mong.	82.55	7	10	0.45	OES	Miniaev 1980	16
17	Urbiun III	Tuva	89.755	8	0.045	2.2	OES	Miniaev 1980	17
18	Tepsei VII	Minus.	97.342	0.048	w	1.8	OES	Miniaev 1980	18
19	Tepsei VII	Minus.	89.984	0.006	0.01	10	OES	Miniaev 1980	19
20	Razliv III	Minus.	94.539	0.016	0.045	5.4	OES	Miniaev 1980	20
21	Krasnyi Iar	Minus.	98.974	0.004	0.022	1	OES	Miniaev 1980	21
22	Krasnyi Iar	Minus.	98.29	0.36	0.6	0.75	OES	Miniaev 1980	22
23	Utinka	Minus.	89.94	1.7	0.76	7.6	OES	Miniaev 1980	23
24	Kosogol hoard	Minus.	90.6	0.3	0.1	9	OES	Miniaev 1980	24
25	Kosogol hoard	Minus.	100.000	0.000	0.000	0.000	OES	Miniaev 1980	25
26	Kosogol hoard	Minus.	95.6	0.1	0.3	4	OES	Miniaev 1980	26
27	Kosogol hoard	Minus.	93.000	0.000	0.000	7	OES	Miniaev 1980	27
28	Kosogol hoard	Minus.	82.8	0.05	0.15	17	OES	Miniaev 1980	28
29	Kosogol hoard	Minus.	89.000	0.000	0.000	11	OES	Miniaev 1980	29
30	Kosogol hoard	Minus.	87.000	0.000	0.000	13	OES	Miniaev 1980	30
31	Kosogol hoard	Minus.	97.82	0.03	0.15	2	OES	Miniaev 1980	31
32	Kosogol hoard	Minus.	93.990	0.01	0.000	6	OES	Miniaev 1980	32

No.	Site	Region	Cu	Sn	Pb	As	Method	Reference	Publ. ID
33	Kosogol hoard	Minus.	96.1	3	0.3	0.6	OES	Miniaev 1980	33
34	Kosogol hoard	Minus.	86.980	0.02	0.000	13	OES	Miniaev 1980	34
35	Kosogol hoard	Minus.	87.000	0.000	0.000	13	OES	Miniaev 1980	35
36	Kosogol hoard	Minus.	86.990	0.01	0.000	13	OES	Miniaev 1980	36
37	Kosogol hoard	Minus.	95.6	0.3	0.1	4	OES	Miniaev 1980	37
38	Kosogol hoard	Minus.	98.500	0.000	0.000	1.5	OES	Miniaev 1980	38
39	Solenoozero	Minus.	97.28	0.22	0.5	2	OES	Miniaev 1980	39
40	Solenoozero	Minus.	90.325	0.045	0.03	9.6	OES	Miniaev 1980	40
41	Solenoozero	Minus.	95.3	0.78	0.12	3.8	OES	Miniaev 1980	41
42	Tabat	Minus.	96.39	0.018	0.092	3.5	OES	Miniaev 1980	42
43	Mar'iasova	Minus.	95.848	0.042	0.11	4	OES	Miniaev 1980	43
44	Minus. Basin	Minus.	98.18	0.25	0.17	1.4	OES	Miniaev 1980	44
45	Minus. Basin	Minus.	98.58	0.18	0.14	1.1	OES	Miniaev 1980	45
46	Mar'iasova	Minus.	98.61	0.22	0.07	1.1	OES	Miniaev 1980	46
47	Beiskoe	Minus.	96.475	0.035	0.19	3.3	OES	Miniaev 1980	47
48	Krapovina	Minus.	98.19	0.21	0.6	1	OES	Miniaev 1980	48
49	Tabat	Minus.	95.716	0.01	0.074	4.2	OES	Miniaev 1980	49
50	Mar'iasova	Minus.	98.551	0.03	0.019	1.4	OES	Miniaev 1980	50
51	Mar'iasova	Minus.	98.651	0.031	0.018	1.3	OES	Miniaev 1980	51
52	Malaia Inia	Minus.	95.995	0.000	0.005	4	OES	Miniaev 1980	52
53	Izykh	Minus.	96.299	0.001	0.000	3.7	OES	Miniaev 1980	53
54	Malaia Inia	Minus.	97.998	0.002	0.000	2	OES	Miniaev 1980	54
55	Izykh	Minus.	97.500	0.000	0.000	2.5	OES	Miniaev 1980	55
56	Minus. Basin	Minus.	98.67	0.13	0.1	1.1	OES	Miniaev 1980	56
57	Mar'iasova	Minus.	95.960	0.000	0.04	4	OES	Miniaev 1980	57
58	Izykh	Minus.	96.6	1.4	1.3	0.7	OES	Miniaev 1980	58
59	Mar'iasova	Minus.	98.747	0.035	0.018	1.2	OES	Miniaev 1980	59
60	Kaly	Minus.	98.174	1.5	0.026	0.3	OES	Miniaev 1980	60
61	Bol'shoi Telek	Minus.	97.299	0.001	0.000	2.7	OES	Miniaev 1980	61
62	Minus. Basin	Minus.	93.72	0.2	0.08	6	OES	Miniaev 1980	62
63	Minus. Basin	Minus.	90.747	0.24	0.013	9	OES	Miniaev 1980	63
64	Minus. Basin	Minus.	96.498	0.002	0.000	3.5	OES	Miniaev 1980	64
65	Minus. Basin	Minus.	91.58	0.009	0.011	8.4	OES	Miniaev 1980	65
66	Minus. Basin	Minus.	92.18	0.01	0.01	7.8	OES	Miniaev 1980	66
67	Minus. Basin	Minus.	98.171	0.009	0.02	1.8	OES	Miniaev 1980	67
68	Grishkin Log	Minus.	92.435	0.005	0.16	7.4	OES	Miniaev 1980	68
69	Nov. Chernaia	Minus.	97.65	0.25	1.5	0.6	OES	Miniaev 1980	69

No.	Site	Region	Cu	Sn	Pb	As	Method	Reference	Publ. ID
70	Kaptyrevo	Minus.	92.985	0.008	0.007	7	OES	Miniaev 1980	70
71	Minus. Basin	Minus.	88.987	0.006	0.007	11	OES	Miniaev 1980	71
72	Oznachennoe	Minus.	94.8	2	2.8	0.4	OES	Miniaev 1980	72
73	Minus. Basin	Minus.	93.771	0.015	0.014	6.2	OES	Miniaev 1980	73
74	Beiskoe	Minus.	87.95	10	0.05	2	OES	Miniaev 1980	74
75	Verkhov'ia Tesa	Minus.	95.278	0.015	0.007	4.7	OES	Miniaev 1980	75
76	Shushenskoe	Minus.	95.7	0.5	2	1.8	OES	Miniaev 1980	76
77	Syda	Minus.	93.981	0.009	0.01	6	OES	Miniaev 1980	77
78	Ulus Kostin	Minus.	87.67	0.25	0.08	12	OES	Miniaev 1980	78
79	Minus. Basin	Minus.	95.086	0.024	0.19	4.7	OES	Miniaev 1980	79
80	Abakanskoe	Minus.	91.2	0.5	3.8	4.5	OES	Miniaev 1980	80
81	Abakanskoe	Minus.	98.853	0.007	0.14	1	OES	Miniaev 1980	81
82	Beresh	Minus.	97.22	0.28	0.6	1.9	OES	Miniaev 1980	82
83	site unknown	Minus.	92.33	0.33	0.14	7.2	OES	Miniaev 1980	83
84	Kokorevo	Minus.	97.64	0.45	0.11	1.8	OES	Miniaev 1980	84
85	Sackler Coll.	Coll.	83.4	0.000	8.8	7.8	XRF	Chase/Douglas 1997	72.2.442
86	Sackler Coll.	Coll.	78	2	20	0	XRF	Chase/Douglas 1997	72.2.443
87	Sackler Coll.	Coll.	96	0.000	1	3	XRF	Chase/Douglas 1997	V-3032
88	Sackler Coll.	Coll.	69.8	6.4	22	1.8	XRF	Chase/Douglas 1997	V-3925
89	Sackler Coll.	Coll.	98.07	0.57	1.3	0.06	XRF	Chase/Douglas 1997	V-7000
90	Sackler Coll.	Coll.	67.52	6.8	25	0.68	XRF	Chase/Douglas 1997	V-7008
91	Sackler Coll.	Coll.	51.9	10.1	38	0	XRF	Chase/Douglas 1997	V-7009
92	Sackler Coll.	Coll.	92.74	1.36	3.6	2.3	XRF	Chase/Douglas 1997	V-7013
93	Sackler Coll.	Coll.	73.5	13.5	13	0	XRF	Chase/Douglas 1997	V-7015
94	Sackler Coll.	Coll.	91.9	3.5	3.4	1.2	XRF	Chase/Douglas 1997	V-7021
95	Sackler Coll.	Coll.	100	0.000	0.000	0	XRF	Chase/Douglas 1997	V-7024
96	Sackler Coll.	Coll.	83.83	3	1.17	12	XRF	Chase/Douglas 1997	V-7052
97	Sackler Coll.	Coll.	70.7	7.3	22	0	XRF	Chase/Douglas 1997	V-7074
98	Sackler Coll.	Coll.	87.6	1.7	0	10.7	XRF	Chase/Douglas 1997	V-7148
99	Coll. Liu	Coll.	84.94	4.211	3.624	0.163	PIXE	Miniaev 2002	66
100	Coll. Liu	Coll.	83.046	0.796	0.394	5.354	PIXE	Miniaev 2002	69
101	Coll. Liu	Coll.	69.569	2.282	4.2	17.089	PIXE	Miniaev 2002	70
102	Coll. Liu	Coll.	61.983	15.631	18.035	0.028	PIXE	Miniaev 2002	71
103	Coll. Liu	Coll.	60.507	13.476	15.199	0.065	PIXE	Miniaev 2002	72
104	British Mus.	Coll.		0.22	1.3	0.000	OES	Pollard et al. 2018b	1950 11-16 2
105	British Mus.	Coll.		3.8	11.1	0.75	OES	Pollard et al. 2018b	1950 11-16 3
106	British Mus.	Coll.		0.57	1.3	0.000	OES	Pollard et al. 2018b	1950 11-16 4

No.	Site	Region	Cu	Sn	Pb	As	Method	Reference	Publ. ID
107	British Mus.	Coll.		0.66	0.000	0.000	OES	Pollard et al. 2018b	1950 11-16 6
108	British Mus.	Coll.		6.9	12.5	0.17	OES	Pollard et al. 2018b	1950 11-16 8
109	British Mus.	Coll.		6.8	14.2	0.31	OES	Pollard et al. 2018b	1950 11-16 9
110	British Mus.	Coll.		4.6	5.3	0.27	OES	Pollard et al. 2018b	1950 11-16 11
111	British Mus.	Coll.		0.91	2.8	0.21	OES	Pollard et al. 2018b	1936 11-18 140
112	British Mus.	Coll.		4.7	10.5	0.24	OES	Pollard et al. 2018b	1936 11-18 149
113	Baga Gazryn ch.	Mong.	97	0.000	1	2	SEM-EDS	Park et al. 2011	6
114	Terezin, 12	Tuva	93	0	0	7	XRF	Khavrin 2011	Tab. 1 (17.1)

Table 3

Chart of published metal compositional data of bronzes (except for belt plaques) from Mongolia, Transbaikal area and the Minusinsk Basin from the Late Iron Age (Xiongnu period); compiled by Ursula Brosseder and Yiu-Kang Hsu.

ID	Site	Region	Artifact	Cu	Sn	Pb	As	Method	Reference	Publ. ID
1	Baga Gazryn ch.	Mong.	belt plaque	97	0.000	1	2	SEM-EDS	Park et al. 2011	6
2	Baga Gazryn ch.	Mong.	arrowhead	97	0.000	0.000	w	SEM-EDS	Park et al. 2011	7
3	Baga Gazryn ch.	Mong.	button	94	0.000	0.000	6	SEM-EDS	Park et al. 2011	11
4	Baga Gazryn ch.	Mong.	fastener	94	0.000	0.000	6	SEM-EDS	Park et al. 2011	12
5	Baga Gazryn ch.	Mong.	fragment	88	8	0.000	4	SEM-EDS	Park et al. 2011	18
6	Baga Gazryn ch.	Mong.	button	90	10	0.000	0.000	SEM-EDS	Park et al. 2011	25
7	Baga Gazryn ch.	Mong.	vessel	90	3	6	1	SEM-EDS	Park et al. 2011	29
8	Baga Gazryn ch.	Mong.	crossbow bolt	92	2	4	2	SEM-EDS	Park et al. 2011	30
9	Baga Gazryn ch.	Mong.	arrowhead	79	6	12	3	SEM-EDS	Park et al. 2011	32
10	Baga Gazryn ch.	Mong.	crossbow bolt	76	9	15	0.000	SEM-EDS	Park et al. 2011	34
11	Baga Gazryn ch.	Mong.	crossbow bolt	75	10	15	0.000	SEM-EDS	Park et al. 2011	35
12	Baga Gazryn ch.	Mong.	ornament	86	10	4	0.000	SEM-EDS	Park et al. 2011	36
13	Baga Gazryn ch.	Mong.	ornament	91	7	2	0.000	SEM-EDS	Park et al. 2011	37
14	Baga Gazryn ch.	Mong.	ring	70	5	25	0.000	SEM-EDS	Park et al. 2011	38
15	Baga Gazryn ch.	Mong.	button	79	14	7	0.000	SEM-EDS	Park et al. 2011	39
16	Baga Gazryn ch.	Mong.	fragment	81	12	7	0.000	SEM-EDS	Park et al. 2011	40
17	Baga Gazryn ch.	Mong.	button	82	14	4	0.000	SEM-EDS	Park et al. 2011	41
18	Baga Gazryn ch.	Mong.	pendant	79	8	13	0.000	SEM-EDS	Park et al. 2011	42
19	Baga Gazryn ch.	Mong.	fragment	84	9	7	0.000	SEM-EDS	Park et al. 2011	43
20	Baga Gazryn ch.	Mong.	pendant	79	9	12	0.000	SEM-EDS	Park et al. 2011	44
21	Baga Gazryn ch.	Mong.	pendant	78	9	13	0.000	SEM-EDS	Park et al. 2011	45
22	Baga Gazryn ch.	Mong.	prill	97	0.000	0.000	3	SEM-EDS	Park et al. 2011	46
23	Baga Gazryn ch.	Mong.	prill	97	0.000	0.000	3	SEM-EDS	Park et al. 2011	47
24	Baga Gazryn ch.	Mong.	prill	91	6	0.000	3	SEM-EDS	Park et al. 2011	48
25	Baga Gazryn ch.	Mong.	prill	91	6	0.000	3	SEM-EDS	Park et al. 2011	49
26	Egiin gol	Mong.	cauldron	66.76	2.35	30.51	0.38	SEM-EDS	Hsu unpubl.	M-108
27	Egiin gol	Mong.	cauldron	98.37	0.58	0.78	0.27	SEM-EDS	Hsu unpubl.	M-109
28	Gol Mod 2	Mong.	chariot flower	90.4	0.000	0.7	8.9	SEM-EDS	Park et al. 2018	16
29	Gol Mod 2	Mong.	chariot flower	92.6	0.000	0.000	7.4	SEM-EDS	Park et al. 2018	12
30	Gol Mod 2	Mong.	chariot flower	91	0.5	1.5	7	SEM-EDS	Park et al. 2018	9
31	Gol Mod 2	Mong.	chariot flower	92.7	1	0.4	5.9	SEM-EDS	Park et al. 2018	4
32	Gol Mod 2	Mong.	chariot flower	90.9	0.9	3	5.2	SEM-EDS	Park et al. 2018	7

ID	Site	Region	Artifact	Cu	Sn	Pb	As	Method	Reference	Publ. ID
33	Gol Mod 2	Mong.	chariot flower	86.9	2.2	5.8	5.1	SEM-EDS	Park et al. 2018	2
34	Gol Mod 2	Mong.	chariot flower	91.8	0.6	3	4.6	SEM-EDS	Park et al. 2018	17
35	Gol Mod 2	Mong.	chariot flower	93.6	0.4	1.8	4.2	SEM-EDS	Park et al. 2018	6
36	Gol Mod 2	Mong.	chariot flower	92	1.3	2.6	4.1	SEM-EDS	Park et al. 2018	11
37	Gol Mod 2	Mong.	chariot flower	93.4	0.000	2.5	4.1	SEM-EDS	Park et al. 2018	14
38	Gol Mod 2	Mong.	chariot flower	91.6	0.7	3.8	3.9	SEM-EDS	Park et al. 2018	19
39	Gol Mod 2	Mong.	chariot flower	93.6	1.3	2.2	2.9	SEM-EDS	Park et al. 2018	3
40	Gol Mod 2	Mong.	chariot flower	91.5	0.7	5	2.8	SEM-EDS	Park et al. 2018	10
41	Gol Mod 2	Mong.	chariot flower	92.1	1.6	4	2.3	SEM-EDS	Park et al. 2018	1
42	Gol Mod 2	Mong.	chariot flower	92.8	2	3	2.2	SEM-EDS	Park et al. 2018	18
43	Gol Mod 2	Mong.	chariot flower	92.8	2.2	3	2	SEM-EDS	Park et al. 2018	8
44	Gol Mod 2	Mong.	chariot flower	92.4	2.2	3.6	1.8	SEM-EDS	Park et al. 2018	21
45	Gol Mod 2	Mong.	chariot flower	90.7	2.9	4.7	1.7	SEM-EDS	Park et al. 2018	5
46	Gol Mod 2	Mong.	chariot flower	92.1	3.5	2.8	1.6	SEM-EDS	Park et al. 2018	20
47	Gol Mod 2	Mong.	chariot flower	92	2.3	4.2	1.5	SEM-EDS	Park et al. 2018	15
48	Gol Mod 2	Mong.	chariot flower	92.1	1.6	5.1	1.2	SEM-EDS	Park et al. 2018	13
49	Dyrestui	Transb.	button	86.6	1	6.6	5.8	OES	Miniaev 1977	316
50	Dyrestui	Transb.	bell pendant	90.6	1.7	2.1	5.6	OES	Miniaev 1977	317
51	Dyrestui	Transb.	bell pendant	92.5	0.8	1.1	5.6	OES	Miniaev 1977	318
52	Dyrestui	Transb.	bell pendant	88.6	1.6	2	7.8	OES	Miniaev 1977	319
53	Dyrestui	Transb.	bell pendant	83	1.6	0.4	15	OES	Miniaev 1977	320
54	Dyrestui	Transb.	button	97	0.3	2.2	0.5	OES	Miniaev 1977	321
55	Dyrestui	Transb.	bell pendant	89.6	1.5	2.5	6.4	OES	Miniaev 1977	322
56	Dyrestui	Transb.	plaque	77.46	11	11	0.54	OES	Miniaev 1977	323
57	Dyrestui	Transb.	buckle	79.66	8	12	0.34	OES	Miniaev 1977	324
58	Dyrestui	Transb.	bell pendant	89.8	0.7	2.5	7	OES	Miniaev 1977	325
59	Dyrestui	Transb.	button	97.76	0.54	0.1	1.6	OES	Miniaev 1977	326
60	Dyrestui	Transb.	button	97.59	0.74	0.17	1.5	OES	Miniaev 1977	327
61	Dyrestui	Transb.	button	86.76	0.94	7.6	4.7	OES	Miniaev 1977	328
62	Dyrestui	Transb.	button	96.2	0.4	2.7	0.7	OES	Miniaev 1977	329
63	Dyrestui	Transb.	appliqué	87.9	7.6	4	0.5	OES	Miniaev 1977	330
64	Dyrestui	Transb.	bell	90.15	8.6	1	0.25	OES	Miniaev 1977	331
65	Dyrestui	Transb.	coin	86.52	3	9.6	0.88	OES	Miniaev 1977	332
66	Dyrestui	Transb.	ring	83.66	7.2	8.4	0.74	OES	Miniaev 1977	333
67	Dyrestui	Transb.	ring	99.08	0.06	0.12	0.74	OES	Miniaev 1977	334
68	Dyrestui	Transb.	ring	92.06	0.94	2.5	4.5	OES	Miniaev 1977	335
69	Dyrestui	Transb.	ring	94.9	0.3	1.8	3	OES	Miniaev 1977	336

ID	Site	Region	Artifact	Cu	Sn	Pb	As	Method	Reference	Publ. ID
70	Dyrestui	Transb.	buckle fragm.	75.98	24	0.02	0.000	OES	Miniaev 1977	337
71	Dyrestui	Transb.	buckle fragm.	96.9	0.6	1.6	0.9	OES	Miniaev 1977	338
72	Dyrestui	Transb.	small buckle	92.4	3.4	2.7	1.5	OES	Miniaev 1977	431
73	Dyrestui	Transb.	belt ring	82.3	8.4	8	1.3	OES	Miniaev 1977	432
74	Dyrestui	Transb.	belt ring	89.84	0.47	0.09	9.6	OES	Miniaev 1977	433
75	Dyrestui	Transb.	button	94.4	0.3	1.1	4.2	OES	Miniaev 1977	434
76	Dyrestui	Transb.	button	98.11	0.09	0.1	1.7	OES	Miniaev 1977	435
77	Dyrestui	Transb.	button	98.112	0.094	0.094	1.7	OES	Miniaev 1977	436
78	Dyrestui	Transb.	button	96.98	0.1	0.22	2.7	OES	Miniaev 1977	437
79	Dyrestui	Transb.	button	94.1	0.8	1.3	3.8	OES	Miniaev 1977	438
80	Dyrestui	Transb.	button	94.15	0.45	1	4.4	OES	Miniaev 1977	439
81	Dyrestui	Transb.	pendant	92.8	1.7	3	2.5	OES	Miniaev 1977	440
82	Dyrestui	Transb.	pendant	92.4	3.1	3.7	0.8	OES	Miniaev 1977	441
83	Dyrestui	Transb.	pendant	92.4	4	2.8	0.8	OES	Miniaev 1977	442
84	Dyrestui	Transb.	cowrie imit.	77.6	16	5.8	0.6	OES	Miniaev 1977	443
85	Dyrestui	Transb.	cowrie imit.	78.8	11	9	1.2	OES	Miniaev 1977	444
86	Dyrestui	Transb.	cowrie imit.	85.07	12	2.5	0.43	OES	Miniaev 1977	445
87	Dyrestui	Transb.	wuzhu coin	84.9	3.7	11	0.4	OES	Miniaev 1977	446
88	Dyrestui	Transb.	wuzhu coin	88.7	3.3	7.6	0.4	OES	Miniaev 1977	447
89	Dyrestui	Transb.	wuzhu coin	82.42	6	11	0.58	OES	Miniaev 1977	448
90	Dyrestui	Transb.	bead	92.6	7	0.4	0.000	OES	Miniaev 1977	449
91	Dyrestui	Transb.	bead	97.42	2.2	0.38	0.000	OES	Miniaev 1977	450
92	Dyrestui	Transb.	strap distr.	92.03	0.17	4.5	3.3	OES	Miniaev 1977	451
93	Dyrestui	Transb.	strap distr.	90.93	0.27	4.5	4.3	OES	Miniaev 1977	452
94	Dyrestui	Transb.	strap distr.	90.73	0.27	5	4	OES	Miniaev 1977	453
95	Dyrestui	Transb.	strap distr.	85.9	0.5	7.4	6.2	OES	Miniaev 1977	454
96	Dyrestui	Transb.	strap distr.	93.03	0.27	4	2.7	OES	Miniaev 1977	455
97	Dyrestui	Transb.	solid bell	93.6	0.8	2.5	3.1	OES	Miniaev 1977	456
98	Dyrestui	Transb.	bell pendant	64.55	22	13	0.45	OES	Miniaev 1977	457
99	Dyrestui	Transb.	bell pendant	87.4	7.6	3	2	OES	Miniaev 1977	458
100	Dyrestui	Transb.	bell pendant	89.7	3.4	5.2	1.7	OES	Miniaev 1977	459
101	Dyrestui	Transb.	bell pendant	99.335	0.045	0.15	0.47	OES	Miniaev 1977	460
102	Dyrestui	Transb.	bell pendant	84.7	4	8	3.3	OES	Miniaev 1977	461
103	Dyrestui	Transb.	bell pendant	94.97	0.23	1.1	3.7	OES	Miniaev 1977	462
104	Dyrestui	Transb.	ring	98.41	0.09	0.9	0.6	OES	Miniaev 1977	463
105	Dyrestui	Transb.	ring	96.41	0.45	0.84	2.3	OES	Miniaev 1977	464
106	Dyrestui	Transb.	ring	98.546	0.034	0.12	1.3	OES	Miniaev 1977	465

ID	Site	Region	Artifact	Cu	Sn	Pb	As	Method	Reference	Publ. ID
107	Dyrestui	Transb.	arrowhead	78.6	6	7.6	7.8	OES	Miniaev 1977	466
108	Dyrestui	Transb.	cauldron	77	9.4	13	0.6	OES	Miniaev 1977	467
109	Dyrestui	Transb.	button	95.4	1.2	1	2.4	OES	Sergeeva 1981	44
110	Cheremu. Pad'	Transb.	bell	90.13	3.67	5	1.2	OES	Sergeeva 1981	50
111	Cheremu. Pad'	Transb.	mirror	89.54	6.85	3.25	0.36	OES	Sergeeva 1981	68
112	Cheremu. Pad'	Transb.	mould	99.969	0.03	0.001	0.000	OES	Sergeeva 1981	72
113	Dyrestui	Transb.	bell	76.7	3.3	10	10	OES	Sergeeva 1981	45
114	Dyrestui	Transb.	button	85.72	1.58	10	2.7	OES	Sergeeva 1981	46
115	Dyrestui	Transb.	buckle	91.15	3.14	5	0.71	OES	Sergeeva 1981	49
116	Dyrestui	Transb.	ring	91.41	2.14	6	0.45	OES	Sergeeva 1981	51
117	Dyrestui	Transb.	plaque	76.35	10	10	3.65	OES	Sergeeva 1981	52
118	Dyrestui	Transb.	ring	79.4	4.2	10	6.4	OES	Sergeeva 1981	67
119	Dyrestui	Transb.	suspension	95.65	0.85	1.9	1.6	OES	Sergeeva 1981	142
120	Dyrestui	Transb.	suspension	98.659	0.021	0.32	1	OES	Sergeeva 1981	145
121	Dyrestui	Transb.	buckle	98.86	0.14	0.89	0.11	OES	Sergeeva 1981	149
122	Dyrestui	Transb.	buckle	98.681	0.069	0.93	0.32	OES	Sergeeva 1981	152
123	Dyrestui	Transb.	buckle	97.533	1.2	1.2	0.067	OES	Sergeeva 1981	157
124	Dyrestui	Transb.	buckle	97.96	0.85	0.79	0.4	OES	Sergeeva 1981	160
125	Dyrestui	Transb.	cowrie	96.36	1.4	1.6	0.64	OES	Sergeeva 1981	165
126	Dyrestui	Transb.	ring	97.681	0.089	0.63	1.6	OES	Sergeeva 1981	217
127	Dyrestui	Transb.	unknown	99.52	0.14	0.3	0.04	OES	Sergeeva 1981	220
128	Dyrestui	Transb.	bead	98.216	1.3	0.46	0.024	OES	Sergeeva 1981	222
129	Dyrestui	Transb.	bell	95.66	0.21	0.93	3.2	OES	Sergeeva 1981	226
130	Il'movaia Pad'	Transb.	button	82.8	2.4	10	4.8	OES	Sergeeva 1981	47
131	Il'movaia Pad'	Transb.	button	91.642	0.078	8	0.28	OES	Sergeeva 1981	48
132	Il'movaia Pad'	Transb.	mirror	86.7	6.8	6	0.5	OES	Sergeeva 1981	69
133	Il'movaia Pad'	Transb.	buckle	99.305	0.015	0.5	0.18	OES	Sergeeva 1981	214
134	Il'movaia Pad'	Transb.	buckle	98.45	0.05	1.1	0.4	OES	Sergeeva 1981	214a
135	Il'movaia Pad'	Transb.	buckle	98.623	0.087	0.79	0.5	OES	Sergeeva 1981	214b
136	Il'movaia Pad'	Transb.	buckle	98.922	0.088	0.47	0.52	OES	Sergeeva 1981	214c
137	Il'movaia Pad'	Transb.	buckle	98.534	0.046	1	0.42	OES	Sergeeva 1981	214f
138	Ust'-Kiakhta	Transb.	plaque	99.29	0.05	0.16	0.5	OES	Sergeeva 1981	215
139	Ust'-Kiakhta	Transb.	plaque	98.745	0.076	0.079	1.1	OES	Sergeeva 1981	216
140	Kosogol hoard	Minus.	strap end	99.49	0.01	0.000	0.5	OES	Miniaev 1978	172
141	Kosogol hoard	Minus.	strap end	95	0.000	0.000	5	OES	Miniaev 1978	173
142	Kosogol hoard	Minus.	strap end	89	0.000	0.000	11	OES	Miniaev 1978	176
143	Kosogol hoard	Minus.	strap end	81.87	0.03	0.1	18	OES	Miniaev 1978	175

ID	Site	Region	Artifact	Cu	Sn	Pb	As	Method	Reference	Publ. ID
144	Kosogol hoard	Minus.	strap end	90	0.5	0.5	9	OES	Miniaev 1978	174
145	Kosogol hoard	Minus.	button	91	0.000	0.000	9	OES	Miniaev 1978	186
146	Kosogol hoard	Minus.	ring	97.4	0.5	0.1	2	OES	Miniaev 1978	189
147	Kosogol hoard	Minus.	button	96.5	0.3	0.2	3	OES	Miniaev 1978	170
148	Kosogol hoard	Minus.	cauldron	98.15	0.2	0.15	1.5	OES	Miniaev 1978	191
149	Kosogol hoard	Minus.	cauldron	90.49	0.5	0.01	9	OES	Miniaev 1978	194
150	Kosogol hoard	Minus.	cauldron	89.9	0.1	0.000	10	OES	Miniaev 1978	198
151	Kosogol hoard	Minus.	cauldron	98.6	0.2	0.2	1	OES	Miniaev 1978	200
152	Kosogol hoard	Minus.	cauldron	98.85	0.2	0.2	0.75	OES	Miniaev 1978	201
153	Kosogol hoard	Minus.	cauldron	97.5	0.3	0.2	2	OES	Miniaev 1978	202
154	Kosogol hoard	Minus.	cauldron	98.65	0.15	0.2	1	OES	Miniaev 1978	203
155	Kosogol hoard	Minus.	fragment	97.2	0.3	0.5	2	OES	Miniaev 1978	212
156	Kosogol hoard	Minus.	fragment	92.5	0.5	0.000	7	OES	Miniaev 1978	213
157	Kosogol hoard	Minus.	fragment	97	0.8	0.2	2	OES	Miniaev 1978	217
158	Kosogol hoard	Minus.	fragment	99.39	0.1	0.01	0.5	OES	Miniaev 1978	219
159	Kosogol hoard	Minus.	ingot	97.7	0.8	0.5	1	OES	Miniaev 1978	211
160	Kosogol hoard	Minus.	fragment	98.85	0.3	0.1	0.75	OES	Miniaev 1978	223
161	Kosogol hoard	Minus.	fragment	99.5	0.2	0.000	0.3	OES	Miniaev 1978	224
162	Kosogol hoard	Minus.	fragment	96.3	0.5	0.2	3	OES	Miniaev 1978	226
163	Kosogol hoard	Minus.	fragment	99.33	0.07	0.1	0.5	OES	Miniaev 1978	229
164	Kosogol hoard	Minus.	fragment	96.6	0.2	0.2	3	OES	Miniaev 1978	237
165	Kosogol hoard	Minus.	fragment	98.8	0.1	0.1	1	OES	Miniaev 1978	238
166	Kosogol hoard	Minus.	ingot	98.5	0.5	0.2	0.8	OES	Miniaev 1978	234
167	Kosogol hoard	Minus.	ingot	98	0.8	0.2	1	OES	Miniaev 1978	235
168	Kosogol hoard	Minus.	fragment	98.75	0.4	0.1	0.75	OES	Miniaev 1978	206
169	Kosogol hoard	Minus.	ornament	82.4	17	0.1	0.5	OES	Miniaev 1978	187
170	Kosogol hoard	Minus.	ornament	82.2	17	0.2	0.6	OES	Miniaev 1978	188
171	Kosogol hoard	Minus.	belt plaque	81.15	18	0.1	0.75	OES	Miniaev 1978	178
172	Kosogol hoard	Minus.	ornament	84.49	15	0.01	0.5	OES	Miniaev 1978	180
173	Kosogol hoard	Minus.	ring	91.3	7	0.2	1.5	OES	Miniaev 1978	185
174	Kosogol hoard	Minus.	ornament	93.95	5	0.3	0.75	OES	Miniaev 1978	176a
175	Kosogol hoard	Minus.	ornament	94.4	5	0.1	0.5	OES	Miniaev 1978	171
176	Kosogol hoard	Minus.	ornament	96.1	3	0.3	0.6	OES	Miniaev 1978	165
177	Kosogol hoard	Minus.	fragment	93.7	3	0.3	3	OES	Miniaev 1978	190
178	Kosogol hoard	Minus.	fragment	94.5	2	0.5	3	OES	Miniaev 1978	221
179	Kosogol hoard	Minus.	fragment	95.2	1.5	0.3	3	OES	Miniaev 1978	215
180	Kosogol hoard	Minus.	fragment	97.7	1	0.3	1	OES	Miniaev 1978	216

ID	Site	Region	Artifact	Cu	Sn	Pb	As	Method	Reference	Publ. ID
181	Kosogol hoard	Minus.	fragment	97.1	1.5	0.4	1	OES	Miniaev 1978	218
182	Kosogol hoard	Minus.	fragment	97.49	2	0.01	0.5	OES	Miniaev 1978	222
183	Kosogol hoard	Minus.	fragment	95.3	4	0.1	0.6	OES	Miniaev 1978	227
184	Kosogol hoard	Minus.	ingot	92.15	7	0.15	0.7	OES	Miniaev 1978	231
185	Kosogol hoard	Minus.	ingot	82.8	15	0.2	2	OES	Miniaev 1978	233
186	Kosogol hoard	Minus.	ingot	89.6	7	0.4	3	OES	Miniaev 1978	236
187	Kosogol hoard	Minus.	ingot	93.95	2	0.05	4	OES	Miniaev 1978	239
188	Kosogol hoard	Minus.	ingot	93.5	2	0.5	4	OES	Miniaev 1978	240
189	Kosogol hoard	Minus.	ingot	93.7	2	0.3	4	OES	Miniaev 1978	241
190	Kosogol hoard	Minus.	ingot	94.75	2	0.25	3	OES	Miniaev 1978	230
191	Kosogol hoard	Minus.	ingot	82.6	15	0.4	2	OES	Miniaev 1978	232
192	Kosogol hoard	Minus.	fragment	96.9	2	0.1	1	OES	Miniaev 1978	195
193	Kosogol hoard	Minus.	fragment	81.2	15	0.8	3	OES	Miniaev 1978	242
194	Kosogol hoard	Minus.	fragment	96.8	1	0.2	2	OES	Miniaev 1978	204
195	Kosogol hoard	Minus.	fragment	96.7	1	0.3	2	OES	Miniaev 1978	205
196	Kosogol hoard	Minus.	fragment	96.8	1	0.2	2	OES	Miniaev 1978	207
197	Kosogol hoard	Minus.	fragment	95.2	1.5	0.3	3	OES	Miniaev 1978	208
198	Kosogol hoard	Minus.	fragment	94.2	1.5	0.3	4	OES	Miniaev 1978	209
199	Kosogol hoard	Minus.	fragment	96.7	1	0.3	2	OES	Miniaev 1978	210
200	Kosogol hoard	Minus.	ornament	83	17	0.000	0.000	OES	Miniaev 1978	179
201	Kosogol hoard	Minus.	ornament	83	17	0.000	0.000	OES	Miniaev 1978	182
202	Kosogol hoard	Minus.	ornament	85	15	0.000	0.000	OES	Miniaev 1978	183
203	Kosogol hoard	Minus.	ornament	83	17	0.000	0.000	OES	Miniaev 1978	184
204	Kosogol hoard	Minus.	cauldron	99.86	0.04	0.000	0.1	OES	Miniaev 1978	192
205	Kosogol hoard	Minus.	cauldron	99.88	0.02	0.000	0.1	OES	Miniaev 1978	193
206	Kosogol hoard	Minus.	cauldron	100	0.000	0.000	0.000	OES	Miniaev 1978	196
207	Kosogol hoard	Minus.	ingot	99.7	0.1	0.000	0.2	OES	Miniaev 1978	228
208	Kosogol hoard	Minus.	cauldron	89	1	8	2	OES	Miniaev 1978	197
209	Kosogol hoard	Minus.	fragment	93	1	2	4	OES	Miniaev 1978	214
210	Kosogol hoard	Minus.	ingot	96.25	1	2	0.75	OES	Miniaev 1978	225
211	Kosogol hoard	Minus.	ornament	76	16	5	3	OES	Miniaev 1978	181

Bibliography

Ackerman 1946 Ackerman, Phyllis. "Early Textile Production in China," in *Bulletin of the Needle and Bobbin Club* 30, 1/2, 1946, 58–69.

Adams 2014 Adams, Noël. *Bright Lights in the Dark Ages: The Thaw Collection of Early Medieval Ornament.* New York: Giles, 2014.

Akishev 1978 Akishev, Kimal' A. *Kurgan Issyk: Iskusstvo sakov Kazakhstana.* Moscow: Iskusstvo, 1978.

Akishev 2006 Akishev, Kimal' A. "Golden Warrior: The Sun God, Shaman, or Mythological hero." In Chang and Guroff 2007, 57–62.

Alekseev and Bokovenko 2005 Alekseev, Andreï Iu., and Nikolaï A. Bokovenko. *Evraziia v skifskuiu ėpokhu: Radiouglerodnaia i arkheologicheskaia khronologiia.* Saint Petersburg: Institut istorii material'noĭ kul'tury RAN, 2005.

Alekseev et al. 2001 Alexeev, Andreï I., Ludmilla L. Barkova, and Ludmilla K. Galanina. *Nomades des Steppes: Les Scythes, VIIe–IIIe siècle av. J.-C.* Paris: Éditions Autrement, 2001.

Allsen 1997 Allsen, Thomas T. *Commodity and exchange in the Mongol Empire: A cultural history of Islamic textiles.* Cambridge, New York, Melbourne: Cambridge University Press, 1997.

Allsen 2006 Allsen, Thomas T. *The Royal Hunt in Eurasian History.* Philadelphia: University of Pennsylvania Press, 2006.

Amandry 1965 Amandry, Pierre. "Un motif 'skythe' en Iran et en Grèce," in *Journal of Near Eastern Studies* 24, 3, 1965, 149–60.

Amiet 1980 Amiet, Pierre. *Art of the Ancient Near East.* New York: Harry N. Abrams, 1980.

Amitai and Biran 2005 Amitai, Reuven, and Michal Biran, eds. *Mongols, Turks, and Others: Eurasian Nomads and the Sedentary World.* Leiden and Boston: Brill, 2005.

Amitai and Biran 2015 Amitai, Reuven, and Michal Biran, eds. *Nomads as Agents of Cultural Change: The Mongols and their Eurasian Predecessors.* Honolulu: University of Hawai'i Press, 2015.

An Zhimin and An Jiayuan 2008 An Zhimin, and An Jiayuan. "Zhongguo zaoqi huangjin zhipin de kaoguxue yanjiu," in *Kaogu xuebao* 2008.3, 291–310.

Ancient Culture 2009 *Monggol, ch'owŏn e p'in kodae munhwa (= The Ancient Culture of Mongolia. = Mongolyn ėrtniĭ soël).* Catalogue of the exhibition at Busan Museum, March 5 – May 17, 2009. Busan, 2009.

Andersson 1929 Andersson, Johan G. "Der Weg über die Steppen," in *Bulletin of the Museum of Far Eastern Antiquities* 1, 1929, 143–63.

Andersson 1932 Andersson, Johan G. "Hunting Magic in the Animal Style," in *Bulletin of the Museum of Far Eastern Antiquities* 4, 1932, 221–317.

Andersson 1933 Andersson, Johan G. "Selected Ordos-Bronzes," in *Bulletin of the Museum of Far Eastern Antiquities* 5, 1933, 143–54.

Anthony 2007 Anthony, David W. *The Horse, the Wheel, and Language: How Bronze-Age Riders from the Eurasian Steppes Shaped the Modern World.* Princeton and Oxford: Princeton University Press, 2007.

Ariadne Galleries 1998 *Treasures of the Eurasian Steppes: Animal Art from 800 BC to 200 AD.* Text by Tina Pang. Exhibition catalogue. New York: Ariadne Galleries, Inc., 1998.

Armbruster 2009 Armbruster, Barbara. "Gold Technology of the Ancient Scythians: Gold from the Kurgan Arzhan 2, Tuva," in *ArcheoSciences* 13, 2009, 187–93.

Art animalier 2012 *Art animalier: Collections de Haute Asie du Musée Cernuschi; Iran, Caucase et steppes orientales.* Paris: Paris Musées/Findakly, 2012.

Artamonov 1973 Artamonov, Mikhail I. *Sokrovishcha sakov: Amu-Dar'inskiĭ klad. Altaĭskie* *kurgany. Minusinskie bronzy. Sibirskoe zoloto.* Moscow: Iskusstvo, 1973.

Aruz and Fino 2012 Aruz, Joan, and Elisabetta Valtz Fino, eds. *Afghanistan: Forging Civilizations Along the Silk Road.* New York: The Metropolitan Museum of Art, 2012

Aruz and Wallenfels 2003 Aruz, Joan, and Ronald Wallenfels. *Art of the First Cities: The Third Millennium BC from the Mediterranean to the Indus.* New York: The Metropolitan Museum of Art, 2003.

Aruz et al. 2000 Aruz, Joan, Ann Farkas, Andrei Alekseev, and Elena Korolkova, eds. *The Golden Deer of Eurasia: Scythian and Sarmatian Treasures from the Russian Steppes.* New York: The Metropolitan Museum of Art, 2000.

Aruz et al. 2006 Aruz, Joan, Ann Farkas, and Elisabetta Valtz Fino, eds. *The Golden Deer of Eurasia: Perspectives on the Steppe Nomads of the Ancient World.* The Metropolitan Museum of Art Symposia. New York: The Metropolitan Museum of Art, 2006.

Aruz et al. 2008 Aruz, Joan, Kim Benzel, and Jean M. Evans. *Beyond Babylon: Art, Trade, and Diplomacy in the Second Millennium BC.* New York: The Metropolitan Museum of Art, 2008.

Aruz et al. 2014 Aruz, Joan, Sarah B. Graff, and Yelena Rakic. *Assyria to Iberia at the Dawn of the Classical Age.* New York, New Haven, and London: Yale University Press, 2014.

Bachmann 1994 Bachmann, Werner. "Die skythisch-sarmatische Harfe aus Olbia: Vorbericht zur Rekonstruktion eines unveröffentlichten, im Kriege verschollenen Musikinstruments." In Otte, Marcel, ed. *Sons originels: Préhistoire de la musique.* Études et recherches archéologiques de l'Université de Liège 61. Liège: Université de Liège, 1994, 111–34.

Bagley 1999 Bagley, Robert. "Shang Archaeology." In Loewe and Shaughnessy 1999, 124–231.

Baipakov 1998 Baipakov, Karl. "Il Kazakhstan nell'eta del ferro." In Popescu, Grigore Arbore, Chiara Silvi Antonini, and Karl Baipakov. *L'uomo d'oro: La cultura delle steppe del Kazakhstan dall'eta del bronzo alle grandi migrazioni.* Milan: Electa, 1998, 39–52.

Barber 2014 Barber, Elizabeth. "More light on the Xinjiang Textiles." In Mair and Hickman 2014, 33–39.

Barbier 1996 Barbier, Jean Paul. *Art des Steppes: Ornements et pièces de mobilier funéraire scytho-sibérien dans les collections du Musée Barbier-Mueller.* Geneva: Musée Barbier-Mueller, 1996.

Barbier-Mueller 2008a Barbier-Mueller, Jean Paul. "L'Art des Steppes: Introduction." In Mattet 2008, 162–75.

Barbier-Mueller 2008b Barbier-Mueller, Jean Paul. "L'Art des Saces dans le Haut Indus." In Mattet 2008, 196–205.

Barbier-Mueller 2013 Barbier-Mueller, Jean Paul. "Review of International Auctions 2012," in *Arts and Cultures* 14, 2013, 222–51.

Barkova 1987 Barkova, Liudmila L. "Obraz orlinogolovogo grifona v iskusstve drevnego Altaia: po materialam Bol'shikh Altaĭskikh kurganov," in *Arkheologicheskiĭ sbornik* (Ėrmitazha) 28, 1987, 5–29.

Barkova and Pankova 2005 Barkova, Liudmila L., and Svetlana V. Pankova. "Tattooed Mummies from the Large Pazyryk Mounds: New Findings," in *Archaeology, Ethnology and Anthropology of Eurasia* 22, 2005.2, 48–59.

Basilov 1989 Basilov, Vladimir N., ed. *Nomads of Eurasia.* Seattle: University of Washington Press, 1989.

Baumer 2012 Baumer, Christoph. *The History of Central Asia: The Age of the Steppe Warriors.* Vol. 1. London and New York: I. B. Tauris, 2012.

Beck et al. 2014 Beck, Ulrike, Mayke Wagner, Xiao Li, and Pavel E. Tarasov. "The invention of trousers and its likely affiliation with horseback riding and mobility: A case study of late second millennium BC finds from Turfan in eastern Central Asia," in *Quaternary International* 348, October 2014, 224–35.

Beifang 1995 Zhongguo qingtongqi quanji bianji weiyuanhui, ed. *Beifang minzu.* Zhongguo qingtongqi quanji 15. Beijing: Wenwu chubanshe, 1995.

Beijing and Shanxi 1994 Beijing daxue kaogu xuexi, and Shanxi sheng kaogu yanjiusuo. "Tianma-Qucun: Beizhao Jin hou mudi dierci faxue," in *Wenwu* 1994.1, 4–28.

Belenitsky 1968 Belenitsky, Aleksandr M. *Central Asia*. Paris, Geneva, and Munich: Nagel, 1968.

Bellezza 2004 Bellezza, John Vincent. "Metal and Stone Vestiges: Religion, Magic and Protection in the Art of Ancient Tibet," in *asianart.com. The on-line journal for the study and exhibition of the arts of Asia*, April 29, 2004, http://www.asianart.com/articles/vestiges/index.html (last accessed March 31, 2021).

Bellezza 2010 Bellezza, John Vincent. "Rare collectable artifacts from Upper Tibet," in *Flight of the Khyung*, December 2010, http://www.tibetarchaeology.com/december-2010/ (last accessed March 31, 2021).

Bellezza 2012 Bellezza, John Vincent. "A brief introduction to the tiger in Tibetan culture," in *Flight of the Khyung*, August 2012, http://www.tibetarchaeology.com/august-2012/ (last accessed March 31, 2021).

Bellezza 2014 Bellezza, John Vincent. *The Dawn of Tibet*. London: Rowman and Littlefield, 2014.

Bellezza 2016a Bellezza, John Vincent. "A Preliminary Study of the Origins and Early Development of Bronze Metallurgy on the Western Tibetan Plateau. Part 1: The 'Eurasian animal style', an art historical perspective," in *Flight of the Khyung*, February 2016, http://www.tibetarchaeology.com/february-2016/ (last accessed March 31, 2021).

Bellezza 2016b Bellezza, John Vincent. "A Preliminary Study of the Origins and Early Development of Bronze Metallurgy on the Western Tibetan Plateau. Part 2: Intercultural contacts in the Bronze Age and Iron Age, an archaeometallurgical perspective," in *Flight of the Khyung*, March 2016, http://www.tibetarchaeology.com/march-2016/ (last accessed March 31, 2021).

Bellezza 2020 Bellezza, John Vincent. *Tibetan Silver, Gold and Bronze Objects and the Aesthetics of Animals in the Era before Empire: Cross-cultural Reverberations on the Tibetan Plateau and Soundings from other Parts of Eurasia*. BAR International Series 2984. Oxford: BAR Publishing, 2020.

Bemmann et al. 2009 Bemmann, Jan, Hermann Parzinger, Ernst Pohl and Damdinsüren Tseveendorzh, eds. *Current Archaeological Research in Mongolia: Papers from the First International Conference on "Archaeological Research in Mongolia" held in Ulaanbaatar, August 19th–23rd, 2007*. Bonn Contributions to Asian Archaeology 4. Bonn: vfgarch, 2009.

Berdnikova et al. 1991 Berdnikova, V. I., Viktor M. Vetrov, and Iu. P. Lykhin. "Skifo-sibirskiĭ stil' v khudozhestvennoĭ bronze Verkhneĭ Leny," in *Sovetskaia Arkheologiia* 1991.2, 196–206.

Biran 2015 Biran, Michal. "Introduction: Nomadic Culture." In Amitai and Biran 2015, 1–9.

Boardman 1980 Boardman, John. "Greek gem engravers, their subjects and style." In Porada, Edith, ed. *Ancient Art in Seals*. Princeton: Princeton University Press, 1980, 101–19.

Boardman 2010 Boardman, John. *The Relief Plaques of Eastern Eurasia and China: The 'Ordos Bronzes', Peter the Great's Treasure, and Their Kin*. BAR International Series 2146. Oxford: Archaeopress, 2010.

Boardman 2012 Boardman, John. "Tillya Tepe: Echoes of Greece and Rome." In Aruz and Fino 2012, 102–11.

Bogdanov 2004 Bogdanov, Evgeniĭ S. "The Origin of the Image of a Predator Coiled Up in a Ball in the 'Eastern Province' of the Scythian World," in *Archaeology, Ethnology and Anthropology of Eurasia* 20, 2004.4, 50–56.

Bogdanov 2006 Bogdanov, Evgeniĭ S. *Obraz khishchnika v plasticheskom iskusstve kochevykh narodov Tsentral'noĭ Azii: Skifo-sibirskaia khudozhestvennaia traditsiia*. Novosibirsk: IAĖT SO RAN 2006.

Bogdanov 2007 Bogdanov, Evgeniĭ S. "Zur Kunst des skythisch-siberischen Kulturkreises. Raubtierdarstellungen der Nomaden Zentralasiens," in *Eurasia Antiqua* 13, 2007, 199–214.

Bogdanova-Berezovskaia 1966 Bogdanova-Berezovskaia, I. V. "Khimicheskiĭ sostav metallicheskikh predmetov iz Tulkharskogo mogil'nika." In: Mandel'shtam, Anatoliĭ M. *Kochevniki na puti v Indiiu*. Materialy i issledovaniia po arkheologii SSSR 136. Moscow, and Leningrad: Nauka, 1966, 225–30.

Bokovenko 1995a Bokovenko, Nikolai A. "The Tagar Culture in the Minusinsk Basin." In Davis-Kimball et al. 1995, 296–314.

Bokovenko 1995b Bokovenko, Nikolai A. "Tuva during the Scythian Period." In Davis-Kimball et al. 1995, 262–81.

Bokovenko 2006 Bokovenko, Nikolay. "The emergence of the Tagar culture," in *Antiquity* 80, 310, 2006, 860–79.

Bone 2015 Bone, Mike. "In Steppe," in *Inside the Gardens*, Denver: Denver Botanic Gardens, Spring (April–June), 2015, 12.

Bower 2014 Bower, Bruce. "First pants worn by horse riders 3,000 years ago," in *Science News*, May 30, 2014, 16.

Brinker 1975 Brinker, Helmut. *Bronzen aus dem alten China*. Sonderausstellung im Haus am Kiel. Zürich: Museum Rietberg, 1975.

Bronzes Chinois 1934 *Bronzes Chinois des dynasties Tcheou, Ts'in et Han*. Paris: Musée de l'Orangerie, 1934.

Brosseder 2007 Brosseder, Ursula. "Fremde Frauen in Ivolga?" In Blečić, Martina, Matija Črešnar, Bernhard Hänsel, Anja Hellmuth, Elke Kaiser, and Carola Metzner-Nebelsick, eds. *Scripta Praehistorica in Honorem Biba Teržan*. Situla 44. Ljubljana: Narodni muzej Slovenije, 2007, 883–93.

Brosseder 2011 Brosseder, Ursula. "Belt Plaques as an indicator of East-West Relations in the Eurasian Steppe at the turn of the millennia." In Brosseder and Miller 2011, 349–424.

Brosseder 2015 Brosseder, Ursula. "A Study on the Complexity and Dynamics of Interaction and Exchange in Late Iron Age Eurasia." In Bemmann, Jan, and Michael Schmauder, eds. *Complexity of Interaction along the Eurasian Steppe Zone in the First Millennium CE*. Bonn Contributions to Asian Archaeology 7. Bonn: vfgarch, 2015, 199–332.

Brosseder and Miller 2011 Brosseder, Ursula, and Bryan K. Miller, eds. *Xiongnu Archaeology: Multidisciplinary Perspectives of the First Steppe Empire in Inner Asia*. Bonn Contributions to Asian Archaeology 5. Bonn: vfgarch, 2011.

Brosseder and Miller 2018 Brosseder, Ursula, and Bryan K. Miller. "Global Networks and Local Agents in the Iron Age Eurasian Steppe." In: Boivin, Nicole, and Michael Frachetti, eds. *Ancient Globalization and the "People Without History"*. Cambridge: Cambridge University Press, 2018, 162–83.

Bruneau and Bellezza 2013 Bruneau, Laurianne, and John V. Bellezza. "The Rock Art of Upper Tibet and Ladakh – Inner Asian cultural adaptation, regional differentiation and the 'Western Tibetan Plateau Style'," in *Revue d'Etudes Tibétaines* 28, 2013, 5–161.

Bunker 1979 Bunker, Emma C. "Alligators or Crocodiles in Ancient China," in *Oriental Art* 25, 3, 1979, 340–41.

Bunker 1981 Bunker, Emma C. "The Ancient Art of Central Asia, Mongolia and Siberia." In Moorey 1981, 139–85.

Bunker 1986 Bunker, Emma C. "Diverse Cultural Encounters in the Art of the Steppes," in *Society of Asian Art Newsletter,* San Francisco: Asian Art Museum of San, Francisco, fall, 1986.

Bunker 1988 Bunker, Emma C. "Lost Wax and Lost Textile: An Unusual Ancient Technique for Casting Gold Belt Plaques." In Maddin, Robert, ed. *The beginning of the use of Metals and Alloys: Papers from the Second International Conference on the Beginning of the Use of Metals and Alloys, Zhengzhou, China, 21–26 October 1986*. Cambridge: MIT Press, 1988, 222–27.

Bunker 1989 Bunker, Emma C. "Dangerous Scholarship: On Citing Unexcavated Artifacts from Inner Mongolia and North China," in *Orientations* 20, 1989.6, 52–59.

Bunker 1990a Bunker, Emma C. "Ancient Ordos Bronzes." In Rawson and Bunker 1990, 291–357.

Bunker 1990b Bunker, Emma C. "Ancient Ordos Bronzes with Tin-Enriched Surfaces," in *Orientations* 21, 1990.1, 78–80.

Bunker 1990c Bunker, Emma C. "Bronze Belt Ornaments from North China and Inner Mongolia." In Bothmer, Dietrich von, ed. *Glories of the Past: Ancient Art from the Shelby White and Leon Levy Collection*. New York: The Metropolitan Museum of Art, 1990, 65–72.

Bunker 1991a Bunker, Emma C. "The Chinese Artifacts among the Pazyryk Finds," in *Source: Notes in the History of Art* 10.4, 1991, 20–24.

Bunker 1991b Bunker, Emma C. "Sino-Nomadic Art: Eastern Zhou, Qin and Han Artifacts made for Nomadic Taste." In *Proceedings of the International Colloquium on Chinese Art History 1991.* Vol. 2. Taipei: National Palace Museum, [1992], 569–90.

Bunker 1992a Bunker, Emma C. "Gold Belt Plaques in the Siberian Treasure of Peter the Great: Dates, Origins, and Iconography." In Seaman, Gary, ed. *The Nomad Trilogy 3: Foundations of Empire; Archaeology and Art of the Eurasian Steppes.* Los Angeles: Ethnographic Press, University of Southern California, 1992, 201–22.

Bunker 1992b Bunker, Emma C. "Significant Changes in Iconography and Technology among Ancient China's Northwestern Pastoral Neighbors from the Fourth to the First Century BC," in *Bulletin of the Asia Institute* 6, 1992, 99–115.

Bunker 1993 Bunker, Emma C. "Gold in the Ancient Chinese World: A Cultural Puzzle," in *Artibus Asiae* 53, 1/2, 1993, 27–50.

Bunker 1994a Bunker, Emma C. "The Metallurgy of Personal Adornment." In White, Julia M., and Emma C. Bunker, with contributions by Chen Peifen. *Adornment for Eternity: Status and Rank in Chinese Ornament.* Denver: Denver Art Museum and the Woods Publishing Co., 1994, 31–54.

Bunker 1994b Bunker, Emma C. "A New Dilemma: Recent Technical Studies and Related Forgeries," in *Orientations* 25, 1994.3, 90.

Bunker 1994c Bunker, Emma C. "The Enigmatic Role of Silver in China," in *Orientations* 25, 1994.11, 73–78.

Bunker 1997 Bunker, Emma C., with Richard Kimball, and Julie Segraves. "Gold Wire in Ancient China," in *Orientations* 28, 1997.3, 94–95.

Bunker 1998 Bunker, Emma C. "Cultural Diversity in the Tarim Basin Vicinity and its Impact on Ancient Chinese Culture." In Mair 1998, 604–18.

Bunker 1999a Bunker, Emma C. "In search of Liao Culture," In Bunker et al. 1999, 11–38.

Bunker 1999b Bunker, Emma C. "Liao Dynasty Personal Ornaments." In Bunker et al. 1999, 203–09.

Bunker 2001a Bunker, Emma C. "The Cemetery at Shanpula, Xinjiang. Simple Burials: Complex textiles." In Keller and Schorta 2001, 15–45.

Bunker 2001b Bunker, Emma C. "Fabulous Creatures from the Taklamakan Desert: Shanpula Textiles at the Abegg-Stiftung," in *Orientations* 32, 2001.6, 60–62.

Bunker 2006 Bunker, Emma C. "Northern China in the First Millennium BC. *Beifang* Artifacts as Historical Documents," in *Arts and Cultures* 6, 2006, 90–123.

Bunker 2008 Bunker, Emma C. "Art Nomade des Steppes Eurasiennes à l'Est de l'Oural et en Siberie Centrale." In Mattet 2008, 176–83.

Bunker 2009 Bunker, Emma C. "First-Millennium BCE *Beifang* Artifacts as Historical Documents." In Hanks, Bryan K., and Katheryn M. Linduff, eds. *Social Complexity in Prehistoric Eurasia: Monuments, Metals, and Mobility.* Cambridge: Cambridge University Press, 2009, 272–95.

Bunker and Ternbach 1970 Bunker, Emma C., and Joseph Ternbach. "A Variation of the 'Lost-Wax' process," in *Expeditions* 12, 3, 1970, 41–43.

Bunker et al. 1970 Bunker, Emma C., Bruce Chatwin, and Ann R. Farkas. *"Animal Style" Art from East to West.* New York: The Asia Society, 1970.

Bunker et al. 1997 Bunker, Emma C., Trudy Kawami, Katheryn M. Linduff, and Wu En. *Ancient Bronzes of the Eastern Eurasian Steppes: The Arthur M. Sackler Collection.* Sackler/Freer Gallery, Smithsonian Institution. New York: Abrams, 1997.

Bunker et al. 1999 Bunker, Emma C., with Julia M. White, and Jenny F. So. *Adornment for the Body and Soul: Ancient Chinese ornaments from the Mengdiexuan collection (= Jin cui liu fang: Mengdiexuan zang Zhongguo gudai shi wu).* Hong Kong: Hong Kong University Museum and Art Gallery, 1999.

Bunker et al. 2002 Bunker, Emma C., with James C. Y. Watt and Zhixin Sun. *Nomadic Art of the Eastern Eurasian Steppes: The Eugene V. Thaw and Other New York Collections.* New York: The Metropolitan Museum of Art, and New Haven: Yale University Press, 2002.

Cahill 1994 Cahill, Suzanne. "Boya Plays the Zither: Two types of Chinese Bronze Mirrors in the Donald H. Graham Jr. Collection." In Toru Nakano, *Bronze Mirrors From Ancient China: Donald H. Graham Jr. Collection.* Honolulu: Orientations, 1994, 50–59.

Cahill 2009 Cahill, Suzanne, ed. *The Lloyd Cotsen Study Collection of Chinese Bronze Mirrors.* Vol. 1. Catalogue. Monumenta archaeologica 25. Los Angeles: Cotsen Occasional Press, 2009.

Cao Wei 2012 Cao Wei, and Qinshi huangdiling bowuyuan ed. *Mengya, Chengzhang, Ronghe: dongzhou shiqi beifang qingtong wenhua zhencui.* Xi'an: Sanqin chubanshe, 2012.

Carter et al. 2013 Carter, Martha, Sidney Goldstein, Prudence O. Harper, Trudy S. Kawami, and Pieter Meyers. *Splendors of the East: Antiquities from the al-Sabah Collection.* London: Thames and Hudson, 2013.

Cavalli-Sforza 1996 Cavalli-Sforza, Luca L. "The spread of agriculture and nomadic pastoralism: insights from genetics, linguistics and archaeology." In Harris, David R., ed. *The Origins and Spread of Agriculture and Pastoralism in Eurasia.* London: University College London Press, 1996, 51–69.

Chang and Guroff 2007 Chang, Claudia, and Katharine S. Guroff, eds. *Of Gold and Grass, Nomads of Kazakhstan.* Exhibition catalogue Bethesda, MD: Foundation for International Arts and Education, 2007.

Chang Kwang-chih 1986 Chang, Kwang-chih. *The Archaeology of Ancient China.* New Haven, London: Yale University Press, 1986.

Chase and Douglas 1997 Chase, W. T., and J. G. Douglas. "Technical Studies and Metal Compositional Analyses of Bronzes of the Eastern Eurasian Steppes from the Arthur M. Sackler Collection." In Bunker et al. 1997, 306–18.

Chen Chien-wen 1998 Chen, Chien-wen. "Further Studies on the Racial, Cultural, and Ethnic Affinities of the Yuezhi." In Mair 1998, 767–84.

Cheng Te-k'un 1963 Cheng, Te-k'un. *Chou China.* Archaeology in China 3. Cambridge and Toronto: W. Heffer and Sons and University of Toronto Press, 1963.

Cherednichenko and Fialko 1988 Cherednichenko, Nikolaĭ N., and Elena E. Fialko. "Pogrebenie zhritsy iz Berdianskogo kurgana," in *Sovetskaia Arkheologiia* 1988, 2, 149–66.

Chernykh 1992 Chernykh, Evgeniĭ N. *Ancient Metallurgy in the USSR: The Early Metal Age.* Cambridge: Cambridge University Press, 1992.

Chernykh 2009 Chernykh, Evgeniĭ N. "Ancient metallurgy in the Eurasian steppes and China: Problems of interaction." In Mei Jianjun and Rehren 2009, 3–8.

Chernykh et al. 2004 Chernykh, Evgeniĭ N., Sergeĭ V. Kuz'minykh, and L. B. Orlovskaia. "Ancient Metallurgy in Northeast Asia: From the Urals to the Saiano-Altai." In Linduff 2004, 15–36.

Chlenova 1963 Tchlenova, Natal'iia L. "Le cerf scythe," in *Artibus Asiae* 26, 1963, 27–70.

Chlenova 1967 Chlenova, Natal'iia L. *Proiskhozhdenie i ranniaia istoriia plemen tagarskoĭ kul'tury.* Moscow: Nauka, 1967.

Chlenova 1976 Chlenova, Natal'iia L. *Karasukskie kinzhaly.* Moscow: Nauka, 1976.

Chlenova 1992 Chlenova, Natal'iia L. "Kul'tura plitochnykh mogil." In Moshkova, Marina G., ed. *Stepnaia polosa aziatskoĭ chasti SSSR v skifo-sarmatskoe vremia.* Moscow: Nauka, 1992, 247–54.

Chlenova 1994 Chlenova, Natal'iia L. "On the Degree of Similarity between Material Culture Components within the 'Scythian World'." In Genito 1994, 499–540.

Christian 1998 Christian, David. *A History of Russia, Central Asia and Mongolia 1. Inner Eurasia from Prehistory to the Mongol Empire.* Oxford: Blackwell, 1998.

Christie's 1988 *Fine Chinese Ceramics and Works of Art.* Christie's New York Sale 6720 catalogue, Thursday 1 December 1988. New York: Christie's, 1988.

Christie's 1990 *Fine Chinese Ceramics and Works of Art.* Christie's London Sale 4431 catalogue, Monday 10 December 1990. London: Christie's, 1990.

Christie's 1994 *Fine Chinese Works of Art.* [Including Property from the Collection of Edgar and Hedwig Worch.] Christie's New York Sale

7910 catalogue, Thursday 2 June 1994. New York: Christie's, 1994.

Christie's 2004 *Fine Chinese Ceramics and Works of Art.* Christie's New York Sale 1354 catalogue, Wednesday 24 March 2004. New York: Christie's, 2004.

Christie's 2010 *Fine Chinese Ceramics and Works of Art: Including Property from the Arthur M. Sackler Collections.* Christie's New York Sale 2405/2297 catalogue, Thursday 25 and Friday 26 March 2010. New York: Christie's, 2010.

Craddock 2009 Craddock, Paul. *Scientific Investigation of Copies, Fakes and Forgeries.* Amsterdam et al.: Elsevier, 2009.

Čugunov et al. 2004 Chugunov, Konstantin, Hermann Parzinger, and Anatoli Nagler. "Arzhan 2: la tombe d'un prince scythe en Sibérie du Sud. Rapport préliminaire des fouilles russo-allemandes de 2000–2002," in *Arts Asiatiques* 59, 2004, 5–29.

Čugunov et al. 2006 Čugunov, Konstantin V., Hermann Parzinger, and Anatoli Nagler. *Der Goldschatz von Aržan: Ein Fürstengrab der Skythenzeit in der südsibirischen Steppe.* Munich: Schirmer Mosel, 2006.

Čugunov et al. 2010 Čugunov, Konstantin V., Hermann Parzinger, and Anatoli Nagler. *Der skythenzeitliche Fürstenkurgan Aržan 2 in Tuva.* Archäologie in Eurasien 26. Steppenvölker Eurasiens 3. Mainz: Philipp von Zabern, 2010.

Cultural Exchange 2020 Wang Xudong, and Thomas Pritzker, eds. *Cultural Exchange Along the Silk Road. Masterpieces of the Tubo Period (7th – 9th Century).* Beijing: China Tibetology Publishing House, 2020.

Cunliffe 2015 Cunliffe, Barry. *By Steppe, Desert, and Ocean: The Birth of Eurasia.* Oxford: Oxford University Press, 2015.

Curtis 1978 Curtis, John E. 1978. "Some Georgian Belt Clasps." In Denwood, Philip, ed. *Arts in the Eurasian Steppelands: A Colloque Held 27–29 June 1977.* London: University of London School of Oriental and African Art, Percival David Foundation of Chinese Art, 1978, 88–120.

David-Weill Sale 1972 Ratton, Charles, ed. *Collection D. David-Weill: Bronzes antiques des steppes et de l'Iran; Ordos, Caucase, Asie Centrale, Louristan.* Sale catalogue, Wednesday 28 and Thursday 29 June 1972. Paris: Hotel Drouot, 1972.

Davis-Kimball 2006 Davis-Kimball, Jeannine. "Filippovka's 'poor relatives': ancient and modern nomads." In Aruz et al. 2006, 92–101.

Davis-Kimball et al. 1995 Davis-Kimball, Jeannine, Vladimir A. Bashilov, and Leonid T. Yablonsky. *Nomads of the Eurasian Steppes in the Early Iron Age.* Berkeley: Zinat Press, 1995.

Davydova 1995 Davydova, Antonina V. *Ivolginskiĭ arkheologicheskiĭ kompleks. I. Ivolginskoe gorodishche.* Arkheologicheskie pamiatniki Siunnu 1. Saint Petersburg: AziatIKA, 1995.

Davydova and Miniaev 2003 Davydova, Antonina V., and Sergeĭ S. Miniaev. *Kompleks arkheologicheskikh pamiatnikov u sela Durëny (= Archaeological sites near Dureny village).* Arkheologicheskie pamiatniki Siunnu 5. Saint Petersburg: AziatIKA, 2003.

Davydova and Miniaev 2008 Davydova, Anthonyna, and Sergey Minyaev. *Khudozhestvennaia bronza siunnu: Novye otkrytiia v Rossii (= The Xiongnu Decorative Bronzes: New Discoveries in Russia).* Arkheologicheskie pamiatniki Siunnu 6. Saint Petersburg: Publishing House "Gamas," 2008.

De Krim 2014 *De Krim: Goud en geheimen van de Zwarte Zee.* Allard Pierson Museum 4. Amsterdam: Wbooks, 2014.

Delbanco 1983 Delbanco, Dawn Ho. *Art from Ritual: Ancient Chinese Bronze Vessels from the Arthur M. Sackler Collections.* Washington DC: The Arthur M. Sackler Foundation, 1983.

Dėvlet 1980 Dėvlet, Marianna A. *Sibirskie poiasnye azhurnye plastiny, II v. do n. ė – I v. n. ė.* Arkheologiia SSSR. Svod Arkheologicheskikh istochnikov D4–7. Moscow: Nauka, 1980.

von Dewall 1967 von Dewall, Magdalene. "New Data on Early Chou Finds: Their Relative Chronology in Historical Perspective." In *Qingzhu Li Ji xiansheng qishisui lunwenji*, vol. 2. Taipei: Qinghua xuebaoshe, 1967, 503–70.

DeWoskin 1982 DeWoskin, Kenneth J. *A Song for One or Two: Music and the Concept of Art in Early China.* Ann Arbor: Center for Chinese Studies, The University of Michigan, 1982.

and the Development of Early Nomadic Polities. Ph Dissertation, University of Pittsburgh, 2010.

Hsing I-Tien 2017 Hsing, I-Tien. "Qin-Han China and the Outside World." In Sun, Zhixin J., ed. *Age of Empires: Art of the Qin and Han Dynasties.* New Haven: Yale University Press, and New York: The Metropolitan Museum of Art, 2017, 63–73.

Hsu 1999 Hsu, Cho-yun. "The Spring and Autumn Period." In Loewe and Shaughnessy 1999, 545–86.

Hsu et al. 2016 Hsu, Yiu-Kang, Peter J. Bray, Peter Hommel, Mark A. Pollard, and Jessica Rawson. "Tracing the flows of copper and copper alloys in the Early Iron Age societies of the eastern Eurasian steppe," in *Antiquity* 90, 350, 2016, 357–75.

Hsu et al. 2020 Hsu, Yiu Kang, Benjamin Sabatini, Noost Bayarkhuu, Tsagaan Turbat, Pierre-Henri Giscard, and Sabine Klein. "Discerning social interaction and cultural influence in Early Iron Age Mongolia through archaeometallurgical investigation," in *Archaeological and Anthropological Sciences* 12, 11, 2020, https://doi.org/10.1007/s12520-019-00952-y (published January 6, 2020; last accessed March 31, 2021).

Huang Xiaofeng and Liang Xiaoqing 1985 Huang Xiaofeng, and Liang Xiaoqing. "Gansusheng Huachixian faxian toudiao jin daishi," in *Wenwu* 1985.5, 40.

Huang Zhanyue 1996 Huang Zhanyue. "Guanyu Liangguang chutu Beifang dongwu wen paishi wenti," in *Kaogu yu wenwu* 1996.2, 55–60.

Hubei 1989 Hubeisheng Bowuguan. *Zeng Hou Yi mu.* 2 vols. Beijing: Wenwu chubanshe, 1989.

Il'iukov 2016 Il'iukov, Leonid S. "Krestovidnye bliakhi rannego zheleznogo veka iz stepeĭ Vostochnoĭ Evropy." In Balakhvantsev, Archil S., and Sergeĭ V. Kullanda, eds. *Kavkaz i step' na rubezhe ėpokhi pozdneĭ bronzy i rannego zheleza: Materialy mezhdunarodnoĭ nauchnoĭ konferentsii, posviashchennoĭ pamiati Mariĭ Nikolaevny Pogrebovoĭ (Moskva, 25–27 aprelia 2016 g.).* Moskow: Institut Vostokovedeniia RAN, 2016, 80–84.

Indrisano and Linduff 2013 Indrisano, Gregory G., and Katheryn M. Linduff. "Expansion of the Chinese Empire into the Northern Frontier (ca. 500 BCE–0 CE): A case study from South-Central Inner Mongolia." In Areshian, Gregory E., ed. *Empires and Diversity: On the Crossroads of Archaeology, Anthropology, and History.* Los Angeles: Cotsen Institute of Archaeology, University of California, 2013, 164–207.

Itina and Iablonskiĭ 1997 Itina, Marianna A., and Leonid. T. Iablonskiĭ. *Saki Nizhneĭ Syrdar'i: po materialam mogil'nika Iuzhnyĭ Tagisken.* Moscow: Rosspen, 1997.

Ivantchik 2005 Ivantchik, Askold I. "Early Eurasian Nomads and the Civilizations of the Ancient Near East (Eighth–Seventh centuries BCE)." In Amitai and Biran 2005, 103–26.

Jacobson 1984 Jacobson, Esther. "The Stag with Bird-headed Antler Tines: A Study in Image Transformation and Meaning," in *Bulletin of the Museum of Far Eastern Antiquities* 56, 1984, 113–80.

Jacobson 1985 Jacobson, Esther. "Mountains and Nomads: A Reconsideration of the Origins of Chinese Landscape Representation," in *Bulletin of the Museum of Far Eastern Antiquities* 57, 1985, 133–80.

Jacobson 1995 Jacobson, Esther. *The Art of the Scythians: The Interpretation of Cultures at the Edge of the Hellenic World.* Handbuch der Orientalistik, Abt. 8, Zentralasien, vol. 2. Leiden: E. J. Brill, 1995.

Jacobson 2006a Jacobson, Esther. "The Issyk Headdress: Symbol and Meaning in the Iron Age Nomadic Culture." In Chang and Guroff 2007, 63–70.

Jacobson 2006b Jacobson, Esther. "The Filippovka Deer: Inquiry into their North Asian Sources and Symbolic Significance." In Aruz et al. 2006, 182–95.

Jacobson-Tepfer 2001 Jacobson-Tepfer, Esther. "Cultural Riddles: Stylized Deer and Deer Stones of the Mongolian Altai," in *Bulletin of the Asia Institute* 15, 2001, 31–56.

Jäger and Kansteiner 2011 Jäger, Ulf, and Sascha Kansteiner. *Ancient Metalwork from the Black Sea to China in the Borowski Collection.* Ruhpolding, Mainz: Franz Philipp Rutzen, 2011.

Janse 1935 Janse, Olov. "L'Empire des Steppes et les relations entre l'Europe et l'Extrême-Orient dans l'Antiquité," in *Revue des Arts Asiatiques* 9, 1, 1935, 9–26.

Jeong et al. 2018 Jeong, Choongwon, Shevan Wilkin, Tsend Amgalantugs, … Bruno Frohlich, Jessica Hendy, and Christina Warinner. "Bronze Age population dynamics and the rise of dairy pastoralism on the eastern Eurasian steppe," in *PNAS* 115, 48, 2018, E11248–55. https://doi.org/10.1073/pnas.1813608115 (published November 5, 2018; last accessed March 31, 2021).

Jeong et al. 2020 Jeong, Choongwon, Ke Wang, Shevan Wilking, … Myagmar Erdene, Jessica Hendy, and Christina Warinner. "A Dynamic 6,000-Year Genetic History of Eurasia's Eastern Steppe," in *Cell* 183.4, 2020, P890–904.E29. https://doi.org/10.1016/j.cell.2020.10.015 (published November 5, 2020; last accessed March 31, 2021).

Jettmar 1967 Jettmar, Karl. *Art of the Steppes.* Revised edition. New York: Crown Publishers, 1967.

Jettmar 1971 Jettmar, Karl. "Metallurgy in the Early Steppes," in *Artibus Asiae* 33, 1/2, 1971, 5–16.

Jettmar 1972 Jettmar, Karl. "Review article of Bunker et al. 1970," in *Artibus Asiae* 34, 4, 1972, 256–58.

Jettmar 1994 Jettmar, Karl. "Body-painting and the Roots of the Scytho-Siberian Animal Style." In Genito 1994, 3–15.

Ji Naijun 1989 Ji Naijun. "Yan'an diqu wenguanhui shoucang de Xiongnu wenwu," in *Wenbo* 1989.4, 72–73.

Jian et al. 2006 Jian Hong-En, Li Xiao, Zhao You-Xing, David K. Ferguson, Francis Hueber, Subir Bera, Wang Yu-Fei, Zhao Liang-Cheng, Lui Chang-Jiang, Li Cheng-Sen. "A new insight into *Cannabis sativa* (Cannabaceae) utilization from 2500-year-old Yanghai Tombs, Xinjiang, China," in *Journal of Ethnopharmacology* 108.3, 2006, 414–22.

Jiao Tianlong 2018 Jiao Tianlong, *Dialogue with the Ancients. 100 Bronzes of the Shang, Zhou, and Han Dynasties. The Shen Zhai Collection*, ed. by Patrick K. M. Kwok, with essays by Jiao Tianlong, Wang Tao, Eugene Y. Wang, Li Feng, Allison R. Miller, and Sarah Wong, Wanchai, Hong Kong: Select Books, 2018.

Jin Fengyi 1982 Jin Fengyi. "Lun Zhongguo dongbei diqu hanquren qingtong duanjiande wenhua yicun (shang)," in *Kaogu xuebao* 1982.4, 387–426.

Jin Fengyi 1990 Jin Fengyi. "Shanrong muzang chenhequan," in *Beijing kaogu* 1990, 8, 2–7.

Jin Yu Huanian 2012 *Jin Yu Huanian: Shaanxi Hancheng chutu Zhou dai Rui Guo wenwu zhenpin.* Shanghai: Shanghai shuhua chubanshe, 2012.

John 2006 John, Gudrun. *Tibetische Amulette aus Himmels-Eisen: das Geheimnis der Toktschaks, Thog lcags.* Rahden/Westf.: Leidorf, 2006.

Jundushan 2007 Beijing shi wenwu yanjiusuo. *Jundushan mudi: Yuhuangmiao.* Vols. 1–4. Beijing wenwu yu kaogu xi lie congshu. Beijing: Wenwu chubanshe, 2007.

Karlbeck 1955 Karlbeck, Orvar. "Selected Objects from Ancient Shou-chou," in *Bulletin of the Museum of Far Eastern Antiquities* 27, 1955, 41–129.

Karlgren 1945 Karlgren, Bernhard. "Huai and Han," in *Bulletin of the Museum of Far Eastern Antiquities* 13, 1945, 1–125.

Kawami 2013 Kawami, Trudy S. "Cosmopolitan Splendor: The First Millennium BCE in West Asia." In Freeman 2013, 71–82.

Kawami et al. 2016 Kawami, Trudy S., Daniel Prior, and Robert S. Wicks. "A Gift of Steppe Bronzes from the Arthur M. Sackler Foundation to the Miami University Art Museum," in *The Silk Road* 14, 2016, 175–85.

Keightley 1990 Keightley, David N. "Early Civilization in China: Reflections on How China Became Chinese." In Ropp, Paul S., ed. *Heritage of China.* Berkeley: University of California Press, 1990, 15–54.

Kelekna 2009 Kelekna, Pita. *The Horse in Human History.* New York: Cambridge University Press, 2009.

Keller and Schorta 2001 Keller, Dominik, and Regula Schorta, eds. *Fabulous Creatures from the Desert Sands: Central Asian woolen Textiles from the Second Century BC to the Second Century AD.* Riggisberger Berichte 10. Riggisberg: Abegg-Stiftung, 2001.

Kessler 1993 Kessler, Adam T., ed. *Empires beyond the Great Wall: The Heritage of Ghenghis Khan.* Los Angeles: Natural History Museum of Los Angeles County, 1993.

Khavrin 2011 Khavrin, Sergei V. "Metal of the Xiongnu period from the Terezin cemetery, Tuva." In Brosseder and Miller 2011, 537–38.

Kilunovskaya and Leus 2018 Kilunovskaya, Marina, and Pavel Leus. "Recent Excavations of Xiongnu Graves on the left bank of the Ulug-Khem in Tuva," in *The Silk Road* 18, 2018, 1–20.

Knauer 1998 Knauer, Elfriede R. *The Camel's Load in Life and Death: Iconography and ideology of Chinese pottery figurines from Han to Tang and their relevance to trade along the silk routes.* Kilchberg, Zurich: Akanthus, 1998.

Knauer 1999 Knauer, Elfriede R. "Le Vêtement des Nomades Eurasiatiques et sa Posterité," in *Comptes Rendus des Séances de l'Académie des Inscriptions et Belles-Lettres* 143, 4, 1999, 1141–87.

Kohl 2007 Kohl, Philip L. *The Making of Bronze Age Eurasia.* Cambridge: Cambridge University Press, 2007.

Kohl 2014 Kohl, Philip L. "Concluding Comments: Reconfiguring the Silk Road or When does the Silk Road Emerge and How Does it Qualitatively Change over Time?" In Mair and Hickman 2014, 89–94.

Kokuritsu Hakubutsukan 2005 *Tōkyō Kokuritsu Hakubutsukan shozō: Chūgoku hoppōkei seidōki.* Tokyo: Kokuritsu Hakubutsukan, 2005.

Korolkova 2006 Korolkova, Elena. "Camel Imagery in Animal Style Art." In Aruz et al. 2006, 196–207.

Kost 2012 Kost, Catrin. "Eurasian Steppe Bronzes (rediscovered)," in *The Silk Road* 10, 2012, 146–50.

Kost 2014 Kost, Catrin. *The Practice of Imagery in the Northern Chinese Steppe (5th–1st centuries BCE).* Bonn Contributions to Asian Archaeology 6. Bonn: vfgarch, 2014.

Kost 2017 Catrin Kost. "Heightened Receptivity: Steppe Objects and Steppe Influences in Royal Tombs of the Western Han Dynasty," in *Journal of the American Oriental Society* 137, 2, 2017, 349–81.

Kovalev 1992 Kovalev, Aleksandr. "Kontakte zwischen der Ordos-Region, Mittelasien und Sibirien: «Karasuk-Dolche», Hirschsteine und die Nomaden der Chinesischen Annalen im Altertum," in Höllmann and Kossack 1992, 46–87.

Kovalev 2009 Kovalev, Alekseĭ A. "Culture of Central Plain and the South," in *E'erduosi Qingtongqi* 2009, 383–414.

Kubarev 1987 Kubarev, Vladimir D. *Kurgany Ulandryka.* Novosibirsk: Nauka, 1987.

Kulikov et al. 2010 Kulikov, Vadim E., Elena Iu. Mednikova, Iulia I. Elikhina, and Sergeĭ S. Miniaev. "An Experiment in Studying the Felt Carpet from Noyon uul by the Method of Polypolarization," in *The Silk Road* 8, 2010, 63–68.

Kull 1997 Kull, Brigitte. "Tod und Apotheose: Zur Ikonographie in Grab und Kunst der jüngeren Eisenzeit an der unteren Donau und ihrer Bedeutung für die Interpretation von 'Prunkgräbern'," in *Bericht der Römisch-Germanischen Kommission* 78, 1997, 197–466.

Kuper et al. 2015 Kuper, Konstantin Ė., Natal'ia V. Polos'mak, and Liudmila P. Kundo. "Examination of a bimetal artifact from the Xiongnu tomb." In Murakami, Yasuyuki, and Iuriĭ N. Esin. *Ancient Metallurgy of the Sayan-Altai and East Asia: Materials of the 1st international scientific conference dedicated to the memory of Doctor of Historical Sciences, Professor Yakov Ivanovich Sunchugashed (Abakan, September 23–27, 2015).* Vol. 1. Abakan, Ehime: Ehime University Press, 2015, 117–24.

Kuz'mina 2007 Kuzmina, Elena. *The Prehistory of the Silk Road.* Philadelphia: University of Pennsylvania Press, 2007.

Lally & Co. 1996 Lally, James J. & Co. *Early Dynastic China: Works of Art from Shang to Song.* March 26 to April 26, Catalogue. New York, 1996.

Lally & Co. 2011 Lally, James J. & Co. *Oriental Art: Ancient Chinese Bronzes.* March 19 to April 9, 2011. Catalogue. New York, 2011.

Lawergren 1990 Lawergren, Bo. "The Ancient Harp from Pazyryk," in *Beiträge zur Allgemeinen und Vergleichenden Archäologie* 9/10, 1990, 111–18.

Lawergren 1993 Lawergren, Bo. "Lyres in the West (Italy, Greece) and East (Egypt, The Near East), ca. 2000 to 400 BC," in *Opuscula Romana* 19, 6, 1993, 55–76.

Lawergren 1994 Lawergren, Bo. "Counting strings on Ancient Egyptian Chordophones." In Homo-Lechner, Catherine, and Annie Bélis, eds.

La Pluridisciplinarité en archéologie musicale. Vol. 2. Paris: Editions de la Maison des Sciences de l'Homme, 1994, 519–33.

Lawergren 1997 Lawergren, Bo. "To Tune a String: Dichotomies and Diffusion between the Near and Far East." In Magnusson, Börje, ed. *Ultra Terminum Vagari: Scritti in onore di Carl Nylander.* Rome: Edizoni Quasar, 1997, 175–92.

Lawergren 2000 Lawergren, Bo. "Strings." In So 2000a, 65–85.

Lawergren 2001 Lawergren, Bo. "Iran." In Sadie, Stanley, ed. *The New Grove Dictionary of Music and Musicians.* Second ed., vol. 12, 2012, 523–30.

Lawergren 2002 Lawergren, Bo. "Harps, Lutes, and Music along the Silk Road: A First Millennium Migration," in *The Silk Road Project. Arts and Humanities Programs at Cal Performances, University of California, Berkeley.* April 2002, 52–55.

Lawergren 2003a Lawergren, Bo. "Western Influences on the Early Chinese *Qin*-Zither," in *Bulletin of the Museum of Far Eastern Antiquities* 75, 2003, 79–109.

Lawergren 2003b Lawergren, Bo. "The Metamorphosis of the Qin, 500 BC–500 CE," in *Orientations* 34, 5, 2003, 31–38.

Lawergren 2007 Lawergren, Bo. "The Iconography and Decoration of the Ancient Chinese Qin-zither (500 BCE to 500 CE)," in *Music in Art* 32, 1/2, Spring/Fall, 2007, 47–62.

Lawergren 2008 Lawergren, Bo. "Angular Harps through the Ages: A Causal History." In Both, Arnd A., Ricardo Eichmann, Ellen Hickmann, and Lars-Christian Koch, eds. *Challenges and Objectives in Music Archaeology. Papers from the 5th Symposium of the International Study Group on Music Archaeology at the Ethnological Museum, State Museums Berlin, 19–23 September, 2006.* Studien zur Musikarchäologie 6. Orient-Archäologie 22. Rahden/Westf.: Leidorf, 2008, 261–81.

Lawergren 2016 Lawergren, Bo. "The *Qin* Excavated in Warring States Period Sites." In Eichmann, Ricardo, Lars-Christian Koch, and Fang Jianjun, eds. *Sound – Object – Culture – History. Papers from the 9th Symposium of the International Study Group on Music Archaeology at the Ethnological Musem, State Museums Berlin, 9–12 September, 2014.* Studien zur Musikarchäologie 10. Orient-Archäologie 37. Rahden/Westf.: Marie Leidorf GmbH, 2016, 115–23.

Lawergren 2018 Lawergren, Bo. "Music." In Álvarez-Mon, Javier, Pietro Basello, and Yasmina Wicks, eds. *The Elamite World.* London and New York: Routledge, 2018, 781–800.

Lawergren 2019a Lawergren, Bo. "Provenience of *Qin* Tuning Keys in China, ca. 400–100 BCE," in Eichmann et al. 2019, 99–111.

Lawergren 2019b Lawergren, Bo. "Music." In Dien, Albert E., and Keith N. Knapp, eds. T*he Cambridge History of China, volume 2. The Six Dynasties, 220–589.* Cambridge: Cambridge University Press, 2019, 698–720.

Lawton 1982 Lawton, Thomas. *Chinese Art of the Warring States Period: Change and Continuity (480–221 BCE).* Washington DC: Freer Gallery of Art, 1982.

Lebedynsky 2006 Lebedynsky, Iaroslav. *Les Saces: Les Scythes d'Asie; VIII siècle av. J.-C. – IV siècle apr. J.-C.* Paris: Errance, Éditions France, 2006.

Legrand 2004 Legrand, Sophie. "Karasuk Metallurgy, Technological Development and Regional Influence." In Linduff 2004, 139–56.

Legrand 2006 Legrand, Sophie. "The emergence of the Karasuk culture," in *Antiquity* 80, 310, 2006, 843–79.

Legrand 2008 Legrand, Sophie. "Sorting Out Men and Women in the Karasuk Culture." In Linduff and Rubinson 2008, 153–74.

Leidy 2012 Leidy, Denise Patry. "Links, Missing and Otherwise: Tillya Tepe and East Asia." In Aruz and Fino 2012, 112–21.

Leskov 1990 Leskov, Aleksandr M. *Grabschätze der Adygeen. Neue Entdeckungen im Nordkaukasus.* Munich: Hirmer, 1990.

Leskov 2008 Leskov, Aleksandr M. *The Maikop Treasure.* Philadelphia: University of Pennsylvania Museum of Archaeology and Anthropology, 2008.

Leus 2011 Leus, Pavel M. "New Finds from the Xiongnu period in Central Tuva. Preliminary Communication." In Brosseder and Miller 2011, 515–36.

Li Gang 2011 Li Gang. *Zhongguo Beifang Qingtongqi de ouya caoyuan wenhua yinsu (= The*

Culture Elements of Eurasian Steppes in the Bronzes of North China). Beijing: Wenwu chubanshe, 2011.

Li Xiaoqing and Nan Baosheng 2003 Li Xiaoqing (Gansusheng Bowuguan, Wen Bowuguan yuan), and Nan Baosheng (Qingshuixian Bowuguan, Wen Bowuguan yuan). "Gansu Qingshuixian Liuping jinnian faxian de beifangxi qingtongqi ji jinshipian," in *Wenwu* 2003.7, 4–17.

Li Xiating et al. 1996 Li Xiating, and Liang Ziming, with Robert Bagley. *Houma tao fan yishu = Art of the Houma Foundry*. Institute of Archaeology of Shanxi Province (IASP). Princeton: Princeton University Press, 1996.

Li Xueqin 1985 Li Xueqin. *Eastern Zhou and Qin Civilizations*. New Haven: Yale University Press, 1985.

Li Xueqin 2000 Li Xueqin. *The Glorious Traditions of Chinese Bronzes*. Catalogue of an exhibition held at the Singapore Ancient Civilizations Museum. Singapore: National Heritage Board, 2000.

Li Yiyou 1959a Li Yiyou. "Neimenggu Helin'geerxian chutu de tongqi," in *Wenwu* 1959.6, 79.

Li Yiyou 1959b Li Yiyou. "Neimenggu Zhaowuda meng chutu de tongqi diaocha," in *Kaogu* 1959.6, 276–77.

Li Yiyou and Wei Jian 1994 Li Yiyou, and Wei Jian, eds. *Neimenggu wenwu kaogu wenji*, 2 vols. Beijing: Zhongguo Dabaike Quanshu chubanshe, 1994.

Li Zebin 2013 Li Zebin. "Fashion and Rituals of the Han Dynasty: Cultural Relics of the Royal Houses of Jiangsu," in *Orientations* 44, 2013.6, 83–87.

Liaoning and Zhongguo 1973 Liaoning sheng Zhaowudameng wenwu gongzuozhan, and Zhongguo kexueyuan kaogu yanjiusuo dongbei gongzuodui. "Ningcheng xian Nanshangen de shiguomu," in *Kaogu xuebao* 1973.2, 27–39.

Lieh-Tzu 1990 *The Book of Lieh-tzŭ: A Classic of the Tao*, translated by Angus C. Graham. New York: Columbia University Press, 1990.

Lin Yun 2008 Lin Yun. "Lun ouya caoyuan de juanqu dongwuwen." In *Lin Yun xueshu wenji. 2*. Beijing: Kexue chubanshe, 2008, 129–42.

Linduff 1997 Linduff, Katheryn M. "Archaeological overview." In Bunker et al. 1997, 18–98.

Linduff 2003 Linduff, Katheryn M. "A Walk on the Wild Side: Late Shang Appropriation of Horses in China." In Levine, Marsha, Colin Renfrew, and Katie Boyle, eds. *Prehistoric Steppe Adaptation and the Horse*. Cambridge: McDonald Institute for Archaeological Research, 2003, 139–62.

Linduff 2004 Linduff, Katheryn M., ed. *Metallurgy in Ancient Eastern Eurasia from the Urals to the Yellow River*. Lampeter, Ceredigion, Wales: The Edwin Mellen Press, 2004.

Linduff 2006 Linduff, Katheryn M. "Imaging the Horse in Early China: From the Table to the Stable." In Olsen, Sandra L., Susan Grant, Alice M. Choyke, and László Bartosiewicz, eds. *Horses and Humans: The Evolution of Human-Equine Relationships*. British Archaeological Reports. International Series 1560. Oxford: Archaeopress 2006, 303–22.

Linduff 2008 Linduff, Katheryn M. "The Gender of Luxury and Power among the Xiongnu in Eastern Eurasia." In Linduff and Rubinson 2008, 175–211.

Linduff 2009 Linduff, Katherine M. "Production of Signature Artifacts for the Nomad Market in the State of Qin During the Late Warring States Period in China (4th–3rd century BCE)." In Mei Jianjun and Rehren 2009, 90–96.

Linduff 2011 Linduff, Katheryn M. "Symmetrically Confronted Dragons at the Frontier of Metal Production in the Eastern Asian Northern Borderlands." Conference presentation, *Emergence of Bronze Age Societies: A Global Perspective*, November 8–10, 2011, at the Baoji Museum of Bronzes, Shaanxi Province, PRC, Session: "Contacts and Trade."

Linduff 2015 Linduff, Katheryn M. "What's Mine is Yours: The Transmission of Metallurgical Technology in Eastern Eurasia and East Asia." In Srinivasan, Sharada, Srinivasa Ranganathan, and Alessandra R. Giumlia-Mair, eds. *Metals and Civilizations: Proceedings of the Seventh International Conference on the Beginnings of the Use of Metal and*

Linduff 2018 Linduff, Katheryn M. "Technoscapes and the Materialization of Ideas in Metal in the Inner Asian Frontier (ca. 3000–1500 BCE)." In Linduff et al. 2018, 35–71.

Linduff and Hanks 2009 Linduff, Katheryn M., and Bryan K. Hanks. *Social Complexity in Prehistoric Eurasia: Monuments, Metals and Mobility.* Cambridge: Cambridge University Press, 2009.

Linduff and Rubinson 2008 Linduff, Katheryn M., and Karen S. Rubinson, eds. *Are All Warriors Male? Gender Roles on the Ancient Eurasian Steppe.* Gender and archaeology series 17. Lanham, MD: Rowman & Littlefield, AltaMira Press, 2008.

Linduff and Rubinson 2013 Linduff, Katheryn M., and Karen S. Rubinson. "Gender Archaeology in East Asia and Eurasia." In Bolger, Diane, ed. *A Companion to Gender Prehistory.* Blackwell Companions to Anthropology. Malden, Oxford, Chichester: Wiley-Blackwell 2013, 351–71.

Linduff and Rubinson 2014 Linduff, Katheryn M., and Karen S. Rubinson. "Transfer of Metallurgical Technology and Objects across Eurasia and Northern China in the late 1st millennium BCE – early 1st millennium CE." In Molodin, Viacheslav I. and Andreĭ V. Epimakhov, eds., *Ariĭ stepeĭ Evrazii: Ėpokha bronzy i rannego zheleza v stepiakh Evrazii i na sopredel'nykh territoriiakh; Sbornik pamiati Eleny Efimovny Kuz'minoĭ (= The Aryans in the Eurasian Steppes: The Bronze and Early Iron Ages in the Steppes of Eurasia and Contiguous Territories; Elena Kuz'mina Memorial Volume).* Barnaul: Altai State University Press, 2014, 110–23.

Linduff and Sun 2004 Linduff, Katheryn M., and Yan Sun, eds. *Gender and Chinese Archaeology.* Walnut Creek, CA: AltaMira Press, 2004.

Linduff and Wu 2005 Linduff, Katheryn M., and Mandy Jui-man Wu. "The Construction of Identity: Remaining Sogdian in Eastern Asia in the 6th Century." In Jones-Bley, Karlene, Martin E. Huld, Angela Della Volpe, and Miriam Robbins Dexter, eds. *Proceedings of the Seventeenth Annual UCLA Indo-European Conference October 27–28, 2005, Journal of Indo-European Studies*, Monograph Series 52, Washington, DC: Institute for the Study of Man, 2006, 219–46.

Linduff et al. 2000 Linduff, Katheryn M., Han Rubin, and Sun Shuyun, eds. *The Beginnings of Metallurgy in China.* Chinese Studies 11. Lampeter, Ceredigion, Wales: The Edwin Mellen Press, 2000.

Linduff et al. 2018 Linduff, Katheryn M., Yan Sun, Wei Cao, Yuanqing Liu, *Ancient China and its Eurasian Neighbors: Artifacts, Identity, and Death in the Frontier, 3000–700 BCE.* Cambridge: Cambridge University Press, 2018.

Linrothe 2016 Linrothe, Rob. *Seeing into Stone: Pre-Buddhist Petroglyphs and Zangskar's Early Inhabitants.* Berlin, New Delhi: Studio Orientalia, 2016.

Litvinskiĭ 1972 Litvinskiĭ, Boris A. *Drevnie kochevniki "kryshi mira."* Moscow: Nauka, 1972.

Litvinskiĭ 1984 Litvinskij, Boris A. *Eisenzeitliche Kurgane zwischen Pamir und Aral-See.* Materialien zur Allgemeinen und Vergleichenden Archäologie 22. Munich: C. H. Beck, 1984.

Liu Bing 2006 Liu Bing, ed. *Chifeng bowuguan: Wenwu dian cang.* Hohhot: Yuan fang chubanshe, 2006.

Liu Dezhen and Xu Junchen 1988 Liu Dezhen, and Xu Junchen. "Gansu Qingyang Chunqiu Zhanguo muzang de qingli," in *Kaogu* 1988.5, 413–24.

Liu Xinru 2010 Liu Xinru. *The Silk Road in World History.* Oxford: Oxford University Press, 2010.

Liu Yang 2013 Liu Yang. "Nomadic Influences in Qin Gold," in *Orientations,* 44, 2, 2013, 119–25.

Liu Yang et al. 2012/2013 Liu Yang, Edmond Capon, Albert Dien, Jeffrey Riegel, Eugene Wang, and Yuan Zhongyi. *China's Terracotta Warriors: The First Emperor's Legacy.* Minneapolis Institute of Arts, Seattle, Washington: University of Washington Press, 2012/2013.

Lobell and Powell 2013 Lobell, Jarrett A., and Eric A. Powell. "Ancient Tattoos," in *Archaeology,* November/December, 2013, 41–46.

Loehr 1949 Loehr, Max. "Ordos Daggers and Knives: New Material, Classification and Chronology. First Part: Daggers," in *Artibus Asiae* 12, 1949, 23–83.

Loehr 1951 Loehr, Max. "Ordos Daggers and Knives: New Material, Classification and Chronology. Second Part: Knives," in *Artibus Asiae* 14, 1/2, 1951, 77–162.

Loehr 1955 Loehr, Max. "The Stag Image in Scythia and the Far East," in *Archives of the Chinese Art Society of America* 9, 1955, 63–76.

Loehr 1956 Loehr, Max. *Chinese Bronze Age Weapons: The Werner Jannings Collection in the Chinese National Palace Museum, Peking.* Ann Arbor: University of Michigan Press, 1956.

Loehr 1967–68 Loehr, Max. "The Fate of Ornament in Chinese Art," in *Archives of Asian Art* 21, 1967–68, 8–19.

Loehr 1975 Loehr, Max. *Ancient Chinese Jades from the Grenville L. Winthrop Collection in the Fogg Art Museum, Harvard University.* Cambridge, Mass.: Fogg Art Museum, 1975.

Loewe and Shaughnessy 1999 Loewe, Michael, and Edward L. Shaughnessy, eds. *The Cambridge History of Ancient China. From the Origins of Civilization to 221 BC.* Cambridge: Cambridge University Press, 1999.

Lubo-Lesnichenko 1969 Lubo-Lesnichenko, Evgeniĭ I. "Kitaĭskie lakovye izdeliia iz Noin-Uly," in *Trudy Gosudarstvennogo Ėrmitazha* 10, 1969, 267–77.

Lucas and Kouřimský 1977 Lucas, Randolph, and Jiří Kouřimský, eds. *The Illustrated Encyclopedia of Minerals and Rocks.* London: Octopus Books, 1977.

Lullo 2013 Lullo, Sheri A. "Shame on You! For These People, Tattoos were never on the Wish List," in *Dig*, 11, 6, 18, Master FILE Premier, EBSCO host, viewed 5 February 2013.

Luo Feng and Han Kongle 1990 Luo Feng, and Han Kongle. "Ningxia Guyuan jinnian faxian de beifangxi qingtongqi," in *Kaogu* 1990.5, 403–18.

Lü Buwei 2000 *The Annals of Lü Buwei: a complete translation and study by John Knoblock and Jeffrey Riegel.* Stanford: Stanford University Press, 2000.

MacDonald 1985 MacDonald, David, ed. *The Encyclopedia of Mammals.* New York: Facts on File Publications, 1985.

Madsen 2010 Madsen, Axel. *Silk Roads: The Asian Adventures of Clara and André Malraux.* London: I. B. Tauris, 1990, reprint by Tauris Parke Paperbacks in India by Replika Press, 2010.

McGovern 1939 McGovern, William M. *The Early Empires of Central Asia: a study of the Scythians and the Huns and the role they played in the world history: with special references to the Chinese sources.* Chapel Hill: University of Carolina Press, 1939.

Mair 1998 Mair, Victor H., ed. *The Bronze Age and Early Iron Age Peoples of Eastern Central Asia,* vol. 1. Washington: The Institute for the Study of Man, in collaboration with The University of Pennsylvania Museum Publications, 1998.

Mair and Hickman 2014 Mair, Victor, and Jane Hickman, eds. *Reconfiguring the Silk Road. New Research on the East-West Exchange in Antiquity.* Philadelphia: University of Pennsylvania Press, 2014.

Major 1993 Major, John S. *Heaven and Earth in Early Han Thought: Chapters Three, Four and Five of the Huainanzi.* Albany: State University of New York Press, 1993.

Major and So 2000 Major, John S., and Jenny F. So. "Music in Late Bronze Age China." In So 2000a, 13–33.

Makarewicz 2017 Makarewicz, Cheryl A. "Winter is coming: seasonality of ancient pastoral nomadic practices revealed in the carbon (δ^{13}C) and nitrogen (δ^{15}N) isotopic record of Xiongnu caprines," in *Archaeological and Anthropological Sciences* 9, 2017, 405–18. https://doi.org/10.1007/s12520-015-0289-5 (published October 8, 2015; last accessed March 31, 2021).

Makarewicz 2018 Makarewicz, Cheryl A. "Stable isotopes in pastoralist archaeology as indicators of diet, mobility, and animal husbandry practices." In: Ventresca Miller, Alicia R., and Cheryl A. Makarewicz, eds. *Isotopic investigations of pastoralism in prehistory.* Themes in Contemporary Archaeology 4. London and New York: Routledge, Taylor & Francis Group, 2018, 141–58.

Maoxian and Aba 1994 Maoxian Qiangzu bowuguan, and Aba Zangzu Qiangzu zizhizhou wenwu guanlisuo. "Sichuan Maoxian Moutuo yihao shiguanmu ji peizangkeng qingli jianbao," in *Wenwu* 1994.3, 4–52.

Marazov 1998 Marazov, Ivan, ed. *Ancient Gold: The Wealth of the Thracians. Treasures from the Republic of Bulgaria.* New York: Harry N. Abrams, 1998.

Masterpieces 2019 *Masterpieces of Early Chinese Gold and Silver.* Christie's New York Sale 18338 catalogue, Thursday, 12 September 2019. New York: Christie's, 2019.

Matsumoto 2018 Matsumoto, Keita. *Yūrashia sōgen chitai no seidōki jidai (= The Bronze Age in the Eurasian Steppes = Ėpokha bronzy v stepiakh Evrazii = Ou-Ya caoyuan di dai de qingtongqi shidai).* Fukuoka: Kyūshū Daigaku Shuppankai, 2018.

Matsumoto et al. 2019 Matsumoto, Keita, Tsend Amgalantugs, and Lochin Ishtseren. "The Bronze Daggers and Knives in the Collection of the South Gobi Museum and the Middle Gobi Museum, and their historical meanings," in *Bulletin of the Yokohama Museum of EurAsian Cultures* 7, 2019, 23–36.

Mattet 2008 Mattet, Laurence, ed. *Le profane et le divin: Arts de l'Antiquité de l'Europe au Sud-Est asiatique.* Geneva: Musée Barbier-Mueller, 2008.

Mayor 1994 Adrienne Mayor. "Guardians of the Gold," in *Archaeology* 47, November/December, 1994, 52–58.

Mei Jianjun 2006 Mei, Jianjun. "The Material Culture of the Iron Age Peoples in Xinjiang, Northwest China." In Aruz et al. 2006, 132–46.

Mei Jianjun and Rehren 2009 Mei, Jianjun, and Thilo Rehren, eds. *Metallurgy and Civilization: Eurasia and Beyond.* London: Archetype Publications, 2009.

Menghin et al. 2007 Menghin, Wilfried, Hermann Parzinger, Anatoli Nagler, and Manfred Nawroth, eds. *Im Zeichen des goldenen Greifen: Königsgräber der Skythen.* Eine Ausstellung des Deutschen Archäologischen Instituts und des Museums für Vor- und Frühgeschichte, Staatliche Museen zu Berlin. Munich, Berlin, London, New York: Prestel, 2007.

Meyer 2015 Meyer, Karl E., and Shareen Blair Brysac. *The China Collectors: America's Century-long Hunt for Asian Art Treasures.* New York: Palgrave MacMillan, 2015.

Meyers 1997 Meyers, Pieter. "Ancient Chinese Gold: Is It Really Old?" in *Orientations*, 28, 3, 1997, 117–18.

Michaelson 1999 Michaelson, Carol. *Gilded Dragons. Buried Treasures from China's Golden Ages.* London: British Museum Press, 1999.

Miller 2016 Miller, Bryan K. "Xianbei Empire." In MacKenzie, John M. *The Encyclopedia of Empire.* Chichester: Wiley Blackwell, 2016, 1–2.

Miller and Brosseder 2012 Miller, Bryan K., and Ursula Brosseder. "Beasts of the North: Global and Local Dynamics as Seen in Horse Ornaments of the Steppe Elite," in *Asian Archaeology* 1, 2012, 94–112.

Miniaev 1976 Miniaev, Sergeĭ S. "Baktriĭskie latuni v siunnuskikh pamiatnikakh Zabaĭkal'ia." In: *Baktriĭskie drevnosti.* Leningrad: Nauka, 1976, 109–10.

Miniaev 1977 Miniaev, Sergeĭ S. "Rezul'taty spektral'nogo analiza bronzovykh izdeliĭ Dyrestuĭskogo mogil'nika," in *Arkheologiia Iuzhnoi Sibiri* 7, 1977, 43–52.

Miniaev 1978 Miniaev, Sergeĭ S. "Rezul'taty spektral'nogo analiza Kosogol'skogo klada." In: Matiushchenko, V. I., and N. A. Tomilov, eds. *Ėtnokul'turnaia istoriia naseleniia Zapadnoĭ Sibiri.* Tomsk: Izdatel'stvo Tomskogo Universiteta, 1978, 26–45.

Miniaev 1980 Miniaev, Sergeĭ S. "Proizvodstvo i rasprostranenie poiasnykh plastin-priazhek s zoomorfnymi izobrazheniiami (po dannym spektral'nogo analiza)," In Dėvlet 1980, 29–34.

Miniaev 1981 Miniaev, Sergeĭ S. "Bronzovye izdeliia Noin-Uly (po rezul'tatam spektral'nogo analiza)," in *Kratkie Soobshcheniia* 167, 1981, 39–43.

Miniaev 1983 Miniaev, Sergeĭ S. "Proizvodstvo bronzovykh izdeliĭ u siunnu." In: Kiriushin, Iuriĭ F., ed. *Drevnie gorniaki i metallurgi Sibiri. Mezhvuzovskiĭ sbornik.* Barnaul: Altaĭskiĭ gosudarstvennyĭ universitet, 1983, 47–65.

Miniaev 1996 Miniaev, Sergei. "Archéologie des Xiongnu en Russie: Nouvelles découvertes et quelques problèmes," in *Arts Asiatiques* 51, 1996, 5–12.

Miniaev 1998 Miniaev, Sergeĭ S. *Dyrestuĭskiĭ mogil'nik.* Arkheologicheskie pamiatniki Siunnu 3. Saint Petersburg: Evropeĭskiĭ dom, 1998.

Miniaev 2002 Miniaev, Serguey. "Some short comments on metal compositional analyses of bronzes from this private collection." In Miniaev and Smolarski 2002, 99–102.

Miniaev 2013 Miniaev, Sergei S. "On the Interpretation of Certain Images on Deer Stones," in *The Silk Road* 11, 2013, 54–59.

Miniaev 2016 Miniaev, Sergei S. "Production of Bronze Wares among the Xiongnu," in *The Silk Road* 14, 2016, 147–165.

Miniaev and Smolarski 2002 Miniaev, Serguey, and Philippe Smolarski. *Art of the Steppes.* Brussels: Foundation Richard Liu, 2002.

Minns 1930 Minns, Ellis H. "Small Bronzes from Northern Asia," in *The Antiquaries Journal* 10, 1, 1930, 1–23.

Mir kochevnikov 2013 *Mir kochevnikov: Iz arkheologicheskikh kollektsiĭ Gosudarstvennogo Èrmitazha (= The nomad world: from the archaeological collections of the State Hermitage).* Katalog vystavki. Saint Petersburg: Slavia, 2013.

Mo Jiangping et al. 1997 Mo Jiangping, Huang Mingyang, Qin Longfang, and Lu Handi. "The origin of Kaiputai iron-copper deposit in Yuxu, Xinjiang, China," in *Dizhi yu kantan = Geology and Exploration* 1997.4, 7–12.

Molodin et al. 2012 Molodin, Viacheslav I., Hermann Parzinger, and Damdiinsüren Tsėvėėndorzh. *Zamërzshie pogrebal'nye kompleksy pazyrykskoĭ kul'tury na iuzhnykh sklonakh Saĭliugema (Mongol'ski Altai).* Moscow: ID Triumf print, 2012.

Moorey 1967 Moorey, Peter R. S. "Some Ancient Metal Belts: Their Antecedents and Relatives," in *Iran* 5, 1967, 83–99.

Moorey 1971 Moorey, Peter R. S. *Catalogue of the Ancient Persian Bronzes in the Ashmolean Museum.* Oxford: Clarendon Press, 1971.

Moorey 1974 Moorey, Peter R. S. *Ancient Bronzes from Luristan.* London: British Museum Publications, 1974.

Moorey 1981 Moorey, Peter R. S., and Glenn Markoe, eds. *Ancient Bronzes, Ceramics and Seals: The Nasli Heeramaneck Collection of Ancient Near Eastern, Central Asiatic and European Art; Gift of the Ahmanson Foundation.* Essays by Peter R. S. Moorey, Emma C. Bunker, Edith Porada, and Glenn Markoe, Exhibition catalogue Los Angeles: Los Angeles County Museum of Art 1981.

Moortgat 1969 Moortgat, Anton. *The Art of Ancient Mesopotamia.* London and New York: Phaidon, 1969.

Mostra d'arte cinese 1954 *Mostra d'arte cinese (= Exhibition of Chinese art): Catalogo.* Venezia, Palazzo Ducale, 1954. Venice: Alfieri, 1954.

Moutuo report 2012 Maoxian Qiangzu bowuguan, Chengdu wenwu kaogu yanjiusuo, and Aba Zangzu Qiangzu zizhizhou wenwu guanlisuo. *Maoxian Moutuo yihao shiguanmu.* Beijing: Wenwu chubanshe, 2012.

Muscarella 2006 Muscarella, Oscar White. "Bronze Socketed Arrowheads and Ethnic Attribution." In Aruz et al. 2006, 154–59.

Musée Cernuschi 2000 *Arts de l'Asie au musée Cernuschi.* Paris: Éditions des musées de la Ville de Paris, 2000.

Narasimhan et al. 2019 Narasimhan, Vagheesh M., Nick Patterson, Priya Moorjani, … Michael Frachetti, Ron Pinhasi, and David Reich. "The formation of human populations in South and Central Asia," in *Science* 365, 6457, 2019, eaat7487. http://dx.doi.org/10.1126/science.aat7487 (published September 6, 2019; last accessed March 31, 2021).

Nazari 2005 Nazari, Maziar. "The Khur Agate Field, Central Iran." In *Symposium on Agate and Cryptocrystalline Quartz, September 10–13, 2005. Golden, CO. Program and Abstracts.* Denver: Friends of Mineralogy, Colorado Chapter, 2005.

Neimenggu 1989 Neimenggu wenwu kaogu yanjiusuo. "Liancheng Chunxian Yaozi mundi," in *Kaogu xuebao* 1989.1, 57–81.

Neimenggu and Neimenggu 1977 Neimenggu bowuguan, and Neimenggu wenwu gongzuodui. "Neimenggu Zhungeerqi Yulongtai de Xiongnu mu," in *Kaogu*, 1977.2, 111–14.

Nelson 1995 Nelson, Sarah Milledge, ed. *The Archaeology of Northeast China: Beyond the Great Wall.* London: Routledge, 1995.

Nelson 2008 Nelson, Sarah Milledge. "Horses and Gender in Korea. The Legacy of the Steppe on the Edge of Asia." In Linduff and Rubinson 2008, 111–27.

Ningcheng et al. 1985 Ningchengxian wenhuaguan, Zhongguo shehui kexueyan, Yanjiu shengwu, Kaoguxi dongbei, and Kaogu zhuanye. "Ningchengxian xin faxian de Xiajiadian shangceng wenhua muzang jiqi xiangguan yiwu de yanjiu," in *Wenwu ziliao congkan* 9, 1985, 23–58.

Ningxia 1988 Ningxia wenwu kaogu yanjiusuo. "Ningxia Tongxinxian Lijiataozi Xiongnu mu qingli jianbao," in *Kaogu yu wenwu* 1988.3, 17–20.

Ningxia 1995 Ningxia wenwu kaogu yanjiusuo. "Ningxia Pengbao Yujiazhuang mudi," in *Kaogu xuebao* 1995.1, 79–107.

Ningxia 2002 Ningxia Huizu zizhiqu wenwu kaogu yanjiusuo. "Ningxia Pengyangxian Zhangjiecun Chunqiu Zhanguo mudi," in *Kaogu* 2002.8, 14–24.

Ningxia and Ningxia 1993 Ningxia wenwu kaogu yanjiusuo, and Ningxia Guyuan bowuguan. "Ningxia Guyuan Yanglang qingtong wenhua mudi," in *Kaogu xuebao* 1993.1, 13–56.

Ningxia et al. 1988 Ningxia wenwu kaogu yanjiusuo, Zhongguo shehui kexueyuan kaogusuo, Ningxia kaoguzu, and Tongxin xian wenwu guanlisuo. "Ningxia Tongxin Daodunzi Xiongnu mudi," in *Kaogu xuebao* 1988.3, 333–356.

Novgorodova 1970 Novgorodova, Ėleonora A. *Tsentral'naia Aziia i karasukskaia problema*. Moscow: Nauka, 1970.

Novgorodova 1980 Nowgorodova, Eleonora. *Alte Kunst der Mongolei*. Translated by Lisa Schirmer. Leipzig: E. A. Seemann, 1980.

Novgorodova 1984 Novgorodova, Ėleonora A. *Mir petroglifov Mongolii*. Moscow: Nauka, 1984.

Novgorodova 1989 Novgorodova, Ėleonora A. *Drevniaia Mongoliia: Nekotorye problemy khronologii i ėtnokul'turnoĭ istorii*. Moscow: Nauka, 1989.

O'Donoghue 1990 O'Donoghue, Diane M. "Reflection and Reception: The Origins of the Mirror in Bronze Age China," in *Bulletin of the Museum of Far Eastern Antiquities* 62, 1990, 5–183.

Olsen 2008 Olsen, Sandra. L. "The Inception of Horse Pastoralism," in *General Anthropology. Bulletin of the General Anthropology Division, American Anthropological Association* 15, 1, 2008, 5–6.

Oriental Bronze Metallurgist 1978 *The Art of the Oriental Bronze Metallurgist: China, Japan (1500–1911)*. Miami: Lowe Art Museum, 1978.

Orlando 2020 Orlando, Ludovic. "The Evolutionary and Historical Foundation of the Modern Horse: Lessons from Ancient Genomics," in *Annual Review of Genetics* 54, 2020, 563–81.

Pan Ling 2008 Pan Ling. "Lun lushi de niandai ji xiangguan wenti," in *Kaogu xuebao* 2008.3, 311–35.

Pan Ling 2011 Pan Ling. "A Summary of Xiongnu Sites within the Northern Periphery of China." In: Brosseder and Miller 2011, 463–74.

Pan Ling 2015 Pan Ling. "The Transformation of Cultural Exchange between North China and the Eurasian Steppe from the late Warring States Period to the Middle Western Han," in *Asian Archaeology* 3, 2015, 95–106.

Pan Ling forthcoming Pan Ling. *Xifeng Xichagou mude*. Beijing: Wenwu chubanshe, forthcoming.

Park et al. 2011 Park, Jang-Sik, William Honeychurch, and Amartuvshin Chunag. "Ancient bronze technology and nomadic communities of the middle Gobi Desert, Mongolia," in *Journal of Archaeological Science* 38, 2011, 805–17.

Park et al. 2018 Park, Jang-Sik, Diimaajav Erdenebaatar, and Gelegdorj Eregzen. "The implication of the metallurgical traditions associated with Chinese style wagons from the royal Xiongnu tomb at Golmod 2 in Mongolia," in *Archaeological and Anthropological Sciences* 10, 7, 2018, 1535–46.

Parzinger 2006 Parzinger, Hermann. *Die frühen Völker Eurasiens vom Neolithikum bis zum Mittelalter*. Historische Bibliothek der Gerda Henkel Stiftung. Munich: C. H. Beck, 2006.

Parzinger et al. 2009 Parzinger, Hermann, Viacheslav I. Molodin, and Damdinsüren Tseveendorzh. "New Discoveries in Mongolian Altai: The Warrior Grave of the Pazyryk Culture at Olon-Güüriin-Gol 10." In: Bemmann et al. 2009, 203–20.

Pearl 1967 Pearl, Richard M. "Minerals of India," in *Mineral Digest. The Journal of Mineralogy* 2, 1967.

Rudenko 1966 Rudenko, Sergeĭ I. *Die Sibirische Sammlung Peters I.* 2nd edition. Moscow, Leningrad: Verlag der Akademie der Wissenschaften der UdSSR, 1966.

Rudenko 1970 Rudenko, Sergei I. *Frozen Tombs of Siberia: The Pazyryk Burials of Iron Age Horsemen.* Berkeley and Los Angeles: University of California Press, 1970.

Salmony 1933 Salmony, Alfred. *Sino-Siberian Bronzes in the Collection of C. T. Loo.* Paris: C. T. Loo, 1933.

Salmony 1934 Salmony, Alfred. "Les Plaquettes de Bronze de Minussinsk," in *Gazette des Beaux-Arts* 11, 1934, 1–12.

Salviati 1996 Salviati, Filippo. "Archaeology on China's Northern Frontier," in *Minerva* July/August, 1996, 24.

Schachner 2007 Schachner, Andreas. *Bilder eines Weltreichs: Kunst- und kulturgeschichtliche Untersuchungen zu den Verzierungen eines Tores aus Balawat (Imgur-Enlil) aus der Zeit von Salmanassar III, König von Assyrien.* Subartu 20. Turnhout: Brepols, 2007.

Schafer 1950 Schafer, Edward H. "The Camel in China down to the Mongol Dynasty," in *Sinologica* 2, 3, 1950, 165–94.

Schafer 1963 Schafer, Edward H. *The Golden Peaches of Samarkand: A Study of T'ang Exotics.* Berkeley and Los Angeles: University of California Press, 1963.

Schiltz 1975 Schiltz, Véronique. *Or des Scythes: Trésors des musées soviétiques.* Paris: Editions des Musées Nationaux, 1975.

Schiltz 1994 Schiltz, Véronique. *Les Scythes et les nomades des steppes: VIIIe siècle avant J.-C. – Ier siècle après J.-C.* Paris: Gallimard, 1994.

Schiltz 2001 Schiltz, Véronique. *L'Or des Amazones: Peuples nomades entre Asie et Europe; VIe siècle av. J.-C. – IVe siècle apr. J.-C.* Paris: Musée Cernuschi, 2001.

Schiltz 2008 Schiltz, Véronique. "L'Art Scythe de la Sibérie au Nord de la Mer Noire." In Mattet 2008, 186–95.

Schorta 2001 Schorta, Regula. "A group of Central Asian Woolen Textiles in the Abegg-Stiftung Collection." In Keller and Schorta 2001, 79–117.

Scott 2011 Scott, David A. "The technical analysis of Chinese mirrors." In von Falkenhausen 2011, 198–233.

Semenov 2003 Semënov, Vladimir A. *Suglug-Khem i Khaĭyrakan: Mogil'niki skifskogo vremeni v Tsentral'no-tuvinskoĭ kotlovine.* Saint Petersburg: Nauka, 2003.

Sergeeva 1981 Sergeeva, Nadezhda F. *Drevneĭshaia metallurgiia medi iuga Vostochnoĭ Sibiri.* Novosibirsk: Nauka, 1981.

Shaanxi 1980 Shaanxi sheng Yongcheng kaogu gongzuodui. "Shaanxi Fengxiang Baqitun Qingou muzang fajue jianbao," in *Wenwu ziliao congkan* 3, 1980, 67–85.

Shaanxi 1986 Shaanxi Zhouyuan kaogudui. "Huangdui Xizhou mudi zhuantan qingli jianbao," in *Wenwu* 1986.8, 56–68.

Shaanxi 2003 Shaanxi sheng kaoguxue yanjiusuo. "Xi'an beijiao Zhanguo zhu tong gongjiang mu fajue jianbao," in *Wenwu*, 2002.9, 4–14.

Shaanxi and Baoji 1988 Shaanxi sheng kaogu yanjiusuo Baoji gongzuozhuan, and Baoji shi kaogu gongzuodui. "Shaanxi Longxian Bianjiazhuang wu hao Chunqiu mu fajue jianbao," in *Wenwu* 1988.11, 14–23.

Shanghai Museum 1998 *Xinjiang weiwu'er zizhiqu silu kaogu zhenpin.* Catalogue of an exhibition held at Shanghai Museum in 1998. Shanghai: Yi wen chubanshe, 1998.

Shanghai Museum 2012 Shanghai Museum, and Shaanxi sheng kaogu yanjiusuo, eds. *Jinyu huanian: Shaanxi Hancheng chutu Zhoudai Ruiguo wenwu zhenpin.* Shanghai: Shanghai shuhua chubanshe, 2012.

Shanpula 2001 Xinjiang Weiwu'er zizhiqu bowuguan, and Xinjiang wenwu kaogu yanjiusuo. *Zhongguo Xinjiang Shanpula: Gudai Yutian wen ming de tishi yuyanjiu (= Sampula in Xinjiang of China: Revelation and Study of Ancient Khotan Civilization).* Urumqi: Xinjiang renmin chubanshe, 2001.

Shanxi 1987 Shanxi sheng kaogu yanjiusuo Houma gongzuozhan. "Jinguo shiqi zuofang yizhi fajue jianbao," in *Wenwu* 1987.6, 73–81.

Shao and Yang 2016 Shao Huiqiu, and Yang Jianhua. "The Northern Zone and Mongolian Plateau Metallurgical Province: The Cultural Foundations of the Xiongnu Confederation," in *Asian Archaeology* 4, 2016, 47–67.

Shape of Beauty 2018 *The Shape of Beauty: Sculpture from the Collection of Howard and Saretta Barnet.* Sotheby's New York Sale NO9855 catalogue, 14 May 2018. New York: Sotheby's, 2018.

Shelach 2008 Shelach, Gideon. "He who eats the horse, She who rides it? Symbols of Gender Identity on the Eastern Edges of the Eurasian Steppe." In Linduff and Rubinson 2008, 93–109.

Shelach 2009 Shelach, Gideon. *Prehistoric Societies on the Northern Frontiers of China: Archaeological Perspectives on Identity Formation and Economic Change during the First Millennium BCE.* Approaches to Anthropological Archaeology. London: Equinox Press, 2009.

Shelach-Lavi 2015a Shelach-Lavi, Gideon. *The Archaeology of Early China, From Prehistory to the Han Dynasty.* New York: Cambridge University Press, 2015.

Shelach-Lavi 2015b Shelach-Lavi, Gideon. "Steppe Land Interactions and their effects on Chinese Cultures during the Second and early First Millennia BCE." In Amitai and Biran 2015, 10–31.

Shen et al. 2015 Shen Hui, Wu Xinhua, Tang Zihua, Zhou Xinying, Sun Nan, and Li Xiaoqiang. "Wood Usage and Fire Veneration in the Pamir, Xinjiang, 2500 yr BP." *PLoS ONE* 2015, 10(8): e0134847. https://dx.doi.org/10.1371/journal.pone.0134847 (published August 26, 2015; last accessed March 31, 2021).

Shennan 1994 Shennan, Stephen. *Archaeological Approaches to Cultural Identity.* London: Routledge, 1994.

Sherratt 2007 Sherratt, Andrew. "Alcohol and its Alternatives: Symbol and Substance in Pre-Industrial Cultures." In Goodman, Jordan, Paul E. Lovejoy, and Andrew Sherratt, eds. *Consuming Habits: Global and Historical Perspectives on How Cultures Define Drugs,* London: Routledge, 2007, 11–45.

Shih Hsio-Yen 1980 Shih Hsio-Yen. "The Western Regions, Serindia, and Middle Asia," paper prepared for the conference China's Past Unearthed: The Reconciliation of the New Discoveries and the Historical Records of the Early Imperial Period, March 26–28, 1980.

Shishlina et al. 2014 Shishlina, Natal'ia I., D. S. Kovalev, and Èl'mira R. Ibragimova. "Catacomb culture wagons of the Eurasian steppes," in *Antiquity* 88, 340, 2014, 378–94.

Simpson and Pankova 2017 Simpson, St. John, and Svetlana Pankova. *The BP exhibition of Scythians, Warriors of Ancient Siberia.* London: Thames and Hudson, 2017.

Sinor 1975 Sinor, Denis. *What is Inner Asia?* Bloomington: Indiana University, Asian Studies Research Institute, 1975.

Sinor 1990 Sinor, Denis. "Introduction: the concept of Inner Asia." In: Sinor, Denis, ed. *The Cambridge History of Early Inner Asia.* Cambridge et al.: Cambridge University Press, 1990, 1–18.

So 1980 So, Jenny F. "New Departures in Eastern Zhou Bronze Designs: The Spring and Autumn Period." In Wen Fong, ed. *The Great Bronze Age of China: An Exhibition from the People's Republic of China.* Exhibition catalogue. New York: Metropolitan Museum of Art, 1980, 251–301.

So 1995 So, Jenny F. *Eastern Zhou Ritual Bronzes from the Arthur M. Sackler Collections.* Washington DC: Arthur M. Sackler Foundation, 1995.

So 1997 So, Jenny F. "The Ornamented Belt in China," in *Orientations*, 28, 3, 1997, 70–78.

So 2000a So, Jenny F., ed. *Music in the Age of Confucius.* Washington, DC: Freer Gallery of Art and Arthur M. Sackler Gallery, Smithsonian, 2000.

So 2000b So, Jenny F.. "Different Tunes, Different Strings: Court and Chamber Music in Ancient China," in *Orientations*, 31, 5, 2000, 26–34.

So 2014 So, Jenny F. "Foreign/Eurasian Elements in Pre-imperial Qin Culture: Materials, Techniques and Types." In Liu, Yang, ed. *Beyond the First Emperor's Mausoleum: New Perspectives on Qin Culture.* Minneapolis: Minneapolis Institute of Arts, 2014, 193–212.

So 2015 So, Jenny F. "Bronze Weapons, Harness and Personal Ornaments: Signs of Qin's Contacts with the Northwest," in *Orientations*, 62, 10, 2015, 36–43.

So 2019 So, Jenny F. "Connecting Friend and Foe: Western Zhou Personal Regalia in Jade and Colored Stones," in *Archaeological Research in Asia* 19, 2019, 100–08.

So and Bunker 1995 So, Jenny F., and Emma C. Bunker. *Traders and Raiders on China's Northern Frontier.* Arthur M. Sackler Gallery, Smithsonian Institution: Washington DC, and Seattle: University of Washington Press, 1995.

So and Xin 2015 So, Jenny F., with Chu Xin, and a contribution by Chi Jo-hsin. *Chinese Jades from the Cissy and Robert Tang Collection.* Hong Kong: Art Museum, Institute of Chinese Studies, The Chinese University of Hong Kong, 2015.

Soper 1941 Soper, Alexander C., "Early Chinese Landscape Painting," in *Art Bulletin* 23, 2, June 1941, 141–64.

Sotheby 1975 *Fine Chinese ceramics, jades and works of art.* Sotheby Parke Bernet New York Sale 3799 catalogue, 25 October 1975. New York: Sotheby Parke Bernet, 1975.

Sotheby's 1994 *Fine Chinese Ceramics, Furniture and Works of Art.* Sotheby's New York Sale 6631 catalogue, Monday 28 and Tuesday 29 November 1994. New York: Sotheby's, 1994.

Speiser 1953 Speiser, Werner. *Ostasiatische Kunst und Chinoiserie. Ausstellung der Stadt Köln.* Staatenhaus, 28 June to 16 August. Cologne: Lang, 1953.

Sponsel 2012 Sponsel, Leslie E. *Spiritual Ecology. A Quiet Ecology.* Santa Barbara: Praeger, 2012.

Spycket 1972 Spycket, Agnès. "La musique instrumentale mésopotamienne," in *Journal des savants* 1972, 3, juillet-septembre, 153–209.

Stark 2008 Stark, Sören. *Die Alttürkenzeit in Mittel- und Zentralasien. Archäologische und historische Studien.* Nomaden und Sesshafte 6. Wiesbaden: Dr. Ludwig Reichert, 2008.

Stark 2012 Stark, Sören. "Nomads and Networks: Elites and their Connections to the outside world." In Stark and Rubinson 2012, 107–38.

Stark and Rubinson 2012 Stark, Sören, and Karen S. Rubinson, with Zainolla S. Samashev and Jennifer Y. Chi. *Nomads and Networks: The Ancient Art and Culture of Kazakhstan.* New York: Institute of the Ancient World at New York University, and Princeton: Princeton University Press, 2012.

Stepanova 2006 Stepanova, Elena V. "Ėvoliutsiia konskogo snariazheniia i otnositel'naia khronologiia pamiatnikov Pazyrykskoĭ kul'tury," in *Arkheologicheskie vesti* 13, 2006, 102–50.

Stevens et al. 2016 Stevens, Chris J., Charlene Murphy, Rebecca Roberts, Leilani Lucas, Fabio Silva, and Dorian Q. Fuller. "Between China and South Asia: A Middle Asian corridor of crop dispersal and agricultural innovation in the Bronze Age," in *The Holocene* 26, 2016, 1541–55.

Stöllner and Samašev 2013 Stöllner, Thomas, and Zajnolla Samašev, eds. *Unbekanntes Kasachstan. Archäologie im Herzen Asiens. Katalog der Ausstellung des Deutschen Bergbau-Museums Bochum vom 26. Januar bis zum 30. Juni 2013.* 2 vols. Veröffentlichung aus dem Deutschen Bergbau-Museum Bochum 192. Bochum: Deutsches Bergbau-Museum, 2013.

Stronach 2005 Stronach, David. "The Arjan Tomb: Innovation and Acculturation in the last days of Elam," in *Iranica Antiqua* 50, 2005, 180–96.

Sturman 1985a Sturman, Peter C. "Wild Beasts and Winged Immortals: Early Representations of Landscape in China. Part 1," in *The National Palace Museum Bulletin* 20, 2, May/June 1985, entire issue.

Sturman 1985b Sturman, Peter C. "Wild Beasts and Winged Immortals: Early Representations of Landscape in China. Part 2," in *The National Palace Museum Bulletin* 20, 3, 1985, July/August, entire issue.

Sturman 1985c Sturman, Peter C. "Wild Beasts and Winged Immortals: Early Representations of Landscape in China. Part 3," in *The National Palace Museum Bulletin* 20, 4, September/October 1985, entire issue.

Su Bai 1977 Su Bai. "Dongbei Neimenggu diqu de Xianbei yiji," in *Wenwu* 1977.5, 42–54.

Sullivan 1953 Sullivan, Michael. "On the Origin of Landscape Representation in Chinese Art," in *Archives of the Chinese Art Society of America* 7, 1953, 54–65.

Sun Wei 2007 Sun Wei. *Xianbei kaoguxue wenhua yanjiu.* Beijing: Kexue chubanshe, 2007.

Takahama et al. 2006 Takahama, Shu, Toshio Hayashi, Masanori Kawamata, Ryuji Matsubara, and Diimaajav Erdenebaatar. "Preliminary Report of Archaeological Investigations in Ulaan Uushig (Uushigiin Övör) in Mongolia," in *Bulletin of Archaeology, The University of Kanazawa* 28, 2006, 61–102.

Tang Yanling 2005 Tang Yanling. *Non-metallic deposits of Xinjiang, China*. Beijing: Geological Publishing, 2005.

Thornton et al. 2002 Thornton, Christopher P., Carl C. Lamberg-Karlovsky, Martin Liezers, and Suzanne M. M. Young. "On Pins and Needles: Tracing the Evolution of Copper-base Alloying at Tepe Yahya, Iran, via ICP-MS Analysis of Common-place Items," in *Journal of Archaeological Science* 29, 2002, 1451–60.

Tian Guangjin 1976 Tian Guangjin. "Taohongbala de Xiongnu mu," in *Kaogu xuebao* 1976.1, 131–44.

Tian and Guo 1986 Tian Guangjin and Guo Suxin. *E'erduosi shi qingtongqi*. Beijing: Wenwu chubanshe, 1986.

Tokyo National Museum 1997 *Daisogen no kiba minzoku: Chugoku hoppo no seidoki (= Mounted Nomads of Asian Steppe: Chinese Northern Bronzes)*. Tokyo: Kokuritsu Hakubutsukan, 1997.

Törbat 2018a Törbat, Tsagaan, ed. *Mongol ba büs nutgiĭn bugan khöshööniĭ soël: Ėrdėm shinzhilgėėniĭ katalog*, vol. 1. Ulaanbaatar: ShUA-iĭ tüükh, Arkheologiĭn khürėėlėgiĭn Ėrdmiĭn zövlöliĭn batalsnaar, 2018.

Törbat 2018b Törbat, Tsagaan, ed. *Mongol ba büs nutgiĭn bugan khöshööniĭ soël: Ėrdėm shinzhilgėėniĭ katalog*, vol. 2. Ulaanbaatar: ShUA-iĭ tüükh, Arkheologiĭn khürėėlėgiĭn Ėrdmiĭn zövlöliĭn batalsnaar, 2018.

Törbat and Tsėvėėndorzh 2016 Törbat, Tsagaan, and Damdiĭnsürėn Tsėvėėndorzh, eds. *Mongol Altaĭn mönkh tsėvdgiĭn bulsh. Mongolyn pazyrykiĭn soël (= Eiskurgan des Monoglischen Altaj. Pazyryk Kultur der Mongolei)*. Ulaanbaatar, 2016.

Trésors de la Chine ancienne 2015 *Trésors de la Chine ancienne de la collection David David-Weill*. Sotheby's Paris Sale 1537 catalogue, 16 December 2015. Paris: Sotheby's, 2015.

Tseng 2017 Tseng, Lillian Lan-ying. "Princely Tombs in Han China: New Discoveries from Dayunshan and Nanchang," in *Orientations* 48, 2, 2017, 103–09.

Tsunoda 1954 Tsunoda Bun'ei, Takashi Okazaki, Seiichi Masuda, and Hironori Ueda. *Ancient Art of the Northern Eurasia*. Kyoto: Shugeisha Press, 1954.

Turkin 2003 Turkin, G. V. "Plitochnye mogily padi Olzonteĭ," in *Izvestiia laboratorii drevnikh tekhnologiĭ* 1, 2003, 74–112.

Turner 1941 Turner, Ralph. *The Great Cultural Traditions. The Foundations of Civilization. Vol. 1. The Ancient Cities*. New York and London: McGraw Hill Book Co., 1941.

Turpan et al. 2019 Turpanshi wenwuju, Xinjiang wenwu kaogu yanjiusuo, Turpanxue yanjiuyuan, and Turpan bowuguan eds. *Xinjiang Yanghai Mudi*. Beijing: Wenwu chubanshe, 2019.

UNESCO 1976 *The Scythians; nomad goldsmiths of the open steppes. The UNESCO Courier, December 1976*. Paris: UNESCO, 1976 (entire issue).

Ventresca Miller and Makarewicz 2019 Ventresca Miller, Alicia R., and Cheryl A. Makarewicz. "Intensification in pastoralist cereal use coincides with the expansion of trans-regional networks in the Eurasian Steppe," in *Scientific Reports* 9: 8363, 2019. https://doi.org/10.1038/s41598-018-35758-w (published June 10, 2019; last accessed March 31, 2021).

Ventresca Miller et al. 2020 Ventresca Miller, Alicia R., Ashleigh Haruda, V. Varfolomeev, Aleksandr A. Goryachev, and Cheryl A. Makarewicz. "Close management of sheep in ancient Central Asia: evidence for foddering, transhumance, and extended lambing seasons during the Bronze and Iron Ages," in *STAR: Science & Technology of Archaeological Research* 6, 1, 2020, 41–60. https://doi.org/10.1080/20548923.2020.1759316 (published May 12, 2020; last accessed March 31, 2021).

Volkov 1995 Volkov, Vitali V. "Early Nomads of Mongolia." In Davis-Kimball et al. 1995, 319–32.

Volkov 2002 Volkov, Vitali V. *Olennye kamni Mongolii*. Moscow: Nauchnyĭ mir, 2002.

Wade 2013 Wade, Nicholas. "24,000-Year-Old Body Shows Kinship to Europeans and American

Indians," in *New York Times*, November 20, 2013, 8.

WAGNER AND BUTZ 2007 Wagner, Mayke, and Herbert Butz. *Nomadenkunst: Ordosbronzen der Ostasiatischen Kunstsammlung.* Museum für Asiatische Kunst, Staatliche Museen zu Berlin. Mainz: Philipp von Zabern, 2007.

WALLACE 2012 Wallace, Leslie V. "Representations of Falconry in Eastern Han China," in *Journal of Sport History*, 39, 1, 2012, 99–109.

WALLACE 2018 Wallace, Leslie V. "A Biographical Approach to the Study of the Mounted Archer Motif during the Han Dynasty." In Allard, Francis, Yan Sun, and Katheryn M. Linduff, eds. *Memory and Agency in Ancient China: Shaping the life history of Objects.* Cambridge, United Kingdom: Cambridge University Press, 2018, 197–215.

WALSH 2016 Walsh, Declan. "King Tut's Dagger Made of 'Iron From the Sky,' Researchers Say," *New York Times*, June 3, 2016, A7. http://www.nytimes.com/2016/06/03/world/middleeast/king-tuts-dagger-made-of-iron-from-the-sky-researchers-say.html (last accessed March 31, 2021).

WANG BINLU 1983 Wang Binlu. *A Chinese Zither Tutor, The Mei-an ch'in-pu.* Translated with commentary by Fredric Lieberman. Washington: University of Washington Press, 1983.

WANG BO 2003A Wang Bo. "Xinjiang Qiemo Zhagunluke yi hao mudi fajue baogao," in *Kaogu xuebao* 2003.1, 89–136.

WANG BO 2003B Wang Bo. "Xinjiang Zhagunluke konghou," in *Wenwu* 2003.2, 56–62.

WANG BO AND LU LIPENG 2016 Wang Bo and Lu Lipeng. "Current Understanding of Zaghunluq Second- and Third-Period Cultures." In Zaghunluq 2016, 73–84.

WANG FEI 2009 Wang Fei. *Beifang Caoyuan E'erduosi Qingtongqi.* Hohhot: Neimenggu wenhua chubanshe, 2009.

WATSON 1962 Watson, William. *Ancient Chinese Bronzes.* London: Faber and Faber, 1962.

WATSON 1971 Watson, William. *Cultural Frontiers in Ancient East Asia.* Edinburgh: University Press, 1971.

WATSON 1972 Watson, William. "The Chinese Contribution to Eastern Nomad Culture in the Pre-Han and Early Han Periods," in *World Archaeology* 4, 2, 1972, 139–49.

WEBER 1973 Weber, George W., Jr. *The Ornaments of the Late Zhou Bronzes.* New Brunswick, NJ: Rutgers Unversity Press, 1973.

WEI JIAN 2004 Wei Jian, ed. *Neimenggu diqu Xianbei muzang de faxian yu yanjiu.* Beijing: Kexue chubanshe, 2004.

WHITE 1934 White, William Charles. *Tombs of Old Lo-Yang: A Record of the Construction and Contents of a Group of Royal Tombs at Chin-ts'un, Honan, probably dating 550 BC.* Shanghai: Kelly & Walsh Ltd., 1934.

WHITFIELD 2004 Whitfield, Susan, ed., with Ursula Sims-Williams. *The Silk Road: Trade, Travel, War and Faith.* Chicago: Serindia, 2004.

WILKIN ET AL. 2020A Wilkin, Shevan, Alicia Ventresca Miller, William T. T. Taylor, … Nicole Boivin, Christina Warinner, and Jessica Hendy. "Dairy pastoralism sustained eastern Eurasian steppe populations for 5,000 years," in *Nature Ecology & Evolution* 4, 2020, 346–55. https://doi.org/10.1038/s41559-020-1120-y (published March 2, 2020; last accessed March 31, 2021).

WILKIN ET AL. 2020B Wilkin, Shevan, Alicia Ventresca Miller, Bryan K. Miller, … Erdene Myagmar, Nicole Boivin and Patrick Roberts. "Economic Diversification Supported the Growth of Mongolia's Nomadic Empires," in *Scientific Reports* 10, 3916, 2020. https://doi.org/10.1038/s41598-020-60194-0 (published March 3, 2020; last accessed March 31, 2021).

WILLIAMS AND OGDEN 1994 Williams, Dyfri, and Jack Ogden. *Greek Gold: Jewellery of the Classical World.* London: British Museum Press, 1994.

WINDFUHR 2006 Windfuhr, Gernot. "The Stags of Filippovka: Mithraic Coding on the Southern Ural Steppes." In Aruz et al. 2006, 46–81.

WINTERNITZ 1967 Winternitz, Emanuel. *Musical Instruments and their Symbolism in Western Art.* London: Faber and Faber, 1967.

WONG 2017 Wong, Raphael. "Carpets, Chariots and the State of Qin," in *Orientations*, 48, 1, 2017, 60–70.

WORLD'S OLDEST WRITING 2016 "The World's Oldest Writing," in *Archaeology*, 69, 3, 2016, 26–33.

Wu En 1985 Wu En. "Yin zhi Zhouchu de beifang qingtongqi," in *Kaogu xuebao* 1985.2, 135–56.

Wu En 1987 Wu En. "Shilun Handai Xiongnu yu Xianbei yiji de qubie." In *Zhongguo kaogu xuehui diliuci nianhui lunwenji*. Beijing: Wenwu chubanshe 1987, 136–50.

Wu En 1997 Wu En. "Some Xianbei Sites." In Bunker et al. 1997, 300–305.

Wu En 2003 Wu En. "Lun Menggu lu shi de niandai ji xiangguan wenti," in *Kaogu yu wenwu* 2003.1, 21–30.

Wu En 2007 Wu En Yue Situ. *Beifang caoyuan kaoguxue wenhua yanjiu: Qingtong shidai zhi zaoqi tieqi shidai*. Beijing: Kexue chubanshe, 2007.

Wu En 2008 Wu En Yue Situ. *Beifang caoyuan kaoguxue wenhua bijiao yanjiu: Qingtong shidai zhi zaoqi Xiongnu shiqi*. Beijing: Kexue chubanshe, 2008.

Wu En and Wagner 1999 Wu En and Mayke Wagner. "Bronzezeitliche Zugleinenhalter in China und Südsibirien," in *Eurasia Antiqua* 5, 1999, 111–13.

Wu Hsiao-yun 2013 Wu Hsiao-yun. *Chariots in early China: Origins, cultural interaction, and identity*. BAR International Series 2457. Oxford: Archaeopress, 2013.

Wu Hung 1984 Wu Hung. "A Sampan Shan Chariot Ornament and the Xiangrui Design in Western Han Art," in *Archives of Chinese Art* 37, 1984, 38–59.

Wu Hung 1986 Wu Hung. "Buddhist Elements in Early Chinese Art," in *Artibus Asiae* 47, 3/4, 1986, 263–352.

Wu Jui-man 2015 Wu, Mandy Jui-man. "Contact and Exchange in Northern China: A Case Study on the Tomb of a Zoroastrian-Sogdian, Kang Ye (512–571 CE)," in *Asian Archaeology* 3, 2015, 107–28.

Wu Xiaolong 2013 Wu Xiaolong. "Cultural hybridity and social status: elite tombs on China's Northern Frontier during the third century BCE," in *Antiquity* 87, 335, 2013, 121–36.

Wu Xiaolong 2017 Wu, Xiaolong. *Material Culture, Power, and Identity in Ancient China*. New York, Cambridge: Cambridge University Press, 2017.

Wu Yuehua 2018 Wu Yuehua. "Shanggu qinzhen de xingzhi he yuanli kaolue," in *Zhongguo yinyue xue* 2018.1, 55–66.

Xiajiadian 2007 *Hagajŏm Sangch'ŭng Munhuwaŭi Ch'ŏngdonggi* (= *Xiajiadian shangceng wenhua de qingtongqi*). Han-Chung kongdong haksul chosa pogosŏ, vol. 2. Seoul: Koguryŏ Yŏn'gu Chaedan, 2007.

Xie Jin 2005 Xie Jin. "Reflection upon Chinese Recently Unearthed Konghous in Xin Jiang Autonomous Region," http://musicology.cn/news/news_299.html (published June 28, 2005; last accessed March 31, 2021).

Xinjiang 1998 *Xinjiang weiwu'er zizhiqu silu kaogu zhenpin*. Catalog of an exhibition organized by and held at Shanghai Museum 1998. Shanghai: Yiwen chubanshe, 1998.

Xinjiang 1999 *Xinjiang wenwu guji daguan* (= *A grand view of Xinjiang's cultural relics and historic sites*). Urumqi: Xinjiang meishu sheying chubanshe, 1999.

Xinjiang Tulufanxue 2011 Xinjiang Tulufanxue yanjiuyuan, and Xinjiang wenwu kaogu yanjiusuo. "Xinjiang Shanshan Yanghai mudi fajue baogao," in *Kaogu xuebao* 2011.1, 99–150.

Xinjiang Wenwu 2004 Xinjiang wenwu kaogu yanjiusuo, and Tulufan diqu wenwuju. "Shanshan xian Yanghai yihao mudi fajue jianbao," in *Xinjiang wenwu* 2004.1, 1–27.

Xinyang 1986 *Xinyang Chu mu*. Beijing: Wenwu chubanshe, 1986.

Xirong Yizhen 2014 Gansu sheng wenwu kaogu yanjiusuo. *Xirong Yizhen: Majiayuan Zhanguo mudi chutu wenwu*. Beijing: Wenwu chubanshe, 2014.

Xu 1996 Xu, Jay. "Summary of Chapter I." In Li Xiating et al. 1996, 75–85.

Xu Junchen and Liu Dezhen 1985 Xu Junchen, and Liu Dezhen. "Gansu Ningxian Yucun chutu Xizhou Qingtongqi," in *Kaogu* 1985.4, 349–64.

Yablonsky 1995a Yablonsky, Leonid T. "Written Sources and the History of Archaeological Studies of the Saka in Central Asia." In Davis-Kimball et al. 1995, 193–97.

Yablonsky 1995b Yablonsky, Leonid T. "The Material Culture of the Saka and Historical

Reconstruction." In Davis-Kimball et al. 1995, 201–39.

Yan Jinzhu 1985 Yan Jinzhu. "Shanxi Jixian chutu Shang dai qingtongqi," in *Kaogu* 1985.9, 848–49.

Yan Shizong and Li Huairen 1992 Yan Shizong, and Li Huairen. "Ningxia Xiji faxian yizuo qingtong shidai muzang," in *Kaogu*, 1992.6, 573–75.

Yang Jianhua 2009 Yang Jianhua. "Zhongguo beifang Dong Zhou shiqi liang zhong wenhua yicun bianxi: Lianlun Rong Di yu Hu de guanxi," in *Kaogu xuebao* 2009.3, 155–84.

Yang Jianhua 2011 Yang Jianhua. "Gender Relationship among the 'Xiongnu' as reflected in burial practices." In Brosseder and Miller 2011, 244–59.

Yang Jianhua and Linduff 2012 Yang Jianhua, and Katheryn M. Linduff. "A Contextual Explanation for 'Foreign' or 'Steppic' Factors Exhibited in Burials at the Majiayuan Cemetery and the Opening of the Tianshan Mountain Corridor," in *Asian Archaeology* 1, 2012, 73–84.

Yang Ningguo and Qi Yuezhang 1999 Yang Ningguo, and Qi Yuezhang. "Ningxia Pengyangxian jinnian chutu de Beifang xi qingtongqi," in *Kaogu* 1999.12, 38–47.

Yang Yuanzheng 2014 Yang Yuanzheng. "The Subdivided Qin." In *The 8th Symposium of the International Study Group on Music Archaeology (ISGMA 2014) in Suzhou and Beijing, China, 20–25 October 2012*. Studien zur Musikarchäologie 9. Orient-Archäologie 33. Rahden/Westf.: Leidorf, 2014, 117–28.

Yang Yuanzheng 2015a Yang Yuanzheng. "*Taotie*, Dragon, Phoenix, and Farmer: A highly decorated *Qin* excavated from Jiuliandun," in *Early China* 38, 2015, 129–50.

Yang Yuanzheng 2015b Yang Yuanzheng. "Finding the Key: Tuning Keys Discovered from the Imperial Collection of Emperor Huizong (r. 1100–1126)," in *Music in Art: International Journal for Music Iconography* 40, 2015, 1–2, 275–84.

Yang Yuanzheng 2016 Yang Yuanzheng. "Typological Analysis of the Chinese *Qin* in the Late Bronze Age," in *The Galpin Society Journal* 69, 2016, 137–51.

Yang Yuanzheng 2019 Yang Yuanzheng. "The *Se* and *Qin* Excavated from the Tomb of Liu He, 59 BCE." In Eichmann et al. 2019, 155–63.

Yatsenko 2012 Yatsenko, Sergey A. "Yuezhi on Bactrian Embroidery from Textiles found at Noyon uul, Mongolia," in *The Silk Road* 10, 2012, 39–48.

Yikezhaomeng 1992 Yikezhaomeng wenwu gongzuozhan. "Yijinhuoluoqi Shihuigou faxian de E'erduosi shi wenwu," in *Neimenggu wenwu kaogu* 1992, 6/7, 91–96.

Yinxu 1980 *Yinxu Fu Hao mu*. Hongguo tianye kaogu bao gao ji 23. Beijing: Wenwu chubanshe, 1980.

Yu Ping and Dai Ge 1985 Yu Ping, and Dai Ge. "Shaanxisheng bowuguan shoucang de Xiongnu tongpaishi," in *Wenbo* 1985.5, 38–42.

Zaghunluq 2016 Xinjiang Uygur Autonomous Region Museum. *Textile Treasures of Zaghunluq*. Contributions by Wang Bo, Wang Mingfang, Minawar Happar, and Lu Lipeng, translated by Martha Avery. Riggisberg: Abegg-Stiftung, 2016.

Zavitukhina 1983 Zavitukhina, Mariia P. *Drevnee iskusstvo na Enisee: Skifskoe vremia; publikatsiia odnoĭ kollektsii*. Leningrad: Iskusstvo, 1983.

Zhang Liangren 2017 Zhang Liangren. "The Transmission of Karasuk Metallurgy to the Northern China," in *Shide Xuebao* 1, 2017, 100–24.

Zhang Wenling 2012 Zhang Wenling. *Huangjin caoyuan: Gudai Ouya caoyuan wenhua tanwei (=The Golden Steppes)*. Shanghai: Shanghai guji chubanshe, 2012.

Zhao Ji 1990 Zhao Ji, ed. *The Natural History of China*. New York: McGraw Hill, 1990.

Zhao et al. 2019 Zhao Meiying, Hongen Jiang, and Christopher Joel Grassa. "Archaeobotanical studies of the Yanghai cemetery in Turpan, Xinjiang, China," in *Archaeological and Anthropological Sciences* 11, 2019, 1143–53.

Zheng Shaozong 1991 Zheng Shaozong. "Luelun Zhongguo beibu Changcheng didai faxian de dongwu wen qingtong shipai," in *Wenwu chunqiu* 1991.4, 1–32.

Zhongguo 1959 Zhongguo kexueyuan kaogu yanjiusuo. *Shancunling Guoguo mudi = The Cemetery of the State of Kuo at Shang Ts'un Ling*. Archaeological

Excavations at the Yellow River Reservoirs Report Nr. 3. Beijing: Kexue chubanshe, 1959.

Zhongguo 1975 Zhongguo kexueyuan kaogu yanjiusuo Neimenggu gongzuodui. "Nincheng Nanshan'gen yizhi fajue baogao," in *Kaogu xuebao* 1975.1, 117–40.

Zhongguo 1984 Zhongguo kexueyuan kaogu yanjiusuo Neimenggu gongzuodui. "Neimenggu Aohanqi Zhoujiadi mudi fajue jianbao," in *Kaogu* 1984.5, 417–26.

Zhongguo 1993 Zhongguo shehui kexueyuan kaogu yanjiusuo. *Kaogu jinghua: Zhongguo shehui xueyuan kaogu yanjiusuo 40 nian jinian*. Beijing: Kexue chubanshe, 1993.

Zhongguo and Hebei 1980 Zhongguo Shehui kexueyuan kaogu yanjiusuo, and Hebeisheng wenwu guanlichu. *Mancheng Hanmu fajue baogao,* 2 vols. Zhongguo tianya kaogu baogaoji kaoguxue zhuankan. Ser. 4, 20. Beijing: Wenwu chubanshe, 1980.

Index of Places

Aba 阿坝 (Aba Tibetan and Qiang Autonomous Prefecture), Sichuan, 408–411
Abakanskoe, 445, 495
Afghanistan, 15, 19, 189, 374
Afrasiab, 416
Africa, north, 244
Aidinghu 艾丁湖, Gaochang 高昌 district, Xinjiang, 138
Ak-Alakha, 50–51, 195, 238–40
Akbeit, 378
Alagou 阿拉沟, Turpan 吐鲁番 prefecture, Xinjiang, 236
Ala-Tey, 434
Almaty, 98, 193, 375, 388
Altai (Mountains), Altai region, 15, 22, 24, 28–29, 40, 51, 82, 116–17, 124, 138, 174–76, 191, 193, 195, 197, 199, 202, 206, 210, 218–20, 224, 232–42, 258–60, 268–70, 298, 356, 360, 372, 375, 470
Aluchaideng 阿鲁柴登, Hanggin 杭锦 banner, Inner Mongolia, 192, 196
Amur (river, valley), 45, 186
Anatolia, 185, 268
Anhui 安徽 (province), 302, 310
Ansai 安塞 district, Shaanxi, 164
Anyang 安陽, Henan, 31–32, 38
Aohan 敖汉 banner, Inner Mongolia, 62
Arabian Peninsula, 244
Aral (lake), 375
Arzhan, 29, 64, 74, 142–44, 150, 184–85, 197
Asia: eastern Asia, northeastern Asia, 140, 185, 198, 265, 268, 440; north Asia, northwest Asia, 18; south Asia; southwestern Asia, 24, 199; western Asia, West Asia, 24, 142, 154, 187, 198, 238, 255, 258, 265–68, 274, 281, 402, 466
Assyria, 473
Azerbaijan, 15
Bactria, 415, 421
Baga Gazryn chuluu, 439, 449–51, 453–54, 456–57, 496–97

Baikal (lake), 77, 83; Baikal area, 47, 49, 186
Baoji 宝鸡, Shaanxi, 187
Baqitun 八旗屯, Fengxiang 凤翔 county, Shaanxi, 252
Bashadar, 40, 116–17, 174–77, 199, 202, 210, 258, 360
Beijing 北京, 38, 76–77, 79–80, 84, 96; north of Beijing, 54, 84–86, 90, 100–108, 141, 183, 187, 250
Beikang 北康, Xi'an 西安, Shaanxi, 191, 322
Beiskoe, 494–95
Beixinbao 北辛堡, Huailai 怀来 county, Hebei, 136
Berel', 184, 220–22, 246, 388
Beresh, 495
Bianjiazhuang 边家庄, Long 陇 county, Shaanxi, 152
Birja, 68
Black Sea, 15, 77, 258, 470; Black Sea region, 50, 81, 83, 92, 98–99, 153, 189, 238, 312, 376–77, 380, 394, 398
Bobrov, 83
Bojishan 簸箕山, Jiangsu, 292
Bol'shoi Telek, 494
Bulgaria, 376, 400
Buryatia, 340–42
Byblos, 183
Caomiao 草庙, Pengyang 彭阳 county, Ningxia, 214
Carpathian Mountains, 15
Caspian Sea, 45, 190
Caucasus, 142, 394; north Caucasus, 83, 142, 392; northwestern Caucasus, 375
Central Asia, 15, 17, 64, 81, 94–96, 189–90, 193, 195, 197, 216, 244, 258–59, 262, 265–68, 276, 281, 312, 374–75, 453, 466, 468–69
Central Plains, 13, 25, 28, 120, 188, 290–92, 300–302, 308–10, 440, 480
Chang'an 长安, Xi'an 西安, Shaanxi, 402
Changsha 长沙, Hunan, 368, 460
Changzhi 长治, Shanxi, 354
Chaoyang 朝阳 county, Liaoning, 54
Chawuhu 察吾呼, Hejing 和静 county, Xinjiang, 110

Cheremukhovaia Pad', 500

Chifeng 赤峰, Inner Mongolia, 45, 47, 51, 68, 76, 324

Chilikty (Shilikty), 83, 196, 380

China, 14, 282, 294–96, 374, 402, 420–21, 456–58, 468, 472, 480–82, 484; central China, 320, 440; north-central China, 40, 42; northeast China, 38, 52, 58–74, 79, 88, 92–96, 292, 316, 324–30, 340, 350, 430, 441, 447; northern China, 83, 173, 280, 282, 286–90, 312, 320–22, 332, 344–46, 352, 354, 360, 364–72, 418, 434, 440–41, 449, 462; northwest China, 32–36, 79, 86, 141, 143, 150, 158–70, 174, 177, 181, 199, 202–34, 238–52, 266–68, 272, 356–58, 362, 375, 462; south China, 278, 283, 300–302, 440, 462; southwest China, 377, 406; western China, 416

Da'an 大安 county, Jilin, 352

Dabaiyang 大白阳, Xuanhua 宣化 county, Hebei, 304

Dabuzishan 大堡子山, Li county, Gansu, 181

Daling 大凌 (river), 54

Danube, lower, 400

Daodunzi 倒墩子, Tongxin 同心 county, Ningxia, 286, 294, 298, 304, 314, 340, 344

Dian 滇 (lake); lake Dian region, 377, 406–8

Dianzixiang 店子乡, Inner Mongolia, 116

Dniepr (river), 196

Dureny, 455, 493

Dvoretzky, 62

Dyrestui, 283, 328, 334–38, 344–46, 372, 421, 424, 427, 439, 443, 445, 447, 449–50, 452–53, 455–57, 493, 498–500

Dzhungaria, 15

Edsin gol, Ejin gol (Ruo 弱 river), Gansu and Inner Mongolia, 242

Egiin gol, 497

Elam, 467, 469

Erlanhugou 二兰虎沟, Chayouhou 察右后 banner, Inner Mongolia, 340

Erlitou 二里頭, Henan, 25

Eshnunna, 467

Eurasia, 19, 23, 45, 83, 98, 114, 140, 180, 189, 193, 196–98, 220, 255–56, 258, 261, 268, 278, 282, 360, 380, 466, 468; central Eurasia, 15, 24, 197, 274, 374; eastern Eurasia, 10, 13–15, 28, 64, 98, 222, 404, 414; northeastern Eurasia, 44, 82, 96; northern Eurasia, 27, 31, 44, 83, 281; northwestern Eurasia, 197, 230, 238, 280; western Eurasia, 98, 197, 282, 374, 398

Eurasian steppe(s), 9, 10, 17, 24, 26, 28, 62, 80–81, 88, 100, 114, 134–36, 141, 182, 185–86, 189–90, 192–93, 196–97, 199, 208, 212, 230, 236–38, 255, 263, 268, 374, 398, 408, 419, 441; eastern Eurasian steppes, 10, 13, 22, 28, 148, 183–86, 348; northeast(ern) Eurasian steppes, 263; northern Eurasian steppes, 98, 377; western Eurasian steppes, 142

Europe, southeastern, eastern, 15, 45, 185, 376, 398, 466

Fanjiayaozi 范家窑子, Horinger 和林格尔 county, Inner Monolia, 118–19, 122–24, 138

Fengxiang 凤翔 county, Shaanxi, 252

Fenshuiling 分水岭, Changzhi 长治, Shanxi, 354

Filippovka, 196–97

Gansu 甘肃 (province); Gansu region, 79, 138, 158, 190–92, 195, 200, 224, 232, 250–52, 362; Gansu (Hexi) Corridor, 187–90, 193, 195; northeastern Gansu, 190; northwestern Gansu, 189; southeastern Gansu, 112–13, 180, 210, 231; southern Gansu, 181

Ganzibao 甘字堡, Huailai 怀来 county, Hebei, 77, 96, 104

Georgia, 396

Girsu, Iraq, 62

Gobi (desert), 187, 208, 445, 447, 449, 451, 493

Gol Mod, 439, 449–50, 453, 457, 497–48

Grishkin Log, 494

Guangdong 广东 (province), 263, 278–80, 298, 312–14

Guangxi 广西 (Guangxi Zhuang Autonomous Region), 294

Guangzhou 广州, Guangdong, 263, 298

Guchin-Us sum, Övörkhangai aimag, Mongolia, 130

Guizhou 贵州 (province), 377, 406

Gujarat, 188

Gumarovo, 83

Guodian 郭店, Jingmen 荆门, Hubei, 465

Guoxianyaozi 崞县窑子, Liangcheng 凉城 county, Inner Mongolia, 118–20, 124, 134

Guyuan 固原, Ningxia, 193, 199, 206, 210, 218, 226–28, 242, 356

Hancheng 韩城, Shaanxi, 182

Hanggin 杭锦 banner, Inner Mongolia, 130, 141, 192, 196

Hattin Sum cf. Khadain-sume,

Hebei 河北 (province), 11, 32, 44, 104–6, 130, 136, 232, 286, 304, 308, 312, 320, 360, 364; northern Hebei, 76–77, 82–83, 90–92, 96, 102, 108, 130, 136, 164–66, 346; northwestern Hebei, 143; southern Hebei, 187

Hechuan 河川, Guyuan 固原, Ningxia, 206

Heilongjiang 黑龙江 (province), 44, 122–23

Hejing 和静 county, Xinjiang, 110

Henan 河南 (province), 32, 40, 62, 76, 79–80, 110, 180, 182

Hetian 和田 (Khotan), Xinjiang, 195, 259, 274

Hexi 河西 (Gansu) Corridor, 187–90, 193, 195

Himalaya(s), 408

Hohhot 呼和浩特, Inner Mongolia, 115, 128, 136

Horinger 和林格尔 county, Inner Mongolia, 112–13, 118–19, 122–24

Houbaoshi 后宝石, Da'an 大安 county, Jilin, 352

Houma 侯马, Shanxi, 119, 122, 143, 158–68, 250, 272, 354, 482

Huailai 怀来 county, Hebei, 77, 96, 104, 136

Huanghe 黄河 (river); Yellow river, 36, 181, 187, 314

Hubei 湖北 (province), 256, 263, 459–60, 465

Hulugou 葫芦沟, Beijing, 76 77

Hunan 湖南 (province), 368, 460

Hunyuan 浑源 county, Shanxi, 119, 122, 250

Il'movaia Pad', 453, 456, 500

Imereti, 396

India, 185, 188, 421

Inner Asia, 9–15, 17, 20–21, 23–24, 26–27, 29–32, 38, 44–45, 72, 80, 82, 110, 116, 118–19, 122, 138, 141–43, 158, 173, 180, 188–89, 191, 198, 282, 336–38, 374, 376–77, 436, 443, 449–50, 455; eastern Inner Asia, 202

Inner Asian artifacts, 12, 17, 19, 31, 40, 50, 112, 115, 119, 189, 316, 374, 420, 436, 438–39, 443

Inner Asian borders, 15, 81, 112

Inner Asian Mountain Corridor, 11, 15, 17

Inner Eurasia, Inner Eurasian world, 15, 17, 22, 25, 28, 31, 50–51, 79, 81, 86, 198, 204, 258, 262, 377; Inner Eurasian Frontier, 9, 24–25, 195

Inner Mongolia 内蒙古 (Inner Mongolia Autonomous Region), 13, 32, 45, 50, 82, 94, 102, 115, 118–20, 123–24, 130, 138, 162, 192, 195, 202, 230, 316, 320, 324, 340, 348, 352, 412, 438–39; east(ern) Inner Mongolia, 350; northeast(ern) Inner Mongolia, 106; northern Inner Mongolia, 348; south-central Inner Mongolia, 112–13, 115, 119–36, 178; southeast(ern) Inner Mongolia, 44, 46, 51–52, 58–62, 66, 70, 76, 79, 186, 349; southwest(ern) Inner Mongolia, 112–13, 141–46, 152–56, 170–73, 176–77, 195–96; western Inner Mongolia, 192, 199, 232, 306, 318

Iran, 83, 173, 186, 197, 248, 259, 266, 402–4, 467–69; central Iran, 188; eastern Iran, 377, 404; western Iran, 376, 402

Irkutsk, 47, 49, 52, 148, 418

Issyk, 193, 255, 274, 375, 380

Ivolga, 418, 447, 452, 455–56, 493

Izykh, 494

Japan, 468

Ji 吉 county, Shanxi, 34

Jiangsu 江苏 (province), 292

Jilin 吉林 (province), 44, 352

Jingjiecun 旌介村, Shanxi, 38

Jirzankal (Ji'erzankale) 吉尔赞喀勒, Xinjiang, 261

Jundushan 军都山, 76–79, 81, 84–88, 94, 100, 108–10, 173, 183, 187, 250, 254

Jungar 准格尔 banner, Inner Mongolia, 142, 146, 154, 173, 192–93, 230–32

Kaly, 494

Kaptyrevo, 495

Kartli, western, 396

Kazakhstan, 15, 19, 80, 98, 184, 189, 193, 195, 220, 246, 255, 274, 375, 380, 388; eastern Kazakhstan, 83, 196; northeast Kazakhstan, 388; northern Kazakhstan, 23; southeast, southeastern Kazakhstan, 38

Keerqin Zuoyi Zhong 科尔沁左翼中 banner, Zhelimu 哲裏木 League, Inner Mongolia, 352

Kelermes, 81, 83, 92

Khadain-sume (Hattin Sum), Zhangbei 张北, Hebei, 106, 130

Khövsgöl aimag, Mongolia, 122

Khotan (Hetian 和田), Xinjiang, 195, 259, 274

Khur, 188

Kokorevo, 495

Korea, 44, 468

Korsukov, Kachugsky district, 47

Kosogol, 439, 449, 493–94, 500–502

Kostromskaia, 83, 99
Krapovina, 494
Krasnyi Iar, 493
Kuban region, 375–76, 390
Kumtag 库姆塔格 (desert), 471
Kyrgyzstan, 15, 374
Ladakh, 412
Leigudun 擂鼓墩, Suizhou 随州, Hubei, 256, 265, 459–60
Li 禮 county, Gansu, 181
Liangcheng 凉城 county, Inner Mongolia, 102, 112–13, 115–20, 124–38, 141, 162
Liangdaicun 梁带村, Hancheng 韩城, Shaanxi, 182
Liaoning 辽宁 (province), 44, 54, 76, 283, 292–96, 304, 324, 330, 434, 441, 445; western Liaoning, 90, 102–4
Lijiataozi 李家套子, Tongxin 同心 county, Ningxia, 338
Litoï, 83
Liujiahe 刘家河, Pinggu 平谷 district, Beijing, 38
Liyu 李峪, Hunyuan 浑源 county, Shanxi, 119, 122, 250
Liyuan 梨园, Weining 威宁 county, Guizhou, 406
Long 陇 county, Shaanxi, 152
Longhua 隆化 county, Hebei, 90
Luanping 滦平 county, Hebei, 77, 102
Luoyang 洛陽, Henan, 180, 480–81
Luristan, 376, 402
Maikop, 142, 150, 375–76, 390–92
Majiayuan 马家塬, Gansu, 192, 232
Malaia Inia, 494
Manchuria, 11, 13, 15, 47, 99, 283, 439
Manhanshan 蛮汉山, Liangcheng 凉城 county, Inner Mongolia, 102, 115
Mao 茂 county, Aba 阿坝 prefecture, Sichuan, 408–11
Maoqinggou 毛庆沟, Liangcheng 凉城 county, Inner Mongolia, 102, 115–20, 124–38, 141, 162
Mar'iasova, 494
Mawangdui 马王堆, Changsha 长沙, Hunan, 368, 460
Mediterranean, 29, 468
Mesopotamia, 88, 183, 185, 255, 258–59, 466–67, 469, 471–72
Minusinsk, 68, 98, 116, 174, 449
Minusinsk Basin, 15, 25, 47, 83, 118, 138, 332–36, 424, 438–41, 443, 445, 447, 449–50, 452, 456–57, 493–95, 500–502
Mongolia, 10, 12, 14–15, 19, 22, 32, 47–49, 51, 64, 81–83, 94–96, 99, 150, 184, 186, 189, 268, 282–83, 314, 324–26, 330, 334–36, 340, 344, 372, 410, 412, 416, 421, 434, 437–41, 443, 445, 447, 449–51, 455, 457, 493, 496–98; central Mongolia, 22; eastern Mongolia, 56, 62, 82, 334; northern Mongolia, 22, 82, 118, 122, 138, 302, 439; northwest Mongolia, 138; south-central Mongolia, 64, 130, 439; southeastern Mongolia, 58; western Mongolia, 22
Mongolian Plateau, 64
Moutuo 牟托, Mao 茂 county, Aba 阿坝 prefecture, Sichuan, 408–11
Nalin'gaotu 纳林高兔, Shenmu 神木 county, Shaanxi, 174, 192–93
Nanshan'gen 南山根, Ningcheng 宁城 county, Inner Mongolia, 46, 58, 62, 70, 186, 412
Nanyue 南越 (kingdom), 263, 278–80, 298, 314
Near East, 14, 27, 81, 98, 114, 116, 122, 140, 183, 185, 468
Nimrud, 259, 471
Nineveh, 469
Ning 宁 county, Gansu, 79, 158, 250–52
Ningcheng 宁城 county, Inner Mongolia, 46, 50–51, 58–62, 66, 70, 186, 412
Ningxia 宁夏 (Ningxia Hui Autonomous Region), 112–13, 180, 189–91, 193, 195, 199–222, 226–31, 242–44, 286, 294–98, 304, 310, 314, 338–40, 344, 356
Northern Zone, 15, 51, 74
Novaia Chernaia, 494
Noyon Uul, 302, 421, 439, 453, 456
Övörkhangai aimag, Mongolia, 130
Olbia, 258–59, 262, 376, 398, 468–70, 472
Olon-Guriin gol, 318
Ongniud 翁牛特 banner, Inner Mongolia, 316
Ordos 鄂尔多斯 (river), 204; Ordos loop, 66, 310; Ordos region, area, 13, 15, 80, 83, 98, 112–13, 120, 141–43, 152–56, 173, 186, 189–90, 192, 194–95, 202, 226, 230–31, 283, 286, 294–304, 328, 334–36, 375, 412, 418–19, 439, 447; southern Ordos (region), 440; southwest Ordos (region), 308–10, 314, 320, 338

Index of Places | 537

Ordos Desert, 130, 141, 170, 174, 187, 192
Oznachennoe, 495
Pacific Ocean, 15
Pakistan, 374
Pamir(s), Pamir Mountains, 374, 378–84
Paozi 泡子, Ongniud 翁牛特 banner, Inner Mongolia, 316
Pazyryk, 22, 29, 40, 51, 88, 117, 176, 185, 195, 199, 210–12, 232, 236, 258, 260, 262, 266, 318, 372, 468–70, 472
Pengyang 彭阳 county, Guyuan 固原, Ningxia, 190, 193, 204, 214
Persepolis, 184, 190, 374
Persia, western, 118, 402
Pinggu 平谷 district, Beijing, 38
Pingyang 平洋, Tailai 泰来 county, Heilongjiang, 122
Polkanovo, 493
Pontic-Caspian steppes, 23
Qiemo 且末 (Qarqan) county, Xinjiang, 27, 256, 259–61, 469–70, 472
Qingshui 清水, Gansu, 224, 362
Qingyang 庆阳 plateau, Gansu, 112–13, 180, 200, 210
Qingzigou 苘子沟, Xingzhou 兴洲, Luanping 滦平, Hebei, 77
Rajpipa, Gujarat, 188
Ratanpur, Gujarat, 188
Razliv, 493
Russia, 82, 150, 189, 196, 224, 268, 376
Sagly-Bazhy, 130, 191, 208
Sagly Valley, 138
Saianskaia, 83
Sandaowan 三道湾, Qahar Youyi Hou 察哈尔右翼后 banner, Inner Mongolia, 349
Sanmenxia 三门峡, Henan, 62, 79–80, 182
Sava, 493
Sayan Mountains, 150
Shaanxi 陕西 (province), 141, 143, 152, 182, 187, 189–90, 192, 230, 252, 302, 322, 402, 416; northern Shaanxi, 32, 112–13, 164, 174, 192–93, 230; northwestern Shaanxi, 170; southwestern Shaanxi, 152
Shandong 山东 (province), 76
Shangcunling 上村岭, Henan, 62, 79–80, 110, 182
Shangdongcun 上东村, Ji 吉 county, Shanxi, 34

Shanpula 山普拉, Xinjiang, 29, 195, 197, 274
Shanshan 鄯善 county, Xinjiang, 261, 470, 472
Shanxi 山西 (province), 11, 32–38, 141, 143, 164, 168, 272, 354, 428; northern Shanxi, 76, 120, 250; southern Shanxi, 119, 122, 158–60, 164–66, 182, 250, 268
Sharagol, 493
Shenmu 神木 county, Shaanxi, 174, 192–93, 230
Shiertaiyingzi 十二台营子, Chaoyang 朝阳 county, Liaoning, 54
Shihuigou 石灰沟, Yijinhuoluo 伊金霍洛 banner, Inner Mongolia, 199, 202
Shijiazhuang 石家莊, Hebei, 308
Shilikty (Chilikty), 83, 196, 380
Shilou 石楼 county, Shanxi, 36
Shiraz, 190
Shiyang 石羊, Sichuan, 320
Shouzhou 壽州, Anhui, 310
Shuanggudui 双古堆, Anhui, 302
Shuoxian 朔县 (Shuocheng 朔城 district), Shanxi, 428
Shushenskoe, 495
Siberia, 32, 40, 68, 81, 83, 98, 184–86, 189, 195–97, 246, 375, 412, 441; central Siberia, 15; eastern Siberia, 418; southeastern Siberia, 15; southern Siberia, 11 12, 14 15, 19, 32, 45, 47, 51 52, 56, 64, 113, 116, 118, 124, 136, 140, 143, 150, 186, 199, 202, 206–8, 224, 232, 258, 268, 282–83, 332, 380, 421, 424, 434, 438, 447
Sichuan 四川 (province), 298, 320, 408–11; western Sichuan, 377
Siniavka, 83
Solenoozero, 494
Subao 苏堡, Xiji 西吉 county, Ningxia, 310
Sükhbaatar (province, aimag), 56
Suglug-Khem, 130
Suide 绥德 county, Shaanxi, 32
Suizhou 随州, Hubei, 256, 265, 459–60
Sujigou 苏计沟, Jungar 准格尔 banner, Inner Mongolia, 142, 146
Syda, 495
Syr Darya, Syr Darya region, 375, 386
Tabat, 494
Tagisken-South, 375, 386
Taihang 太行 Mountains, 11, 15; east of Taihang, 13, 44–46, 50–51, 60, 76, 96, 106, 114–15, 119,

130–31, 186, 286, 308–10, 439–40; west of Taihang, 13, 36, 45, 50–51, 80, 106, 112–16, 118–19, 126–36, 230, 283, 314, 404
Tailai 泰来 county, Heilongjiang, 122
Tajikistan, 15, 374, 378–84
Taklamakan 塔克拉玛干 (desert), 471
Taldykorgan, 38
Taohongbala 桃红八拉, Hanggin 杭锦 banner, Inner Mongolia, 130, 141
Tarim 塔里木 Basin, 259, 469–70
Tashkurgan 塔什库尔干, Xinjiang, 261
Tepsei, 493
Terezin, 344, 447, 496
Tianma-Qucun 天马–曲村, Shanxi, 182
Tianmiliang 添密梁, Inner Mongolia, 350
Tibet, 411–12
Tibetan Plateau, 408–11
Tongxin 同心 county, Ningxia, 286, 294, 298, 304, 314, 338–40, 344
Toupaizi 头牌子, Inner Mongolia, 340
Transbaikal area, Transbaikalia, 15, 62, 66, 80, 82, 283, 314, 328, 330, 334–36, 340–46, 418, 421, 424–27, 437, 439–41, 443, 447, 449–51, 455, 457, 493, 498–500
Transcaucasia, 396
Tuekta, 191, 218–20
Turkmenistan, 15
Turpan 吐鲁番 prefecture; Turpan Basin, 236, 261
Tuva (republic), 15, 29, 64, 82, 130, 138, 142–44, 150, 184, 191, 193, 197, 208, 324–26, 344, 434, 445, 447, 493, 496
Uïgarak, 375, 386
Ukok Plateau, 50–1
Ulaanbaatar, 83
Ulandryk, 206, 224–28, 268
Ul'skiĭ aul, 83
Ulus Kostin, 495
Ur, 27, 88, 183, 258, 262, 468
Ural(s); southern Ural region, 26, 83, 197, 290
Urbiun, 324, 493
Ust'-Kiakhta, 500
Utinka, 445, 493
Uushgiĭn Övör, 47, 49, 82, 122
Uyuk, 150
Uzbekistan, 15, 416
Verkh-Kaldzhin, 195

Verkhneudinsk (= Ulan-Udė), 330
Verkhniaia Koia, 83
Verkhniaia Rutkha, 83
Verkhov'ia Tesa, 495
Waertugou 瓦尔吐沟, Jungar 准格尔 banner, Inner Mongolia, 154
Xiajiadian 夏家店, 45, 47; Lower Xiajiadian, 38, 47; Upper Xiajiadian, 45–47, 49, 51–52, 60, 64, 68–72, 76, 80, 94, 186
Xi'an 西安, Shaanxi, 152, 191, 302–4, 322, 402
Xianbei 鲜卑 mountains, 348
Xianyang 咸阳, Shaanxi, 416
Xiaoheishigou 小黑石沟, Ningcheng 宁城 county, Inner Mongolia, 46, 50–51, 66, 70
Xichagou 西岔沟, Xifeng 西丰 county, Liaoning, 292–94, 304, 324, 330, 434, 441, 445
Xietuncun 谢屯村, Ansai 安塞 district, Shaanxi, 164
Xigoupan 西沟畔, Jungar 准格尔 banner, Inner Mongolia, 192–93, 232
Xiliangguang 西梁垙, Yanqing 延庆 district, Beijing, 76–77
Xincun 辛村, Jun 浚 county, Henan, 40
Xingzhou 兴洲, Luanping 滦平, Hebei, 77
Xinjiang 新疆 (Xinjiang Uyghur Autonomous Region), 15, 19, 28–29, 110–13, 138, 180, 188, 193, 195, 197, 236, 256, 258–62, 274, 334, 468–73
Xinzhuangtou 辛庄头, Yi 易 county, Hebei, 232, 286, 360, 364
Xiufengcun 锈峰村, Wushan 巫山 county, Chongqing 重庆, Sichuan, 298
Yanghai 洋海, Shanshan 鄯善 county, Xinjiang, 261, 470, 472
Yangzi 扬子 (river), 257
Yanqing 延庆 district (county), Beijing, 54, 76–80, 84, 96, 108, 250
Yanxiadu 燕下都, Yi 易 county, Hebei, 194
Yellow River cf. also Huanghe, 36, 187, 314; Yellow river basin, 181
Yi 易 county, Hebei, 194, 232, 286, 360, 364
Yijinhuoluo 伊金霍洛 banner, Inner Mongolia, 199, 202
Yinniugou 饮牛沟, Liangcheng 凉城 county, Inner Mongolia, 120
Yinshan 阴山 (mountain range), 115
Yinshanling 银山岭, Pingle 平乐 county, Guangxi, 294

Index of Places | 539

Yinxu 殷墟, Anyang 安陽, Henan, 31
Yucun 遇村, Ning 宁 county, Gansu, 79, 158, 250–52
Yuhuangmiao 玉皇庙, Yanqing 延庆 district, Beijing, 54, 76–80, 84, 96
Yulin Fu 榆林府, Shaanxi, 170
Yulongtai 玉隆太, Jungar 准格尔 banner, Inner Mongolia, 142, 146, 173, 230–31
Yunnan 云南 (province), 377, 406–8
Zaghunluq 扎滚鲁克, Qiemo 且末 county, Xinjiang, 27, 256, 259–61, 469–70, 472
Zaporozh'e, 196
Zavkhan, 493
Zhangbei 张北 (Hattin Sum, Khadain-sume), Hebei, 106, 130–31
Zhangjiakou 张家口, Hebei, 77, 83
Zhangjiapo 张家坡, Chang'an 长安 district, Xi'an 西安, Shaanxi, 402
Zhangjiecun 张街村, Pengyang 彭阳 county, Ningxia, 190, 204, 214
Zhelimu 哲裏木 League, Inner Mongolia, 352
Zhoujiadi 周家地, Aohan banner 敖汉, Inner Mongolia, 62
Ziwiyeh, 83
Zorgol, 340
Zuny gol, 49

Picture Credits

All photographs are by Rainer Wolfsberger, Zurich, with the exception of the following:

Küsnacht/Zurich, Art Conservation® Thomas Becker: X-ray images of entries 96–99.

London, © The Trustees of the British Museum: figs. 49, 51.

Riggisberg, Abegg-Stiftung (photo: Christoph von Viràg): fig. 22.

David Salmon, UK: fig. 27.

St Petersburg, © The State Hermitage Museum (photo by Vladimir Terebenin): figs. 2, 10.

Washington, DC, Freer Gallery of Art and Arthur M. Sackler Gallery, the Smithsonian's National Museum of Asian Art, Department of Conservation and Scientific Research: Appendix 2, pp. 481–84.

Xi'an, Shaanxi History Museum: fig. 16.

Landscape photography from central Mongolia (frontispiece, pp. 16, 48, 121): Ursula Brosseder, Rheinische Friedrich-Wilhelms-Universität Bonn.

Maps (figs. 1, 4, 13, 14, 23–26, 32–35): Ursula Brosseder with the help of Lara Fabian, Albert-Ludwigs-Universität Freiburg; base map from naturalearthdata.com.

Reproductions from publications:

Andersson 1932, pl. 29.8–9: fig. 15.

Barkova and Pankova 2005, 51, fig. 4 (drawing by Elena Stepanova): fig. 20.

Chlenova 1994, 530 fig. 11: fig. 12.

E'erduosi Qingtongqi 2006, 175: fig. 17.

Lawergren 2003a, 107, fig. 11; 109, fig. 14: figs. 44, 50.

Lawergren 2003b, 32–33, fig. 2; 34, figs. 3, 4; 36, fig. 6: figs. 41–43, 46.

Lawergren 2019a, 110, fig. 8: fig. 45.

Miniaev 1998, tabl. 1–3, 5: fig. 37.

Ningxia 2002, 21, fig. 11.10: fig. 18.

Polos'mak and Barkova 2005, 90, fig. 2.60: fig. 8.

Rashid 1984, figs. 62 and 73: fig. 47.

So 2000a, figs. 3.3, 3.4a, 3.5: fig. 21.

So and Bunker 1995, 49, figs. 16–17: fig. 5 A, B; 59 fig. 23: fig. 19.

Takahama et al. 2006, 102 pl. 20.1: fig. 11

Törbat 2018b, 345 no. 1040; 422 no. 1148: fig. 7.

Zaghunluq 2016, 159: fig. 3.

Zhongguo 1959, 27 fig. 21: fig. 9.

Drawing by Iwona Jaworowska Frei, after Berdnikova et al. 1991, fig. 2–7: fig. 6.

Copy editor: Regula Schorta
English editors: John Stevenson, Chad Jorgenson

Bibliografische Information der Deutschen Nationalbibliothek
Die Deutsche Nationalbibliothek verzeichnet diese Publikation in der Deutschen Nationalbibliografie; detaillierte bibliografische Daten sind im Internet über https://dnb.dnb.de abrufbar.
Bibliographic information published by the Deutsche Nationalbibliothek
The Deutsche Nationalbibliothek lists this publication in the Deutsche Nationalbibliografie; detailed bibliographic data are available in the Internet at https://dnb.dnb.de

For further information about our publishing program consult our website https://www.harrassowitz-verlag.de
© Otto Harrassowitz GmbH & Co. KG, Wiesbaden 2022
This work, including all of its parts, is protected by copyright. Any use beyond the limits of copyright law without the permission of the publisher is forbidden and subject to penalty. This applies particularly to reproductions, translations, microfilms and storage and processing in electronic systems.

Design and Typesetting: Franziska Schott & Marco Schibig
Binding: bubu, Mönchaltorf
Printed on FSC certified paper
Printing and Lithographs: Abächerli Media AG, Sarnen
Printed in Switzerland
ISBN 978-3-447-11848-4